flavors of
GREECE

flavors of GREECE

ROSEMARY BARRON

Interlink Books

An imprint of Interlink Publishing Group, Inc.
Northampton, Massachusetts

First American edition published in 2004 by

INTERLINK BOOKS
An imprint of Interlink Publishing Group, Inc.
46 Crosby Street, Northampton, MA 01060
www.interlinkbooks.com

Originally published by Grub Street, London, England

Library of Congress Cataloging-in-Publication Data

Barron, Rosemary.
 Flavors of Greece / Rosemary Barron. — 1st American ed.
  p. cm.
 ISBN 1-56656-520-0 (Hardback)
 1. Cookery, Greek. I. Title.
 TX723.5.G8B37 2003
 641.59495 — dc22

                                                                    2003016825
                                                                         CIP

Printed and bound in Korea

To request our complete 40-page full-color catalog,
please call us toll free at **1-800-238-LINK,** visit our
website at **www.interlinkbooks.com,** or write to
Interlink Publishing
46 Crosby Street, Northampton, MA 01060
e-mail: info@interlinkbooks.com

Contents

FOREWORD

It is impossible for me to think of Greece without thinking of the colors, sights, aromas, and, above all, the flavors of Greek cooking. So many of my happy memories of the country are linked with food enjoyed in the company of good Greek friends or of new food experiences associated with out-of-the-way or exotically beautiful places – high in the mountains, by the glistening blue Aegean Sea, or in medieval ports, picturesque villages, or the heart of cosmopolitan Athens.

Yet my interest in this fascinating, many-layered, cuisine began by accident: On an archaeological dig on Crete, cut off by rugged mountain passes from all but the most durable of supplies, my fellow "diggers" and I found ourselves eating the same foods our "subjects" had enjoyed some four thousand years earlier. This was the beginning of a passionate and lifelong curiosity about Greek food and its history, and its place in our own culinary culture.

Fifteen years after this first prophetic encounter, I was back on Crete, this time to set up a cooking school. *Kandra Kitchen* was based in an old house that, 450 years earlier, had been rebuilt with stone rescued from a ruined monastery. Its wood-burning oven still worked, the huge wine press remained intact, remnants of once-elegant antique columns supported the steps, and the flagstone floor was gloriously shiny and worn. *Kandra Kitchen*'s program ensured that each student enjoyed Greek foods, wines, and culture within the daily, seasonal, and festive rhythms of village life. I did, however, make one contribution to this otherwise idyllic state of affairs – I installed a "state-of-the-art" kitchen, at that time the only one on Crete, to provide the "classroom" for testing and experimenting with Cretan foods and dishes.

Kandra Kitchen attracted enormous interest, in the United States (where I was living at the time) and Canada in particular, and the six years I ran the school on Crete and on Santorini (Cyclades) were very happy ones for me.

The constraints of family life, although perfectly enjoyable in their own way, prevented further long-term travel, so I turned to writing, teaching, and lecturing on Greek foods and culinary culture, past and present. My "itchy-feet" were reasonably well-taken care of though, as these new activities entailed plenty of travel – to the United States and Greece, to Canada, Australia, France, Argentina, Thailand, and elsewhere. During this time, I wrote *Flavors of Greece*.

I hope my recipes here will pay some tribute to the wonderful spirit of friendliness that has engulfed me, and warms any visitor in Greece; that they will revive happy memories in those who have already traveled to

Greece or her islands and in the Greeks who now live abroad.

As a visitor to Greece I was automatically awarded the status of a *xsenos*, which means a "stranger-friend"; with this comes, for any traveler, the "protection of the gods" and a magnificent welcome to match. Such a welcome always includes the sharing of food. You are not just given food by Greeks but asked to share with them the food they enjoy (somehow there is always enough!). In few other countries are food and its traditions so much part of the fabric of life, playing an important role in the rituals associated with birth and death and everything in between.

Of course, just because a recipe is ancient, there is no guarantee that it will taste wonderful. But, with Greek food, much of it does. When I open a recipe book I often recall that the first recorded collection of recipes dates from the days of ancient Greece, that Greeks established the first schools for chefs, and that a fastidious Greek gourmet invented the fork. And each time I hear the issues of the day discussed over dinner, my mind is drawn back to the scholarly dinners of antiquity when food, philosophy, and conversation were considered inseparable companions.

My hope is that some of this enthusiasm for Greek food and culinary history will inspire my readers to discover more about both. Perhaps too it will persuade others to visit that beautiful and hospitable country and experience the delights of Greek food for themselves.

Rosemary Barron

INTRODUCTION

Those who know Greece, even if only from a brief acquaintance, are aware that there is a vigorous culinary tradition in the country, with a distinct identity and character. There is a robust regional and local cuisine and an informed and lively interest in food and flavor. All these aspects are linked, in an amazing continuity of tradition, with the ancient world of over two thousand years ago.

Ancient Greece is universally accepted as the cradle of Western civilization, with its highly developed political and social system and rich intellectual and cultural life. In such a civilization could it have been possible that food and its preparation would not have been taken seriously? A remote possibility indeed. In fact, the ancient Greeks regarded cooking as both an art and a science and throughout the ancient world Greek chefs were accorded the status and reputation that French chefs now enjoy. The principles and practice of fine cooking and gastronomy as we know them today were first established in the abundantly stocked and highly creative kitchens of ancient Greece, and modern Greeks still enjoy the foods and tastes that inspired the chefs of antiquity.

What makes the style and flavor of Greek food essentially different from that of other Mediterranean countries? To discover that we need to take a brief look at the country's history, since Greek cooking is greatly influenced by the twists and turns of its turbulent past.

Until around 3500 B.C. the early inhabitants of Greece grilled the food they had gathered, hunted, and fished over wood fires, baked it in glowing embers, or, like their Etruscan neighbors, cooked it in clay ovens. But with the advent of what has been called the "Greek miracle" – the budding of the sophisticated Minoan civilization on the islands of Crete and Santorini – Greek cuisine began to develop a strongly individual style.

At the height of its influence (around 1700 to 1400 B.C.) the Minoan state dominated the Aegean, and its culture spread throughout the Mediterranean. Trade links with North Africa brought dates and onions to the islands and forests were cleared to make way for widespread planting of vines and olives. Then, as now, Crete was a true "Garden of Eden," producing some of the richest honey and sweetest fruits to be found anywhere, so it is no coincidence that the first sweetmeats were made in Minoan kitchens. The well-known Mediterranean sweetmeat *membrillo*, made from quince paste, is almost undoubtedly Minoan in origin, although it is often thought to come from Spain. Quinces were grown on Crete before the days of the ancient Greeks and archaeological research has established that the Minoans made pastes from fruits.

The creative and organizational skills of the Minoans, and their systematic approach to land cultivation and trade, laid the foundations for the successful economy of classical Greece and, as the Greek civilization developed, so also did a culinary culture. Gastronomy became a subject for serious study, and skilled technicians were required to put into practice the food theories formulated by scholars. These technicians, soon highly regarded as chefs, developed many of the cooking techniques and basic sauces we still use. Just as importantly, civilized Greek society developed the framework in which we enjoy food – the art of dining and of dinner party conversation.

As classical Greece declined and the Roman Empire grew in power and influence, Rome supplanted Athens as the center of the civilized world. Educated and affluent Romans, anxious to improve their gastronomic and cultural standards, employed Greek teachers for their children and Greek chefs in their kitchens. Under the tutelage of Greek chefs the Romans developed their own distinctive cuisine and laid the foundations of Italian cooking, which, of course, has many similarities with Greek food.

Later, the expansion of the Byzantine Empire, with its center in Constantinople (now Istanbul), spread the influence of Greek cooking northward and eastward throughout the Balkans and the area that is now Turkey. Even today, many Turkish and Eastern Mediterranean communities rely on Greek bakers and pastry cooks for a variety of breads, pastries, and sweetmeats. In its turn, Greek cuisine absorbed Balkan and Eastern influences.

Then came the dark years, when Greece found itself at the mercy of a succession of invaders. Parts of the country were occupied in turn by Franks, Venetians, and Ottomans, who all influenced native food, and smaller invasions – for example, by the Vlachs and Slavs – brought new flavorings, such as paprika, to occupied towns and villages.

After the fall of Constantinople in A.D. 1453 Greece was under the sway of the expansionist Ottoman Empire. This occupation naturally brought a renewed Eastern influence to bear on Greek food, although this influence was not so profound as is generally thought. During this period (which lasted until 1830), Greeks were forced to use Turkish names for foods and dishes; this practice has led to a widespread, but mistaken, belief that Greek dishes with Eastern-sounding names, for example *dolmades* and *borekakia*, are, of Turkish origin. Four hundred years of culinary habits based on expediency have left Greece with a legacy of native foods with Turkish names and a few dishes, such as *moussakas*, that are popular in both countries.

During the Turkish occupation many Greek chefs took refuge in monasteries, both for their own safety and to safeguard centuries of culinary knowledge and practice. To distinguish them from the monks, who wore the black hats still associated with the Greek Orthodox church, they wore tall white toques – the chef's hat now familiar throughout the world and an accepted professional symbol.

Over the centuries, migrations, invasions, trade customs, and personalities all have contributed to the magnificent expansion of the early Greek diet of olives, wheat, figs, grapes, wild greens, fish, and a little meat, to the colorful abundance evident in Greek food today. Lemons, potatoes, eggplants, tomatoes, spinach, and okra, for example, none native to Greece, were introduced over the centuries as a result of trade, war, or occupation. Even in our own century, drastic changes have taken place in Greek culinary life. A brief German occupation during World War II was responsible for a devastating reduction of the Greek Jewish community and thus its influence on food, and today the European Union, although, of course, not similar in tragic human terms, is making a decisive impact on Greek agriculture and food choices. The production of "ancient" crops is giving way to the demands and patterns of mechanization and export, and inexpensive foods from other European countries are replacing more expensive traditional ones. In many towns, for example, the transatlantic hamburger is unfortunately supplanting the centuries-old *souvlaki* as a favorite street food. However, fine imaginative cooking and good natural ingredients are still to be found in Greece if the visitor cares to look beyond the bland hodgepodges commonly offered to tourists.

Greek tables today

Greek food is inspired by the heady perfumed fragrances that float on the Greek air. Then there is the color and novelty of Greek food. On shopping trips to the market, shapes, textures, and colours assault the senses, excite and entice – glossy multicolored vegetables and lush juicy fruits; plump nuts and seeds; boxes of dried fruits; strangely shaped sausages and meats from every part of an animal; sea-fresh fish you have never seen before; barrels of salted fish and *tarama*; hard and soft cheeses, crumbly white or creamy golden, some wrapped in animal skins; and more kinds of olives and beans than you ever imagined. Even the water in Greece seems special; Greeks say that some dishes, particularly those based on vegetables, cannot be made properly outside Greece because the water is not the same.

In the villages the traditional way of dining is still observed, and very pleasant and relaxed it is. A table is set up in a courtyard and on it is spread a variety of *mezedes* for guests and family to nibble on for an hour or two while they chat and wind down. Every meal is preceded by *mezedes*, "to prepare the stomach for the onslaught to come," as one ancient Greek writer explained. When the *mezedes* are finished, bread, salad, and a main course are placed in the center of the table. Vegetables are usually served later, separate from the main course. Family and guests alike are expected to help themselves to the food provided and to pass their wine glasses to the host to be filled.

But there are strict rules of etiquette at work here, very different from our own. For example, taking large helpings of everything at the start of the meal, to show appreciation of the food, would actually be an insult to the host, implying that there might not be enough food to go around! Instead, the diners help themselves to the same dish several times, proving to the host that they are enjoying themselves and the food he/she offers.

Even the most sophisticated world-traveled Greek approaches a village table laden with foods such as wild greens, spit-roasted lamb, and sweet cheese pies with relish and enthusiasm. At such a feast he instinctively feels in touch with generations of Greeks who have enjoyed these traditional aromas and tastes before him; these are the flavors of home and here he knows he will find good companionship and a special communal pleasure and appreciation.

The preparation of food for others, a generous and loving activity, is experienced at its most lavish and hospitable at a Greek table; no one is ever turned away.

Feasting and fasting, richness and frugality, especially among traditional and religious Greeks, is still the pattern of gastronomic life; food cannot be truly valued unless, at some other time, it has been denied. Hence, the strict observance of the Lenten and Advent fasts, and the explosion of rich ingredients and exotic flavors lavished on Easter and Christmas meals.

Dining in Greece is an activity that stimulates all the senses; the food – aromatic, pungent, and colorful – is consumed with great gusto. Whether the occasion is an ordinary family supper or a splendid festive celebration the dining table is the place to enjoy each other's company. At home, in a taverna, or at a restaurant, a meal is accompanied by animated conversation, and appreciation of the food is loud and unequivocal. Good food entwines people in a bond that remains long after the meal is finished.

This brief introduction to Greek gastronomic history and present-day culinary practices gives just a shadowy outline of the rich character and tradition of the country's cuisine. The way to really appreciate the variety, flavor, and sheer pleasure of the best Greek food is to try it. And since much of this is to be found in out-of-the-way tavernas or on domestic tables, rather than in ritzy restaurants, trying your hand at some of the regional and national specialities in this book is the ideal introduction to the expressive Greek attitude to food and cooking, and the unpretentious, flavorful foods that Greeks delight in. From appetizers to desserts you will find strength and subtlety, verve and vigor in these flavors of Greece and discover the wonderful legacy that Greek cooks of the past have left us.

Traditional flavors on modern tables

For me, Greek food is beautiful in its honesty, its healthy indifference to trends (although many basic tenets of traditional Greek cooking are now both medically approved and highly fashionable) and in its ability to promote a feeling of well-being in everyone at the table. In this book you will find no *haute cuisine* but plenty of fine food. Many recipes are simple, based on good fresh ingredients and the aromatic scents of the Greek countryside; many are highly flavored; all taste even better when shared with friends. The preparation of most of these dishes is straightforward; most do not call for unreasonable culinary artistry and skill. And each recipe is in some way personal to me and evokes wonderful memories of the person who gave it to me.

When we serve Greek food at home, some traditional customs can pose problems. Our guests, used to spending less time relaxing before dinner, can easily misjudge the pace of the meal and become quite full just on *mezedes*. Thus, it is better to serve just a few *mezedakia* such as olives, *feta* cheese, salted almonds, and peppered figs with drinks. Then, at the table, serve two or three more substantial *mezedes* as a first course.

In traditional Greek homes no separate first or soup courses are served (a soup is usually served as a complete meal), so the main course is served immediately after the *mezedes*. This does not mean that you have to do the same: I often serve a few *mezedes*, followed by a soup or vegetable casserole, bread, and salad. Fresh fruit or perhaps pudding or ice cream usually completes the meal. After the meal, and away from the dining table, Greeks often enjoy honey-rich pastries, sweetmeats, or syruped fruits (*glyka*) with coffee. For us these treats make delectable desserts.

If you find balancing your Greek menu a problem you may find my menu planner helpful (see page 353). As you become more familiar with Greek food, however, you will begin to recognize instinctively which dishes complement each other best.

MACEDONIA

Thessalonika

THASOS

Sea of Marmara

Mt. Athos

• Meteora

Metsovo

SPORADES

TURKEY

CORFU

LESBOS

Aegean Sea

IONIAN
ISLANDS

KHIOS

Mt. Olympia

Athens

Corinth

SAMOS

ZAKYNTHOS

Náfplion

PELOPONNESE

THE CYCLADES

DODECANNESE

KOS

Kalamata

Ionian Sea

SANTORINI

RHODES

Sea of Crete

Hania

Iraklion

CRETE

Mediterranean Sea

N

THE GREEK KITCHEN

Ingredients

Olives / *Elies*

For modern Greeks olives and bread are the basic necessities of life, as they have been for centuries. The olive groves of modern Greece – still, mysterious, and peaceful places – date back to around 450 B.C. when olive oil was first recognized as a valuable export commodity and the land was given over to olive cultivation. As Lawrence Durrell put it, olives have "a taste older than meat, older than wine. A taste as old as cold water."

Olives thrive in the Mediterranean climate of long hot summers and mild winters with only short periods of frost. The difference in flavor and texture are to some extent influenced by their situation – olives grown on the arid rocky hillsides, for example, tend to be small and the richest flavored, while those grown on the coastal plains are fatter and fleshier.

The taste is also affected by the degree of ripeness when an olive is picked and by the curing method used. Some Greek producers, using centuries-old methods, still supply olives of a very high standard and a great diversity of flavor. In each olive-producing area the local people delight in the flavor variation that makes their olives different from others and, they claim, better.

All olives are bitter and inedible when picked. As an olive matures it changes from green to black. Most olives are picked when young or just mature but, if local taste and custom dictates, some olives are harvested at a very late stage when their skins are leathery and wrinkled. In the two-stage traditional curing process the olives are first soaked in water for 3–30 days to remove any bitterness, then immersed in brine, the strength of which determines the saltiness of the cured olive. Occasionally the olives are packed into rock salt rather than steeped in brine.

Olives are usually harvested in autumn and considered sufficiently cured by early spring. They are then packed in either fresh brine, brine and vinegar, olive oil, or olive oil and vinegar for storage. They can be used straight from the pot or marinated in herbs, lemon juice or vinegar, and olive oil to serve as a *meze*.

It is worth seeking out imported Greek olives to give an authentic flavor to the recipes in this book. Although there are only a few commercially important types of olive grown in Greece, regional preferences for ripeness and curing method, as well as the local environment, give an imposing

1

variety of olives for sale. Most are not exported and can only be sampled in their place of origin, but here is a list of those more commonly available in Greek shops, good supermarkets, and speciality shops:

Amfissa From the olive groves surrounding Delphi. Picked when ripe and oil-rich, Amfissa olives are round and black with a mellow, pleasantly nutty flavor. Perfect with cheese and crusty country bread.

Atalanti Large, luscious, and fruity olives in shades of purple and greenish-purple. Atalanti are gathered half-ripe and cured in brine. The effort and time required to produce these lovely olives means that they are particularly at risk to modern lye-curing methods; check before buying. Exquisitely flavored, they can be served straight from their brine or sprinkled with a few drops of red wine vinegar, olive oil, and a little dried *rigani* or thyme.

Cracked Green The ubiquitous countryside olives, picked just before their color changes from light to dark green. This olive too is at risk from modern "shortcuts" in curing; buy from a reputable supplier. Strong and sharp, they are an ideal *meze* to serve with ouzo. Or marinate them for a few hours in olive oil, a few drops of red wine vinegar, bay leaves, a little crushed coriander, and slivered garlic.

Elitses Tiny, sweetly-flavored, purple-brown olives, similar in appearance and taste to Niçoise olives; they are grown extensively on Crete. Use whenever a mildly flavored olive is called for.

Khourmades Named for their shape and appearance, *khourmades* ("dates") are large, dark brown, and attractively wrinkled. Some of the best come from the island of Chios where they take pride of place on the *meze* table.

Ionian Green Grown on the Ionian islands, picked young, and cured in a light brine. Lovely mild, mellow olives to serve just as they are. Or sprinkle with lemon juice, olive oil, and a little finely chopped preserved lemon and parsley.

Kalamata Probably the most famous Greek olives and a favorite the world over: Large and glossy, purple-black, almond-shaped, and with a distinctive flavor from the red wine vinegar used in the curing. Good Kalamatas are meaty and firm, at their best 4–5 months after curing, but can be kept longer. Named for the town of Kalamata (at the entrance to the Messenia Valley in the western Peloponnese), they are the perfect olive for many salads, and especially good marinated.

To use these olives in cooking, first blanch them for 5 seconds in boiling water.

Nafplion Grown in the eastern Peloponnese and picked in September when young and under-ripe. Their mild and slightly nutty flavor is good in salads and Nafplion is the traditional olive to serve with *taramosalata*. Occasionally I like to mix them with a little finely chopped preserved lemon, olive oil, and crushed coriander.

Thasos or Throumbes Grown on the island of Thasos in the northern Aegean, these olives are salt-cured (a process that produces a wrinkled skin and concentrated flavor), then stored in olive oil. They are excellent with *myzithra* cheese.

Volos Smooth, round brown olives of varying size from the province of Thessaly in central Greece. Their unusual color and appearance make them an ideal *meze* olive and they are especially good with the strong country flavors of sausages and offal meats, or *kephalotyri* cheese.

When buying olives be guided by your nose! Regardless of the curing method used, good olives smell fresh and intriguingly complex, never overwhelmingly salty. Unfortunately, it is now legal to lye-cure (steep in sodium hydroxide) and dye olives in Greece; lye-curing means that the one- to four-month natural fermentation period can be completed in a few hours. Avoid flavorless lye-cured or dyed olives by buying only those labelled "naturally cured" or "naturally fermented," and without the additive ferrous gluconate (or iron gluconate).

Left in the storage solution, olives can be kept for months, although all are best eaten as soon as possible after buying.

Olive Oil / *Elaiolatho*

Three significant factors influence the quality of olive oil: the growing conditions, the timing of the harvest, and, probably the most important, the way they are harvested – the olives should be picked, sorted, and pressed with care and precision, preserving as much of the fine natural flavor as possible.

Cold-pressed olive oil is made by spreading olive pulp on mats that fit in layers into a wooden press. A weight is placed on the top mat and the pressure releases the oil into a vat below. This exquisite oil, unfortunately, is becoming hard to find, even in Greece, for it is time-consuming to prepare. Extra virgin olive oil (defined by its low acidity, less than 1 percent) is made from the pulp of just-ripe olives and has the best flavor for salads. The pressed oil, standard cold-pressed or extra virgin, is left to settle for a few days to a week, then decanted into crocks, ready for the kitchen.

There have been, of course, modern advances in olive production – picking and oil extraction are now mechanized and there are chemicals available to "persuade" the olives to ripen and fall. But a machine cannot distinguish between ripe, just-ripe, and under-ripe olives nor strip trees on rocky hillsides where the best-tasting olives grow. Nor can mass production, relying on chemicals to accelerate filtering, "improve" flavor, and lengthen shelf life, yield an oil with anything approaching the rich quality, beautiful green-gold color, and fruity flavor of oils produced by traditional methods.

Olive oil of the highest quality can be expensive, but there is no substitute for it in good cooking. When buying olive oil, use the same discernment as you would when buying wine. Look for a young oil, with a fruity, immediately recognizable, aroma and taste and a good balance of flavor, and buy only a small quantity at first. Although the best village oil does have a distinctive green-gold color, it is a mistake to use only the color criterion when buying – unscrupulous producers have been known to alter the color with additives.

Greek olive oils are finally achieving the recognition they have long deserved. Greece, the third largest olive oil producing country in the world (making about 18 percent of total production), produces 75 percent of the world's extra virgin olive oil, and Greeks consume more olive oil than anyone else (about 53 gallons per person each year). The unique, richly-flavored olive oils of Crete and the Peloponnese, in particular, are worth searching for here. The ancient Greeks considered the best olive oil to be from slightly under-ripe olives, and both these regions of antiquity produce a special olive oil (*agourelaio*) from green olives, picked in the late autumn, at the start of the harvest. Buy olive oil only from shops where there is a high turnover and where the oil has been carefully stored in airtight containers, away from heat or sunlight. In your own kitchen, store olive oil in a dark cool place – it does not require refrigeration.

Greeks appreciate fine olive oil and demand high standards from commercial brands. If economy in the kitchen is an issue, it's worth keeping both extra virgin and virgin olive oil on hand. Use the extra virgin olive oil in salads and in dishes requiring a last-minute addition of oil; use the less expensive virgin olive oil in cooked dishes or for deep-fat frying (virgin olive oil has none of the "debris" left in extra virgin oils).

Sea Salt / *Alati tis Thalassas*

Salt was important in the ancient world, both to enliven frugal diets and as a preservative, but in recent years we have become more aware of the health risks associated with too much salt. However, it is possible to use salt to gain maximum taste advantage without endangering health. For example, adding lemon juice to salt strengthens its flavor, so you can use less salt but retain the taste, and relatively small quantities of strongly salted foods (such as olives) satisfy the body's natural requirements for this important mineral.

Sea salt, the type commonly used in Greece, is a wonderful flavor-enhancer, and it also contains other trace minerals beneficial to health. When a villager explains how to make a dish, salt is never far from the top of his or her list of ingredients. It is considered a digestive, an appetizer, and has an ability to balance and mellow flavors. It also deepens color and aroma and has the effect of drawing out liquid – which is why villagers always add salt to grilled food after cooking, not before.

Sea salt is more expensive than other types but you use less of it. It's a good idea to keep two varieties of sea salt in your kitchen – fine-grain for most cooking, and coarse-grain for some dishes and for the table.

Vinegar / *Xsithi*

Only wine vinegar, mainly that made from red wine, is used in the Greek kitchen and it's a commodity that is taken seriously. As much care is taken over vinegar making as wine making and often the village winemaker has a dual role as the local supplier of good vinegar. In one old village house I once occupied, a huge earthenware pot stood in a corner of the courtyard – this contained the village vinegar supply and during the day villagers would stop by for a ladleful of vinegar, sometimes bringing a little wine to top off the pot.

One of the first food additives, vinegar is a digestive, a preservative, and a versatile flavoring agent. There is an enormous difference in flavor between good and poor wine vinegars, and it is an important distinction since the quality of the vinegar affects the quality of the dishes and sauces made with it. The quality depends primarily on the quality of the wine converted or soured by the vinegar "mother" – a self-perpetuating colony of harmless bacteria that float around in the wine while slowly acidifying it.

To make your own wine vinegar Stand a large glazed earthenware crock on a shelf or in a corner, and add leftover red wine whenever you have any available. When you have about 2 1/2 cups, add 4 tablespoons good-quality red wine vinegar, loosely cover the crock to keep it dust-free but open to the air, and leave undisturbed for a week or two. A "mother" will form. Continue adding red wine, tasting occasionally to see if you are satisfied with the vinegar. Once you are, decant most of it into bottles and seal. Add more red wine to the "mother," which will continue to grow – eventually you will need to break it up and donate bits to your friends!

If you cannot find aged red wine vinegar imported from Greece, or make your own, substitute Italian balsamic vinegar, but use less than is called for in the recipe.

Wine in Cooking / *Krasi sti Magiriki*

Wine does not feature in Greek recipes as often as you might expect.
As an old winemaker on the island of Santorini once told me, wine is made
to drink! Nevertheless, red wine's ability to tenderize tough cuts of meat is
used to full effect in casseroles, and traditional nectar-sweet wines are used
to flavor sweet dishes. Madeira can be used in place of sweet Greek wines
such as Samos or Mavrodaphne, which can sometimes be difficult to find.

Yogurt / *Yiaourti*

Fresh milk, a controlled temperature, and the help of two friendly
bacteria (*lactobacillus bulgaricus* and *streptococcus thermophilus*) are the
essential requirements for making yogurt. A rich source of minerals and
vitamins, especially vitamin B, yogurt can also taste wonderful. The best
deliciously thick and creamy versions have a refreshing taste and luxurious
texture, totally different from the thin and lusterless product that too often
passes as yogurt on our supermarket shelves.

Yogurt is used throughout the Balkan region and the Middle East as a
tenderizer, to enrich stews, to make sauces, and in salads, desserts, and
cakes. And the food-curious visitor to Greece very soon discovers what
I consider to be the best snack in the world – a plate of thick white sheep's
milk yogurt covered with fragrant Hymettus honey.

The best yogurt I have ever tasted was made in the small Cretan village
of Vrisses. It was sold in unglazed flat-bottomed bowls for which each
customer paid a deposit; if you brought back the bowl all you had to pay
for next time was the yogurt. That memorable yogurt was made from
sheep's milk but village yogurt is also made from goat's milk, which gives a
different, less creamy, sharper flavor.

The easiest way to ensure that you have a good supply of flavorful
yogurt is to make it yourself. Despite the complicated instructions often
given for yogurt making, it's really very simple. All you need is good-
quality fresh milk, a few tablespoons of live yogurt starter, and a fairly
warm (about 75–80°F) draft-free spot.

Live yogurt starter can be bought in Greek or health food shops. Once
you have made your first batch, you save some of it to use as a starter for
the second batch, and so on. The taste of your finished yogurt depends
largely on this starter; 1– to 2–day-old starter will produce a mildly sweet
version, 5– to 6–day-old starter a sharper, tarter one. Every month or two
you will need a new starter (the bacteria gradually lose their potency).
Taste is also affected by the length of time yogurt is incubated – the longer
you leave it, the stronger the result.

Both the texture and flavor of Greek yogurt is difficult to reproduce
outside the countries of the Near East. Experiment with the milk you have

available to find what works best for you. Yogurt added to cooked dishes or salads must be thick; thin yogurt can be strained for a few hours to remove excess water. Left longer to strain, it becomes a delicious creamy cheese.

To make your own yogurt
Makes 4 cups yogurt

4 cups organic whole milk
3 tablespoons live yogurt culture, at room temperature

Heat the milk to just under a boil and pour into a glass, ceramic, or earthenware bowl. Let cool, uncovered, to about 110°F (you should be able to comfortably leave your finger in the milk for a count of five). A skin will have formed on the surface (this makes a special treat later, with honey). To retain the skin, push a little of it to one side and spoon the yogurt into the milk. For yogurt with a textured crust, cover the bowl loosely, if at all; for yogurt without a crust, cover the bowl with a plate.

Set aside for 10–12 hours in a warm draft-free spot, such as an oven with a pilot light, until thick and creamy. Cover and refrigerate for up to 4 days. (Remember to make another batch of yogurt before finishing the bowl.)

Do not be put off if your first few attempts are disappointing. Your yogurt may not set – in which case make sure that the incubating spot is warm enough and the temperature is constant; if your yogurt still does not set, you need to begin again with a new starter. Or it may curdle – the most common causes of curdling are incubating yogurt in a place that is too warm or for too long a period.

Strained Yogurt Line a sieve with two layers of cheesecloth and set over a bowl. Pour in 4 cups yogurt, pull up the sides of the cheesecloth, and tie together to make a bag. Hang the bag over the bowl in a cool place and let drain for 3 hours. Do not drain the yogurt in the refrigerator or it will set firm rather than just thickening. Give the bag an occasional squeeze to remove as much water (whey) as possible. (You can use the whey in a soup or casserole.) Refrigerate in an airtight container for up to 5 days. (Makes about 3 cups.)

Yogurt Cheese Strain 4 cups yogurt and return the bag to the sieve. Open the cheesecloth and stir in 1/4–1/2 teaspoon fine-grain sea salt if liked. Fold the cheesecloth over the yogurt, place a heavily weighted plate on top, and set aside for 2 hours. Transfer to the refrigerator and let sit another 2 hours.

Dry the cheesecloth bag with paper towels and, leaving the cheesecloth in place, refrigerate the yogurt cheese in an airtight container for up to 4 days.

For breakfast, serve with honey, fresh fruit, and crusty bread. For lunch, sprinkle with extra virgin olive oil, a little freshly ground pepper, and/or finely chopped fresh herbs such as parsley and oregano. (Makes about 1 cup.)

Cheeses / *Tyria*

Greece produces relatively few types of traditional cheese but each has a distinctive flavor. In the villages cheese is made according to local practices that determine its unique character. For this reason, Greek cheeses are rarely named: to a villager, cheese is cheese! Some of the finest Greek cheeses come from the island of Crete, where sheep and goats graze on herb-covered foothills and where cool mountain temperatures provide an ideal environment for storing and ripening cheese to perfection.

The best-known Greek cheese, *feta*, suffers from an unfortunate form of flattery – it is now made in several northern European countries. This *feta*, usually made from cow's milk and in an industrialized environment, bears no comparison to the true *feta* of the Greek countryside.

Below is a short guide to the traditional cheeses referred to in this book, as well as the ones a visitor to Greece is most likely to find. Most are available here from Greek or Middle Eastern shops, and some are available from our better supermarkets:

Anthotyro A soft, delicate, very pale yellow cheese, made from goat's milk – a speciality of the island of Crete. Its name means "blossom cheese" in Greek, because the curds "bloom" as they rise to the surface on stirring. Soured or aged *anthotyro* is the cheese that gives Cretan pies their unique flavor. You can make a decent substitute by adding finely grated *feta* to drained and sieved cottage cheese (use 1 part *feta* to 4 parts cottage cheese).

Batsos A white, semi-hard brine cheese made from sheep's or goat's milk, *batsos* is not exported. But if you visit the wine-producing area of Naoussa, in the Peloponnese, try *batsos* with the local olives and a glass of Naoussa wine.

Feta The most famous Greek cheese, sometimes known in Greece as farmhouse cheese. Made from sheep's milk, *feta* is white and crumbly with a slightly sour, salty flavor – a pleasant, moderately priced table cheese. In isolated villages it is still made traditionally by pouring fresh unpasteurized sheep's milk into large leather pouches that are left hanging through the heat of the day. This process quickly curdles the milk, separating it into curds and whey. The curds are scooped out and packed into small baskets, the whey combined with salt to make brine, and the cheese is then stored in this brine for a week or two.

Although cheesemakers throughout Greece use the same basic method to make *feta*, there are marked regional variations. A good *feta* has a flaky texture and a mildly salty, fresh flavor. When you buy *feta* ask for some of the brine in which it is stored – the cheese can be refrigerated in this for up to 2 weeks longer, but without it your *feta* will only last a few days. Buy only Greek *feta*; many other countries now make this cheese but do not always use the distinctively flavored sheep's milk and the result is a vastly inferior product. *Feta* is best eaten young (ripened for a month or two); if ripened longer it becomes unpleasantly salty. Enjoy *feta* just as it is or sprinkle it with a little olive oil and dried *rigani* or fresh oregano and serve it as a *meze* or with grilled dishes. With the exception of Shrimp in a Pot with Feta Cheese (page 113) and Baked Eggplants with Tomatoes and Feta Cheese (page 200), I do not recommend using *feta* in cooked dishes, as cooking dissipates its fresh flavor.

Galotyri A distinctive soft and creamy cheese made from sheep's milk in late summer. The best is said to come from the mountain villages of Epirus in central Greece. *Galotyri* ("milk-cheese") is naturally fermented in crocks, goatskins or barrels for up to two months, and rich with the flavors of the local flora. A thick smooth texture (similar to that of yogurt) and tart flavor makes *galotyri* a deliciously refreshing snack or dessert; serve with figs, or other ripe fruits, and honey.

Graviera A mild-tasting, slightly salted cheese made from sheep's or cow's milk. Similar in both texture and flavor to Gruyère cheese, *graviera* is used mostly in sauces (page 156 and page 240). The best *graviera* is produced in the Cretan mountains, and this is served as a traditional and delicious accompaniment to fresh or poached fruits.

Halloumi A soft or semi-hard creamy-white cheese from Cyprus. This salty goats' milk cheese is often flavored with mint or cilantro. It is very good grilled and sprinkled with lemon juice as a *meze*.

Kasseri *Kephalotyri*'s milder and creamier cousin, known to Greeks as "factory cheese" since it is reconstituted from the curds of *kephalotyri*. However, it is often a perfectly acceptable, good-tasting cheese – always taste before buying.

Kaskavali A sheep's milk cheese made in the north of Greece, and in the Balkans. Its distinctive flavor is derived from the curds being heated before salting and pressing. With its thin rind, pale yellow color and herbal flavor, *kaskavali* is a very pleasant *meze* cheese.

Kephalotyri Named for its head-like shape, *kephalotyri* is a hard, pale yellow cheese made from unpasteurized sheep's or goat's milk. The curds are rubbed with salt, then returned to the mold for 3 days for a rind to form. Young *kephalotyri* is a good table cheese; one around 8 months old or more makes excellent Fried Cheese (page 38), and aged *kephalotyri* is perfect for grating over *macaronia* dishes.

Kopanisti This cheese is ripened in earthenware crocks called *kopanisti* – hence the name. It is a blue cheese, made only on the islands. Freshly made curds are cut and wrapped in cloth, then left to dry to develop a bluish-green mold. This mold, along with salt, is kneaded into the curds and left to ripen. With a light peppery flavor, *kopanisti* is a perfect *meze* cheese, a wonderful complement to Thasos olives.

Lathotyri One of Greece's best-known regional cheeses, *lathotyri* is produced only on the islands of Lesbos and Zakynthos. Each cheese is made in the shape of a miniature barrel and stored for 1–3 months in olive oil, hence its Greek name, "oil-cheese." True *lathotyri* is delicious, but there are many inferior imitations on the market.

Manouri A fresh *manouri* cheese, made in the spring by Cretan shepherds, is one of the great flavors of the Greek kitchen. *Manouri* is sweet, creamy-white, with a buttery, slightly "earthy" flavor – it is the perfect dessert cheese. Serve with rich, aromatic Greek honey and fresh figs or other seasonal fruit, or enjoy the cheese for breakfast with Currant Bread (page 264) and fresh fruit.

Metsovo Also excellent for the *meze* table are two cheeses made in the Pindus mountain village of Metsovo. One type of *metsovo* is a light flaky goat's milk cheese flavored with whole black peppercorns, the other an unusual smoked sheep's milk cheese.

Megithra *Megithra*, made only on the Cycladic islands, is one of the few Greek cheeses that has anything added to the curds. When the curds are cut for the first time, herbs, usually oregano or thyme, are mixed in, and the curds are pressed into a goatskin and left to mature for 4 months or more.

Myzithra Made from the whey from *feta* or *kephalotyri*. Fresh sheep's or goat's milk is added to the whey, then the curds are separated and poured into cheesecloth-lined baskets, with light weights placed on top. After one or two days this young fresh *myzithra*, sometimes known as *anari*, is ready to enjoy. During the autumn, winter, and early spring these flavorful unsalted cheeses, still displaying the indentations of the baskets, are sold in every Greek market. Unfortunately, young *myzithra* is not exported, but fresh ricotta is a reasonable substitute – or you can make your own (recipe follows). The *myzithra* widely available here is a pale yellow semi-hard cheese with a mildly nutty, almost buttery flavor. This is aged *myzithra*, about three months old, and a perfect grating cheese for *macaronia* dishes.

Toulomotyri Matured for three months encased in animal hide, *toulomotyri* ("skin-cheese") does not look like the most appetizing cheese in the world. But if you visit Greece and are offered a chance to sample this glorious cheese, please do. It's a cheese with an ancient pedigree – a pure white sheep's curd cheese, semi-soft, a little sour, even strangely musty, and truly delicious with sweet wine and fruit. The whey leftover from making *toulomotyri* is used to make a tangy version of *manouri* (see above).

Fresh Cheese
Myzithra

Makes approximately ½ pound cheese

....

8 ¾ cups organic whole milk
    or **other milk of choice**
Juice of 1 small lemon, strained

....

Line a sieve with 2 layers of cheesecloth and set over a bowl. Bring the milk to a boil in a stainless steel saucepan. Immediately remove from heat, add the lemon juice, and stir with a wooden spoon until the curds separate from the whey. If they do not separate, return the saucepan to very low heat and stir until they do. Pour slowly through the cheesecloth and set aside for 15 minutes to drain. Refrigerate the whey for later use in soups or casseroles. Fold the cheesecloth over the curds, place a weighted plate on top, and let drain for 1 hour. For a firmer cheese, refrigerate overnight with the weight in place. Dry the cheesecloth bag with paper towels and refrigerate it in an airtight container. For the freshest flavor, use within 2 days but it can be kept for up to 5 days.

Serve with honey, fresh fruit, and crusty bread. Or sprinkle with extra virgin olive oil, *rigani* (see page 13), fine-grain sea salt, and cracked black pepper, and serve with olives and bread.

Butter / *Voutiro*

In the hot Greek climate fresh sweet butter is a rare commodity. But when you do find it, made from sheep's or goat's milk and rather like clotted cream in texture, it tastes wonderful. According to some Greeks, goat's milk butter, which quickly develops a rather "high" aroma and flavor, is an essential flavoring for *macaronia*.

In Greek cooking butter does not generally play an important flavoring role, except in pastries. Unsalted butter can be used but clarified butter is the traditional choice and produces the finer flavor. Butter can be clarified in large quantities and, once processed, it keeps for several months in the refrigerator.

To clarify butter Melt 2 pounds butter in a heavy saucepan over low heat. When it begins to foam, gently stir in 4 tablespoons cracked wheat. Cook over low heat until the butter no longer steams (this indicates that all the water is expelled), remove from the heat, and set aside for 30 minutes.

Carefully decant into a container, leaving the salt and other residues on the bottom of the saucepan with the cracked wheat. You can also clarify butter by straining it through 3 layers of cheesecloth, but decanting produces the clearer, more satisfactory, result.

Herbs and Spices / *Votana ke Aromata*

It would be difficult to imagine Greek food without the characteristic aromatic pungency of a wide range of fresh herbs and spices. Parsley, cilantro, and mint, fresh from the kitchen garden, are used in large quantities; wild herbs (*rigani*, marjoram, thyme, sage, and fennel), with a fresh concentrated strength, are gathered from the dry rocky hillsides.

Listed below you will find information on the herbs and spices most commonly used in the Greek kitchen and in these recipes.

Various factors, such as climate, soil, time of year, and length of storage, all affect the pungency of any herb or spice you use. Thus, I have given guidance on seasonings for each dish but feel free to adjust the amounts specified – let your own taste be the final judge.

Dill / *Anithos* Quickly glancing at bunches of fresh herbs in a Greek market, it is easy to mistake the gentle fronds of dill for fennel; their seasons overlap. But dill is earlier and a darker green. In early spring dill is a favorite flavoring in soups or dishes made with *avgolemono* sauce.

Bay Laurel / *Dafni* An indispensable flavoring in both savory and sweet dishes, bay laurel is pungent and strong. Its Greek name is a legacy from myth – Daphne had the misfortune to be turned into a bay laurel tree by the sun god Apollo!

Rosemary / *Dendrolivano* or *Arismari* Rosemary grows wild throughout Greece and the best aromatic rosemary, with beautiful tiny purple-blue flowers, is said to grow on the dry hills close to the sea. Rosemary is used in Greek cooking mainly to aromatize roasts and grilled meats and fish – a few sprigs of fresh rosemary make a perfect basting brush.

Anise / *Glykaniso* The seeds of the anise bush, a member of the hemlock family, are used to flavor ouzo, breads (see page 263), cookies, and cakes. Anise is available in Greek and Middle Eastern shops; buy only in small quantities as it quickly loses its flavor.

Cumin / *Kimino* Cumin is a member of the same botanical family as fennel, dill, and coriander. For the sweetest, most pungent flavor, buy the dried seeds whole, and grind them when needed. In Greek cooking cumin gives a very special character to roast pork and lentil dishes.

Coriander / *Koriandron* Coriander has been cultivated in Greece since antiquity. Fresh coriander leaves, cilantro, are a stimulating aromatic in dried bean dishes and vegetables cooked à la greque (see pages 191 to 193); the pulverized dried seeds are a popular flavoring for pork (see pages 170, 171, 173, and 174). Ground coriander quickly loses its perfumed pungency, so store the seeds whole and pulverize them only when needed. The ancients believed a cordial of cilantro, garlic, and wine to be an effective aphrodisiac. Dried coriander seeds are also used to preserve meat (*pastourmas*, see page 349) and to flavor sausages.

Parsley / *Maidanos* or *Petroselino* Few savory Greek dishes do not require parsley. Flat-leaf parsley, which is measured by the handful in Greek cooking, has a more delicate appearance and milder flavor than the more common curly-leaf variety. Greeks regard parsley as a true tonic (it contains iron, minerals, and vitamins A and C) and consider it a natural deodorizer, absorbing the smell of other strong flavors such as wine, garlic, and vinegar. Take a minute or two to strip the leaves from the parsley stalks before use to prevent any trace of bitterness in your finished dish.

Marjoram / *Mandzurana* Pot marjoram (*origanum onites*) is the type most commonly used in Greek cooking. It is a smaller, more delicate herb than its botanical cousin, sweet or "garden" marjoram (*origanum hortensis*), which has a markedly different flavor. There can be confusion over the two so be sure to check which one you are buying if you wish to avoid disappointment in your finished dish. Marjoram is the essential flavoring in many lamb dishes and in *loukoumia* (known to us as Turkish delight).

Fennel / *Marathon* In spring, new shoots of fennel flavor an exquisite Fennel Bread (page 257). Later, the silky fronds are added to salads, wild greens, pies, and beet dishes. During early autumn the seeds are collected and dried, to be used in fish dishes, sweet breads, and pork dishes all through the year. The flavor is similar to licorice.

Mastic / *Mastiha* The resin collected from the bark of a small bush, mastic is a flavoring unique to the Eastern Mediterranean. It is sold as small hard granules – pulverize them in a clean coffee grinder or mortar, with double the quantity of sugar, before using. Mastic flavors cookies (page 285), breads (page 260), drinks (page 337), and rice pudding (page 300).

Oregano / *Rigani* Greek oregano is a stronger, sharper version of the familiar imported Italian herb. The word *oregano* is from the Greek, meaning "joy of the mountains," and *oreganum heracleoticum*, the herb known to the ancient Greeks, covers the hills and mountain slopes of Greece and perfumes the air. You can find large bunches of dried *rigani* in Greek shops; it is worth seeking out to give an authentic flavor to these recipes. Use the leaves on salads, on grilled foods, and in casseroles, and throw the twigs on a barbecue fire. Italian oregano (*oreganum vulgare*) can be substituted but will not provide the characteristic pungency associated with *rigani*.

Celery / *Selino* Celery is a very popular flavoring in meat and fish casseroles, soups, and pickles. The celery available to the Greek cook is wild celery; its natural habitat is marshland near the sea but in Greece it is semicultivated. The leaves, similar in appearance to flat-leaf parsley, are a beautiful shade of dark green; they have a mild, almost sweet, flavor, without any trace of the slightly bitter aftertaste of the pale leaves of large cultivated celery. During spring and summer Greek and Chinese shops stock wild celery; if unavailable, use the darkest leaves of rib celery, but first blanch them in boiling water.

Mint / *Thiosmos* or *Mentha* Several varieties of this deliciously refreshing herb are popular in Greece. Water mint is the type most commonly used in cooking dishes such as stuffed tomatoes. Peppermint, spearmint, lemon mint, and corn mint are all used to make fragrant herbal teas. Our nearest equivalent for cooking is fresh garden mint (use only the young tender leaves). Dried spearmint is delicious in *tsatsiki* (page 54).

Savory / *Throumbi* There are two types of this fragrant herb. Winter savory (*satureia hortensis*) is a favorite herb for flavoring grilled dishes, especially lamb and pork. Delicate summer savory (*satureia thymbra*) is rarely used in Greek cooking but it makes a soothing and popular tea.

Thyme / *Thymari* The thyme most widely available in Greece, the type that covers the dry limestone hills and is the source of the wonderful fragrance and flavor of Hymettus honey, is too strong to be used in cooking. But in the hillside villages, a gentler, sweeter version grows and this is used a great deal in the kitchen. It flavors game and pork as no other herb can.

Basil / *Vasilikos* Pots of sweetly fragrant basil, believed to keep flies away, are a common sight in Greece, but this herb is rarely used in cooking except in cakes and breads celebrating important religious events. The reasons for this are lost in folklore and myth, although basil's Greek name, meaning "kingly," may give us a clue; but it is also known as the "devil plant" and is associated with misfortune.

The herbs detailed above are all grown in Greece, but it was trade in other aromatics that helped create the wealth on which classical Greece thrived. These were mainly spices, some introduced through trade with Egypt, others brought back from eastern military campaigns by Alexander the Great.

Cinnamon / *Kanella* Produced from the bark of the cinnamon tree this heady spice is used to maximum advantage in the Greek kitchen. A favorite flavoring in lamb dishes (it is essential for magnificent *moussakas*), it also lends a delectable fragrance to cakes, syrups, cookies, and pies. Whole cinnamon sticks can be stored almost indefinitely; ground cinnamon is easier to use but be sure to buy only small quantities at a time since it quickly loses its pungency.

Nutmeg and Mace / *Moskhokario* Deep-yellow nutmegs are the hard seeds of soft fruit; mace is nutmeg's lacy reddish-orange natural covering. Nutmeg, rich and pungent, is best stored whole and grated, as needed; mace has a milder, less acrid flavor, and ground mace is fine for cooking. Both impart a lovely fragrance to sauces and casseroles.

Cloves / *Moskokarfi* Spicy cloves, the unopened flower buds of the clove tree, have a powerful fragrance. Whole cloves are used to perfume syrups, decorate cookies, and impart an unforgettable fragrance to beef casseroles; ground cloves add a delicious flavor to cookies.

Pepper / *Piperi* Pungent black pepper is generally preferred to the stronger, less subtle white. Invest in a good-quality pepper mill – ready-ground pepper is no substitute for freshly ground. I find it useful to have three pepper mills: one for black pepper, one for white, and one for a mixture of the two.

Vanilla / *Vanillia* Vanilla, the dried pod of a tropical orchid, is a relative newcomer to the Greek kitchen (used only since the medieval period) but is an essential flavoring in many cakes and pastries. Buy only good-quality pure vanilla extract. You can also make vanilla sugar by keeping a vanilla bean in a jar of granulated or superfine sugar.

Carob / *Xsilokerata* Carob is now better known as "health-food chocolate," a substitute for the real thing. But at other times in its long history, it had considerable economic importance (its seeds were the original carat measurement used by jewelers). In antiquity, carob was a favorite flavoring in confections. On Crete, the world's largest exporter of carob, it is now mostly used in wine production or to make syrup.

In addition to these aromatic flavorings, such spices as caraway seeds, paprika, aniseed, allspice, cayenne pepper, mustard seeds, and dry mustard appear in many Greek dishes.

With the exception of cinnamon, all spices should be bought whole, if possible, and ground in a spice grinder or electric coffee grinder, as required. Buy in small quantities and store in airtight jars away from the light to minimize loss of the spice's oil. It is this oil that aromatizes and flavors food.

Capers / *Kapari*

In the spring, the small tender leaves of the spindly wall-hugging caper bush, a native of the eastern Mediterranean, are picked; in early summer the tight flower buds, varying in size from tiny currants to small olives, are gathered. Leaves and buds are thoroughly cleaned and dried, then pickled in white wine vinegar aromatized with bruised fennel seeds. The capers can be eaten after one month or stored in the pickling liquid for up to a year. Capers give incomparable zest and character to grilled foods (especially lamb), beef casseroles, and fish dishes. Sprinkled with a little olive oil they can also be served as part of a *meze* table. Caper leaves make a pretty and edible garnish or flavoring. Buy small capers packed by a reputable supplier; some of the larger ones on the market are actually nasturtium buds.

Nuts / *Karythia*

Almonds (*amigdala*) have probably been cultivated in Greece for as long as the grape, the fig, and the olive and they feature in many ancient and traditional recipes. Eaten instead of meat and dairy products during religious fasts they are also symbols of long life and happiness. For festive sugar-coated almonds – and to flavor preserves – the Jordan, or "bitter," almond is used. For all other purposes the "sweet" almond is the type of choice.

Almonds are the central ingredient in rich Greek cakes such as *kataifi* (page 270), in Garlic Almond Sauce (page 313), and a soft marzipan sweetmeat called *amigdalota*. Pounded with sugar to a sweet paste, they are used to make *soumada*, a delicious syrupy drink. On Crete almonds are believed to prevent a hangover and are eaten in large handfuls before any serious raki drinking begins. These nuts are sold on every street corner, either salted or coated with honey.

Karythia is the Greek word for nuts but it is also the name for the walnut, popular throughout Greece. During autumn newly ripe walnuts are everywhere – served with ouzo or raki, made into cakes, sprinkled over desserts, and pounded into a creamy sauce – *karythesaltsa* (page 316). Very young walnuts are preserved for the winter – either in salt and vinegar to serve as a *meze* or in honey to nibble with coffee.

Waxy white pine nuts (*koukounaria*), from the cones of the stone pine, are a delicate and essential ingredient in a favorite *pilafi* (see page 227) and make a delicious sauce (see page 317). Since the stone pine bears fruit only every three years and the nuts have to be extracted from their tough outer covering by hand, pine nuts are expensive even in Greece.

Hazelnuts (*foundouki*), sold by every street vendor, are used to make wonderful cookies. On the vendor's tray there are also purple-skinned, green-fleshed pistachio nuts (*fistikia*); their delicate sweet perfume scents elegant creamy desserts (see page 303) and often replaces sesame seeds in *pasteli*, a popular sweet.

Store-bought ground nuts are, of course, easy for the cook. But in terms of moistness and flavor it is worth shelling, skinning, and grinding nuts yourself. The skins are easily removed after dipping the nuts into boiling water, and a food processor or blender makes easy work of grinding (use a clean coffee grinder for small quantities or treat yourself to an antique nut grinder).

Honey / *Meli*

According to legend, honey was literally a lifesaver for Zeus, the king of the ancient Greek gods. His father, Cronos, had a nasty habit of murdering his male offspring to prevent them from threatening his omnipotence and power. Keeping the baby Zeus quiet, therefore, was vital; spoonfuls of sweet and fragrant honey did the trick! Perhaps this is why honey-candied fruits were once a favorite sacrificial offering to the gods.

For Greeks the best honey comes from Mount Hymettus; clear and thick, it is perfumed with the thyme blossom that covers the mountain slopes. Most Greek honeys have a herbal bouquet although a few hint at the more floral notes of almond or citrus blossom. Honey contains natural minerals and trace elements beneficial to health and its aroma and pungency are so satisfying that only small amounts are needed. So, for a variety of reasons, honey is a healthier sweetener than sugar.

Honey and bread is a quick, nutritious snack; add honey to yogurt and you have a meal fit for the gods. Pungent blends of honey and vinegar are traditional flavorings for Greek casseroles, vegetables, and fish, and what would phyllo pastry be without its luscious drenching of honey syrup?

If it proves difficult to find Hymettus honey, unfiltered herb or orange blossom honey are good substitutes.

Lemons / *Lemonia*

The clear sharp tang of lemon was unknown to the ancient Greeks; this pretty fruit made its first appearance in Greece at the time of the thirteenth-century Crusades. But it would be difficult now to imagine Greece without its profusion of lemon trees, or a Greek meal without the color and piquant flavor lemons bring.

Lemon juice is an essential ingredient in many marinades and sauces, and it is the perfect complement to rich fruity olive oil. A small bunch of lemon leaves makes an exquisitely perfumed basting brush for grilled foods, and lemon zest and juice give a refreshing pungency to syrups and savory dishes. And what would a platter of tiny fried fish, *kephtedes*, or *souvlakia* be without their garnish of bright lemon wedges? Oil extracted from lemon zest is also a fragrant flavoring in sweet pies and cakes, and pretty rolled strips of zest make a luscious sweetmeat.

To make the most of versatile lemons it's a good idea to invest in three inexpensive kitchen implements – a zester (to remove tiny strips of zest), a wooden reamer (to quickly juice a lemon), and a stripper (to remove small sections of zest for flavoring or garnish). Empty lemon halves, pierced with a skewer and dipped into olive oil, make perfect natural basters for grilled fish and other dishes.

From every Greek lemon harvest some fruit is set aside to be preserved. Lightly treated with salt and stored in olive oil, lemons acquire a lively and distinctive flavor, perfect as a last-minute addition to casseroles, beans, and liver and fish dishes. Save the olive oil used as a preservative – it adds a delicious flavoring to salads and grilled dishes.

Preserved Lemons

5 large lemons (organic, if possible)
5 tablespoons coarse-grain sea salt *or* kosher salt
Extra virgin olive oil, to cover the lemons
Dried *rigani* (see page 13), marjoram, *or* thyme sprigs *or* large bay leaves

If you have unsprayed lemons you need only to rinse them well. Otherwise, cover the lemons with boiling water and set aside to cool. Drain, then cover with cold water. Set aside for 2 days, changing the water 3 or 4 times. Dry the lemons, cut off a thin slice from each end, and cut lemon into 1/4 inch slices. Remove any seeds with the point of a small knife, spread the slices on a plate, and sprinkle with the salt. Cover and refrigerate 24 hours.

Layer the slices in glass or earthenware jars and pour over any of the brine (salt water) left on the plate. Place the herb sprigs or bay leaves on top of the lemons, wedging them under the rims of the jars, and pour over enough oil to cover. The sprigs keep the slices immersed and flavor the olive oil. Cover tightly with plastic wrap and let sit at room temperature for at least 2 weeks. Refrigerate after opening, and use within 3 months.

Oranges / *Portokalia*

Navel and Seville are the types of oranges generally found in Greek kitchens. Navel oranges, large, juicy, sweetly perfumed, and thick-skinned, are on every dining table during their season. The skins are made into sweetmeats (see Candies, page 19) or preserves, or the zest dried to flavor cakes and casseroles. To dry the zest, remove the orange part of the skin in long strips and dry in a very low oven or in the sun. Hang the strips in the kitchen – they will add a lovely scent to the room – and break off pieces as you need them. (Treat lemon zest the same way.)

Seville oranges have a bitter flavor so cannot be eaten straight from the tree. Tiny ones, however, are preserved whole in a thick honey or sugar syrup as a delicious treat. The juice from larger oranges is used in dishes such as Pork in Aspic (page 35).

The blood orange, not widely popular on the Greek mainland, is more appreciated on the islands. Similar to a navel orange in taste, the flesh of a blood orange is a startling deep blood red. Its juice makes an unusual mayonnaise and a vibrantly colored drink.

Orange extract is used to flavor cookies and cakes; orange blossom infused to make a headily perfumed essence or "water" to flavor syrups, and also made into exquisite preserves. There is no substitute for orange extract or orange-flower water; the best brands are available in speciality shops.

Candies / *Zakharota*

Candies, confections, and/or sweetmeats, are a legacy of antiquity. The word candy is derived from *Candia*, the ancient name for Crete, where it was considered that the best honey and honeyed fruits originated. The confections so beloved by the ancients were sweet and fragrant, and many of these are still made in Greece in exactly the same way. The most popular are *pasteli* (Honey Sesame Sweetmeats, page 309), Moustalevria Sweetmeats flavored with cinnamon (page 307), sugared almonds, *loukoumia* (known to us as Turkish delight), and a sweet paste made from the quince. A more modern sweetmeat, very simple and economical to produce at home, can be made from the zest of oranges, lemons, or grapefruit.

Candied Citrus Zest / *Portokaloflioutho glyko*

Cut oranges lengthways into 8 or 10 segments, lemons into 6, and grapefruit into 12. Remove the flesh with a small paring knife. Weigh the zests and measure out an equal quantity of sugar; set aside.

Place the zests in a large saucepan, cover with cold water, and bring to a boil. Drain and repeat the process 3 times. Drain, cover with cold water, and set aside for 2 hours. Drain, and thoroughly dry with paper towels.

Thread a trussing or other large needle with thin kitchen string and tie a large knot at the end. Roll each piece of zest into a spiral and thread onto the string, passing the needle through the zest so it will not unravel. Thread no more than 18 zests onto each length of string, and tie the two ends together.

Place the sugar and half its volume of water in a large heavy saucepan. Slowly bring to a boil, stirring until the sugar is dissolved. Simmer 5 minutes, then add the strings of zest. Simmer uncovered for 30 minutes or until a needle will easily pierce the zests. Remove from the syrup and set aside to cool.

Carefully pull out the string. The zests will be left intact. Boil the syrup until it just reaches the light thread stage (230°F) on a candy thermometer. Stir in the juice of 1 small lemon and pour this syrup over the zests. Store the extra syrup in a covered container for up to 1 month.

To serve, remove the zests from the syrup and coat each one with honey, preferably Hymettus, or granulated sugar.

Ingredients at Home

In some recipes here I use ingredients that consumers and consumer groups today may rightly question on health grounds. I find that if I know the source of my ingredients, I feel secure in using them. I buy meat only when I can be assured of the standards of the farm where it was raised; vegetables and greens I cannot grow myself I buy from local farms or from the organic section in my local supermarket; I've found a source of organic milk and grains and I make my own yogurt and bread; a local farm, where the chickens appear as happy as I would imagine chickens are able to be, provides my eggs and poultry. I most enjoy ingredients grown or produced close to home for I know I am not only eating fresh food, but also food that has not suffered all the manhandling entailed in our modern packaging/storing methods.

Pots, Pans, and Kitchen Tools

Tsoukalia, Tigania, ke Ergalia Kouzinas

The most important, and most frequently used, tool in the Greek kitchen is the mortar and pestle. Greek cooks like to have three – a large walnut mortar in which to pound and blend *salates*, a large marble mortar and pestle for pulverizing nuts and spices, and a small brass or wooden mortar and pestle for bruising herbs. A food processor or blender could do this work quickly and easily, but these machines cannot produce the fine flavor that traditional equipment seems to provide. I also find that the delectable aromas released into the air when herbs and spices are pounded with oils are wonderfully satisfying.

Your repertoire of pots and pans should include the following:

An enamelled cast-iron casserole with a tight-fitting lid, for long slow oven baking. The best is called a *doufeu*. It has an indented lid that can be filled with water to keep the food moist during slow baking. Without the water, the *doufeu* can be used as an ordinary heavy baking dish.

Heavy cast-iron sauté pans, the plainer and heavier the better. (Fancy surfaces soon wear out and also prevent meat from browning properly.) You need one medium-size and one large one, at least.

A cast-iron omelet pan In Greece, a traditional shallow cast-iron pan is preferred as it can be taken straight to the table.

Also useful is a **round aluminum baking dish** (*tapsi*), about 2–3 inches deep and 15 inches in diameter, available in Greek and Middle Eastern shops.

For cooking and serving traditional dishes, nothing can beat **earthenware pots**. They should be glazed on the inside. If kitchen space is limited choose one deep casserole with a lid and one oval or round baking dish. If you can store more, add a deep bean pot (similar to a cassoulet pot), a rectangular dish (for baked *macaronia* dishes), and an unglazed clay pot (which I find produces a wonderful flavor in potatoes and beets).

Pickles and vinegar are best stored in stoneware jars. Stoneware is not, in fact, available in Greek villages but it is a much better material for long-term storage than porous earthenware. Small stoneware or glazed earthenware jars with tight-fitting tops are the most effective containers for dried herbs and spices. You may also like to collect special storage jars for specific ingredients, such as salt-glazed containers for sea salt or a jar with a tap at the base for vinegar.

Three good knives should be a minimum requirement in any serious cook's kitchen: a large chopping knife, a flexible filleting knife, and a paring knife.

The utensil I would least like to be without is a food mill. Unlike a food processor or blender, a food mill produces a delicious texture in soups and vegetable dishes and it can process larger quantities at one time.

A hinged double grill saves work too, making the grilling of small fish and pieces of meat simple.

And a few more:

A balloon whisk and small sauce whisk

A colander and several sizes of strainers

A wide pastry brush, for phyllo

Heavy baking pans

There are other kitchen tools, dishes, and storage pots in common use in Greek village kitchens of interest to serious cooks elsewhere. All have their origins in antiquity but are in daily use in the village. If you enjoy exploring markets you may like to look for a few of the following:

Bread-making equipment

Skafi a wooden trough for mixing and kneading the dough, usually about 3 feet long and 2 feet wide

Koskino a large shallow sieve, for sifting flour

Petromilos a large millstone with a wooden handle, for grinding flour

Tipari a carved wooden seal about 6 inches in diameter, used to imprint "offering" bread for the church

Casserole dishes

Kapamas or *lopas* a glazed earthenware casserole with sloping sides and a conical lid; it gives its name to the dish *kapama kotopoulo* (page 122)

Pithos a beautiful tall earthenware bean pot

Tsentsero a deep earthenware casserole with an elegant lid

Tsouka a round earthenware baking dish without a lid, for baking foods in the *fournos*

Tsoukali a smaller version of the *tsouka*, but with a lid and sometimes a handle

Coffee-making equipment

Briki long-handled, small brass coffee pot; the 4- or 6-cup size is the most useful

Flintzani tiny coffee cups

Milos tou kafe a magnificent coffee grinder, usually brass, but older ones are often made of copper

Grilling equipment

Souvles skewers, 12–18 inches long, often with elaborate cast metal animals at one end, for *souvlakia*

Foufou a beautiful little clay brazier, based on a design used by the Minoans and still found in Cretan villages, for grilling small birds and fish

Mangali a deep metal tray on legs, standing about 2 feet high, for *souvlakia*. The ends of the skewers (*souvles*) rest on the sides of the *mangali*, so no metal grate is needed

Cheese-making equipment

Trikon a deep basket with slightly sloping sides, made in many sizes – the smallest holds a ¹/₂-pound cheese, the largest, a cheese weighing several pounds; lined with cheesecloth, the *trikon* is then filled with curds and left on a tray to drain

Kopanaki wooden paddle for kneading and shaping the curds

And in village courtyards you may be lucky enough to find:

Kazani (colloquial Arabic name) or *lebes* (Greek) the ubiquitous iron cooking pot, used on a tripod over an open fire

Pitharia unglazed storage pots, some standing 4 feet high, and decorated with simple but beautiful designs dating from antiquity

Stamnos a gorgeous squat pot with two handles at the neck, for storing liquids such as vinegar or wine

Souratha similar to the *stamnos*, but with a spout on one side of the neck for easier pouring; with a *souratha* you do not need to master the difficult trick of tilting the large *stamnos* over your shoulder

Amourghi an earthenware cooking pot with cups attached on both sides, to hold the ingredients to be added to the pot during the cooking

Hydria a large earthenware jar with three handles, for carrying and storing water

Kakave a three-legged pot, which gives its name to the dish *kakavia* (fish soup)

Skoupa the appropriately named brush for sweeping the courtyard

My neighbor on the island of Crete, Irina, keeps a traditional kitchen, still using many of these ancient cooking tools. The entrance to her house is through a pretty paved courtyard that serves as an extension of both kitchen and sitting room; on warm days a large dining table is set up here, shaded from the fierce midday sun by a beautiful trellised vine.

Built into the far side of the courtyard wall is a beehive-shaped oven (*fournos*) where all the family baking is done. Nearby are propped a long handled wooden rake and paddle, used for removing baking trays and red-hot embers, and in one corner is a pile of kindling (the rest of the wood, mostly olive, is neatly stacked on the roof). In the corner a small blackened alcove encloses a fireplace and metal tripod supporting a large encrusted black cauldron with a gleaming interior, and a grill rests against the stones surrounding the fire. A small opening in the wall leads to a small stone building where the grape press, olive press, and huge storage jars (*pitharia*) for wine, olive oil, olives, vinegar, and pickles are kept.

Inside the small kitchen, a double burner (fueled by bottled gas) occupies one shelf; this is used mainly to make coffee – a concession to progress that most villagers have made. Four small wall cupboards hold bowls and kitchen tools; casseroles and saucepans are stored outside. Three mortars of varying sizes stand against one wall. A tiny pantry extends beyond the kitchen where preserves, preserved meats, pickles, yogurt, and cheeses are stored, and bunches of herbs and smoked sausages dangle from the ceiling.

A short walk from the house brings you to the delightful kitchen garden where Irina grows the herbs and all the vegetables she needs. Caper bushes cover the surrounding low stone walls and the lush greenery of asparagus and artichoke plants contrasts vividly with the barren hills beyond. In one corner of the garden is a well, tapping a natural spring, and beyond the garden is a small field where Irina's father grows wheat. Along the hillside, beyond the wheat field, are the vines and olive trees that have provided Irina's family with their basic necessities for centuries.

For me the simplicity of Irina's traditional kitchen was a revelation. I quickly discovered that I could produce superb food with very little sophisticated equipment and that there is wonderful satisfaction in working with traditional tools in an atmosphere of calm, tranquility, and order.

About the Recipes

There is a marked gender bias in the preparation and serving of food in Greece. This does not, of course, affect the flavor of the food but it does influence any selection of recipes. The oral tradition in the kitchen, passing recipes from mother to daughter, is still very strong, but men also take a keen interest in food and have their own oral tradition, passing on knowledge and skill in spit roasting, grilling, and oven (fournos) baking from father to son. In hotels, restaurants, and tavernas most chefs are male and, while they have a broad overview of their country's food, their knowledge is often confined to the professional, rather than the domestic, kitchen.

My experience of food and cooking in Greece falls somewhere between all these categories. I learned a great deal about grilling and roasting, for example, from good male cooks in the village where I lived. Through their experience and knowledge I also began to appreciate the particular culinary skills of Greek hunters and fishermen.

And since I lived in a village, I was always welcome in family kitchens – traditionally the woman's domain and a place where men are rarely seen. Here I learned just how pleasurable and creative food preparation can be, and how skilled Greek women cooks are at a range of remarkable vegetable cooking and at bread and pastry making.

Occasionally Athens would lure me. In this cosmopolitan city I enjoyed the company of urban Greek friends, many from families returned from Asia Minor. They too have their food preferences and particular flavoring skills in the kitchen. And I have to thank the chefs, on the mainland and on the beautiful islands, who shared with me their professional secrets and taught me much about the Greek attitude toward food, cooking, and flavor. These combined experiences, city and country, domestic and professional, provided me with the inspiration and information for this selection of recipes.

I have tried to be completely scrupulous in crediting the recipes, but it has not been an easy task. Few people, especially villagers, could be persuaded to give me a recipe I could actually write down, preferring instead to give me an idea (albeit lovingly descriptive) of the "essence" of a dish. Or they would give me a list of ingredients calling for "a little of this, more of that," until the flavor was "just right." Details about traditional dishes such as *stifado* (page 166) or *fassolada* (page 64) tended to follow these lines – how on earth could anyone not know the best way to make and flavor these familiar dishes?

My recipes are the result of tasting and more tasting, until I was satisfied I had reproduced an authentic Greek flavor. Most of the recipes have been adapted to a greater or lesser degree to suit our kitchens and tastes. Where I have used a recipe exactly as it was given to me, or stressed a technique or ingredient in the way it was stressed to me, I have said so and credited the cook who passed the recipe on to me. These were usually the recipes of the chefs, who understood my need for a concise explanation. However, even they tended to answer the question "Why?" with the response, "Because that is the way it has always been done."

APPETIZERS AND FIRST COURSES

Mezedes ke Orektika

Philosophers the ancient Greeks may have been, but they were practical too. They knew, for example, that drinking wine on an empty stomach is not a sensible idea. With characteristic creative logic they made it impossible in Greek society to indulge in such a barbaric practice – by the simple expedient of making delectable mouthfuls of solid food available wherever and whenever drinks were served. From this practical precaution stems the tradition and culture of the *meze*, now, as then, an integral part of the fabric of Greek social life.

Mezedes is usually translated as "appetizers" and, of course, these tempting little dishes are served with drinks as hors d'oeuvres and many make imaginative first courses. But the translation hardly does justice to the sheer range, ingenuity, and delight of *mezedes* nor to their fundamental place in Greek tradition.

Mezedes are available in cafés at any time; for many Greeks meeting friends to enjoy a refreshing drink and a *meze* platter makes a relaxing break in the busy working day. In Greek homes *mezedes* are automatically offered to all visitors, whether friends or stranger.

Guests are expected to help themselves to as much as they like from the *meze* platter and it's the host's duty to make sure empty dishes are replenished with more, or different, *mezedes* as necessary. This is not just politeness but an important social ritual. By providing food, drink, stimulating conversation, and an easy relaxed atmosphere the host demonstrates his/her ability to satisfy both the physical and spiritual needs of his guests. At the *meze* table the food is colorful, intensely aromatic, and highly flavored and the conversation is similarly exuberant, dramatic, and high-spirited.

In his writings, the philosopher Plato gives us a good idea of the range of tastes and texture offered by a well-balanced *meze* table. Laid out before the guests, he says, were platters of radishes, olives, beans, green vegetables, figs, cheese, fresh chickpeas, and myrtle. Here are foods both sweet and savory, fresh and preserved, crunchy and tender, and flavors subtle and strident. The same principle of contrasts is evident in good *meze* platters today – fresh and preserved vegetables, crunchy nuts, soft creamy *salates*, pickles, tiny savory pies and miniature meat patties, crumbly cheese, morsels of fried fish, octopus, or smoked eel, and fresh or dried fruit – the list is practically endless.

Mezedes are perfect for buffets and picnics, make unusual first courses, and are ideal as light lunches. A traditional *meze* table might comprise 25 dishes or more, but for our purposes 12–16 will create a spectacular display. It does take time to organize and cook a good variety of *mezedes*, but the pickled and preserved dishes can be prepared months ahead and many others one or two days before serving. You need provide only a small quantity of each *meze*, but do make sure each is decorated with an attractive edible garnish that enhances both its flavor and appearance.

Mezedes are served everywhere in Greece, from the tiniest bar to the swankiest hotel, and are one of the most enjoyable features of Greek life. Some of the best *mezedes* I've tasted were in one of the crowded *meze* cafés in the back streets of Athens, around the ancient Athinas market. These high-ceilinged, marble-floored cafés ring with the buzz and bustle of humanity, all chaos and confusion. With an attractive *meze* table, ouzo, raki, or wine to drink, and the stimulating company of good friends, you can create something of the atmosphere of those vibrant cafés.

Mezedakia

Small Appetizers
Mezedakia

At the sight of a tray of *mezedakia* – small *mezedes* – tastebuds tingle and eyes light up in anticipation. The bite-size morsels, in a seductive array of colors, textures, and flavors, are tidbits par excellence and Greek cooks assemble *mezedakia* platters with consummate artistry and skill.

On a well-balanced platter you'll find something crunchy (peppery radishes, perhaps, or fresh walnuts), something refreshing (tiny fingers of cucumber or melon or juicy tomato wedges), something salty (olives, capers, pickled eggplant), something savory such as crumbly fresh cheese or tiny fried fish, and sweet treats like dried figs or tiny plump currants.

Serves 8

2 large ripe tomatoes
Large pinch of sugar
Sea salt, to taste
1 cucumber, peeled
12 Amfissa, Thasos, *or* cracked green olives
12 Marinated Olives (page 28) *or* Kalamata olives
8 oz *feta* cheese, cut into slices or cubes
12 radishes, stems trimmed to 1 inch, a few small leaves left in place

And 2 or more of the following:
24 Salted Almonds (page 28)
4–8 Peppered Dried Figs (page 29)
8 Pickled Tiny Stuffed Eggplants (page 327)
8 Spiced Pickled Peppers (page 326)
24 capers, drained
8 salted anchovy fillets (see page 343), rinsed and patted dry *or* small
    sardines packed in olive oil (see page 350)
8 slices smoked ham *or* sausage (see page 179)

A few minutes before serving, core the tomatoes, cut each into 6 or 8 wedges, and sprinkle with sugar and salt. Cut the cucumber in half lengthways, then into 1/2-inch slices to make half-moons.

Keeping each ingredient separate, arrange the *mezedakia* on a large platter, either in concentric circles or as triangular wedges.

Marinated Olives

Elies Marinata

A small barrel of these glistening aromatic olives is a familiar sight in Greek homes. They are easy to prepare and the pungent herbs used in the marinade make the fleshy Kalamata olives irresistible. After the olives are eaten, use the olive oil in salad dressings.

1 pound Kalamata olives
4 tablespoons dried *rigani* (see page 13)
1 tablespoon dried rosemary
1/2 tablespoon dried thyme
1 teaspoon dried marjoram
2-inch strip of orange zest
3 sprigs dried *rigani or* thyme, each about 3 inches long
Extra virgin olive oil, to cover the olives

Spread the olives between layers of paper towels and blot dry to remove most of the brine. Mix together the olives, dried herbs, and orange zest in a bowl. Pack loosely into a glass jar, lay the herb sprigs on top, and add olive oil to cover. Cover tightly and store for 2 days to 1 week.

Salted Almonds

Amigdala Alatismena

Traditional Greek wisdom says that eating salted almonds when you take a drink (or several!) will keep you sober. I have not put this tip to serious test myself so cannot vouch for its success, but I do know that once you've tasted the delicious sweet-sour flavor of these almonds you'll be in no hurry to buy commercially prepared ones again.

2 cups almonds, with brown skins intact
Juice of 2 lemons
3 tablespoons coarse-grain sea salt

Heat the oven to 325°F. Combine the almonds and lemon juice in a nonreactive bowl and set aside for 10 minutes; stir the almonds with a wooden spoon occasionally so they are evenly coated.

Arrange the almonds on a baking pan in a single layer and sprinkle with the salt. Bake 20 minutes, until lightly browned, stirring once or twice. Let cool and serve, or store in small airtight containers for up to 1 month.

Peppered Dried Figs
Sika Piperata

If possible, use fleshy, juicy organic figs imported from southern Greece for this simple *meze*, and prepare three days ahead for the richest flavor.

24 good-quality, moist dried figs
4 tablespoons cracked black pepper
12–18 bay leaves

Trim the fig stems. Gently roll each fig in the pepper to lightly coat.

Cover the bottom of a glass jar with a few of the bay leaves, or make an overlapping circle of leaves on two layers of plastic wrap. Then make alternate layers of figs and bay leaves, finishing with a layer of leaves. Gently press down on the leaves with the palm of your hand, then tightly cover the jar or pull the edges of the plastic wrap together into an airtight packet. Store at room temperature for up to 1 month.

Serve the figs on a bed of bay leaves.

Smoked Fish Salad
Tsirosalata

There is a long tradition of preserving fish in Greece and markets display a variety of brightly colored smoked fish, stacked in decorative layers in wooden crates and barrels. On these market stalls you will also find whole anchovies packed in salt, fish roe in beeswax, sardines in olive oil, bonito in brine, or young mackerel or octopus dried in the sun. Look for preserved fish in Greek stores or delicatessens; this recipe is for smoked fish but you could substitute good-quality tuna, sardines, or anchovies.

Serves 6 to 8

1 large smoked mackerel *or* herring *or* 2 small smoked mackerel
    (about ³/₄ pound total)
2 tablespoons aged red wine vinegar

For serving
1 tablespoon capers, drained
1 tablespoon extra virgin olive oil, or to taste
Coarsely ground black pepper, to taste
2 tablespoons snipped fresh dill *or* chervil *or* 1 tablespoon coarsely
    chopped flat-leaf parsley
Elitses *or* Niçoise olives, drained

Hold the mackerel by its tail above an open flame until the skin blisters and breaks. (Or place under a hot broiler until the skin blisters.) Peel off the skin and discard the head and tail. With a thin-bladed knife, make a slit along the underside of the fish, open it like a book and, with your palm, press firmly to flatten it. Discard the backbone and skeleton. Place the fillets in a bowl, add 1¹/₂ tablespoons of the vinegar, and cover with cold water. Set aside for 10 minutes.

Remove the fillets, discarding the liquid, thoroughly dry with paper towels, and cut into thin strips or bite-size pieces. Arrange on a serving plate and sprinkle with the capers, olive oil, pepper, dill, olives, and the remaining vinegar.

Tiny Fried Fish
Marithes Tiganites

Frugal Greek cooks let nothing go to waste. The tiniest fish of the catch are not worth sending to the market, so a taverna or café close to the harbor is the place to try this mouth-watering *meze*. Tiny fish, freshly caught and crisply fried in olive oil, are piled high on a platter, surrounded with lemon wedges, and served with ouzo or wine. In Greece, delicate little pickerel or anchovies, or the tiniest sardines, are the fish of choice for this dish; whitebait smelt are a good substitute. It's important to choose glossy-looking, very fresh fish since the whole whitebait is eaten, including the bones and head.

Serves 6 to 8

1 pound tiny whitebait smelt
¹/₂ cup all-purpose flour
1 tablespoon chickpea flour

½ tablespoon coarse-grain sea salt, or more to taste
1 tablespoon cracked black pepper, or to taste
Extra virgin olive oil, for frying

For serving
2 large lemons, cut into wedges

Rinse the fish, drain between layers of paper towels, and blot dry. Combine the flours, salt, and pepper in a bowl, add the fish, and toss to coat.

Pour a ½-inch layer of olive oil into a large heavy sauté pan set over low heat. When hot but not smoking, raise the heat to medium-low and add enough fish to fill the pan without overcrowding. Fry until golden brown, turning once, and drain on paper towels. Repeat with the remaining fish.

To serve, pile on a warm platter, garnish with the lemon wedges, and sprinkle with more salt and pepper if desired.

Kephtedakia

Kephtedakia – small, highly flavored meat croquettes or patties, traditionally made with lamb or pork and fried or baked in good olive oil – are popular on *meze* tables whatever the occasion. Delicious warm or cold, tiny *kephtedakia* (about the size of marbles) are the perfect tidbits to serve with ouzo. Make them egg-sized instead and they become *kephtedes*, which, served with a green salad, make an enjoyable and economical main course.

Makes approximately 48 *kephtedakia* or 36 *kephtedes*

2 medium onions, finely chopped
1 pound lean lamb *or* beef *or* a mixture of both, finely ground
1 large potato, peeled and grated
1 cup fresh bread crumbs
2 eggs, lightly beaten
1 tablespoon aged red wine vinegar, or more to taste
4 tablespoons finely chopped flat-leaf parsley
Sea salt *and* freshly ground black pepper, to taste
1 tablespoon ground cumin *or* 1½ tablespoons ground coriander *or* ½
    tablespoon ground cinnamon *or* 2 tablespoons finely grated *kasseri or*
    Parmesan cheese
All-purpose flour, for dredging
Extra virgin olive oil, for frying or baking

For serving
Juice of 1 large lemon

Combine the onion and ½ cup water in a small saucepan, bring to a boil and simmer until the liquid has evaporated, about 6 minutes. Combine the onion, meat, potato, bread crumbs, beaten egg, vinegar, parsley and a generous amount of salt and pepper in a large bowl and add one of the spices or the cheese. With a wooden spoon or your hand, mix until well blended. Add additional vinegar, salt and/or pepper to taste; the mixture should be highly flavored. Cover and refrigerate for 1 hour.

Moisten your hands with cold water and pat them barely dry. Form the meat mixture into ¾-inch patties (or 1½-inch patties for *kephtedes*), flattening each slightly between your palms, and lightly dredge with flour.

To fry, pour a ¼-inch layer of olive oil into a heavy frying pan set over medium-low heat. When the oil is hot but not smoking, add just enough *kephtedakia* (or *kephtedes*) to fit comfortably in a single layer. Fry until golden brown on both sides and drain between 2 layers of paper towels. Repeat with the remainder.

Or, to bake, heat the oven to 325°F and warm 2 or more baking pans. Brush with olive oil and arrange the *kephtedakia* 1 inch apart on the pans. Lightly brush with olive oil and bake 20–25 minutes (25–30 minutes for *kephtedes*), turning once to brown on both sides. Drain between layers of paper towels.

To serve, arrange on a platter and sprinkle with lemon juice.

Note For a buffet or first course, form the meat mixture into 1-inch patties and cook as directed. To serve, combine the following:

....

1 small head of Romaine lettuce, rinsed and cut into thin ribbons (chiffonade) just before serving
6 scallions, trimmed, the best green parts left intact, and thinly sliced
5 tablespoons coarsely chopped flat-leaf parsley
1 tablespoon dried *rigani* (see page 13)

....

Arrange this salad on a platter. Sprinkle with the strained juice of 1 lemon and extra virgin olive oil, salt, and pepper to taste. Pile the *kephtedakia* on top.

Potato Kephtedakia
Patatokephtedakia

In the Cretan port of Aghios Nikolaos there was once a café where, along with the local backgammon players, you would also find a mouth-watering variety of traditional Cretan *mezedes*; the great speciality were these delicious *kephtedakia*. Potato *kephtedakia* may not be sophisticated eating, but the taste is superlative. Serve with a variety of other *mezedes* and *khorta* (see page 221) for a traditional meal, or include them in a buffet or picnic. Larger potato *kephtedes* and a Wild Greens Salad (page 222) make an unusual light lunch.

Makes approximately 30 *kephtedakia* or 24 *kephtedes*

1 pound boiling potatoes
3 tablespoons fresh mint leaves *or* chopped fresh dill
2 tablespoons unsalted butter, melted
1 egg yolk
4 scallions, trimmed and finely chopped
2 tablespoons finely chopped flat-leaf parsley
1 tablespoon freshly squeezed lemon juice
Sea salt *and* freshly ground white pepper, to taste
1½ ounces fine bulgur, *optional*
All-purpose flour, for dredging
About 4 tablespoons extra virgin olive oil, for baking

Scrub the potatoes and cut larger ones in half or into quarters. Place in a saucepan with cold salted water to cover and bring to a boil. Cover, and simmer 15 minutes or until just cooked. Drain, and as soon as the potatoes are cool enough to handle, peel them. Pass through a food mill fitted with the fine disc into a large bowl. Or mash with a potato masher or fork, then push through a strainer into a large bowl. Tear the mint leaves into small pieces. Combine the melted butter and the egg yolk and add to the potatoes, with the mint, scallions, parsley, lemon juice, and salt and pepper. Lightly mix with a fork; refrigerate.

If using the bulgur, combine it with 2 tablespoons flour in a food processor and process until the mixture has a sand-like consistency. Spread enough of the mixture, or all-purpose flour, on a plate to cover. Heat the oven to 375°F and place 2 baking pans in the oven to heat. Moisten your hands with cold water and pat barely dry. Shape spoonfuls of the potato mixture into ¾-inch balls for *kephtedakia*, or a little larger for *kephtedes*. Flatten slightly between your palms and lightly dredge with the bulgur mixture or flour. Brush the hot baking trays with olive oil and arrange the *kephtedakia* 1 inch apart on them. Lightly brush with olive oil and bake 15–20 minutes, turning once to brown on both sides. Drain between layers of paper towels.

Pile on a platter and serve hot or warm.

Potato Kephtedakia with Cheese
Polpetes

On Crete, two favorite cheeses are used to flavor potato *kephtedakia*: either aged *myzithra* cheese or the fresh, slightly sour-tasting, *anthotyro*. *Anthotyro* is available only in Greece, but *feta* makes a good substitute.

Omit the parsley and use dill rather than mint. Add 1½ ounces finely grated aged *myzithra* cheese, or 2 tablespoons finely grated *feta* cheese and 2 ounces well-drained cottage cheese, passed through a strainer, to the potato mixture. Chill, shape into *kephtedakia* or *kephtedes*, and bake and serve as above.

Potato Kephtedakia with Tomatoes
Polpetes me Domates

Make these beautiful little *kephtedakia* when tomatoes are in season. Core, skin, and seed 2 large ripe tomatoes; dice. Place in a strainer set over a bowl, and sprinkle with a large pinch of sugar and a small pinch of salt. Set aside for at least 30 minutes, then press the tomatoes gently but firmly against the sides of the strainer to remove as much juice as possible. Combine the tomato with the potato or potato-cheese mixture just before shaping.

Potato and Vegetable Kephtedakia
Polpetes Lakhanika

Add a puree of spinach, cauliflower, or fresh fava beans to either the potato mixture or the potato-cheese mixture. For each 1 cup potato mixture, add ½ cup vegetable puree.

Note To fry *kephtedakia*, use a light olive oil. To deep-fry, form the mixture into small round patties no more than 1 inch in diameter. Heat the olive oil until hot but not smoking, and fry the *kephtedakia*, a few at a time, until golden brown. Drain between layers of paper towels.

To pan-fry, pour a ¼-inch layer of olive oil into a heavy frying pan set over medium-low heat. Heat until hot but not smoking, and fry the slightly flattened *kephtedakia* in batches until golden brown on both sides. Drain between layers of paper towels and serve hot or warm.

Lamb's Liver with Lemon Juice and Rigani

Sikotakia Tikhanita

Thin squares of tender lamb's liver, lightly fried in a well-flavored olive oil, are a classic of Greek cuisine. Justly so, since that treatment lifts humble liver into the realms of the sublime. If lamb's liver is unavailable, you can substitute calf's liver, although the dish will be less authentic.

Serves 10

1 pound lamb's *or* calf's liver
All-purpose flour, for dredging
5 tablespoons extra virgin olive oil
1 teaspoon paprika
Coarse-grain sea salt *and* cracked black pepper, to taste
Strained juice of 1 large lemon

For serving
2 tablespoons dried *rigani* (see page 13), briefly pounded in a small mortar
1 small bunch flat-leaf parsley, leaves coarsely chopped
1 small red *or* mild onion, cut into thin rings

Trim off any membrane from the liver, cut it into thin slices, and cut the slices into 2-inch squares. Lightly dust with flour and shake off the excess.

Heat 4 tablespoons of the olive oil in a large heavy frying pan and fry the liver over medium-low heat until light brown and slightly crusty on both sides, about 4 minutes. (It should still be moist in the center.) Sprinkle with the paprika, salt and pepper, and half the lemon juice. Reduce the heat to low and cook 1 minute longer.

Transfer to a warm platter and sprinkle with the remaining olive oil and the lemon juice, salt and pepper, to taste, and the *rigani*, parsley, and onion. Serve immediately.

Pork in Aspic

Pikti

A common sight in village kitchens in autumn and winter is a sturdy tripod supporting a well-used blackened pot from which steams the most tantalizing spicy aroma. In the pot, pork and pig's feet simmer gently with herbs and spices. A good *pikti* takes time to prepare, but it is an important traditional dish and will repay your effort. Prepare it at least 4 hours before serving so it will have time to set. It makes a beautiful buffet centerpiece, garnished with olives, radishes, cucumber, and tiny tomatoes. It can also be served as an elegant first course, accompanied by toasted whole wheat bread and black olives or Black Olives and Lentil Salata (page 39). For a satisfying lunch, serve it with Beet Salad with Allspice (page 184), black olives, and crusty bread.

Serves 12 to 14 as a first course, 8 as a light lunch

2 pig's feet, cut into pieces by the butcher
2 pound lean pork on-the-bone (any cut), trimmed of fat
12 black peppercorns
1 tablespoon sea salt
4 bay leaves
3 cloves
1/2 teaspoon dried red pepper flakes
1 tablespoon dried rosemary *or* sage leaves
4–8 oz lean mild ham, *optional*
3–5 tablespoons white wine vinegar
2 egg whites
1 small bunch of flat-leaf parsley, leaves finely chopped
Olive oil, for greasing

Rinse the pig's feet and pork, place in a stockpot, and add water to cover. Bring to a boil and remove any surface froth with a slotted spoon. Add the peppercorns, salt, bay leaves, cloves, red pepper flakes, and rosemary. Reduce the heat, cover, and simmer 1 hour.

Add the ham, cover, and simmer 2–3 hours longer, or until the meat is falling off the bones. Strain, and set aside the meat and bones to cool; discard the seasonings. Strain the stock through 2 layers of cheesecloth into a bowl, set aside to cool, and refrigerate, uncovered, until cold.

Remove and discard the surface layer of hardened fat. Heat the stock until it has just liquefied, then measure it. You should have about 4 cups; if necessary, reduce by rapid boiling. When cool, add 3 tablespoons of the vinegar and the egg whites, and stir with a wooden spoon. Bring to a boil over medium-low heat, stirring constantly, until the egg whites set and become stringy. Simmer a few minutes longer.

Set a fine-meshed strainer lined with 2 layers of cheesecloth over a bowl and strain the stock. You should have about 1 1/2 cups of clear straw-colored aspic. Taste, add more vinegar if desired; the aspic should be quite tangy. Loosely cover and refrigerate.

Remove the meat from the bones and discard the fat, sinew, and bones. Cut the ham and the meat from the pig's feet into tiny chunks and the remaining meat into ¼-inch cubes. Once the aspic has begun to thicken and stick to the sides of the bowl, stir in the meat and parsley. Transfer the mixture to an oiled 1-quart mold, cover, and refrigerate until set, or for up to 3 days.

To serve, dip the mold in a bowl of boiling water for 5 seconds. Invert a serving plate on top and, holding the plate firmly in place, turn upside down to remove from the mold.

Note You can substitute ¼ cup Seville orange juice and the juice of 1 lemon for the vinegar to make a slightly different version of this traditional dish.

Snails in Vinegar
Salingaria me Xsithi

This rather startling *meze* is a speciality of the island of Crete. The islanders enjoy it with plenty of crusty bread and copious quantities of robust local red wine, together with two or three other *mezedes* such as olives, marinated vegetables, and *khorta* (see page 221) to complement the taste and texture of the snails.

Serves 4

2 tablespoons coarse-grain sea salt
24 cleaned snails in their shells, boiled 15 minutes and their protective skins removed (see page 351)
2 tablespoons extra virgin olive oil
Boiling water, to cover the snails
½ cup aged red wine vinegar

For serving
1 small bunch flat-leaf parsley, leaves coarsely chopped

Spread the salt on a plate, press the rim of each snail into it, and set aside.

Add the olive oil to a large heavy sauté pan that will hold all the snails in a single layer and heat it over low heat. Add the snails and gently roll them around with a wooden spoon so they heat through. Add enough boiling water to barely cover the snails and simmer until the water has evaporated, about 12 minutes. Take care not to let the snails burn. Add the vinegar, cover, and cook over very low heat for 5 minutes or until reduced by half, occasionally shaking the pan.

Transfer the snails to a warm platter or individual plates, spoon over the sauce, sprinkle with the parsley, and serve.

Fried Cheese
Saganaki

Saganaki means "two-handled frying pan," and this savory *meze* is named after the dish in which it was originally cooked. Serve bubbling hot, and have ready some olives, *kephtedakia* (page 31), and one or two *salates* then bring on your *saganaki* centerpiece with a flourish.

Serves 6

1/2 pound *kephalotyri or kasseri* cheese (see page 9)
All-purpose flour, for dredging
Extra virgin olive oil, for frying

For serving
Strained juice of 1 large lemon
Finely chopped flat-leaf parsley
Cracked black pepper, to taste

Cut the cheese into 1/4-inch slices with a thin-bladed knife or cheese wire, and cut each slice into rectangles approximately 1 1/2 by 2 inches. Dredge with flour, shaking off any excess, and set aside.

Cover the bottom of a heavy frying pan with a thin layer of olive oil and heat over medium-low heat just until the oil sizzles when you drop in a crumb of cheese; don't allow the oil to reach smoking temperature. Fry the cheese slices, a few at a time, on both sides until golden brown and crusty, about 6 minutes. Drain between layers of paper towels and keep warm in a low oven until all the slices are fried.

Transfer to a warm platter, sprinkle with the lemon juice, parsley, and black pepper, and serve immediately.

Salates

Greek *salates* bear little resemblance to what we know as salads. Most are purees made from fresh or dried vegetables, blended with herbs, spices, and olive oil. Sometimes nuts are substituted for vegetables; the popular *taramosalata* is made from the pureed roe of the mullet fish. With a culinary history stretching back into antiquity, *salates* are attractive additions to a buffet table and offer a variety of interesting flavors and textures. The best *salates* are still made in the traditional way, using a large walnut mortar, which imparts its own special flavor. Blenders and food processors make speedy and simple work of them, but tend to mash the ingredients into a smoother, blander texture than that of the traditional way. Serve two or three *salates* on a *meze* table, accompanied by warm pita or crusty bread and fresh or preserved *mezedakia* such as cucumbers and olives.

Salates are appealing to busy cooks, as many can be made ahead of time, giving the flavors time to mellow and deepen. They are also versatile – Fava Bean Salata (page 40), for example, can be served as an unusual first course. Or, to serve with drinks, spread one or two contrasting *salates* on toast for quick and simple canapés.

Black Olives and Lentil Salata
Elaiosalata

All over Greece olives appear in an infinite variety of guises. In this attractive *salata*, the magnificent flour of oil-cured black olives is at its powerful best. Ideal as a spread for canapés, it's especially good with savory appetizers and Tiny Cracked Potatoes (page 56).

Serves 10 to 12 as a *meze*, 8 as a first course

7/8 cup green lentils, picked over, rinsed, and soaked for 30 minutes in cold
    water to cover
3 ounces oil-cured black olives, pitted
2 tablespoons capers, rinsed and patted dry
2 small anchovy fillets (see page 343), rinsed and patted dry
2 tablespoons dried *rigani* (see page 13)
1 large clove garlic, finely chopped
Juice of 1 large lemon
4 tablespoons extra virgin olive oil, or more to taste

For serving
Oil-cured olives
1 teaspoon dried *rigani*, briefly pounded in a small mortar
Coarsely chopped flat-leaf parsley

Drain the lentils and place in a large saucepan with cold water to cover by 3 inches. Bring to a boil, cover, and simmer 30 minutes, or until they are soft but not disintegrating. Drain, and set aside to cool; shake the colander once or twice to make sure all the lentils are dry.

Place the olives, caper, anchovies, *rigani*, garlic, and lentils in a food processor or blender container. With the machine running, add half the lemon juice, then add the olive oil in a thin steady stream. Add more lemon juice or olive oil to taste and process just until the mixture is thick and creamy.

Spread on a platter and place the olives in the center. Sprinkle with the *rigani* and parsley, and serve.

To make the traditional way Fit a food mill with the fine disc and press all the ingredients through into a large wooden mortar. Pound for 5 minutes, or until well mixed. Add half the lemon juice and then add the olive oil drop by drop, pounding constantly, until you have a thick, creamy purée. The more olive oil you use, the better the flavor. Add more lemon juice to taste.

Note To store, refrigerate for up to 24 hours in an airtight container or store for up to 6 months in small sterilized jars, with a thin layer of olive oil on top of the puree to "seal" it. Before serving, stir in the olive oil.

Fava Bean Salata
Fava

There is no doubt that shelling and skinning fava beans is labor-intensive, but don't let that stop you from making this wonderful classic dish. The earthiness of the beans is sharpened by the lemon juice and yogurt, olive oil gives a creamy texture, and fragrant dill lends pungency. The combination produces a *meze* of surprisingly fine flavor and texture. Or try it as a side dish for roast or grilled pork or lamb.

Serves 8 as a *meze*, 4 as a vegetable dish

3 pounds fava beans in the pod
6 scallions, trimmed, with 2 inches of green left intact
5–6 tablespoons extra virgin olive oil
2 tablespoons finely chopped fresh dill
Sea salt *and* freshly ground black pepper, to taste
Strained juice of 1 small lemon
4 tablespoons Strained Yogurt (page 7)

For serving
Fresh dill sprigs
4–8 Elitses *or* Niçoise olives

Shell the beans, remove their skins, and set aside. Coarsely chop all the scallions, then finely chop 2 tablespoons and set aside for garnish.

Heat 2 tablespoons of the olive oil in a large heavy frying pan over low heat and sauté the scallions for 5 minutes, or until soft. Add the beans, cover, and cook 5 minutes longer, shaking the pan occasionally.

Transfer the beans and scallions to a food processor or blender and add the dill, salt, and pepper. With the machine running, add most of the lemon juice and yogurt, and 2 tablespoons of the remaining olive oil, and process to a puree. If the puree seems too thick, add a few tablespoons of water.

Add lemon juice, yogurt, or olive oil for a sharper, lighter, or deeper flavor, respectively.

Spread on a plate and sprinkle with the reserved scallions and the remaining olive oil and lemon juice. Garnish with dill sprigs and olives and serve at room temperature.

To make the traditional way Prepare the beans in the same way, but finely chop the scallions before sautéing with the beans and dill. Pound the sautéed bean mixture in a large wooden mortar for 10 minutes before adding the remaining ingredients. To obtain a creamier puree, double the quantity of olive oil.

Another Fava Bean Salata
Fava

The success of this traditional country *salata* depends on the quality of the olive oil you use – the better the oil, the richer the flavor. The base is a melting mixture of finely diced carrot, celery, onions, garlic, and bay leaf, sweetened by long slow cooking in the olive oil. It's a distinctive dish that never fails to please, and it improves in flavor if made a day or two ahead. Serve as a *meze*, with bowls of yogurt and *khorta* (see page 221), or as a side dish for roast or grilled meats. If using dried fava beans seems too time-consuming, you can substitute canned lima beans, although the dish will lose some authenticity of flavor.

Serves 8 to 10 as a *meze*, 6 as a vegetable dish

1¼ cups dried fava *or* lima beans, soaked overnight in water to cover, *or* 2 14–ounce cans lima beans, rinsed
6 tablespoons extra virgin olive oil
1 medium onion, finely chopped
1 clove garlic, finely chopped
1 medium carrot, finely diced
½ stick celery, finely diced
2 bay leaves, crumbled
3 tablespoons finely chopped flat-leaf parsley
Sea salt *and* freshly ground black pepper, to taste
1 thick slice coarse-grain white *or* whole wheat bread, crust removed, *and* soaked for 5 minutes in 1–3 tablespoons extra virgin olive oil, to taste
Juice of 1 small lemon

For serving
Large pinch of paprika

Drain the dried beans and place in a large saucepan with cold water to cover. Bring slowly to a boil, reduce the heat, cover, and simmer 5 minutes; drain and rinse the beans. Rinse out the saucepan, return the beans to the pan, and add cold water to cover by 3 inches. Bring to a boil, reduce the heat, cover, and gently simmer 20–25 minutes, or until soft. Drain, reserving ¹/₂ cup of the cooking liquid. Remove the fava bean skins with your fingers and spread the beans between layers of paper towels to dry. (This step is unnecessary if using lima beans.)

Heat half the olive oil in a large heavy pan. Sauté the onion, carrot, garlic, celery, and bay leaves over medium-low heat for 15–20 minutes, until dark golden brown, stirring occasionally with a wooden spoon.

Stir in 2 tablespoons of the parsley, the salt, pepper, beans, and reserved cooking liquid. (If using canned beans, add ¹/₂ cup water.) Cook for 2–3 minutes, until the liquid has evaporated.

Transfer to a food processor or blender and add the bread. With the machine running, add about two-thirds of the lemon juice and most of the remaining olive oil, and process until thick and smooth. Add a few drops of water if the puree seems too thick, and add salt, pepper, olive oil, and/or lemon juice to taste.

Serve on a platter, sprinkled with the remaining parsley and olive oil and the paprika.

To make the traditional way Pound the cooked vegetable-bean mixture and the bread in a large wooden mortar for 5 minutes. Slowly add about two-thirds of the lemon juice and then 4 tablespoons of the olive oil. Pound for 5 minutes longer, and add salt, pepper, olive oil, and/or lemon juice to taste.

Chickpea and Garlic Salata
Revithosalata

The best *revithosalata* has a thick creamy consistency, a spicy coriander tang, and a pleasing mustard color. The flavors of garlic and olive oil, although not overpowering, should be detectable. Serve with *mezedakia*, vegetable appetizers, a bowl of yogurt, and warm pita bread.

Serves 10

1¹/₂ cups chickpeas, soaked overnight in water to cover
2 large cloves garlic, chopped
1 teaspoon ground coriander *or* ¹/₂ teaspoon ground cumin
1 teaspoon sea salt, or more to taste
¹/₂ teaspoon freshly ground black pepper, or more to taste
5 tablespoons extra virgin olive oil
Strained juice of 2 lemons, or to taste

For serving
Finely chopped flat-leaf parsley
1 tablespoon dried *rigani* (see page 13), crumbled
1 teaspoon paprika

Drain the chickpeas and place in a large saucepan with cold water to cover. Bring slowly to a boil, drain, and rinse. Rinse out the saucepan, return the chickpeas to the pan, and add cold water to cover by 3 inches. Bring to a boil, reduce the heat, cover, and gently simmer for 50 minutes, until soft. Drain, reserving 1/2 cup of the cooking liquid and a few whole chickpeas for garnish.

Place the chickpeas, garlic, coriander, salt, and pepper in a food processor or blender. With the machine running, gradually add 4 tablespoons of the olive oil and most of the lemon juice. Add more salt and pepper and the remaining lemon juice if desired and process until smooth and creamy. For a thinner consistency, gradually add some or all of the reserved cooking liquid. (If you plan to store the *salata*, add all the reserved liquid – it will thicken on standing.)

Spread on a platter and sprinkle with the parsley, *rigani*, and reserved whole chickpeas. Combine the paprika and remaining olive oil and sprinkle over the *salata*.

Note To store, refrigerate in an airtight container for up to 2 days.

Salt-Dried Fish Roe Salata
Taramosalata

The ancient Greeks were very fond of this smooth sharp fish pâté and it's just as popular in Greece today. Barrels of salted dried mullet roe, the basic ingredient of *taramosalata*, are a familiar sight in busy fish markets. For Greeks *taramosalata* is a winter dish, especially popular during the Lenten fast when no meat or dairy products are eaten. For us, with jars of *tarama* readily available in Greek and Middle Eastern shops, it can be a year-round treat. Versions vary from region to region, even from cook to cook – some favor the use of just bread, others use potatoes instead, others both. Experiment until you find your favorite combination of ingredients, texture, and flavor. Best made just before serving, *taramosalata* is an attractive buffet dish; served on small plates, garnished with radishes, olives, and cucumber, it makes an elegant first course for a dinner party.

Serves 10 to 12 as a *meze*, 8 as a first course

2 1/4 cups *tarama*
1/2 medium onion, finely grated

3–4 cups fresh bread crumbs (made from good white bread, crusts
  removed)
Juice of 1½ lemons
½ cup extra virgin olive oil, or more to taste

For serving
12 Nafplion *or* other Greek green olives (see page 3)
Finely chopped flat-leaf parsley

Place the *tarama* in a bowl, cover with cold water, and break up any
lumps with your fingers. Set aside for 30 minutes.

Line a strainer with 2 layers of cheesecloth and drain the *tarama* over a
bowl. Gently squeeze the cheesecloth "bag" to remove as much of the salty
water as possible; discard the water. Place the *tarama*, onion, and most of
the bread crumbs in a food processor or blender. With the machine running,
add the juice of 1 lemon, and then add the olive oil in a thin steady stream
and process until the *taramosalata* has the consistency and texture of thick
cream. Add a little cold water if it is too thick, or additional bread crumbs if
too thin. If you prefer a sharper flavor, add some or all of the remaining
lemon juice; for a more mellow taste, add more olive oil.

Serve on a platter, surrounded with the olives and sprinkled with the
parsley.

To make the traditional way With a large wooden mortar and pestle,
pound the *tarama*, most of the bread crumbs, and the onion for 5 minutes,
or until well-mixed. Slowly add the lemon juice and ⅝ cup olive oil, and
pound for 5 minutes longer. Add a little cold water if the mixture seems
too thick, or additional bread crumbs if too thin.

Note You can substitute 1 pound mashed potato for the bread crumbs
or use a mixture of potatoes and bread crumbs. Use a mortar and pestle –
potatoes lose their firm texture if processed.

Grilled Eggplant Salata
Melitzanosalata

For this *salata*, egplants are first grilled, then the soft cooked flesh is
scooped from the shells and mixed with an aromatic blend of tomato,
rigani, onion, garlic, lemon juice, and seasoning. A food processor will
make fast work of this unusual dish – but a smoky flavor is essential so the
eggplants must be grilled, not baked.

Serves 10 to 12

1 large ripe tomato, skinned, seeded, and diced

3 or 4 large unblemished eggplants (about 3 pounds total)
1 tablespoon dried *rigani* (see page 13)
2 tablespoons finely chopped mild onion
1–2 cloves garlic, crushed
Sea salt *and* freshly ground white pepper, to taste
Juice of 1 small lemon
4 tablespoons Strained Yogurt (page 7)
4 tablespoons coarsely chopped flat-leaf parsley
4 tablespoons extra virgin olive oil

For serving
6 small capers, drained and rinsed
Large pinch of paprika

Heat the grill. Drain the diced tomato in a strainer.

Trim the stem ends from the eggplants, make 6 small slits in each eggplant, and place on the grill 2–3 inches from the heat source. Grill for about 15 minutes, until the skins scorch, turning them carefully so they brown evenly on all sides. Test by inserting the point of a knife into the center of each eggplant – they should be very soft. Set aside to cool.

When the eggplants are cool enough to handle, carefully scrape out the flesh from the skins and, with a teaspoon, remove and discard as many of the seeds as possible (there's no need to be too fussy). Gently squeeze the flesh between paper towels to remove excess moisture.

Place the *rigani*, onion, garlic, salt and pepper, and lemon juice in a food processor or blender and process a few seconds, until well-mixed and finely chopped but not pulverized. Add the tomato, eggplants, and 3 tablespoons each of the yogurt and parsley, and pulse 2 or 3 times to mix. Add the olive oil in a thin steady stream, continuing to pulse – but stop just before the mixture is smooth. Add salt and pepper, lemon juice, and/or olive oil to taste. Transfer to a serving bowl, cover tightly, and chill for at least 1 hour.

To serve, spoon the remaining yogurt on top of the *salata* and sprinkle with the capers, paprika, and the remaining parsley.

To make the traditional way Grill the eggplants over the embers of a wood fire. Let cool, then remove the flesh and seeds, and cut the flesh into tiny cubes. Pound the onion, garlic, and salt and pepper in a large wooden mortar for 5 minutes. Add the eggplants, tomato, *rigani*, lemon juice, yogurt, and parsley. Pound 5 minutes longer, or until well pulverized. Add the olive oil in a thin steady stream, still pounding, until the mixture is thick and well combined. Although the quantities of the other ingredients remain the same, 2 or 3 tablespoons more olive oil are needed to obtain the right consistency – this is one reason why traditionally made *melitzanosalata* has a deeper, more interesting, flavor.

Sweet and Spicy Tomato Salata
Domatosalata

Anastasia, a friend on the island of Khios, taught me how to make this appetizing *salata*. The dish has a charm all its own, especially when served in a shallow bowl with a swirl of creamy white yogurt and a sprinkling of glossy fresh parsley or cilantro for garnish. You can also use the *salata* as a rich tomato sauce, perfect with baked or grilled fish, meat *pilafi*, and *macaronia* dishes.

Serves 6

4 tablespoons extra virgin olive oil
1 large onion, finely chopped
3 pounds firm ripe tomatoes, skinned and diced, juices reserved
1 tablespoon tomato paste diluted with 2 tablespoons water
1½ teaspoons ground cinnamon, or to taste
1 large clove garlic, finely chopped
Sea salt, to taste
½ teaspoon freshly ground black pepper, or more to taste
Pinch of cayenne pepper
2 tablespoons aromatic honey, such as Hymettus
1–2 tablespoons aged red wine vinegar *or* 1 tablespoon light balsamic
  vinegar

For serving
2 tablespoons Strained Yogurt (page 7), *optional*
Finely chopped flat-leaf parsley *or* a few fresh cilantro leaves

Heat the olive oil in a large heavy frying pan and sauté the onion over medium-low heat for 10 minutes or until soft; do not let it brown. Add the tomatoes and their juices, tomato paste, cinnamon, garlic, cayenne pepper, salt, and pepper. Raise the heat and boil uncovered 30–40 minutes, until most of the liquid has evaporated, stirring occasionally with a wooden spoon. The puree should be thick enough to remain separated for a few seconds when you draw the spoon across the bottom of the pan. Add the honey, reduce the heat, and cook, stirring occasionally, for 10 minutes longer, until thick and slightly syrupy. Be careful not to let it burn. Remove from the heat and set aside to cool.

Stir in half the vinegar, taste, and add more cinnamon, salt, pepper, cayenne pepper, and/or vinegar if desired.

Transfer to a shallow bowl, add a swirl of the yogurt in the center, sprinkle with the parsley, and serve.

Note To store, refrigerate for up to 1 week in an airtight container or store for up to 3 months in small sterilized jars "sealed" with a thin layer of olive oil. Use this oil in salad dressings or other dishes, or stir into the *salata* before serving.

Eggplant and Other Vegetable Appetizers

Eggplant Appetizers
Melitzanes Mezedes

Eggplants are such a characteristic ingredient of Mediterranean cuisines that it may be a surprise to learn that they are not native to the region but instead originated in tropical Asia. In Greece, eggplants form the basis of an infinite variety of simply prepared delicacies – baked, they lend a subtle earthy flavor and richness to casseroles and other dishes; stuffed with aromatic or spicy fillings, they become satisfying main courses; and pureed into delicate creamy *salates* they have pride of place on a good *meze* table. For simple snacks eggplant slices can be fried plain in olive oil or dipped in fritter batter and fried.

Visit any Greek market in early summer and displayed before you is the abundance, variety, and splendor of the exotic eggplant: skillfully stacked in huge geometric piles, glossy skins gleaming in the sun, small round eggplants nestle next to thin elongated varieties and bulbous pear shapes. Their variegated colors create a feast for the eye, ranging from pure pearly white and white streaked with green to the deepest velvet purple and black.

Reject any eggplant with bruised or wrinkled skin and check that the stem end looks fresh and the prickly calyx firm and bright. Fresh eggplant feels heavy in your hand and the skin should be glossy and tight. Size and shape do not affect flavor, so choose according to the requirements of your recipe.

Eggplant contains a bitter juice that must be removed before cooking. Cut the vegetable in half or into slices or cubes, sprinkle the cut surfaces with salt, and let drain in a colander for about one hour. The cut surfaces will then be covered by droplets of pale brown liquid, which you can remove by patting the pieces with paper towels. Remove as much moisture as you can. This salting and drying process not only seasons the eggplant but also prevents it from absorbing too much olive oil during cooking. Eggplants and olive oil are, however, natural partners, so do not be tempted to skimp on the amounts called for in these recipes. A Greek friend says that olive oil helps the "shy" eggplant to discover its "true talkative personality" – and I agree with him.

Grilled Eggplants
Melitzanes Skharas

An informal supper that always pleases friends is simplicity itself to prepare: grilled eggplants, a tasty fish *meze*, juicy olives, *feta* cheese, plenty of bread, and a glass or two of ouzo. Each guest receives a whole eggplant and, according to taste, adds a dressing of olive oil, lemon juice, and seasonings to the eggplant's delicious smoky-flavored flesh.

---

1 eggplant per person (4–5 inches long)

For serving
Small jug of extra virgin olive oil
Lemon wedges
Coarse-grain sea salt *and* freshly ground black pepper

Heat the grill.

Trim the ends from each eggplant and make 6 small slits in the skin to allow moisture to drain during grilling. Place on a grilling tray 2–3 inches from the heat source and grill, using tongs to turn carefully, until lightly charred and blistered on all sides, about 10 minutes. Drain briefly on paper towels.

Slit open each eggplant from one end to the other, taking care not to let any charred pieces of skin fall inside, and press the ends to open them slightly.

Arrange on a platter or individual plates and serve immediately. Pass around the olive oil, lemon wedges, salt, and pepper grinder.

Fragrant Eggplants with Olives
Melitzanes Aromatikes

Turning everyday ingredients into special treats is a traditional Greek skill, as this popular *meze* demonstrates. Eggplant slices are simply fried or grilled, but the last-minute addition of good red wine vinegar, succulent olives, bright green parsley, and perfumed *rigani* creates a colorful dish

with a highly unusual flavor. Serve with thick yogurt in which to dip the eggplant slices.

Serves 4

3 medium eggplants (about 1 1/4 pounds), each about 2 inches in diameter
Sea salt, to taste
Extra virgin olive oil, for frying or grilling

For serving
3 tablespoons aged red wine vinegar, or to taste
12 Elitses *or* Niçoise olives, drained
2 tablespoons finely chopped flat-leaf parsley
1 tablespoon dried *rigani* (see page 13), briefly pounded in a small mortar
Cracked black pepper, to taste

Trim off the ends from the eggplants and cut into 1/4-inch slices. Sprinkle with salt and set aside for 1 hour to "sweat."

To grill, arrange a grill rack about 3 inches above hot coals, or heat a broiler. Thoroughly dry the eggplant slices with paper towels and brush on both sides with olive oil. Grill 1–2 inches from the heat source until dark golden brown on both sides; don't worry if they blacken in places.

Or, to fry, cover the bottom of 1 or 2 large heavy frying pans with a thin layer of olive oil and heat over medium-low heat. Fry the eggplant slices, a few at a time, until golden brown on both sides. Drain between layers of paper towels.

Arrange the slices in an attractive pile on a platter. Just before serving, sprinkle with the vinegar, olives, parsley, *rigani*, and salt and pepper. Serve hot, warm, or at room temperature (within 1 hour of cooking).

Eggplants with Zucchini and Artichoke Hearts
Tiganita Lakhanika

In early summer, when zucchini and artichokes are at their crunchy best, these delectable vegetable fritters appear on taverna tables throughout Greece, as part of a *meze* table, or as a simple lunch. Garlic adds the finishing touch – these fritters are traditionally served with a powerful garlicky sauce.

Serves 12 as a *meze*, 6 as a light lunch

3 medium eggplants (about 1 pound total)
Sea salt
1 pound medium zucchini
12 small *or* 6 medium artichokes
1 lemon, cut in half
All-purpose flour, for dredging
2 cups fresh fine bread crumbs
3 eggs
Freshly ground black pepper, to taste
Extra virgin olive oil, for frying

For serving
5 tablespoons coarsely chopped flat-leaf parsley
1 tablespoon dried *rigani* (see page 13)
Finely grated zest of ½ lemon
Juice of 1 large lemon
12 Elitses *or* Niçoise olives, drained
Garlic Almond Sauce (page 313) *or* Potato Skordalia (page 314)

Trim off the stem ends of the eggplants and cut into ¼-inch lengthways slices. Cut these crosswise in half or into quarters, sprinkle with 1 tablespoon salt, and set aside for 45 minutes to "sweat." Wipe the zucchini and cut into ¼-inch crosswise slices. Sprinkle with 1 tablespoon salt and set aside.

Prepare a large bowl of ice water. Trim the stalks of the artichokes and remove the tough outer leaves. With a sharp knife, slice off the top third of each artichoke to expose the choke. Scoop out the fuzzy part with a small spoon and trim off any remaining leaves from the heart. Cut large hearts in half or into quarters. Rub all the cut surfaces with a half-lemon, place in the bowl of ice water, and add the lemon halves to the bowl.

Spread the flour on one plate and the bread crumbs on another. Break the eggs into a small bowl, add salt and pepper to taste, and lightly beat together with a fork. Place 2 large heavy frying pans over low heat and add olive oil to make a thin layer. With paper towels, dry enough eggplant slices to make a single layer in the frying pans. Lightly dust with flour and shake off any excess. Dip the slices first in the egg mixture, then in the breadcrumbs, to coat on both sides. When the oil is hot but not smoking, fry the eggplant slices until light golden brown on both sides, about 6 minutes. Drain between layers of paper towels, and repeat with the remaining eggplant and the zucchini slices.

Add enough olive oil to one of the frying pans to make a ¼-inch layer. When the oil is hot, fry the artichoke hearts until light golden brown on all

Opposite: Mezedakia: Peppered Dried Figs, Salted Almonds, Marinated Olives, Radishes

sides. Drain between layers of paper towels. Chop the parsley, *rigani*, and lemon zest together until well mixed.

To serve, arrange the vegetables on a platter and sprinkle with the lemon juice, olives, and the parsley mixture. Serve hot, warm, or at room temperature, with the garlic sauce.

Note For greater speed, you can deep-fry the vegetables in olive oil but be sure to keep the temperature of the oil just below smoking.

Island Eggplants
Nisiotikes Melitzanes

This hearty eggplant dish from the Greek islands, with its combination of robust contrasting flavors, reflects the Turkish occupations of medieval times. Serve cold as an elegant appetizer or buffet dish or warm as an unusual accompaniment to grilled meats and egg dishes. If possible, make a day ahead to give the flavors time to mellow.

Serves 8 to 10 as a first course, 6 as a vegetable dish

1½ pound medium round eggplants
Sea salt
6 sticks celery, rinsed and tough strings removed
2 red bell peppers, roasted and skinned (see page 343)
½ cup extra virgin olive oil, or to taste
2 large onions, quartered and thinly sliced
1 large clove garlic, minced, *optional*
6 large ripe tomatoes, skinned and diced, juices reserved
1 teaspoon honey
1 tablespoon tomato paste diluted with 2 tablespoons water
3 tablespoons dried *rigani* (see page 13)
½ teaspoon freshly ground black pepper, or more to taste
1 pound tiny potatoes, baked in a clay pot (see page 207) or boiled until
    barely tender, *optional*
1 small bunch flat-leaf parsley, leaves finely chopped
24 Elitses *or* Niçoise olives, rinsed and pitted
2–3 tablespoons capers, rinsed and coarsely chopped
4 salted anchovy fillets, rinsed and finely chopped

For serving
Juice of 1 large lemon

Trim the ends from the eggplants and cut into ¾-inch cubes. Sprinkle the cut surfaces with 1 tablespoon salt and set aside in a colander for 45

Opposite: Grilled Aubergines

minutes to "sweat." Cut the celery into large matchstick strips and blanch in boiling water for 1 minute. Drain under cold running water and set aside. Remove the cores and seeds from the peppers and wipe with paper towels to remove any remaining seeds. Slice lengthways into strips.

Heat half the olive oil in a large sauté pan and sauté the onions over low heat for 10 minutes or until soft. Add the garlic, tomatoes and their juices, honey, tomato paste, *rigani*, and salt and pepper. Raise the heat and lightly boil for 20–30 minutes, until reduced by half. The sauce should remain separated for a second or two when a wooden spoon is drawn across the bottom of the pan.

Meanwhile, in another large sauté or frying pan, heat most of the remaining olive oil over medium heat. Thoroughly dry the eggplants with paper towels and fry 10–15 minutes or until golden brown on all sides. Drain between layers of paper towels and set aside.

Add the celery, peppers, potatoes, parsley, olives, capers, anchovies, and eggplants to the tomato sauce. Stir gently just to combine and cook over very low heat for 5 minutes. Add salt, pepper, and/or the remaining olive oil to taste.

To serve, arrange on a platter or individual plates and sprinkle with the lemon juice.

Note If you intend to reheat the dish, don't add extra salt until just before serving; the salty olives, anchovies, and capers will flavor the other ingredients.

Aromatic Giant Beans
Fassolia Gigantes

This is one of my favorite Greek dishes and one I always associate with impromptu village gatherings in cool courtyards. Whatever the occasion, these beans are always present! Long slow cooking in olive oil sweetens and mellows the vegetables and the dish has a very special nutty flavor.

Serves 10 to 12 as a *meze*, 4 as a light lunch

1¹/₂ cups dried fava beans *or* lima beans, soaked and cooked (see page 42) *or* 2 14-ounce cans lima beans, drained and rinsed
5 tablespoons extra virgin olive oil
1 large onion, cut in quarters and thinly sliced
1 stick celery, finely diced
2 medium carrots, peeled or scrubbed, and finely diced
1 pound ripe tomatoes, skinned and diced, juices reserved
1 teaspoon honey
1 tablespoon ground coriander

2 tablespoons dried *rigani* (see page 13)
1 large clove garlic, finely chopped
Sea salt *and* freshly ground pepper, to taste

For serving
Juice of ½ small lemon, or to taste

Heat half the olive oil in a large heavy pan. Sauté the onion, celery, and carrot over medium-low heat for 20 minutes, or until light golden brown, stirring occasionally with a wooden spoon. Add the tomatoes and tomato juices, honey, coriander, *rigani*, and garlic, and stir well. Simmer until the sauce becomes thick and syrupy and stays separated for a few seconds when the spoon is drawn across the bottom of the pan. Gently stir in the beans, salt (canned beans may not need added salt), and a generous sprinkling of pepper. Cover and simmer 5 minutes longer.

Transfer to a shallow bowl, sprinkle with the lemon juice and the remaining olive oil, and serve hot, warm, or cold.

Meze Salad Medley
Lakhanika Diafora Marianata

This enticing trio of vegetable salads captures all the unmistakable fragrance and flavors of the eastern Mediterranean. Serve with plenty of crusty bread to mop up the delicious sauces.

Serves 10 as a *meze*, 5 to 6 as a light lunch

2 pounds young fava beans in the pod
1 small bunch flat-leaf parsley, leaves coarsely chopped, stalks removed and
  tied in a bundle
Strained juice of 3 lemons, or to taste
Coarse-grain sea salt *and* cracked black pepper, to taste
Large pinch of powdered mustard
1 cup extra virgin olive oil, or to taste
2 tablespoons snipped fresh chervil, *optional*
4 medium artichoke hearts, lightly boiled until tender and cut into quarters
12 ounces slender asparagus, steamed or lightly boiled (see page 182)
2 tablespoons coarsely chopped fresh oregano *or* 1 tablespoon dried *rigani*
  (see page 13)

For serving
1 red bell pepper, roasted and skinned (see page 343), seeded, and cut into
  thin strips

Fill a large saucepan with lightly salted water and bring to a boil. Shell the beans, reserving 2 pods. Add the pods and parsley stalks to the boiling water and boil for 5 minutes. Add the beans and boil for 2 minutes longer. Drain, discarding the pods and parsley stalks. While the beans are still warm, remove the skins. Drain between layers of paper towels and pat dry.

Divide the lemon juice between 3 nonreactive bowls; add salt and a generous amount of pepper to each. Add the mustard to one of the bowls, divide the olive oil between the bowls, and add the chervil (or 1 tablespoon of the parsley) and artichokes to the bowl with the mustard. Add the (remaining) parsley and asparagus to the second bowl, and the oregano and fava beans to the third. Gently stir each mixture, tightly cover, and set aside for 1 hour.

To serve, taste each sauce and add lemon juice, salt, and/or pepper if necessary; the sauces should be highly seasoned. Arrange the vegetables attractively on a flat platter or on individual plates, keeping them separate. Garnish the fava beans with strips of bell pepper.

Yogurt and Cucumber Salad
Tsatsiki

Variations of this crisp refreshing salad are popular throughout an area stretching from northern India to the Balkans and Greece. In the Greek version, large amounts of garlic and flat-leaf parsley are used or, better still, fresh mint, which gives a light fragrant flavor. Serve *tsatsiki* as soon as possible after preparing or it will become watery. Delicious as part of a *meze* table, *tsatsiki* also nicely complements *kephtedes*, *souvlakia*, grilled meats and fried liver (see page 35).

Serves 8 as a *meze*, 4 as a salad

1 large cucumber, peeled
½ tablespoon sea salt, or more to taste
1 cup Strained Yogurt (page 7)
2 tablespoons extra virgin olive oil
1 tablespoon freshly squeezed lemon juice
Freshly ground white pepper, to taste
2 large cloves garlic, finely chopped
5 tablespoons fresh mint leaves *or* coarsely chopped flat-leaf parsley *or*
    2 tablespoons dried mint, crushed

Using a knife, food processor, or mandoline, slice the cucumber into matchstick strips. Sprinkle with salt and set aside in a colander for 1 hour to drain.

Combine the yogurt, olive oil, lemon juice, pepper, and garlic in a large bowl. Cover, and refrigerate.

Just before serving, beat the yogurt sauce with a wooden spoon until smooth. Tear the mint leaves into small pieces. Dry the cucumber by gently squeezing it between paper towels; don't worry if the cucumber bruises – it is more important to avoid a watery salad. Combine with the yogurt mixture and mint, add salt and pepper to taste, and serve.

Leeks the Classic Way
Klassika Prassa

This simple dish features traditional ingredients of the ancient Greek cuisine – spicy coriander, perfumed bay leaves, sweet honey, pungent vinegar, and rich olive oil. A popular *meze* since the days of Homer, it looks beautiful and has an unusual sweet-sour flavor.

Serves 12 as a *meze*, 6 as a first course

12 slender leeks, 1/2 inch in diameter
1/2 cup extra virgin olive oil, or to taste
1 1/2 tablespoons whole coriander seeds, crushed
3 bay leaves
1 teaspoon cracked black pepper
2 tablespoons aromatic honey, such as Hymettus
4 tablespoons aged red wine vinegar
1/2 cup currants *or* small seedless raisins
Coarse-grain sea salt, to taste

For serving
2 tablespoons finely chopped flat-leaf parsley

Slice off the roots and green tops of the leeks. Cut a slit lengthways halfway through each leek, keeping the original shape intact. Hold upright under running water and gently pull the layers apart, one at a time, to wash out any grit or dirt. Shake off any excess water, drain between layers of paper towels, and blot dry.

Place a heavy sauté pan large enough to hold the leeks in a single layer over low heat, and add 3/8 cup of the olive oil, the coriander seeds, bay leaves, and pepper. Cook for 1 minute, until the coriander is aromatic. Add the leeks, turning to coat with the oil and spices.

Combine the honey and vinegar and add to the leeks along with the currants. Cover and bring just to a boil; reduce the heat to very low and simmer 10–15 minutes, or until the leeks are tender but still firm in the center.

Transfer to a serving dish and set aside to cool. Add salt to taste and the remaining olive oil if desired. Sprinkle with the parsley and serve warm or at room temperature.

Note Twelve tender sticks of celery can be substituted for the leeks. Remove the tough strings with a paring knife and cut wide sticks lengthways in half. Cut into 5-inch pieces. Boil for 1 minute in lightly salted water, drain, and add to the aromatic olive oil.

Tiny Cracked Potatoes
Patates Antinaktes

This simple but superbly aromatic dish is a perfect *meze* with yogurt, *khorta* (see page 221), *kephtedakia* (page 31), and Fried Cheese (page 38), or serve it with grilled meats and chicken.

Serves 8 to 10 as a *meze*, 4 as a vegetable dish

....

1½ pounds tiny new potatoes
4 tablespoons extra virgin olive oil
5 tablespoons aged red wine vinegar
4 tablespoons coriander seeds, lightly crushed
Sea salt *and* cracked black pepper, to taste
4 tablespoons coarsely chopped flat-leaf parsley
1 tablespoon small capers, rinsed and patted dry, chopped
1 tablespoon finely grated lemon zest

....

Scrub the potatoes and pat dry. With a heavy kitchen mallet or meat pounder, firmly tap each potato to crack it slightly, taking care not to break it apart.

Heat the olive oil in a large sauté pan with a tight-fitting lid. Add the potatoes in a single layer, cover, and cook for 1 minute over low heat, until light golden brown, shaking the pan frequently.

Drain off most of the oil from the pan. Add the vinegar, coriander, salt, and a generous amount of pepper to the potatoes, cover, and cook over very low heat for 15 minutes, until the potatoes are tender. Take care not to let the potatoes burn. Mix together the parsley, capers, and lemon zest.

Transfer the potatoes to a warm serving dish and sprinkle with the parsley mixture. Serve hot, warm, or at room temperature.

Meze Pies

Fried Cheese Pies
Tyropittes Tighanites

These tiny fried pies are a real taste of Greece. Made with an orange-flavored pastry, they conceal a sweet cheese filling, perfumed with fresh mint. Whenever I serve them to guests, either as a *meze* or light lunch, they disappear very quickly. Fry them in olive oil for the most authentic flavor, or, if you prefer, bake them.

Makes 18 to 24 pies: Serves 8 as a *meze*, 4 to 6 as a light lunch

Pastry
2 cups all-purpose flour
1 teaspoon sea salt, or to taste
½ teaspoon superfine sugar
2 tablespoons virgin olive oil
1 egg white, lightly beaten
4–5 tablespoons strained fresh orange juice, as needed

Filling
5 tablespoons fresh mint leaves
12 ounces fresh *myzithra* cheese (see page 10), crumbled, *or* small-curd cottage cheese, drained and pressed through a fine strainer
About ½ cup finely grated *feta* cheese
1 whole egg *plus* 1 egg yolk, lightly beaten
2 tablespoons honey
2 tablespoons unsalted butter, melted
½–1 teaspoon ground cinnamon, or to taste
Olive oil, for frying

For serving
confectioners' sugar, sifted
Ground cinnamon

To make the pastry, combine the flour, salt, sugar, olive oil, egg white, and 3 tablespoons of the orange juice in a large bowl. Knead for 5 minutes, adding more orange juice if needed to make a smooth and elastic dough. Tightly wrap in plastic wrap and refrigerate for 1 hour.

To make the filling, finely chop the mint leaves and mash together all the filling ingredients with a wooden spoon until well mixed but not smooth.

Divide the dough in half, rewrap 1 portion, and return to the refrigerator. Roll out the pastry on a lightly floured surface and cut out circles with a 2-inch or 4-inch round cutter; or cut into 2x4-inch rectangles. Place 1 heaping tablespoon of filling in the centers of half the 2-inch circles, or all the large circles or rectangles. Brush the edges of the pastry with the remaining orange juice. Cover the 2-inch circles with the remaining small circles, or fold the 4-inch ones in half to make half-moons; fold rectangles in half to make 2-inch squares. Crimp the edges with a fork to seal. Repeat with the remaining pastry and filling.

Pour a 1/2-inch layer of olive oil into a large heavy sauté pan, or heat olive oil in a deep-fat fryer. When the olive oil is hot but not smoking, fry the pastries over medium heat until deep golden brown on both sides; or deep-fry until golden. Drain on paper towels, arrange on a warm platter, sprinkle liberally with the confectioners' sugar and cinnamon, and serve hot or warm.

Note To bake, instead of frying, heat the oven to 350°F. Arrange the pastries 2 inches apart on lightly oiled baking sheets and bake for 15 minutes. Lightly beat 2 egg yolks with 2 tablespoons olive oil and brush the pastries with this glaze; bake 10 minutes longer, or until deep golden brown. Or you can make squares or circles with a little of the filling exposed in the center (see page 274) and bake these.

Baked Cheese and Spinach Pies
Spanakopittes me Tyri

These little pastries, filled with a creamy nutmeg-spiced spinach mixture, are perfect picnic food. You can make them with either pastry dough or with phyllo and they freeze beautifully (freeze before cooking).

Makes 18 to 24 pies: Serves 8 as a *meze*, 4 to 6 as a lunch dish

1 pastry (see page 57) *or* (1–pound) package phyllo pastry (see page 266), thawed if frozen

Filling
1 1/2 pounds fresh spinach
1/2 cup extra virgin olive oil
5 scallions, trimmed, the best green parts left intact, and thinly sliced
1/4 teaspoon grated nutmeg
Sea salt, to taste
1 teaspoon cracked black pepper, or to taste
6 ounces small-curd cottage cheese, drained and pressed through a fine strainer
1/2 cup crumbled *feta* cheese
1 small bunch flat-leaf parsley, leaves coarsely chopped

2 egg yolks, lightly beaten (for pastry pies), *or* 4 tablespoons unsalted butter, melted (for phyllo pies)

If using phyllo, remove from the refrigerator and set aside unopened.

Rinse the spinach in several changes of cold water, discard the stalks and any bruised or tough leaves, and place in a heavy saucepan. Cover and cook, with just the water that clings to the leaves, for 1 minute, until wilted and barely soft. Drain, pressing the greens against the sides of the colander to remove as much liquid as possible. Finely chop the spinach and set aside.

Warm half the olive oil in a heavy sauté pan and sauté the scallions over low heat until soft, about 5 minutes. Stir in the spinach, nutmeg, salt, and pepper and cook 2 minutes. Remove from the heat and drain off any liquid. Add the cottage cheese, *feta* cheese, and parsley, and gently mash together with a fork. Season to taste with salt and pepper.

Heat the oven to 350°F. Make the pies with the pastry as directed on page 57 or with the phyllo as directed on page 267. Arrange 2 inches apart on lightly oiled baking sheets. Brush pastry pies with the remaining olive oil, phyllo pies with a mixture of the olive oil and melted butter. Bake pastry pies for 15 minutes, brush with the beaten egg yolks, and bake 10 minutes longer, or until deep golden brown. Bake phyllo pies 15–20 minutes, or until deep golden brown. Serve hot or warm.

Note If tender young beet greens or chard are available, try the country version of these pies. Substitute 2 pounds of greens for the spinach; discard all tough stalks and bruised or blemished leaves. Prepare as the spinach but cook 3 minutes, or until just soft.

Sesame Spinach Pies
Spanakopittes

These delicious sesame-topped miniature pies and some good fresh cheese are the perfect nibbles to accompany a glass of wine. Or serve them the Cretan way, as a side dish with roast or grilled pork. Wild greens provide the most authentic country flavor, but you can substitute beet greens, chard, or spinach.

Makes 18 to 24 pies: Serves 8 as a *meze*, 4 to 6 as a lunch dish

1 Pastry (see page 57)

Filling
3 pounds young water spinach (*vlita*, see page 221) *or* beet greens *or* ruby chard *or* 2 pounds young fresh spinach
¹/₂ cup extra virgin olive oil

2 medium onions, quartered and thinly sliced
1 teaspoon ground cumin
1 small bunch fresh dill *or* fennel, coarsely chopped
1 teaspoon sea salt, or to taste
1 teaspoon cracked black pepper, or to taste
Juice of 1 small lemon
2 egg yolks, lightly beaten
1 cup sesame seeds

Rinse the greens in several changes of cold water and discard the stalks and any tough or discolored leaves. Boil the water spinach, covered, in 1/2 inch of water for 5 minutes, until barely tender. (Boil beet greens or ruby chard in 1/2 cup water for 2 minutes, spinach in a few tablespoons water for 1 minute.) Drain, and press the greens firmly against the side of the colander to remove excess water.

Heat 6 tablespoons of the olive oil in a heavy sauté pan and sauté the onion over low heat until soft, about 10 minutes. Stir in the cumin. Finely chop the greens, and add to the onions with the dill. Cook 2 minutes longer, and add the salt, pepper, and lemon juice; the mixture should be highly seasoned.

Heat the oven to 350°F. Make the pies as directed on page 57 and arrange them 2 inches apart on lightly oiled baking sheets. Brush with the remaining olive oil and bake 15 minutes. Brush with the beaten egg yolks, liberally sprinkle with the sesame seeds, and bake 8 minutes longer, until deep golden brown. Serve hot or warm.

Variations
♦ Add 1/4 cup cooked rice and 1/4 cup currants to the filling.
♦ Add 2 ounces drained small-curd cottage cheese, pressed through a strainer, and 1/4 cup toasted pine nuts to the filling.
♦ Increase the amount of dill or fennel to 1 large bunch and use 21/2 pounds water spinach or beet greens.

Note To freeze, spread uncooked pies in a single layer on a baking sheet and freeze. Remove from the baking sheet and store in freezer bags. Defrost before baking.

Tiny Vegetable Pies
Bourekakia Lakhanika

Serve these little delicacies as the glorious centerpiece to a *meze* table. Eggplants, zucchini, leeks, onions, or bell peppers can all be used in the filling; next time you grill or bake vegetables, cook a few extra, and cut down on your preparation time the next day. You can make *bourekakia* with either pastry dough or with phyllo.

Makes 18 to 24 pies: Serves 8 as a *meze*, 4 to 6 as a lunch dish

1 Pastry (see page 57) *or* (1-pound) package phyllo pastry (see page 266), thawed if frozen

Filling
1 large eggplant
Coarse-grain sea salt, to taste
6 tablespoons extra virgin olive oil
5 ounces small-curd cottage cheese, drained and pressed through a fine strainer
3/4 cup crumbled *feta* cheese
2 eggs, beaten
1 teaspoon *rigani* (see page 13), briefly pounded in a mortar
1 small bunch flat-leaf parsley, leaves coarsely chopped
1 teaspoon cracked black pepper, or to taste
3 egg yolks, lightly beaten (for pastry pies), *or* 4 tablespoons unsalted butter, melted (for phyllo pies)

If using phyllo, remove the package of dough from the refrigerator and set aside unopened.

Trim the eggplant and cut into 1-inch cubes. Sprinkle with 1 tablespoon salt and set aside in a colander to drain.

Warm 4 tablespoons of the olive oil in a heavy sauté pan. Wipe the cubed eggplant with paper towels and sauté over low heat, turning occasionally, until deep golden brown, about 15 minutes. Drain on paper towels and transfer to a bowl.

Mash the eggplant to a pulp with a fork or potato masher and add the cottage cheese, *feta* cheese, eggs, *rigani*, parsley, and salt and pepper to taste. Continue gently mashing with a fork until well-mixed. Taste, and add salt and pepper if necessary; the mixture should be highly seasoned.

Heat the oven to 350°F. Make the pies with the pastry as directed on page 57 or with the phyllo as directed on page 267. Arrange 2 inches apart on lightly oiled baking sheets. Brush pastry pies with the remaining olive oil, phyllo pies with a mixture of the olive oil and melted butter. Bake pastry pies for 15 minutes, brush with the beaten egg yolks, and bake 10 minutes longer, until deep golden brown. Bake phyllo pies 15–20 minutes, until deep golden brown. Serve hot or warm.

Variations

♦ Substitute 3 medium zucchini, baked (see page 206), grilled or sautéed in olive oil, or 2 medium leeks, thoroughly cleaned, thinly sliced, and lightly sautéed in olive oil, for the eggplant. Take care to drain the zucchini properly to ensure a firm filling and mash as described. Use a small handful of fresh dill instead of parsley and omit the *rigani*.

♦ Substitute 2 medium onions, each one cut in half and slow-roasted or grilled with olive oil, or sliced and gently sautéed until deep golden brown, or 3 medium bell peppers, any color, cut in half, seeds discarded, and roasted or grilled, or sliced and sautéed in olive oil, for the eggplant. Roughly chop the vegetables, and drain on paper towels, before mashing with the cheese.

♦ Substitute 1/4 cup cooked long-grain rice for the cottage cheese, use only 1/4 cup *feta* cheese, and add 2 tablespoons toasted pine nuts and 2 tablespoons currants to the filling.

Marjoram Meat Pies

Kreatopittes

These spicy pastry parcels are a treat, especially good in late spring when lamb has a delicate succulent flavor and marjoram leaves are at their most fragrant. If you have the patience, you'll achieve the best texture and flavor if you chop the meat by hand.

Makes 18 to 24 pies: Serves 8 as a *meze*, 4 to 6 as a lunch dish

Pastry
2 cups all-purpose flour
1 teaspoon sea salt
2 tablespoons extra virgin olive oil
1 egg, lightly beaten
3 tablespoons red wine vinegar *or* yogurt, preferably homemade (see page 7)
3–4 tablespoons cold water

Filling
1/2 cup extra virgin olive oil
2 large onions, chopped
1 1/2 pounds lean lamb *or* beef *or* a mixture of both, finely chopped or
    ground
1/2 cup dry red wine *or* 2 tablespoons red wine vinegar

½ teaspoon coarse-grain sea salt, or to taste
1 teaspoon cracked black pepper, or to taste
1 teaspoon ground cinnamon
¼ teaspoon ground cloves
1 small bunch flat-leaf parsley, leaves finely chopped
2 tablespoons fresh marjoram, chopped, *or* 1 tablespoon dried *rigani* (see
  page 13), crumbled
½ cup lightly toasted pine nuts
2 egg yolks beaten with 1 tablespoon water
½ cup sesame seeds, *optional*

To make the pastry, sift the flour into a large bowl and add the salt, olive oil, egg, and vinegar. Knead for 5 minutes, adding enough of the old water if needed to make a smooth and elastic dough. Tightly wrap in plastic and refrigerate for 1 hour.

To make the filling, heat 3 tablespoons of the olive oil in a large heavy sauté pan and sauté the onion over medium-low heat until golden brown, about 15 minutes, stirring continuously. Add the meat and cook until lightly browned, breaking up any lumps with a wooden spoon. Add the wine and boil until almost evaporated. Stir in the salt, pepper, cinnamon, and cloves, cover, and simmer 15 minutes over very low heat. Add 1 or 2 tablespoons water if the mixture starts to dry out; or, if there is still liquid remaining in the pan, uncover for the last few minutes to let it evaporate. Add the parsley, marjoram, and pine nuts. Season to taste and set aside to cool.

Heat the oven to 350°F. Roll out the pastry on a lightly floured surface, and cut out circles with a 4-inch round cutter or cut into 2x4-inch rectangles. Place 2 scant tablespoons of filling in the center of each shape and brush the edges of the pastry with water. Fold the circles in half to make half-moons or fold the rectangles in half to make 2-inch squares. Crimp the edges with a fork to seal.

Arrange the pies 2 inches apart on a lightly oiled baking sheet and brush with the remaining olive oil. Bake 10 minutes, then brush with the egg yolks and lightly sprinkle with the sesame seeds. Bake 15 minutes longer, until deep golden brown. Serve hot or warm, or cool to room temperature on racks.

Note These can be made with phyllo pastry, but the filling must be moister. Add 2 skinned and diced tomatoes to the meat along with the spices, or add 6 ounces drained cottage cheese, pressed through a strainer, with the pine nuts. Shape into triangles, rolls, or rectangles as directed on pages 273 or into 1 large pie as directed on pages 95–97, and bake as directed in each recipe.

SOUPS

Soupeʃ

For Greeks an ideal one-dish meal is a large bowl of aromatic and hearty soup, accompanied by crusty bread, plenty of local wine, juicy olives, peppery radishes, and soft crumbly cheese. From classical time Greeks have believed in the fortifying powers of good soups and they have a particular reverence for bean soups, which they believe develop physical and mental stamina. These substantial winter soups are especially popular during the Lenten fast.

At the other extreme, the Greek cook is also adept at creating a variety of delicate broths, which make light and elegant first courses. These are usually laced with *avgolemono*, giving them a beautiful pale lemon color.

The most exquisitely flavored soup of this type is *mayeritsa*, the Easter soup made from the offal of the Paschal lamb and flavored with fresh dill and *avgolemono*. Served at the midnight breakfast of Easter morning and at Easter Sunday lunch, *mayeritsa* is a treat not to be missed. It's difficult to reproduce with complete success outside Greece, but if you are in Greece at Easter, don't miss the opportunity to sample it.

An introduction to Greek soups is not complete without some reference to fish soups, staple food on Greek tables, especially on the islands. The most popular of these is *kakavia*, almost certainly the original of *bouillabaise* and introduced into France by occupying Greeks of classical times. You will not, however, find a recipe for this soup in my selection. This is not an oversight but a recognition of the fact that it is almost impossible to reproduce *kakavia* with any kind of authenticity outside Greece since the requisite variety of fish is not available. But if you visit Greece be sure to seek out *kakavia* and discover its delights for yourself.

Bean and Vegetable Soup
Faʃʃola∂a

For the Greeks of antiquity *fassolada* was the staple winter food – not only delicious and aromatic, but nourishing, filling, and easy to make with ingredients on hand. It's still the most popular winter soup in Greece today and it is served in large shallow bowls, accompanied by *feta*, olives, a green salad, crusty bread, and a robust red wine. For best results use top-quality olive oil – it's essential for an authentic flavor.

Serves 6 to 8

··

1½ cups dried cannellini *or* small white beans *or* black-eyed peas, soaked
   for 4 hours in water to cover
½ cup extra virgin olive oil, or to taste
2 medium onions, finely chopped
4 medium carrots, finely diced
2 celery sticks, finely diced
4 sprigs celery leaves (see page 14), lightly chopped, *optional*
2 large cloves garlic, finely chopped
2 tablespoons dried thyme *or rigani* (see page 13) *or* a mixture of both
1 medium bunch flat-leaf parsley, leaves coarsely chopped
Sea salt *and* cracked black pepper, to taste
8¼ cups water *or* Light Meat Stock (page 348) *or* a mixture of both
3 large ripe tomatoes, skinned and diced, juices reserved
1 tablespoon tomato paste diluted with 3 tablespoons water

For serving
Aged red wine vinegar *or* lemon juice, *optional*

··

Drain the beans and place in a large saucepan. Add cold water to cover
by 3 inches, bring slowly to a boil, drain, and rinse. Set aside.

Rinse out the saucepan and set over medium-low heat. Heat 6
tablespoons of the oil and add the onion, carrot, and celery. Sauté for 30
minutes or until pale gold, stirring occasionally with a wooden spoon. Add
the celery leaves (if using), the garlic, thyme, half the parsley, the pepper,
beans, and water. Bring to a boil, cover, and simmer for 1 hour, until the
beans are soft but not disintegrating. Meanwhile, sprinkle the tomatoes
with salt and set aside for 15 minutes.

Stir the tomato paste and tomatoes into the soup, season with salt and
pepper, and simmer for 5 more minutes. Stir in the remaining parsley, olive
oil, and vinegar if desired. Serve hot.

Bean and Vegetable Soup with Spinach
Fassolada me Spanaki

Thoroughly wash 8 ounces young spinach leaves, discard the tough
stalks, and slice the leaves into chiffonade (thin ribbons). Add to the soup
with the tomatoes. Sprinkle 1 tablespoon aged red wine vinegar over each
bowl of soup when serving, and provide each guest with a small bowl of
croutons (page 344).

Green Lentil Soup with Sorrel
Fakes Soupa

Lentil and onion soup does not sound exotic – but add the richness of honey-sweetened ripe tomatoes, the strong sharp tang of sorrel, and a swirl of yogurt and you have a soup in an entirely different class. The trick of adding wild greens to bean soups is a common village practice and works well in softening the texture of lentils and improving their flavor.

Serves 6

4 tablespoons extra virgin olive oil
1 large mild onion, finely chopped
1⅛ cups green lentils, picked over, rinsed, and soaked for 10 minutes in cold water to cover
5 cups light stock (chicken, meat, *or* vegetable, pages 343, 348, or 352) *or* water
2 large ripe tomatoes, skinned, and cut into small cubes
½ teaspoon honey
Sea salt *and* cracked black pepper, to taste
½ pound fresh sorrel

For serving
½ cup Strained Yogurt (page 7)

Heat the olive oil in a heavy saucepan and sauté the onion over low heat for 10 minutes. Drain the lentils and add to the saucepan with the stock. Bring slowly to a boil, cover, and simmer 40 minutes, until the lentils are soft. (Keeping the heat low prevents an unattractive froth from forming.)

Meanwhile, place the tomatoes in a colander set over a bowl, sprinkle with the honey and salt, and set aside to drain. Wash the sorrel in several changes of cold water, strip the leaves from the stalks, and discard any bruised or discolored parts of the leaves.

Drain the lentils over a bowl and set aside the cooking liquid. Transfer the lentils to a food processor or blender, in batches if necessary, and pulse, adding enough reserved cooking liquid (and water if needed) to make a light soup. Return the soup to the rinsed-out saucepan.

Slice the sorrel into chiffonade (thin ribbons) and reserve a few choice strips for garnish. Add the sorrel and the tomatoes to the soup and season with pepper. Simmer 2 minutes, just until the sorrel is soft. Add salt and pepper to taste.

Serve in individual bowls with a spoonful of yogurt in the center of each, and sprinkle with the reserved sorrel.

Aromatic Yellow Split Pea Soup
Aromatiki Soupa

This savory cumin-flavored soup looks elegant, comforts on cold days, and yet is surprisingly refreshing in cold weather.

Serves 4

⋯⋯⋯⋯⋯⋯⋯⋯⋯⋯⋯⋯⋯⋯⋯⋯⋯⋯⋯⋯⋯⋯⋯⋯⋯⋯⋯⋯⋯⋯⋯⋯⋯⋯⋯

$^7/_8$ cup yellow split peas, picked over and rinsed
4 tablespoons extra virgin olive oil
1 medium onion, finely chopped
1 medium carrot, finely diced
1 small celery stick, finely diced
$^1/_2$–1 tablespoon cumin seeds, or to taste, gently heated in a small clean frying pan until their aroma rises, and pulverized in a clean coffee grinder or mortar
$3^3/_4$ cups Chicken Stock (page 343) *or* water
Sea salt *and* freshly ground white pepper, to taste

For serving
4 tablespoons Strained Yogurt (page 7)
Juice of 1 small lemon
Coarsely chopped flat-leaf parsley

⋯⋯⋯⋯⋯⋯⋯⋯⋯⋯⋯⋯⋯⋯⋯⋯⋯⋯⋯⋯⋯⋯⋯⋯⋯⋯⋯⋯⋯⋯⋯⋯⋯⋯⋯

Cover the split peas with cold water and set aside. Heat the olive oil in a large heavy saucepan and sauté the onion, carrot, and celery over medium heat until golden brown, about 20 minutes, stirring occasionally with a wooden spoon. Stir in the cumin and cook 1 minute longer. Drain the split peas and add with the stock. Bring to a boil, cover, and gently simmer 40 minutes or until the peas are soft.

Puree the soup in a food processor or blender or push through the medium disc of a food mill. Add water if necessary to make a light soup. Return to the rinsed-out saucepan, add salt and pepper, and heat slowly. Add more cumin if desired (you should be able to taste the cumin but its flavor should not be overpowering).

Divide the soup between warm individual bowls and place a spoonful of yogurt in the center of each. Sprinkle with lemon juice and parsley and serve hot or warm.

Variations
♦ Add 2 skinned and diced ripe tomatoes to the pureed soup and simmer 5 minutes. Omit the lemon juice.
♦ Serve with golden-brown croutons (page 344) rather than yogurt, and

sprinkle each serving with the parsley and lemon juice and 1 teaspoon finely chopped Preserved Lemons (page 18).

Country Tomato Soup
Soupa Domata

The gentle slow cooking of chopped onion, celery, and carrot, perfumed with thyme, creates a fragrant base for this colorful country soup. Make it when tomatoes are at their sweetest and serve with olives, *feta* cheese, crusty bread, and a green salad.

Serves 4

2 tablespoons extra virgin olive oil
1 large onion, finely chopped
½ small celery stick, finely diced
1 small carrot, finely diced
1 tablespoon dried thyme
1½ pounds ripe tomatoes, skinned and diced, juices reserved
1 teaspoon honey
Sea salt *and* cracked black pepper, to taste
4⅓ cups Chicken Stock (page 343) *or* water
¼ cup small *kritharaki* (see page 245) *or* medium-grain bulgur (see Note)
1 bunch watercress, leaves only, rinsed and coarsely chopped
2 tablespoons finely chopped flat-leaf parsley

For serving
Finely grated *kasseri, kephalotyri, or* Parmesan cheese

Warm the olive oil in a large heavy saucepan set over low heat and sauté the onion, celery, carrot, and thyme until pale golden brown, about 25 minutes; stir occasionally with a wooden spoon. Stir in the tomatoes and their juices, honey, and salt and pepper, and simmer 4 minutes, until the tomatoes are soft. Add the stock and bring to a boil. Add the *kritharaki* (or bulgur) and simmer 4 minutes, until the *kritharaki* is almost cooked. Add the watercress and simmer 1 minute longer. Stir in the parsley and serve immediately, with small bowls of grated cheese.

Note If using the bulgur, first bring a small saucepan of water to a boil over medium heat. Add the bulgur, boil 1 minute, drain, and rinse under cold running water. Set aside until needed.

Chicken Avgolemono Soup
Avgolemono Soupa

A traditional favorite in Greek homes and tavernas, *avgolemono* soup has its origins back in antiquity. It's a most delicious and refreshing soup – light, nourishing, and elegant enough to serve at a dinner party. My version is based on a rich chicken stock enhanced with saffron, which gives a delicate but distinctive flavor. The addition of rice makes a more substantial soup.

Serves 6 to 8

6⅞ cups Rich Chicken Stock (page 343)
¼ cup short-grain rice, *optional*
4 eggs, separated
Juice of 2 large lemons
Sea salt *and* freshly ground white pepper, to taste

For serving
2 tablespoons finely chopped flat-leaf parsley

Bring the stock to a boil in a large saucepan. (If using rice, add to the stock, cover, and simmer 15 minutes, or until the rice is cooked.)

Five minutes before you are ready to serve the soup, whisk the egg whites in a large bowl with a wire whisk or electric mixer until stiff. Whisk in the egg yolks, add the lemon juice, and whisk 1 minute longer. Hold a ladleful of the hot soup broth about 12 inches above the bowl and slowly add it to the eggs and lemon juice, whisking constantly. (This trick helps prevent curdling the egg mixture, because by the time the broth reaches the bowl it is hot but not boiling.) Off the heat, whisk the egg and lemon juice sauce into the soup. Do not return the soup to the heat. Add salt and pepper to taste, sprinkle with the parsley, and serve at once.

Note Once the egg and lemon juice flavoring is added, the soup must not be reheated.

Avgolemono Soup with Kephtedes
Avgolemono Soupa me Kephtedes

This delicate and delicious soup is satisfying without being heavy – ideal for a light lunch. For convenience both the soup broth and the tiny crisp *kephtedes* can be made in advance, but do not combine them until 10 minutes before serving.

Serves 8

½ pound lean lamb, finely minced
1 egg yolk, lightly beaten
1 small onion, finely grated
2 tablespoons finely chopped flat-leaf parsley
½ cup fresh fine bread crumbs, soaked for 5 minutes in 1 tablespoon milk
½ tablespoon aged red wine vinegar
Sea salt *and* freshly ground black pepper, to taste
1 tablespoon olive oil, or more to taste
8¾ cups Light Meat Stock (page 348)
2 egg yolks
Juice of 2 lemons

For serving
Finely chopped flat-leaf parsley

Heat the oven to 375°F.

Combine the lamb, lightly beaten egg yolk, onion, parsley, bread crumbs, vinegar, and salt and pepper, and mix until thoroughly blended. Moisten your hands with cold water and pat barely dry. Shape the meat mixture into small balls the size of your thumbnail; you should have about 3 dozen.

Lightly brush a baking sheet with olive oil and place in the oven for 2 minutes to heat. Arrange the *kephtedes* on the baking sheet and bake 15–20 minutes or until golden brown. Drain between layers of paper towels.

Bring the stock to a boil in a large saucepan. Add the *kephtedes*, reduce the heat, cover, and gently simmer 10 minutes; do not let the soup broth boil. Whisk the egg yolks in a large bowl until pale and frothy, add the lemon juice, and whisk 1 minute longer. Hold a ladleful of the hot broth about 12 inches above the bowl and slowly add it to the eggs, whisking constantly.

With a slotted spoon, transfer the *kephtedes* to a warm soup tureen or divide among warm individual bowls. Off the heat, lightly whisk the egg and lemon juice mixture into the soup. Add salt and pepper to taste, stir in the parsley, ladle the soup over the *kephtedes*, and serve.

The Monks' Onion Soup
Monarcho Soupa

Staple fare in Byzantine monasteries, this soup is based on the humblest ingredients. It was served to the monks to remind them of the virtues of the simple religious life, removed from worldly extravagance. Although it is simple, and easy to prepare, this onion soup has a delicious flavor and makes a warming winter meal.

Serves 4 to 6

2 tablespoons unsalted butter
4 tablespoons extra virgin olive oil
3 large onions, quartered and thinly sliced
Sea salt *and* freshly ground black pepper, to taste
2 thick slices whole wheat bread, crusts removed, and cut into ½-inch dice
3 egg yolks
3 tablespoons aged red wine vinegar *or* 1 tablespoon balsamic vinegar

For serving
Finely chopped flat-leaf parsley
Ground cinnamon, to taste

Heat the butter and 1 tablespoon of the olive oil in a large, preferably enamel, saucepan and sauté the onions over low heat for 20 minutes; stir occasionally with a wooden spoon and don't let the onions brown. Cover, reduce the heat, and cook 50 minutes longer, stirring once or twice. If the onions begin to stick, sprinkle with 1 or 2 tablespoons of water. They will reduce almost to a puree, but should remain very pale. Add 4⅓ cups water, salt, and pepper, and bring to a boil over medium heat. Cover, reduce the heat, and simmer for 15 minutes.

Heat the remaining olive oil in a heavy frying pan and fry the bread cubes over medium-low heat until golden brown on all sides. Drain these croutons between layers of paper towels.

Just before serving, whisk the egg yolks with the vinegar in a large bowl. Hold a ladleful of the hot soup about 12 inches above the bowl and slowly add it to the eggs, whisking constantly; whisk 10 seconds longer. Off the heat, stir the egg mixture into the soup. Add salt and pepper to taste.

Divide the soup between warm individual bowls and sprinkle with the croutons, parsley, and cinnamon. Serve at once.

Note For a more substantial soup, substitute Chicken or Light Meat Stock (page 343 or page 348) for some or all of the water.

LIGHT MEALS

Yevmata Ellafra

Greek cooks have a special talent for creating quick and appetizing snacks and light meals. Often the clue to their enchantment is the sheer simplicity of their preparation and the perfect freshness of the ingredients used.

The satisfying Greek egg dishes are a good example of this skill. I have been delighted by an unpretentious platter of creamy eggs on a laden taverna table, a frittata of zucchini in the cool shade of a perfumed summer garden, and, at a country café buzzing with local gossip, a fragrant herbed omelet enveloping tiny browned diced potatoes.

In summer a colorful variety of stuffed vegetables are served as light meals, and tavernas display tempting trays of vegetable shells bulging with spicy rice or meat fillings. In the villages stuffed vegetables with an olive oil and lemon juice or tomato sauce are slowly baked to a moist mellowness in the baker's oven, producing a wonderful richness of flavor. The amount of olive oil used in the following stuffed vegetable recipes may seem high. But the pungency of good-quality olive oil is essential to flavor both vegetable and filling – without it you will not achieve the richness and depth of taste that's characteristic of these aromatic country meals.

Savory pies, made with crumbly pastry or phyllo, are favorite snacks and light meals too. Every bus or train station and every town square has its pie shop, selling tiny pastries concealing mouthfuls of spicy meat, cheese, chicken, or wild greens. Honeyed nuts or sweet custard fillings are popular too.

Many of the following recipes can be prepared in advance and reheated or served cold, and several, notably the pies, freeze very well (but freeze *before* cooking). Remember too that many *mezedes* and vegetable dishes can also be served as light meals or tasty snacks.

Egg Dishes

A Villager's Eggs
Avga Khoriatiki

An omelet made with just-laid eggs and a handful of pungent fresh wild herbs is a favorite country snack. Villagers are especially fond of wild asparagus, mallow, wild chervil, purslane,wild leeks, zucchini flowers, and wild artichokes in their omelets, and we can enjoy some of these country flovors too. I've found wild chevril in Chinese markets, purslane in a potato field, and mallow alongside country paths.

Serves 2

8 ounces wild asparagus *or* slender young asparagus
2 tablespoons extra virgin olive oil
1 tablespoon freshly squeezed lemon juice
Coarse-grain sea salt *and* cracked black pepper, to taste
4 eggs, lightly beaten

For serving
Coarsely chopped flat-leaf parsley
Lemon wedges

Break off the tough ends of the asparagus stalks at the point where they snap easily and discard. Blanch the asparagus in boiling water for 5 seconds, rinse under cold running water, drain between layers of paper towels, and blot dry. Cut into 2-inch pieces.

Warm the olive oil in a seasoned 9-inch omelet pan or heavy frying pan and sauté the asparagus over medium-low heat until barely tender. Sprinkle with the lemon juice and salt and pepper. Pour the eggs over the asparagus and tilt the pan to distribute evenly. Reduce the heat to low.

When the omelet is lightly set, lift one edge with a spatula to allow any still-liquid egg to flow underneath. Slide out onto a plate, invert the pan over the plate, and, firmly holding both, invert once more so the omelette is upside down in the pan. Cook 20 seconds longer, or until set, and invert onto a warm serving platter. Sprinkle with the parsley and serve at once, with the lemon wedges.

Note To season an omelet pan, sprinkle 2 tablespoons salt over the bottom of the pan and set it over low heat for 5 minutes. The salt will turn light brown as it absorbs all the extraneous substances that inevitably stick to the surface of kitchen utensils. Discard the salt and thoroughly wipe out the pan with paper towels.

Cheese Omelet
Omeleta Tyri

In this tasty dish garlic is used to flavor the cooking oil, giving a robust character to the omelet; the crunchy oven-dried bread crumbs add an unusual nutty texture. Serve with a tomato or bean salad or Beet Salad with Allspice (page 184).

Serves 2

---

2 tablespoons extra virgin olive oil
1 clove garlic, cut into 3 pieces
3 tablespoons dried fine bread crumbs
2 ounces *feta* cheese, crumbled, *or* aged *myzithra*, grated
4 eggs
Freshly ground black pepper, to taste

For serving
1 tablespoon finely chopped flat-leaf parsley
1 scallion, trimmed, and thinly sliced
2 teaspoons fresh oregano, chopped, *or* 1 teaspoon dried *rigani* (see page 13), crumbled
6 Elitses *or* Niçoise olives
Lemon wedges

Heat the olive oil in a seasoned 9-inch omelet pan or heavy frying pan (see page 73). Sauté the garlic for a minute or two over medium-low heat and discard. Add the bread crumbs to the pan and fry until pale golden brown, stirring occasionally. Lightly whisk together the cheese, eggs, and pepper and pour over the bread crumbs, tilting the pan to distribute evenly.

When the omelet is lightly set, lift one edge with a spatula to allow any still-liquid egg to flow underneath. Slide the omelet out onto a warm plate, invert the pan over the plate, and, firmly holding both, invert once more so the omelet is upside down in the pan. Cook 20 seconds longer, until set, and invert onto a warm serving platter.

Mix together the parsley, scallion, and oregano and sprinkle the mixture over the omelet, along with the olives. Serve immediately, with the lemon wedges.

Sausage and Potato Omelet
Omeleta me Loukhanika ke Patates

Make this substantial and spicy omelet with *pastourmas* sausages (see page 178) or Country Sausages (page 179) and whatever fresh herbs are available. Serve with Wild Greens Salad (page 222) and Shepherd's Bread (page 250), or Olive Bread (page 254).

Serves 2

---

3 tablespoons extra virgin olive oil
2 (4-to-5-inch) sausages, casings discarded, cut into ½-inch slices

2 medium boiling potatoes, peeled if desired, cooked and cut into ½-inch
   cubes
5 eggs, lightly beaten
Cracked black pepper, to taste

For serving
2 tablespoons coarsely chopped-flat leaf parsley *or* cilantro *or* dill
Large pinch of ground paprika
Lemon wedges

Heat half the olive oil in a seasoned 9-inch omelet pan or heavy frying
pan (see page 73) and sauté the sausages until lightly browned on both
sides. Drain between layers of paper towels and wipe the pan clean.

Heat the remaining olive oil in the pan and sauté the potato over
medium-low heat until golden brown on all sides, about 6 minutes. Add
the sausages and lightly stir to mix. Pour in the eggs, reduce the heat to
low, and tilt the pan to distribute the eggs evenly. Season with pepper (the
sausages are salty). When lightly set, lift one edge with a spatula to allow
any still-liquid egg to flow underneath. Slide the omelet onto a warm plate,
invert the pan over the plate, and firmly holding both, invert once more so
the omelet is upside down in the pan. Cook 20 seconds longer, or until set,
and invert onto a warm serving platter.

Sprinkle with the parsley and paprika and serve immediately, with the
lemon wedges.

Variations
♦ Add 1 roasted, seeded, and skinned red bell pepper (see page 343), cut
into strips, or 1 medium eggplant or zucchini, cubed and fried, or 1 leek,
thinly sliced and sautéed, to the pan with the potatoes.

Saffron Eggs with Lamb's Kidneys
Avga me Nefra apo Arnaki

I first came across this surprising dish one Easter in a village on the
island of Paxos. This was the speciality of the village café and I must say I
had my reservations about sampling it, but it tasted superb. It is an unusual
dish with a bold conjunction of distinctive flavors; it's well worth trying.
With crusty bread and Wild Greens Salad (page 222), Purslane Salad (page
220), or a green salad, it's an ideal lunch or supper when you want a meal
that's quick and easy but out-of-the-ordinary.

Serves 2

2 or 3 small lamb's kidneys
Sea salt
3 tablespoons aged red wine vinegar
4 tablespoons extra virgin olive oil
6 large flat mushrooms, preferably wild, trimmed and cut into ¼-inch
    slices
¼ teaspoon saffron threads
1 tablespoon hot water
1 teaspoon fresh thyme *or* oregano, finely chopped
1 teaspoon whole coriander seeds, pulverized
½ teaspoon freshly ground black pepper
1 teaspoon honey
4 eggs

For serving
1 tablespoon finely chopped parsley
1 tablespoon finely chopped chives

Slice each kidney horizontally in half to expose the center. Cut out the valves and discard. Cut the kidneys lengthways into ¼-inch slices and place in a bowl with ½ teaspoon salt, half the vinegar, and water to cover. Set aside for 30 minutes.

Heat 1 tablespoon of the olive oil in a heavy frying pan and sauté the mushrooms over medium-low heat for a minute or two. Once they have released some of their water, raise the heat to medium and cook, stirring occasionally, until most of the liquid has evaporated. Set side.

Heat the saffron in a small dry frying pan until aromatic, crumble into the hot water, and set aside. Drain the kidneys and rinse in several changes of cold water until the water runs clear; thoroughly dry with paper towels.

Heat 1 tablespoon of the remaining olive oil in a heavy frying pan and sauté the kidneys over medium heat for about 3 minutes, until lightly browned. Sprinkle with the thyme, coriander, salt, and pepper. Combine the honey and remaining vinegar and add with the mushrooms. Cover, shake gently to mix, and cook for 1 minute, until most of the liquid has disappeared. Set aside and keep warm.

Strain the saffron water, discarding the saffron and reserving the liquid. Lightly beat the eggs and add the strained saffron water, salt, and pepper. Add the remaining olive oil to a seasoned 9-inch omelet pan or heavy frying pan (see page 73) set over medium-low heat. Pour in the eggs and cook, stirring with a fork, until lightly set. Reduce the heat and spoon the warm kidney and mushroom mixture over the eggs.

Sprinkle with the parsley and chives and serve immediately.

Country Vegetable Omelet
Sfongata

A fragrant dish of vegetables and eggs flavored with Mediterranean cheese, a *sfongata* is essentially a frittata. You can use eggplants, potatoes, grilled bell peppers, onions, beans, leeks, or zucchini – whatever you have available. If you include tomatoes your *sfongata* will have a soft and creamy texture. A *sfongata* made without tomatoes, which is easier to maneuver, is usually turned over to brown on both sides. Garnish with tiny olives and parsley and serve with country bread, slices of *feta* or *myzithra* cheese, and Wild Greens Salad (page 222).

Serves 2

5 small firm zucchini (about 1 pound total)
Coarse-grain sea salt
6 tablespoons extra virgin olive oil
1 shallot, finely chopped
1 small clove garlic, minced
2 large ripe tomatoes, skinned, seeded, and diced
Pinch of sugar, *optional*
5 eggs
2 tablespoons finely grated *kephalotyri or* Parmesan cheese
Freshly ground black pepper, to taste
1 teaspoon fresh oregano *or* marjoram, finely chopped

For serving
2 tablespoons coarsely chopped flat-leaf parsley
6 Elitses *or* Niçoise olives, drained

Trim the zucchini and cut into large matchsticks. Sprinkle with 1 teaspoon of salt and set aside for 30 minutes to drain.

Heat half the olive oil in a seasoned 9-inch omelet pan or heavy frying pan (see page 73). Dry the zucchini with paper towels and sauté over medium-low heat for about 8 minutes, until light golden brown. Drain on paper towels. Wipe out the pan and set aside.

Heat 1 tablespoon of the remaining olive oil in a heavy frying pan and cook the shallot and garlic over low heat until soft. Add the tomatoes, sugar, and a pinch of salt and gently boil 1 minute. Set aside.

Whisk together the eggs, cheese, and pepper. Heat the remaining olive oil in the omelet pan over low heat and spread the zucchini over the bottom of the pan. Sprinkle with the oregano, pour the egg mixture over the zucchini, and cook until the eggs are lightly set. Using a slotted spoon, spoon the tomato mixture over the eggs, and season to taste. Sprinkle with the parsley and olives and serve.

Stuffed Vegetables

Tiny Stuffed Vegetables
Mikra Yemista Lakhanika

These tiny stuffed vegetables are miniature works of art, masterpieces of the Greek kitchen. The vegetables used may be tomatoes, eggplants, peppers, onions, artichokes, zucchini, or squash. The main criteria for selection are that they add splashes of brilliant color to the *meze* table (see pages 26 to 27) and are the best available.

For a large gathering, buffet, or picnic these vegetables are a gift. They look spectacular and they're very long suffering, staying fresh and delicious even in hot sunshine and after the first wave of guests has descended on the table. Although the preparation is fairly time consuming, most of it can be done ahead of time. Any of the meatless fillings for stuffed vegetables given on pages 86 and 89 can be used, but my own favorite is the following recipe. Its tantalizing herbal aroma reminds me of villages in the rugged Greek mountains where these highly flavored tiny treats are a speciality.

Serves 12 to 15 as a *meze*, 8 as a first course

2 firm round eggplants, no more than 3 inches long
Sea salt
2 zucchini, 2–3 inches long
3 small squash suitable for stuffing, about 2 inches in diameter *or* another 2 zucchini, 2–3 inches long
3 small bell peppers, green, red, *or* yellow *or* a combination of all three
6 boiling onions, about 1 1/2 inches in diameter
4 small tomatoes
1/2 teaspoon sugar
1/2–3/4 cup extra virgin olive oil
1 small onion, finely grated
1 large clove garlic, finely chopped
1 1/2 teaspoons ground cinnamon *or* 1 tablespoon ground coriander
Freshly ground black pepper, to taste
1 cup long-grain rice, cooked
4 tablespoons finely chopped flat-leaf parsley
2 tablespoons dried *rigani* (see page 13), briefly pounded in a small mortar
1/2 cup currants *or* small dark seedless raisins, *optional*
Juice of 1 lemon

For serving
Lemon wedges

....

Slice off the stem ends of the eggplants, cut lengthways in half, and sprinkle the cut sides with 2 teaspoons salt. Set aside for 30 minutes to "sweat."

Fill a large saucepan with water and bring to a boil. Meanwhile, rinse the zucchini and other squash and rub with a clean dish towel to remove any fuzz. Slice off the stem ends of the zucchini and squash and remove a thin slice from the base of each squash so that they stand upright. Add the zucchini and other squash to the boiling water and lightly boil for 5 minutes, until barely soft. Drain on paper towels and retain the boiling water for the next stage.

Slice off the tops of the peppers, remove the cores and seeds, and rinse the tops and peppers. Peel the onions, slicing off the root and stem ends. Add the peppers, pepper tops and onions to the boiling water. Lightly boil the peppers for 5 minutes or until slightly softened, the onions 3 or 4 minutes longer, until just soft, and drain.

Slice off the tops of the tomatoes and set aside. With a small spoon, scoop out the seeds, sprinkle the insides with the sugar and a pinch of salt, and invert on paper towels to drain. With the point of a small paring knife, push out the centers of the boiled onions, leaving shells of 2 layers. Finely chop the centers.

Place a heavy frying pan over medium-low heat and add 3 tablespoons of the olive oil. Dry the eggplants with paper towels and fry until the cut sides are golden brown and the skins are dark and wrinkled, about 12 minutes. Drain on paper towels.

Cut the zucchini lengthways in half and carefully scoop out the flesh, leaving 1/4-inch shells. Scoop out the flesh of the eggplants and squash. Discard the eggplant seeds and finely dice all the flesh.

Heat the oven to 325°F. Heat 2 tablespoons of the remaining olive oil in a heavy sauté or frying pan. Add the chopped onion, grated onion, and garlic, and sauté over low heat until soft. Add the tomato, eggplant pulp, zucchini and squash pulp, cinnamon, and pepper, stir with a wooden spoon and cook for 1 to 2 minutes. Add the rice, parsley, *rigani*, currants, and half the lemon juice, and gently stir to mix. Add salt and pepper, cinnamon, and/or lemon juice to taste; the mixture should be highly flavored.

Arrange all the vegetable shells in a single layer in a large shallow baking dish. Loosely fill with the rice mixture, taking care not to split the shells. Replace the tops of the tomatoes and peppers and sprinkle all the vegetables with the remaining lemon juice and olive oil to taste. Add 1 cup water to the dish and bake uncovered for 1 hour, until the vegetables are soft; reduce the oven temperature to 300°F if the vegetables start to brown. If necessary, add a little more water to the dish.

Let the vegetables cool in the baking dish, then transfer to a serving plate. Surround with lemon wedges and sprinkle with pan juices and olive oil to taste. Serve at room temperature.

Note If you prefer to use less olive oil, the eggplants can be cut in half and added to the boiling water with the zucchini. Boil 5 minutes and drain on paper towels. Because this dish has an overall mellowness, the rich flavor of eggplants prepared in olive oil is not essential to its success.

Baked Eggplants to Make the Sultan Swoon
Imam Bayildi

Imam Bayildi is of Turkish origin, and there are many stories about how the dish acquired its name. Some say the sultan fainted in blissful pleasure at his first taste of this rich and spicy eggplant dish, others say that he was overcome by the beauty of the young woman who served it to him. Whatever its origins, it is delectable. *Imam Bayildi* is ideal for a large party since it is best made a day ahead to give the flavors time to mellow and deepen. Serve warm for a first course, hot as a side dish for grilled meats, or cold as part of a buffet.

Serves 12 as a first course, 6 as a vegetable dish

12 slender eggplants, about 4 inches long, *or* 6 medium eggplants (about 2½ pounds total)
Coarse-grain sea salt, to taste
1 cup extra virgin olive oil, or to taste
1½ pounds onions, quartered and thinly sliced
2 large cloves garlic, finely chopped
1½ pounds ripe tomatoes, skinned and diced, juices reserved
½ cup currants *or* small dark seedless raisins
1 tablespoon ground allspice
1 small bunch flat-leaf parley, leaves finely chopped
Freshly ground black pepper, to taste
1 tablespoon honey
Juice of 2 lemons
2 tablespoons dried *rigani* (see page 13)

Slice off the ends of the eggplants and cut lengthways in half. Sprinkle the cut sides with salt and set aside for 30 minutes to "sweat."

Heat 4 tablespoons of the olive oil in a heavy sauté pan and sauté the onions over low heat until soft and pale golden brown, about 15 minutes; stir occasionally. Add the garlic and tomatoes with their juices and boil until most of the liquid has evaporated, about 10 minutes. Stir in the currants, allspice, most of the parsley, and salt and pepper to taste, and set aside.

Heat the oven to 325°F. Thoroughly dry the eggplants with paper towels. Place a large heavy frying pan over medium-low heat, add 3 tablespoons of the remaining olive oil, and fry half of the eggplants until the cut sides are a deep golden brown and the skins are dark and wrinkled, about 10 minutes. Drain between layers of paper towels. Add 2 tablespoons of the remaining olive oil to the frying pan, fry the remaining eggplants, and drain on paper towels. With a small spoon, scoop out the eggplant centers, leaving 1/4-inch thick shells. Discard most of the seeds, finely dice the flesh, and stir into the onion and tomato mixture.

Arrange the eggplant shells in a heavy baking dish just large enough to hold them. Divide the filling between them, heaping it a little in the center for an attractive appearance. Combine the honey, lemon juice, and olive oil to taste and drizzle over the eggplants. Sprinkle with the *rigani*, salt, and pepper. Pour 1/2 cup water into the dish and bake uncovered for 45 minutes. Add a little more water to the dish if it appears to be drying out.

Arrange the eggplants on a platter or on individual plates, spoon over any cooking liquid, and sprinkle with olive oil to taste and the remaining parsley.

Note To serve as a main course use large round eggplants, 5–6 inches long and increase the filling by half. Or add 4 ounces cooked rice (Perfect Pilaf, page 226) or lightly browned, finely minced, lean lamb, or a mixture of both, to the filling, adding more currants and allspice to taste; place 1 thin tomato slice on top of each eggplant, to prevent the rice from drying out during baking. Bake uncovered at 325°F for 1 hour.

Imam Bayildi in Grape Leaves
Imam Bayildi me Ambelofila

Using 12 small slender eggplants, fry the eggplants and prepare the filling as directed above. Line a heavy baking dish, just large enough to hold the eggplants in a single layer, with fresh or brine-preserved grape leaves that have been blanched in boiling water (3 seconds for preserved leaves, 5 seconds for fresh), glossy sides facing down. (You will need about 12 large leaves or 18 medium leaves.) Divide the filling between the eggplants and arrange them in the baking dish. Cover with a second layer of blanched grape leaves, glossy sides facing up. Pour the lemon juice, honey, and olive oil mixture over the eggplants; omit the *rigani*. Add ½ cup water to the dish and bake uncovered at 325°F for 1 hour. Add a little more water to the dish if necessary.

To serve, discard the top layer of grape leaves and carefully transfer the eggplants to a platter or individual plates. Serve with lemon wedges.

Stuffed Eggplants with Cinnamon Tomato Sauce
Yemistes Melitzanes

These subtly spiced stuffed eggplants are easy to make. If possible, prepare and bake them a day ahead and gently reheat before serving. This gives the rich flavors a chance to deepen and brings out all the pungent fragrance of herbs and spices. Bell peppers can be substituted for eggplants – in that variation cumin becomes the dominant spice.

Serves 4

2 large *or* 4 medium eggplants (about 1½ pounds total)
Sea salt
¾ cup extra virgin olive oil, or to taste
1 medium onion, finely chopped
½ pound lean lamb, finely minced
1½ teaspoons ground cinnamon
1 cup long-grain rice
1½ cups Chicken *or* Light Meat Stock (page 343 or page 348) *or* water
⅓ cup small dark seedless raisins
1 small bunch flat-leaf parsley, leaves finely chopped
1 large ripe tomato, skinned and cut into 8 slices
1 teaspoon sugar
Cracked black pepper, to taste
1 cup Tomato Sauce (page 321), made with cinnamon and parsley, *and* ½ cup water *or* 4 tablespoons tomato paste diluted with 1¼ cups water

For serving
Juice of 1 lemon

Slice off the ends of the eggplants and cut lengthways in half. Dust the cut sides with salt and set aside for 30 minutes to "sweat."

Heat 3 tablespoons of the olive oil in a heavy saucepan and sauté the

Opposite: A Villager's Eggs

onion over low heat until pale golden, about 12 minutes; stir occasionally. Add the lamb, raise the heat, and cook until lightly browned, breaking up any lumps with a wooden spoon. Stir in the cinnamon, salt (to taste), and the rice. Add the stock, bring to a boil, cover, reduce the heat, and simmer until the liquid has disappeared from the surface, about 15 minutes. Set aside.

Heat the oven to 325°F. Thoroughly dry the eggplants with paper towels. Warm 4 tablespoons of the remaining olive oil in a heavy frying pan and fry the eggplants over medium-low heat until the cut sides are golden brown and the skins are dark and wrinkled, about 10 minutes. Drain between layers of paper towels. With a small spoon, scoop out the flesh, leaving 1/4-inch thick shells. Discard most of the seeds and finely dice the flesh. Stir the eggplant cubes, raisins, and half the parsley into the rice mixture.

Arrange the eggplant shells in a heavy baking dish, just large enough to hold them. Divide the filling between the shells. Place a tomato slice on top of each, sprinkle with the sugar, salt, a generous amount of pepper, and the remaining olive oil. Pour the tomato sauce and water into the dish and bake, uncovered, for 1 hour, basting occasionally with the sauce. Add more water if the dish is in danger of drying out.

To serve, remove the eggplants from the dish with a slotted spoon and set aside. Pour the sauce onto a warm platter, arrange the eggplants on top, and sprinkle with lemon juice and the remaining parsley. Serve hot or warm.

Stuffed Bell Peppers with Tomato Cumin Sauce
Yemistes Strongiles Piperies

Substitute 8 medium green and/or yellow bell peppers for the eggplants, cumin for the cinnamon, and 6 sprigs celery leaves (see page 352), coarsely chopped, for the raisins. Slice off the tops of the peppers, discard the cores and seeds, and rinse out to remove any remaining seeds. Blanch the tops and shells in boiling water for 5 minutes, and drain well. Fill the peppers and replace the tops. Arrange them in a heavy baking dish just large enough to hold them. Sprinkle with the sugar, salt and pepper, and olive oil, and add the sauce and water. Cover and bake for 1 hour, basting the peppers occasionally with the sauce.

Serve sprinkled with the lemon juice and parsley.

Note The peppers can also be simmered in a heavy saucepan on top of the stove. Bring the sauce to a boil, reduce the heat, and simmer for 45 minutes to 1 hour, until tender.

Opposite: Grilled Octopus

Stuffed Eggplants with Green Grape Sauce

Yemistes Melitzanes me Agouritha

This Cretan version of stuffed eggplants is one of my favorite dishes –
substantial enough to feed the hungriest family, yet impressive enough for
an elegant dinner. The rice filling is spiced with cloves, sharpened by the
sauce made from under-ripe green grapes, and exotically colored and
aromatized with saffron. The vine leaves protect the eggplants from drying
out in the oven and, of course, impart a subtle flavor to the dish. Serve
with bowls of Strained Yogurt (page 7), radishes, tiny black Elitses olives,
and Wild Greens Salad (page 222).

Serves 6

3 large *or* 6 medium eggplants (about 2 pounds total)
Sea salt
7/8 cup yellow split peas, picked over, rinsed, and soaked for 3 hours in
    water to cover
1 cup extra virgin olive oil, or to taste
1 medium onion, grated
1/2 pound lean lamb, finely minced
1 teaspoon saffron threads
1/2 teaspoon ground cloves
1 teaspoon cracked black pepper, or to taste
2/3 cup long-grain rice
1 1/4 cups Chicken *or* Light Meat Stock (page 343 or page 348) *or* water
5 tablespoons finely chopped chives *or* the best green parts of scallions
6 tablespoons Green Grape Sauce (page 319) *or* the juice of 1 large lime
1 bunch flat-leaf parsley, leaves finely chopped
1/4 cup brown sugar
Juice of 1 large lemon
16 fresh *or* brine-preserved grape leaves, blanched in boiling water
    (3 seconds for preserved leaves, 5 seconds for fresh) and drained

Slice off the ends of the eggplants and cut lengthways in half. Sprinkle
the cut sides with salt and set aside for 30 minutes to "sweat."

Drain the split peas, place in a medium saucepan with water to cover by
2 inches, and bring to a simmer over medium heat. Reduce the heat and
simmer 20 minutes, or until just tender. Drain and set aside.

Meanwhile, heat 3 tablespoons of the olive oil in a heavy saucepan and
sauté the onion over medium heat until golden brown, about 12 minutes.
Add the meat, raise the heat, and cook until lightly browned, breaking up

any lumps with a wooden spoon. Gently heat the saffron in a small dry frying pan until aromatic, and crumble it into the lamb mixture. Stir in the cloves, pepper, salt (to taste), and the rice. Add the stock and bring to a boil, without stirring. Cover, reduce the heat to low, and cook 15–20 minutes, until all the liquid has been absorbed by the rice.

Heat the oven to 325°F. Thoroughly dry the eggplants with paper towels. Place a large heavy frying pan over medium-low heat, add 3 tablespoons of the remaining olive oil, and fry the eggplants until the cut sides are dark golden brown and the skins are dark and wrinkled, about 10 minutes. (Fry in 2 batches if necessary, adding 2 tablespoons olive oil before frying the second batch.) Drain between layers of paper towels. Scoop out the flesh with a small spoon, leaving 1/4-inch thick shells. Discard most of the seeds and cut the flesh into small cubes. Combine the cubed eggplant, split peas, chives, Green Grape Sauce, three-quarters of the parsley, and the lamb and rice mixture. Season to taste with salt and pepper.

Arrange the eggplant shells in a heavy baking dish just large enough to hold them. Divide the filling between the eggplant shells, heaping the filling in the centers. Combine the sugar, lemon juice, and 1 cup water, and pour into the baking dish. Add more water if necessary to come halfway up the sides of the eggplant shells. Sprinkle the remaining olive oil over the eggplants and cover with the grape leaves, glossy sides facing down.

Bake uncovered for 50 minutes to 1 hour, or until the grape leaves are dry and wrinkled, basting frequently with the liquid in the dish. Add a little more water if the dish is in danger of drying out.

To serve, discard the grape leaves, arrange the eggplants on a warm platter, pour the pan juices over, and sprinkle with the remaining parsley. Serve hot or warm.

Stuffed Onions with Green Grape Sauce
Yemista Kremithia me Agouritha

Served in ancient Greece, this spicy dish is still popular today. Substitute 4 large onions for the eggplants. Peel them, slice off the root and stem ends, and cook in boiling water for 10 minutes; drain. Push out the centers to leave shells of 3 layers, and separate these to make 12 shells. Finely chop 1 of the centers and add it to the rice mixture. (Reserve the remaining centers for another use.)

Arrange the onion shells in a heavy baking dish and divide the filling between them. Pour the sugar-lemon juice mixture over the onions and sprinkle with the olive oil; omit the grape leaves. Bake uncovered until the filling is golden brown, about 1 hour, basting frequently with the liquid in the dish. Serve hot or warm, with the syrupy pan juices poured over.

Serves 2 or 3 per person as a main course or, for an unusual vegetable to accompany grilled meats, omit the lamb, and serve 2 to each person.

Stuffed Bell Peppers with Green Grape Sauce
Yemistes Strongiles Piperies me Agouritha

Substitute 12 small to medium red, yellow, and/or green bell peppers for the eggplants. Slice off the tops, discard the cores and seeds, and rinse out to remove any remaining seeds. Blanch the tops and shells in boiling water for 5 minutes and drain. Divide the filling between the peppers and replace the tops. Add the sugar-lemon juice mixture and sprinkle with the olive oil; cover with grape leaves if desired. Bake uncovered 1 hour, basting frequently with the liquid in the dish. Serve hot or warm, with the pan juices.

Stuffed Bell Peppers Avgolemono
Yemistes Strongiles Piperies Avgolemono

In this recipe a perfumed rice filling is enhanced with *avgolemono* to produce a dish that's both sweetly aromatic and exquisitely beautiful. Choose small bell peppers for a first course, medium-sized ones for a main course – or substitute zucchini or onions if you prefer.

Serves 8 as a first course, 5 as a main course

1 cup extra virgin olive oil
2 tablespoons unsalted butter
3 shallots, finely chopped, *or* 6 scallions, white part only, finely chopped
2 cups long-grain rice
1 teaspoon saffron threads
5 cups Chicken Stock (page 343) *or* water
1 teaspoon sea salt, or to taste
16 small *or* 10 medium yellow, green, *and/or* red bell peppers
2/3 cup small dark seedless raisins
3/4 cup lightly toasted pine nuts
1 tablespoon dried *rigani* (see page 13)
1 small bunch flat-leaf parsley, leaves finely chopped
3 tablespoons finely chopped Preserved Lemons (page 18) *or* the strained juice of 1 lemon

Freshly ground black pepper, to taste
3 eggs
Strained juice of 2 large lemons

Heat 2 tablespoons of the olive oil and the butter in a heavy saucepan
and sauté the shallot over low heat until soft, about 5 minutes. Add the
rice and cook for 1 minute, stirring with a wooden spoon, until opaque.
Heat the saffron in a small dry frying pan until aromatic and crumble it
into 1 cup of the stock. Add the saffron stock, 2 cups of the remaining
stock, and the salt to the rice. Raise the heat and boil uncovered for 8
minutes, until the liquid has disappeared and holes appear in the surface of
the rice. Remove from the heat, cover with 2 layers of paper towels and a
tight-fitting lid, and set aside for 30 minutes in a warm place such as the
back of the stove.

Fill a large saucepan with water and bring to a boil. Slice the tops off the
peppers, discard the cores, and rinse off the seeds from both tops and shells.
Add to the boiling water, cover, and boil 5 minutes. Drain and set aside.

With a fork, lightly mix the raisins, pine nuts, *rigani*, most of the parsley,
the Preserved Lemons, and pepper into the rice. Add salt and lemon juice to
taste. Loosely fill the pepper shells with this mixture and replace the tops.
Arrange upright in a heavy saucepan just large enough to hold them, pour
the remaining olive oil and stock over, and bring to a boil. Cover, reduce the
heat, and simmer 40 minutes to 1 hour, until the peppers are soft, adding
water if the liquid in the saucepan reduces to less than 1 cup.

Ten minutes before serving, whisk the eggs in a large bowl for 2 minutes,
until pale and frothy. Slowly add the lemon juice and whisk for 1 minute
longer. Remove the peppers from the saucepan, reserving the cooking
liquid, and keep warm. Add 1 cup of the reserved liquid to the egg mixture
in a slow steady stream, whisking constantly. Transfer the sauce to a small
heavy saucepan or the top of a double boiler set over hot water. Stir over
low heat until the sauce thickens enough to coat the back of the spoon; do
not allow to boil.

Arrange the peppers on a warm platter or individual plates and pour
over the sauce. Sprinkle with the remaining parsley and serve immediately.

Stuffed Courgettes Avgolemono
Yemista Kolokithia Avgolemono

Substitute 5 medium zucchini, 4–5 inches long (to serve as a main
course), or 8 small zucchini, 3 inches long (to serve as a first course), for
the peppers, and make half the amount of filling. Trim the ends of the
zucchini and rub them with a towel to remove any fuzz. Blanch in boiling

water (5 minutes for large zucchini, 3 minutes for small), and drain. Cut lengthways in half, scoop out the centers with a small spoon, and arrange in a baking dish. Finely chop the flesh and add it to the rice mixture. Add salt, pepper, and lemon juice to taste. Fill the zucchini, pour over the remaining olive oil and stock, and bake uncovered in a preheated oven at 350°F until tender, about 40 minutes; add water if liquid in the dish reduces to less than 1 cup. Make the sauce and serve immediately.

Stuffed Onions Avgolemono
Yemista Kremithia Avgolemono

Substitute 5 large onions (to serve as a main course) or 16 small onions (to serve as a first course) for the peppers. Peel, and slice off both ends. Blanch in boiling water (10 minutes for large onions, 5 minutes for small), drain, and let cool slightly. Push out the onion centers, leaving shells of 2 layers. If using large onions separate the layers to make 10 shells. Arrange the shells in a heavy baking dish. Fill the shells with the rice mixture, piling it high. Pour over the remaining olive oil and stock, and bake uncovered in a preheated oven at 350°F until tender, about 40 minutes for small onions, 1 hour for large, occasionally basting with the stock. Make sure there is always at least 1 cup cooking liquid in the dish; add water if necessary. Make the sauce and serve hot.

Note For a meat filling, sauté ³⁄₄ pound finely minced lean lamb in 2 tablespoons olive oil until lightly browned. Drain on paper towels and sprinkle with a little salt and lemon juice. Stir into the cooked rice mixture with a fork.

Baked Stuffed Tomatoes and Peppers
Yemistes Domates ke Piperies

Huge shallow trays of beautiful stuffed vegetables – tomatoes and multi-colored peppers, zucchini, eggplants, and onions – await the hungry visitor to any taverna. In this recipe either chickpeas or pine nuts can be used to provide an unusual texture. Currants or raisins add a gentle sweetness and fresh mint or *rigani,* a hillside fragrance. Although the vegetables take some time to prepare, they can be baked ahead of time. Serve cold with yogurt, olives, and lemon wedges for a perfect summer lunch.

Serves 8 as a first course, 4 as a main course

....

8 small *or* 4 large ripe tomatoes
¹/₂ tablespoon sugar
Sea salt
8 small *or* 4 medium green bell peppers, roasted, seeded, and skinned
  (see page 343)
¹/₂ cup extra virgin olive oil, or more to taste
1 medium onion, grated
1 teaspoon ground allspice
1 cup long-grain rice, cooked
¹/₂ cup crumbled cooked chickpeas *or* lightly toasted pine nuts
5 tablespoons fresh mint leaves, torn into small pieces at the last minute, *or*
  1¹/₂ tablespoons dried *rigani* (see page 13), crumbled
¹/₂ cup currants *or* small dark seedless raisins
1 small bunch flat-leaf parsley, leaves finely chopped
Juice of 1 lemon
1 cup fresh whole wheat bread crumbs

....

Heat the oven to 325°F. Slice off the tops of the tomatoes and set aside. Scoop out the pulp with a small spoon, discard the seeds, and dice the pulp. Set aside with the juices. Sprinkle the sugar and salt into the tomato shells, invert onto paper towels, and set aside to drain.

Slice off the tops of the peppers, discard the cores, and wipe the seeds off the tops and shells. Drain on paper towels.

Warm 4 tablespoons of the olive oil in a heavy saucepan and sauté the onion over low heat until golden brown, about 12 minutes; stir occasionally. Add the tomato and juices, allspice, pepper, and salt (to taste), and cook 5 minutes, until most of the liquid has evaporated. With a fork, stir in the rice, chickpeas, mint, currants, and half the parsley. Season to taste. Loosely fill the tomatoes and peppers, replace their tops, and arrange them in a heavy baking dish. Sprinkle with the lemon juice and the remaining olive oil; sprinkle the bread crumbs over the tomatoes. Add 1 cup water to the dish and bake uncovered for 40 minutes to 1 hour, until the vegetables are soft and slightly darkened, basting occasionally with the liquid in the dish. Add a little more water to the dish if it appears to be drying out. Let the vegetables cool in the dish.

To serve, arrange the vegetables on a platter and sprinkle with the cooking liquid, olive oil if desired, and the remaining parsley.

Baked Stuffed Eggplants, Tomatoes, and Peppers

Diafora Parayemista

Choose slightly smaller tomatoes and peppers, and add 4 round eggplants, about 4 inches long. Trim off the stems of the eggplants, cut lengthways in half, and fry in 3 tablespoons olive oil until the cut sides are golden brown and the skin is dark and wrinkled. Scoop out the flesh with a small spoon, discard the seeds, and dice the pulp. Add the cubed eggplant and an additional 7/8 cup cooked rice, 1/4 cup pine nuts or crumbled cooked chickpeas, and salt and pepper to taste, to the filling. Arrange the vegetables in a heavy baking dish, divide the filling between them, and replace the tomato and pepper tops. Sprinkle with the lemon juice and olive oil if desired. Sprinkle the bread crumbs over the tomatoes. Add 1 cup water to the dish and bake uncovered for 1 hour, basting frequently with the liquid in the dish. Let the vegetables cool in the dish.

Arrange on a large platter or individual plates, pour over the pan juices, and serve with lemon wedges.

Stuffed Cabbage Leaves in Tomato Sauce

Lakhanodolmades me Saltsa Domatas

In the winter months cabbages, cheap and at their best, are used for a variety of salads and family meals, and this is one of the most popular dishes. The Greek affection for cabbage has a long history: Hippocrates is said to have prescribed it as a cure for colic and Pythagoras to have composed a eulogy on this humble vegetable! Serve with Perfect Pilaf (page 226) or Pilaf with Green Lentils (page 229).

Serves 4

....

1 (1 1/2-to-2-pound) firm white *or* pale green cabbage
4 tablespoons extra virgin olive oil
1 small onion, finely chopped
1/2 pound lean pork *or* beef, finely minced
1 teaspoon ground allspice, or to taste
3 tablespoons lightly toasted pine nuts
4 tablespoons currants
2/3 cup long-grain rice, cooked
Sea salt *and* freshly ground black pepper, to taste
2 tablespoons fresh mint leaves, or to taste

4 tablespoons finely chopped flat-leaf parsley
Juice of 1 lemon *or* 2 tablespoons white wine vinegar
1½ cups Tomato Sauce (page 321), made with parsley and bay leaves

Discard any torn or discolored outer cabbage leaves and, with a sharp paring knife, cut out as much of the core as possible. Cook, covered, in boiling water for 5 minutes, drain and set aside.

Heat half the olive oil in a heavy saucepan and sauté the onion over low heat until soft, about 6 minutes. Raise the heat, add the meat, and sauté until lightly browned, breaking up any lumps with a wooden spoon. Add the allspice, pine nuts, currants, rice, and salt and pepper. Chop the mint and half the parsley together and add to the meat along with the lemon juice. Stir with a fork until well mixed. Add allspice, salt, pepper, and/or mint if desired; the mixture should be highly flavored.

Turn the cabbage upside down. Separate 16–20 leaves from the core with a paring knife by pulling each one down and off. Trim and discard any thick spine and lay the leaves flat between layers of paper towels to dry.

Lay a cabbage leaf on your palm (or on a flat surface), spine side up, and place 1 heaping tablespoon of filling on the bottom third of the leaf. Fold over both sides and, keeping the filling in place with your thumb, firmly roll up from the leaf base to tip; repeat with the remaining leaves and filling. As you finish each stuffed leaf, place it seam side down in a heavy sauté pan large enough to hold all the *dolmades* in a single layer, pressing the rolls tightly against each other.

Pour over the Tomato Sauce and add enough water to come barely to the top of the *dolmades*. Place a heat-resistant plate slightly smaller than the pan on top and set a weight (such as a large can of fruit) on top of the plate. Slowly bring to a boil, reduce the heat, and simmer gently for 1 hour. Add a little more water if the liquid begins to disappear from the surface. Remove from the heat and set aside for 5 minutes with the weight still in place.

Transfer the *dolmades* to a warm platter and pour over the sauce and the rest of the olive oil. Sprinkle with the remaining parsley and serve hot or warm.

Savory Pies

Spinach Pie
Spanakopitta

One of the finest examples of Greek home-cooking, *spanakopitta* is a colorful centerpiece on any table, from a family picnic to an elegant supper.

For a flavor closer to that of the village kitchens, make the pie with beet greens or other *khorta* (see page 221). Serve with olives and a jug of rosé wine (see page 339).

Serves 8–10

Filling
2 pounds fresh spinach
½ cup extra virgin olive oil
8 scallions, trimmed, the best green parts left intact, and thinly sliced *or* 2 leeks, trimmed, thoroughly rinsed and thinly sliced
6 sprigs fresh dill, coarsely chopped
¼ teaspoon grated nutmeg
1 teaspoon cracked black pepper, or to taste
4 ounces small-curd cottage cheese, drained and pressed through a fine strainer
1 cup crumbled *feta* cheese
4 eggs, beaten
1 small bunch flat-leaf parsley, leaves coarsely chopped
Sea salt, to taste

¾ pound phyllo pastry, thawed if frozen
4 tablespoons (½ stick) unsalted butter, melted

Rinse the spinach in several changes of cold water, discard the stalks and any bruised or tough leaves, and place in a heavy saucepan. Cover and cook, with just the water that clings to the leaves, for 1 minute, until wilted and barely soft. Drain, pressing the greens against the sides of the colander to remove as much liquid as possible. Finely chop the spinach and set aside.

Warm half the olive oil in a heavy sauté pan and sauté the scallions over low heat until soft, about 3 minutes (leeks will take a few minutes longer). Stir in the dill, spinach, nutmeg, and pepper and cook 1 minute; remove from the heat. Add the cottage cheese, *feta* cheese, eggs, and parsley, and mash together with a fork. Check the seasonings and add salt and pepper to taste.

Heat the oven to 350°F. Remove the phyllo from the refrigerator and set aside.

In a bowl, combine the melted butter with the remaining olive oil. Divide the phyllo sheets into 2 portions, tightly rewrap one, and refrigerate. Lightly brush a 10-inch square or round baking pan, at least 2 inches deep, with the oil/butter mixture. Line with 1 phyllo sheet, gently pressing it into the sides of the pan, and brush the sheet with the oil/butter. Repeat with the remaining unrefrigerated sheets of pastry, but do not brush the last sheet. Rotate a round pan 60 degrees each time you add a sheet; a square pan 90 degrees. Gently spread the filling over the phyllo and lightly smooth it flat. Fold the edges of the phyllo over the filling and brush with the oil/butter.

Remove the second portion of phyllo from the refrigerator. Lay 1 sheet over the filling, letting the edges hang over the sides of the pan. Lightly brush with the oil/butter mixture, and layer until all the sheets are used; do not brush the last sheet.

Carefully ease your fingers down between the edge of the pie and the sides of the pan, pull the bottom edges of the pie toward the center, and tuck the top sheets in around the bottom of the pie. Liberally brush the top sheet with the remaining oil/butter mixture and, with a sharp knife, score the top 2 sheets of phyllo into rectangles or diamond shapes for serving. Do not score a round pie – this would make it impossible to remove from the pan. Bake 45–50 minutes, until deep golden brown.

When the pie is cooked, immediately cut through the score marks to the bottom of the pan. Serve from the pan or arrange the pieces on a dish. Transfer a round pie to a serving platter: Invert a large plate over the baking pan, turn upside down, remove the pan, and invert a serving platter over the bottom of the pie. Hold firmly and turn right side up.

Serve hot, warm, or cold.

Variation
♦ Substitute young beet greens, ruby chard, or water spinach (see page 221) for the spinach, and cook 3 minutes, or until barely soft, before mixing with the rest of the ingredients. Use leeks instead of scallions.

Aromatic Lamb Phyllo Rolls
Arnaki Tiligmeno me Filo

There are several versions of this delicious and versatile dish. It can be made as small rolls for a buffet or lunch, or as one large round or rectangular pie. It's composed of an aromatic meat layer topped with a spicy cheese mixture, and wrapped in phyllo to make a neat package for baking. Although it sounds complicated, it's not really too difficult to make, and you can prepare the filling a day ahead and refrigerate overnight if you prefer. I like even more exotic versions, with an extra layer of *pilafi*, spinach, or rice or, perhaps, sautéed diced eggplants. Serve with Wild Greens Salad (page 222) or a green salad.

Serves 6

6 tablespoons extra virgin olive oil
6 tablespoons unsalted butter
1 large onion, finely chopped

1½ pounds lean lamb, finely ground
2 large ripe tomatoes, skinned and diced
1 teaspoon honey
1 tablespoon ground cinnamon, or to taste
½ teaspoon sea salt, or to taste
1 teaspoon cracked black pepper, or to taste
4 tablespoons reduced Meat Stock (page 348) *or* robust red wine
1½ tablespoons chopped fresh marjoram *or* 2½ tablespoons dried *rigani*
  (see page 13), crumbled
4 tablespoons finely chopped flat-leaf parsley
6 ounces fresh *myzithra or* small-curd cottage cheese, drained
⅓ cup finely grated *feta* cheese
½ teaspoon grated nutmeg
2 egg yolks
12 sheets phyllo (from a 1-pound package, see page 266)

For serving
confectioners' sugar
Ground cinnamon

Warm 1 tablespoon of the olive oil and 2 tablespoons of the butter in a heavy sauté pan and sauté the onion over low heat until soft, about 8 minutes. Raise the heat, add the meat, and sauté until lightly browned, breaking up any lumps with a wooden spoon. Add the tomatoes, honey, cinnamon, salt, and ½ teaspoon of the pepper, and bring to a boil. Add the stock, bring to a boil, reduce the heat, and simmer 15 minutes, until almost all the liquid has evaporated. Add the marjoram and parsley, and additional cinnamon, marjoram, and pepper to taste (do not add salt at this point, as the cheese mixture is salty). Set aside, or refrigerate for up to 24 hours.

Heat the oven to 375°F. Press the *myzithra* through a strainer into a bowl. Combine with the *feta*, the nutmeg, the remaining ½ teaspoon of pepper, and the egg yolks. Cover and set aside.

Combine the remaining butter and olive oil in a small saucepan, and melt over very low heat. Brush a heavy baking sheet with some of this mixture. Lay the phyllo sheets one on top of another and cut in half crosswise to make 24 sheets. Tightly rewrap half the sheets and refrigerate. Lay 1 of the remaining sheets on a clean work surface with a long end facing you, and brush lightly with the butter mixture. Lay a second sheet on top, brush it with the mixture, and repeat with a third sheet. Lay another sheet on top. Divide the mixture into 6 portions. Place 1 portion on the bottom third of the top phyllo sheet and shape it into a sausage about 8 inches long. Divide the cheese filling into 6 portions and spread 1 portion over the meat. Fold the bottom edges of the phyllo layers over the filling, then fold over the 2 sides and roll up to make a firm neat parcel. Place on the baking sheet and repeat with the remaining phyllo and filling.

Brush the rolls with the remaining butter mixture and bake for 25–30 minutes, until deep golden brown. Drain on paper towels, sprinkle liberally with the confectioners' sugar and cinnamon, and transfer to a warm platter.

Note To make one large round or rectangular pie, use a 1-pound package of phyllo and additional melted butter and olive oil as needed for brushing the sheets. Assemble the pie as directed on pages 96 to 97. Bake for 35–40 minutes, until deep golden brown. Sprinkle liberally with the confectioners' sugar and cinnamon and serve warm.

Cretan Chicken Pie
Tzoulamas

At a wedding feast high in a remote mountain village on Crete, this pie was the magnificent centerpiece to the wedding buffet table laid out in the village square. Around us were the snow-capped mountain peaks, in the distance a brilliant blue sea sparkling in the sunlight. No wonder the *tzoulamas* tasted wonderful! But it tastes almost as good in less romantic settings, can be prepared ahead, and even freezes well (freeze before baking), so don't miss out on it.

A traditional *tzoulamas* is made with layers of crisp pastry (fried in olive oil before the pie is assembled), mildly spiced chicken and rice, fresh mountain cheese, and hot goat's butter. My version replaces the fried pastry with phyllo, the *anthotyro* cheese with *feta* and cottage cheese, and the goat's butter with unsalted butter and lemon juice. Begin the meal with *mezedes* such as Grilled Eggplant Salata (page 44) or *taramosalata* (page 43).

Serves 10 to 12

1 (5-to-6-pound) chicken, cut into serving pieces, skin and fat removed and giblets reserved
1 large onion, chopped
2 carrots, scrubbed, and cut into thick slices
1 large bunch flat-leaf parsley, stalks removed and tied in a bundle, leaves finely chopped
Chicken Stock (page 343) *or* water to cover the chicken
Sea salt *and* freshly ground white pepper, to taste
5 tablespoons extra virgin olive oil
4 shallots, finely chopped
1 tablespoon ground cumin
1⅓ cups long-grain rice
6 bay leaves

Juice of 2 lemons
4 tablespoons finely chopped Preserved Lemons (page 18) *or* the finely
 grated zest of 1 lemon
1 large clove garlic, finely chopped
4 tablespoons capers, rinsed

1 (1-pound) package of phyllo pastry, thawed if frozen
1 cup (2 sticks) unsalted butter
½ cup grated *feta* cheese
¾ pound small-curd cottage cheese, drained
1 cup *plus* 3 tablespoons small dark seedless raisins
1 cup lightly toasted pine nuts

Place the chicken pieces, giblets, onion, carrot, parsley stalks, stock, and
salt and pepper in a large saucepan. Bring slowly to a boil, cover, reduce
the heat, and simmer 40 minutes, until the chicken is cooked. Strain over a
bowl, and strain the cooking liquid once more through cheesecloth. Set
aside 2 cups of the liquid (and refrigerate or freeze the rest for another
use). Discard the vegetables and all the giblets except the liver.

Warm 4 tablespoons of the olive oil in a heavy saucepan and sauté the
shallots over low heat for 10 minutes, or until soft. Add the cumin and cook
1 minute, until aromatic. Stir in the rice, reserved stock, the bay leaves, and
salt (to taste), and bring to a boil without stirring. Cook uncovered for 8
minutes, until holes appear in the surface of the rice and the liquid has
evaporated. Remove from the heat, cover with 2 layers of paper towels and
a tight-fitting lid, and set aside for 30 minutes in a warm place.

Remove the chicken from the bones and cut the meat into almond-sized
pieces. Cut the liver into tiny cubes. Place the chicken and liver in a bowl
and sprinkle with half the lemon juice and pepper to taste. Set aside 2
tablespoons of the parsley and add all but 1 tablespoon of the Preserved
Lemons, the garlic, 3 tablespoons of the capers, and a pinch of salt to the
remaining parsley. Chop to mix. Combine with the chicken, using your
fingers to make sure each piece is coated. Cover and set aside. (The chicken
can be prepared ahead and refrigerated overnight.)

Heat the oven to 375°F. Remove the package of phyllo from the
refrigerator and set aside unopened. (If you have refrigerated the filling,
remove that too.) With a fork, mash the *feta* and cottage cheeses together
in a small bowl. Melt ¾ cup of the butter over very low heat and add the
remaining olive oil.

Divide the phyllo sheets into 2 portions, tightly rewrap one, and
refrigerate. Lightly brush a 10-inch square or round baking pan with the
butter mixture. Line with 1 phyllo sheet, gently pressing it into the sides of
the pan, and brush the sheet with the butter mixture. Repeat with the

remaining unrefrigerated sheets of pastry, but do not brush the last sheet. Turn a round pan 60 degrees each time you add a sheet, a square pan 90 degrees. Spread the rice mixture over the phyllo and then spread with the chicken and parsley mixture. Scatter the cheese mixture over the chicken as evenly as possible, then sprinkle the raisins and pine nuts over the cheese. Sprinkle with a few tablespoons of the chicken stock if the filling seems dry. Fold the edges of the phyllo over the filling and brush with the butter mixture.

Remove the second portion of phyllo from the refrigerator. Lay 1 sheet over the filling, letting the edges hang over the sides of the pan. Lightly brush with the butter mixture, and layer until all the sheets are used; do not butter the last sheet.

Carefully ease your fingers down between the edge of the pie and the sides of the pan, pull the bottom edges of the pie toward the center, and tuck the top sheets in around the bottom of the pie. Liberally butter the top sheet and, with a sharp knife, score the top 2 sheets of phyllo into rectangles or diamond shapes for serving. Do not score a round pie – this would make it impossible to remove from the pan. Bake 35–40 minutes, until deep golden brown.

While the pie is baking, heat the remaining butter in a small saucepan over very low heat for 10 minutes, until foamy and nutty brown; don't let it burn. Strain through cheesecloth into a small bowl, add the remaining lemon juice and set aside in a warm place. Chop the reserved parsley and remaining capers and Preserved Lemons together.

When the pie is cooked, immediately cut through the score marks to the bottom of the pan. Serve from the pan or arrange the pieces on a dish. Transfer a round pie to a serving platter: invert a large plate over the baking pan, turn upside down, remove the pan, and invert a serving platter over the bottom of the pie. Hold firmly and turn right side up. Carefully make a small hole in the center of the pie, pour the brown butter over, and sprinkle with the parsley mixture. Serve at once.

FISH AND SEAFOOD

Psaria ke Psarika Thalassina

For me any mention of Greek fish dishes immediately conjures up images of waterfront tavernas by a sparkling azure sea on a day shimmering with heat and brilliant sunlight. Seated at a rickety table under the welcome shade of a pine tree, you choose the fish that takes your fancy, then relax with an ouzo and *mezedes* while it's prepared. Your anticipation of the treat ahead mounts as a bewildering array of fish dishes, their mouth-watering aromas filling the air, are served to tables around you.

The sheer variety of fish readily available in Greece is amazing. The Greek cook has the choice of over 30 different kinds of fish, plus shellfish and the cephalopods such as octopus and squid, and makes good use of them all. Situated in the warmest part of the Mediterranean, Greece and her islands have enjoyed a wonderfully rich sea harvest since ancient times.

Methods of preparation and presentation have changed remarkably little over the centuries. Fish is always served complete with its head – to Greeks this is the tastiest and most nutritious part. They also prefer many fish dishes to be served warm rather than hot, a practice that many visitors to Greece are not used to.

Most of the dishes included here are very simple to prepare. And, although we may not have the Greek cook's wide choice of fish, in many of these dishes almost any kind of fish steak or whole fish can be substituted.

Crusty Baked Fish
Psaria Plaki sto Fourno

This gloriously aromatic dish is a concoction of olive oil, parsley, tomatoes, and garlic with a crunchy crusty top. Village cooks say *psaria plaki* should be made only with John Dory fish but almost any firm-fleshed fish can be baked this way, using whole fish, steaks, or fillets. You can make a lighter version by substituting white wine or fish stock or chicken stock for some of the olive oil. Serve with lemon wedges.

Serves 4

2 firm-fleshed white fish such as John Dory (see page 346), sea bream, *or* bass (about 1¼ pound each), cleaned and scaled (see page 345) *or* 4 fillets, (6-to-8-ounces each)

Coarse-grain sea salt *and* cracked black pepper, to taste

Juice of 1 lemon

1 cup extra virgin olive oil *or* 5 tablespoons extra virgin olive oil *and* ⁵/₈ cup Light Fish *or* Chicken Stock (page 345 or page 343) *or* dry white wine

3 tablespoons finely chopped fresh oregano *or* thyme *or* 2 tablespoons dried *rigani* (see page 13), crumbled

2 medium onions, cut in half and thinly sliced

1 large clove garlic, finely chopped

1¼ pounds boiling potatoes, peeled and cut into thin slices (boiled 10 minutes if fillets are used)

6 large ripe tomatoes, skinned and cut into slices

3 bay leaves, broken in half

12 Elitses *or* Niçoise olives, rinsed and pitted

For serving

12 sprigs flat-leaf parsley, leaves coarsely chopped

Lemon wedges

....

Dry the fish with paper towels. Make 2 deep parallel incisions on either side of the whole fish. Rub whole fish inside and out, fillets on both sides, with salt and pepper, half the lemon juice, and 1 tablespoon of the olive oil. Sprinkle the cavities of the whole fish, or both sides of the fillets, with 2 tablespoons of the oregano, cover, and set aside for 30 minutes to marinate.

Heat 3 tablespoons of the remaining olive oil in a heavy frying pan and sauté the onions over low heat until pale golden, about 12 minutes. Stir in the garlic, cook 1 minute longer, and set aside.

Heat the oven to 350°F. Brush a heavy deep baking dish with 1 tablespoon of the remaining olive oil. Dry the potato slices with paper towels and arrange about two thirds of them in the bottom of the baking dish. Cover with the onion slices and lay the fish on top. Cover with the tomato slices and sprinkle with any remaining marinade, the bay leaves, and salt and pepper. Arrange the remaining sliced potatoes on top, leaving the tomato slices partially exposed.

Pour the remaining lemon juice and olive oil (or olive oil and stock) over the potatoes, cover, and bake 30 minutes. Reduce the oven temperature to 325°F, uncover, and bake 20–30 minutes longer, until golden brown and crusty. Gently press the olives into the potato-onion crust and bake 5 minutes longer.

Sprinkle with the parsley and the remaining oregano and serve at once.

Corfiot Baked Fish
Bourtheto

This Corfu island speciality is one of the few hot and spicy dishes in Greek cuisine. The Corfiots use small, bony fish, the cheapest in the market. For our taste, fillets of any firm-fleshed white fish such as bass, sea bream, or halibut are probably a better choice – and easier to eat. Or try a popular island alternative – *bourtheto* made with octopus. This colorful country food, traditionally cooked in a shallow earthenware dish, is easy to make and perfect for a leisurely summer lunch.

Serves 4

4 firm-fleshed white fish (about 14 ounces each), cleaned and scaled
    (see page 345) *or* 4 fillets, (about 6–7 ounces each)
Juice of 1 small lemon
Sea salt *and* freshly ground black pepper, to taste
1 large bunch flat-leaf parsley, stalks reserved, leaves finely chopped
½ cup extra virgin olive oil, to taste
3 large mild onions, quartered and thinly sliced
1 large clove garlic, finely chopped
4 tablespoons aged red wine vinegar
1 tablespoon honey
6 tablespoons dry red wine
1 teaspoon cayenne pepper, or to taste
4 large ripe tomatoes, skinned, seeded, and diced
3 bay leaves
1 teaspoon fresh thyme

For serving
24 Elitses *or* 12 Niçoise olives, rinsed and pitted

Dry the fish with paper towels. Rub whole fish inside and out, fillets on both sides, with the lemon juice and salt and pepper. Place in a shallow dish along with the parsley stalks, pour 4 tablespoons of the olive oil over, cover, and set aside for 1 hour to marinate.

Heat 3 tablespoons of the remaining olive oil in a large heavy sauté pan and cook the onions, covered, over low heat until very soft, about 30 minutes; reduce the heat if the onions begin to brown.

Heat the oven to 350°F. Stir the garlic into the onions. Combine the vinegar and honey, add to the pan, and boil until syrupy. Add the wine and boil 1 minute longer. Stir in the cayenne pepper, tomatoes, bay leaves, thyme and half the parsley, and pour into a baking dish. Remove the fish from the marinade, discarding the parsley stalks, and lay the fish on top of the onions. Sprinkle with the remaining olive oil, cover, and bake 20 minutes (fillets) to 30 minutes (whole fish), until the fish is an even white all the way through.

Sprinkle with the olives and remaining parsley and serve hot.

Baked Fish with Garlic and Vinegar
Psari sto Fourno me Xsithi

This is a popular way of cooking a plump whole fish, especially for a small dinner party. The ingredients produce an interestingly sweet but mildly piquant flavor, and the finished dish is elegant and polished. Whole cloves of garlic and sprigs of herbs support the fish in the baking dish and impart fragrance and flavor. The only other requirements are a salad, wine, and plenty of bread to mop up the delicious sauce and roasted garlic.

Serves 4

1 (3-to-3½-pound) sea bass *or* other firm-fleshed white fish, cleaned and scaled, scored (see page 345)
1½ tablespoons coarse-grain sea salt, or to taste
1 tablespoon cracked black pepper
2 bay leaves
1¼ cups extra virgin olive oil
24 cloves garlic (unpeeled), feathery skin rubbed off and stem ends trimmed
6 sprigs dried rosemary *or* thyme *or* rigani (see page 13)
5 tablespoons aged red wine vinegar

For serving
Coarsely chopped flat-leaf parsley
Thasos *or* Kalamata olives

Dry the fish with paper towels and rub inside and out with half the salt and pepper. Place the bay leaves inside the cavity, cover, and set aside for 1 hour.

Heat the oven to 325°F. Liberally brush a heavy baking dish, just large enough to hold the fish, with some of the olive oil. Lay the garlic cloves in the baking dish in a single layer, brush with olive oil, and bake, uncovered, for 20 minutes. Lay the rosemary sprigs over the garlic and lay the fish on top. Whisk together the vinegar and remaining olive oil. Pour half this mixture over the fish and sprinkle with the remaining salt and pepper. Add 4 tablespoons of water to the baking dish, cover loosely with aluminum foil, and bake 15 minutes. Remove the foil and bake 30–40 minutes longer, until the fish is an even white all the way through. Baste the fish and garlic frequently with the remaining vinegar and olive oil mixture, and add a little more water to the dish if the garlic is in danger of burning.

Transfer the fish to a warm platter and surround with the garlic. Spoon over the pan juices and any remaining oil and vinegar sauce, sprinkle with the parsley, and serve the olives in bowls.

Baked Sole in Grape Leaves
Glosses Fournou se Ambelofila

Dover sole is a favorite choice for this dish but other flat fish or slender fillets of bass make fine substitutes. John Dory fillets (page 346) or whole sardines are also delicious cooked this way. The layers of grape leaves keep the delicate fish moist and infuse the dish with their subtle and unique fragrance.

Serves 4

8 fillets of sole, (4-to-5-ounces each) *or* 4 large fish fillets
Juice of 1 lemon
Sea salt *and* freshly ground black pepper, to taste
½ cup extra virgin olive oil, to taste
Fresh *or* brine-preserved grape leaves, to make 2 layers in the baking dish, blanched in boiling water (3 seconds for preserved leaves, 5 seconds for fresh) and drained

For serving
Finely chopped flat-leaf parsley
12 Elitses *or* Niçoise olives, rinsed and pitted, *optional*
Lemon wedges

Dry the fillets with paper towels. Sprinkle both sides with half the lemon juice and salt and pepper, and set aside for 30 minutes.

Heat the oven to 325°F. Brush a shallow earthenware or enameled cast-iron baking dish, just large enough to hold the fillets in a single layer, with some of the olive oil, and cover the bottom of the dish with half the grape leaves, glossy sides up. Brush the leaves with olive oil, lay the fillets on top, and sprinkle with the remaining lemon juice and olive oil. Cover with the rest of the grape leaves, glossy sides down, and sprinkle with 2 tablespoons water. Bake, uncovered, for 20 minutes, until the fillets are an even milky white all the way through.

Discard the top layer of grape leaves. Spoon the pan juices over the fish, sprinkle with the parsley, olives, and pepper, and serve with the lemon wedges.

Fish Spetsai-Style
Psari Spetsiotiko

From the charming island of Spetsai, famous for its fragrant pinewoods, comes this good country dish. The fish is smothered in an aromatic tomato sauce flavored with cinnamon, cloves and garlic, topped with a layer of bread crumbs, and baked until golden and crisp. It can be served hot or cold. Fried or grilled eggplants are a good accompaniment, and resin-flavored retsina is the perfect wine to complement the fish.

Serves 4

2 (1½-pound) sea bream, cleaned and scaled, scored (see page 345)
   or 4 fillets white-fleshed fish such as bass (about 7 ounces each)
Juice of ½ lemon
Coarse-grain sea salt *and* cracked black pepper, to taste
½ cup extra virgin olive oil
1 small onion, finely chopped
2–4 cloves garlic, finely chopped
8 large tomatoes, skinned and diced, juices reserved
1 teaspoon honey
1 3-inch cinnamon stick, broken in half *or* 1 teaspoon ground cinnamon
3 cloves *or* ¼ teaspoon ground cloves
4 tablespoons coarsely chopped flat-leaf parsley
½ cup dry white wine
⅜ cup dried coarse bread crumbs
1 teaspoon dried *rigani* (see page 13)

Dry the fish with paper towels. Rub whole fish inside and out, fillets on both sides, with the lemon juice, salt and pepper, and 2 tablespoons of the olive oil. Cover and set aside.

In a heavy sauté pan heat 2 tablespoons of the remaining olive oil over low heat and sauté the onion until soft, about 6 minutes. Add the garlic, tomatoes with their juices, honey, cinnamon, cloves and half the parsley. Raise the heat to medium-low and simmer until the cooking liquid is reduced by half. Add the wine and boil for 1 minute. Strain the sauce through a coarse strainer into a large bowl, pressing on the solids to extract as much liquid as possible. Measure, and add water if necessary to make 3 cups. Season to taste with salt and pepper. Place the fish in the sauce, turn once or twice to coat, and set aside for 30 minutes.

Heat the oven to 325°F. Brush a baking dish, just large enough to hold the fish, with some of the remaining olive oil, place the fish in it, and pour over the sauce. Sprinkle with olive oil and bake, uncovered, for 20 minutes. Baste the fish with the sauce and sprinkle with the bread crumbs and the rest of the olive oil. Bake 15 minutes longer, until the fish is an even white all the way through and the sauce is thick and syrupy.

Sprinkle with the *rigani* and the remaining parsley, and serve hot or warm.

Sea Bass with Vinegar and Rosemary
Lavrakia Marinata

Sea bass is a favorite taverna dish – best eaten, say the Greeks, at an open-air restaurant close by the sea. The fish, glistening and plump, looks beautiful, while sweet rosemary lends a subtle fragrance. Here the dusting of flour keeps the fish from splitting and flaking during frying and cuts down fish odors in the kitchen. Chickpea flour, available in Greek, Middle Eastern, and health food stores, gives just the right traditional nutty flavor.

Serves 4

4 (1-to-1¼-pound) sea bass, cleaned and scaled (see page 345)
   or 4 (7-ounce) fillets
Juice of ½ lemon
1 teaspoon coarse-grain sea salt, or to taste
½ tablespoon cracked black pepper, or to taste
4 tablespoons chickpea flour *and* 2 tablespoons all-purpose flour *or*
   6 tablespoons all-purpose flour
1 cup extra virgin olive oil, or to taste
1 large clove garlic, cut into slivers, *optional*
5 tablespoons aged red wine vinegar
2 tablespoons hot water
2 tablespoons fresh rosemary
4 bay leaves

For serving
Small sprigs fresh rosemary
Elitses *or* Niçoise olives

Wipe the fish with a damp cloth and rub whole fish inside and out, fillets on both sides, with the lemon juice and half the salt and pepper. Dust with 2 tablespoons of the flour, cover, and set aside for 30 minutes.

Place a large heavy sauté pan over medium-low heat and add half the olive oil. Dust the fish again with half the remaining flour and shake off any excess. When the olive oil is hot but not smoking, fry the fish on both sides until pale golden, about 15 minutes for whole fish, 10–12 minutes for fillets. The fish is cooked if it flakes easily when you insert a thin knife blade into the thickest part of the fish; it should be an even white all the way through. Drain between layers of paper towels. Strain the frying oil through 2 layers of cheesecloth to remove any residue and set aside.

Wipe out the pan with paper towels and return to low heat. Sprinkle the remaining flour over the bottom of the sauté pan and stir a minute or two with a wooden spoon until deep golden brown. Whisk in the reserved frying oil and the remaining olive oil. Add the garlic and cook, stirring, 1 minute longer, until the flour is a deep nutty brown. The flour and oil will not blend together, but the flour will flavor and color the oil. Add the vinegar, water, rosemary, bay leaves and remaining salt and pepper. Whisk to mix, and simmer for 3 minutes.

Return the fish to the sauté pan, cover, and heat through. Transfer to a warm dish, pour over the sauce, and garnish with the rosemary sprigs. Serve hot or warm, with black olives.

Note To serve cold, add ½ cup dry white wine or 1 cup strained Tomato Sauce (page 321), made with parsley and bay leaves, along with the vinegar. Let the sauce cool, then transfer the fish and sauce to a shallow glass or ceramic dish, add olive oil to cover, tightly cover the dish, and refrigerate overnight or for up to 3 days before serving. Turn the fish in the marinade once or twice. Serve as a *meze* or lunch dish.

Red Mullet in Savory Sauce
Barbounia me Saltsa Savori

Red mullet has always been highly prized in Greece. One ancient manuscript lists a 2-pound mullet at the same price as two dozen slaves. Nowadays large red mullet are popular, but it is the smaller fish that have the sweeter flavor. In Greece the liver and cheeks are considered a delicacy – I prefer to do without the liver unless the fish is very fresh. This dish tastes equally delicious hot or cold; the piquant sauce also marries well with filets or steaks of bass, halibut, or sea bream.

Serves 4

8 (8-to-10-ounces each) red mullet, cleaned and scaled (see page 345) *or*
    4 (7-ounce) fillets of bass *or* sea bream
1 teaspoon coarse-grain sea salt, or to taste
½ tablespoon cracked black pepper, or to taste
½ cup extra virgin olive oil
1 large clove garlic, cut into slivers
5 tablespoons aged red wine vinegar
1 teaspoon honey

6 large ripe tomatoes, skinned, seeded, diced, and drained in a colander for
   30 minutes
1/4 teaspoon ground cinnamon
5 tablespoons currants *or* small dark seedless raisins, soaked for 30 minutes
   in 1 tablespoon hot water
4 bay leaves
1 tablespoon fresh thyme, finely chopped *or* 1/2 tablespoon dried thyme,
   crumbled

For serving
4 tablespoons coarsely chopped flat-leaf parsley
2 salted anchovy fillets (see page 343), rinsed, patted dry, and finely chopped

Wipe the fish with a damp cloth and rub whole fish inside and out,
fillets on both sides, with half the salt and pepper. Cover and set aside for
30 minutes.

Place a large heavy sauté pan over medium-low heat, add half the olive
oil, and heat until hot but not smoking. Fry the fish on both sides until
pale golden, about 15 minutes for whole fish, 10–12 minutes for fillets.
The fish is cooked if it flakes easily when you insert a thin knife blade into
the thickest part; it should be an even white all the way through. Drain
between layers of paper towels.

Drain off the olive oil and wipe out the sauté pan with paper towels.
Add half the remaining olive oil and sauté the garlic over low heat just
until fragrant; don't let it brown. Combine the vinegar and honey and add
to the pan, raise the heat, and boil until reduced to about 3 tablespoons.
Add the tomatoes, cinnamon, currants, bay leaves, thyme, and remaining
salt and pepper, lower the heat, and simmer 3 minutes. Return the fish to
the pan, cover, and heat through.

Transfer to a warm platter, pour over the sauce and remaining olive oil,
and sprinkle with the parsley and chopped anchovies. Serve hot or warm.

Note To serve cold, add 1/2 cup dry white wine to the sauté pan once the
vinegar is reduced, boil 1 minute, and then add the tomatoes and
remaining ingredients. Let the sauce cool, transfer the fish and sauce to a
glass or ceramic dish, and add olive oil to cover. Tightly cover the dish, and
refrigerate overnight or for up to 3 days. Turn the fish in the marinade
once or twice. Serve as a *meze* or light lunch dish.

Grilled Fish

Psaria Skharas

Few treats can equal the splendor of a freshly-caught fish grilled over an aromatic charcoal fire and served with a scattering of fresh herbs. Walk along any Greek harborside and you'll find tavernas whose speciality is the daily creation of this culinary masterpiece.

For grilling, Greeks choose a variety of fish and seafood, including red mullet, the colorful members of the bream family, bonito, tuna, and swordfish, delicious little sardines, and lobster, shrimp, octopus, cuttlefish, and squid. Before grilling, fish is often steeped in a well-flavored marinade.

The charcoal should be produced from hardwood (olive wood and vine clippings make the best); it should be moderately hot and have reached what the Greeks call the "digested stage," i.e., lightly covered with grey ash.

Herbs, both fresh and dried, are a fundamental way of flavoring grilled fish, but how you use them is more important than which herbs you choose. Don't be tempted to just throw a handful of bay leaves onto the fire – the acrid smoke they produce will not enhance the flavor or the fish. Sprigs of fresh herbs such as thyme, rosemary, or oregano are used as basting brushes, in marinades, and in sauces; dried *rigani* us used in marinades and at serving time.

The most common problems with grilled fish are drying up and breaking. Guard against this by choosing plump and succulent fish of at least 1¹/₂ pounds in weight (smaller fish are better fried), brush both fish and grill liberally with olive oil before grilling, and take special care over cooking times (this depends on the thickness of the fish, not its length).

Serves 4

2 (1³/₄-to-2¹/₄-pound) *or* 1 (3¹/₂-pound) firm-fleshed fish, cleaned and
    scaled (see page 345) *or* 4 fish steaks, ¹/₂ inch thick (about ¹/₂ pound
    each)
Juice of 1 lemon (reserve 1 juiced lemon half)
Sea salt *and* freshly ground pepper, to taste
4–6 tablespoons extra virgin olive oil, or to taste
6 sprigs fresh oregano
3 bay leaves

For serving
Purslane Salad (page 220) *or* watercress sprigs

Dry the fish with paper towels and score fish larger than 2 pounds so they cook evenly. With a sharp knife, make 2 or 3 deep 2-inch parallel diagonal incisions on each side of the fish. (The heads are always left intact on fish prepared for the grill – the cheeks taste particularly good.) Rub whole fish inside and out, steaks on both sides, with half the lemon juice, salt, and pepper, and 1½ tablespoons of the olive oil. Scatter the oregano and bay leaves over the fish and set aside while you prepare the grill.

Set a grill rack 4–5 inches above hot coals and brush with olive oil, or brush a hinged double grill with olive oil. Brush the fish with some of the remaining olive oil. Combine the remaining lemon juice and olive oil to make a basting sauce. Pierce the lemon half with a skewer and use it as a "baster," dipping it in the sauce. Grill the fish on both sides until cooked through, about 10 minutes for steaks, up to 15 minutes for smaller whole fish, and 25 minutes for larger fish, basting liberally with the sauce.

Spread the Purslane Salad over a warm platter and arrange the fish on top. Sprinkle with the remaining basting sauce, salt, and pepper and serve immediately.

Grilled Marinated Fish
Psari Marinata tis Skhara

Traditionally used by village cooks to preserve freshly caught fish, aromatic marinades inspired by a variety of ingredients continue to add a delightful flavor to grilled fish. Swordfish steaks are particularly good with the marinades given here. Either will give any grilled fish an authentic Greek taste, whether you serve it simply garnished with fresh herbs or accompanied by one of the suggested sauces, along with the Wild Greens Salad (page 222) and Olive Bread (page 254).

Serves 4

....

2 (2-to-2¼-pound) *or* 1 (3½-pound) firm-fleshed fish, cleaned, scaled, and
    scored (see page 345) *or* 4 fish steaks, at least ½-inch thick (about ½
    pound each)
Juice of 1 small lemon (see Note)
Sea salt *and* freshly ground black pepper, to taste
½ cup extra virgin olive oil

Marinade 1
1 large mild onion, thinly sliced
2 tablespoons aged red wine vinegar
Pinch of cayenne pepper

For serving
Coarsely chopped fresh cilantro *or* flat-leaf parsley
Black Olives and Lentil Salata (page 39) *or* Anchovy Sauce (page 324)

Marinade 2
3 shallots, finely chopped
4 sprigs parsley
2 sprigs fresh thyme
Juice of ½ lemon
2 bay leaves

For serving
Finely chopped flat-leaf parsley
Peloponnese Honey Sauce (page 324) *or latholemono* sauce (4 parts extra
   virgin olive oil to 1 part freshly squeezed lemon juice, whisked together,
   with finely chopped fresh thyme or parsley, to taste)

Dry the fish with paper towels. Rub whole fish inside and out, steaks on
both sides, with the lemon juice and salt and pepper. Place in a shallow
ceramic or glass dish and add all the ingredients for either of the marinades
and half the olive oil. Cover and set aside for 1 hour.

Prepare the grill and set a grill rack 4–5 inches above the coals. Brush
the grill, or a hinged double grill, with olive oil. Remove the fish from the
marinade, strain the marinade, and combine with the remaining olive oil.
Remove any onions or herbs sticking to the fish and grill on both sides
until cooked through, about 10 minutes for steaks, up to 15 minutes for
smaller whole fish, and 25 minutes for larger whole fish. Baste occasionally
with the marinade.

Transfer to a warm platter, sprinkle with the cilantro or parsley, and
drizzle with the remaining marinade mixture. Serve immediately and pass
the *salata* or sauce separately.

Note Reserve 1 of the juiced lemon halves for a "baster" (pierce it with
a skewer and dip it in the marinade) or use sprigs of dried *rigani* or fresh
thyme as a basting brush.

Pan-Seared Tuna with Beet Greens
Thonnos Psiti me Khorta

For centuries Greeks have enjoyed this ancient dish, which brings land
and sea together in perfect harmony: from the sea, the rich strongly
flavored oily fish and from the land, the earthy country tones of beet
greens. The combination creates a colorful succulent dish that looks
enticingly exotic, but is very easy to prepare. Surprising as it may sound, a
good dry red wine complements the flavors in this dish best.

Serves 4

4 (8-ounce) tuna *or* swordfish steaks
Coarse-grain sea salt, to taste
1 tablespoon cracked black pepper, or to taste
4–6 tablespoons aged red wine vinegar, or to taste
4 bay leaves
2 sprigs fresh *or* dried thyme
½ teaspoon ground paprika
½ cup extra virgin olive oil, or to taste
1 pound beet greens
1 large clove garlic, cut into slivers

For serving
1 tablespoon small capers, rinsed

Wipe the fish steaks and rub with salt, half the pepper, and 1 tablespoon of the vinegar. Place in a shallow ceramic or glass dish with the bay leaves and thyme, and sprinkle with half the paprika and 1 tablespoon of the olive oil. Cover and set aside 1 hour to marinate.

If the beet greens are young and tender, with bright green leaves, just strip the leaves from the stalks. If the greens are older, with dark green leaves, remove the tough stalks and blanch the leaves in boiling water for 3 minutes. Drain in a colander, pressing out excess moisture.

Heat a heavy cast-iron frying pan or sauté pan over medium-low heat, and add 2 tablespoons olive oil. Remove the fish from the marinade, discarding the bay leaves and thyme, and sear on both sides until the fish is an even color all the way through, about 8–10 minutes. Transfer to a warm platter, cover, and keep warm.

Wipe out the pan with paper towels, return to low heat, and add 1 tablespoon olive oil. Sauté the garlic until golden. Add 3 tablespoons of vinegar to deglaze the pan; it will reduce by half almost immediately. Slice the fresh greens into thin ribbons or coarsely chop the cooked greens and add to the pan with salt and the remaining pepper. Stir with a wooden spoon until tender greens are just cooked or cooked greens are hot.

Transfer to a platter and arrange the fish on top. Sprinkle with the capers, remaining paprika and vinegar, and olive oil to taste. Serve immediately.

Shellfish and Crustaceans

Ostraka ke Ostrakithi

Greeks revel in subtle and innovative blends of taste and texture, but they also know when to leave well enough alone – and the shellfish and crustaceans available to them, deliciously fresh from the sea, need very little help from the cook.

Scallops and cockles and are eaten raw as *mezedes* or made into *pilafi* or soup. Mussels are removed from their shells, coated with egg and bread crumbs, and deep-fried, to be served as a *meze*, with *macaronia*, or in a *pilafi*.

Shrimp are popular throughout Greece and her islands. The fishermen baste them with lemon juice, olive oil, and coarse-grain sea salt and grill them – nothing could be more delicious.

Lobster is the prize catch of the Mediterranean and many Greeks prefer their lobster simply boiled and served with a good mayonnaise or a light *latholemono* sauce – but charcoal-grilled lobster is popular too.

Lobster with Latholemono Sauce
Astakos me Latholemono

The spiny lobster is the most common lobster in Greek waters and many Greeks prefer its flavor to that of the larger lobster (*karavida* [Greek] or *homard*). In homes and tavernas lobster is always presented very simply, with olive oil, lemon juice, and a scattering of fresh parsley or oregano – an especially lovely treat on a warm summer's day.

Serves 4

4 tablespoons wine vinegar
1 tablespoon sea salt
2 (1-to-1¼-pound) live lobsters
Juice of 1 lemon
Large pinch of dry mustard
Sea salt *and* freshly ground black pepper, to taste
½ cup extra virgin olive oil

For serving
Finely chopped fresh oregano *or* flat-leaf parsley

Fill a large saucepan with water and bring it to a boil over high heat; add the vinegar and salt. Add the lobsters, bring back to a boil, reduce the heat slightly, and cook 6 minutes longer. Drain and blot dry.

Devein the lobsters and discard the small sac beneath the heads. Cut in half along the length of the body. Take out the olive-green tomalley and, if there is any, the bright orange coral. Mash the coral (and tomalley, if liked) to a paste with half the lemon juice, the mustard, and salt and pepper. Whisk in the olive oil to make a creamy sauce, and add the remaining lemon juice to taste.

Remove the meat from the tails and chop it into small pieces. Toss with 2 tablespoons of the sauce and stuff the shells with it. If using a variety other than spiny lobster, crack the claws (only the tail meat of the spiny lobster is eaten). Arrange the lobsters attractively on a platter and sprinkle with the oregano. Serve the sauce separately.

Grilled Lobster
Astakos tis Skhara

Small lobsters are the best choice for grilling; their meat stays moist and sweet. If you can prepare your fire using woody rosemary bush branches or olive hardwood you will enjoy grilled lobster with a very special flavor. Better still, have some branches of rosemary ready to throw on the fire just before grilling the lobsters and use several sprigs of rosemary tied together as a basting brush.

Serves 4

Coarse-grain sea salt
6 tablespoons wine vinegar
4 live lobsters
1 cup extra virgin olive oil, to taste
1 teaspoon honey
1/2 teaspoon ground coriander
Crushed black peppercorns, to taste
Juice of 1 lemon

Fill a large saucepan with water and bring to a boil over high heat; add 1 tablespoon salt and 4 tablespoons of the vinegar. Add the lobsters, bring back to a boil, reduce the heat slightly, and boil 3 minutes longer. Drain and blot dry.

Set a grill rack 3 inches above charcoal and brush it with olive oil.

Combine the remaining vinegar, 5 tablespoons of the olive oil, honey, coriander, and salt and pepper and brush the lobsters liberally with this sauce. Grill 20–30 minutes, basting and turning frequently, until the shell can be easily separated from the flesh. Leave the shells in place, but devein each lobster, and discard the small sacs beneath the heads. Remove the orange coral, if there is any, and mash to a paste with the lemon juice and remaining olive oil.

Arrange the lobsters on a serving platter. Serve the remaining sauce separately, and have plenty of napkins on the table.

Shrimp in a Pot with Feta Cheese
Garithes Youvetsi

This is a pretty – and convenient – dish for a dinner party. It can be prepared a few hours ahead of time and baked at the last minute. Serve in individual earthenware dishes for a beautiful presentation and have plenty of country bread on the table for your guests to mop up the delicious sauce.

Serves 4

1½ pounds shrimp in the shell
½ cup extra virgin olive oil
2 onions, quartered and thinly sliced
1 large clove garlic, finely chopped
7 medium ripe tomatoes, 4 of them skinned, seeded, and diced, and the remaining 3 skinned, cored, and cut in thin slices
½ teaspoon honey
¼ teaspoon cayenne pepper, *optional*
½ teaspoon ground cumin
1 tablespoon dried *rigani* (see page 13), crumbled
1 small bunch flat-leaf parsley, leaves coarsely chopped
1 cup dry white wine
Coarse-grain sea salt, to taste
½ tablespoon cracked black pepper, or to taste
¾ pound *feta* cheese, cut into 8 slices

For serving
Lemon wedges

Remove the legs from the shrimp and devein (but do not remove from the shell). Rinse and dry between layers of paper towels. Heat 2 tablespoons of the olive oil in a heavy sauté pan, add the shrimp, cover, and cook 4 minutes over medium-low heat, occasionally giving the pan a vigorous shake. Transfer the shrimp and oil to a bowl, tightly cover, and refrigerate. Wipe out the pan.

Heat the oven to 350°F. Heat half the remaining olive oil in the sauté pan and cook the onions over low heat until soft, about 8 minutes. Add the garlic, diced tomatoes, honey, cayenne pepper, and cumin, raise the heat to medium, and simmer 10 minutes, or until most of the liquid has evaporated. Add the *rigani,* most of the parsley, the wine, salt, and pepper. Cook, stirring occasionally, for about 8 minutes; the sauce should remain separated for a few seconds when a wooden spoon is drawn across the bottom of the pan.

Divide the sauce between 4 individual ovenproof dishes. Peel the shrimp, catching any juices in the bowl. Arrange the shrimp on top of the sauce and sprinkle with the juices. Cover with the tomato and *feta* cheese slices, sprinkle with the remaining olive oil, and bake 15 minutes, until heated through.

Sprinkle with the rest of the parsley and serve hot, with the lemon wedges.

Sea Urchins
Achini

Until recently any cookbook mention of sea urchins would have been of purely academic interest. Now these fascinating sea creatures are becoming popular.

Greeks have enjoyed eating sea urchins since before the time of Homer. They gather only the females since it is the females that yield the distinctive coral (roe) or eggs and they gather sea urchins only at around the time of the full moon, when, for some mysterious reason, they contain the greatest number of eggs.

Serve sea urchins in the shell so guests can scoop out the coral for themselves, or gently detach the coral from the sides of each shell and serve it in small dishes, and offer ouzo, raki, or a jug of chilled dry white wine to drink.

Serves 4

48 very fresh sea urchins (see page 350)

For serving
Lemon wedges *or* aged red wine vinegar

To prepare a sea urchin, wrap one of your hands in a heavy cloth and grip the spike-covered shell, soft side facing upward. Insert a blunt-ended knife into the mouth in the center of this soft side and, with a circular motion, gently scoop out the mouth and the top third of the shell; the shell cracks easily, so care is needed. As you finish preparing each sea urchin, rinse it in a bowl of water; the loose inner grey mass should float out, leaving the roe adhering to the inside of the shell. Check that no spikes have found their way into the shell, and set aside; or scoop the roe out onto a small platter.

Serve immediately, or tightly cover and refrigerate for no more than an hour or two. Serve with lemon wedges.

Octopus, Squid, and Cuttlefish

Khtapothi, Kalamaria, ke Soupia

Octopus, squid, and cuttlefish (the cephalopods) are everyday food in Greece. Inexpensive and nutritious, they appear on taverna menus everywhere, especially on the islands.

Small squid and cuttlefish are the tastiest and the most tender. As a *meze,* these tiny creatures are fried whole to crisp perfection and served just with a little lemon juice and salt. For a main course, squid may be slowly simmered in an aromatic wine or ink sauce.

Larger squid are usually stuffed – popular in Greece are stuffings made with rice, shallots, spinach, and tomatoes; bread crumbs, olives, pine nuts, and currants; or rice, parsley, currants, and pine nuts – and simmered until they are tender and the flavors have blended beautifully. Cuttlefish can also be stuffed, but it is easier to cut it into pieces before cooking. It's from cuttlefish ink that the pigment sepia is extracted (the Greek name for cuttlefish is *soupia)*.

Perhaps the best way to try octopus for the first time is grilled (see page 117). In Greece not only the octopus itself but also the ink sacs are considered *meze* delicacies. Large ink sacs are fried; small ones roasted in an eggplant or onion shell in the embers of a fire. Check the glossary for more information on mastering the art of cleaning and preparing these traditional delicacies.

Octopus in Red Wine
Khtapothi Krasato

Remnants of Minoan and Classical Greek pottery adorned with strange and beautiful octopus-inspired motifs have been found on island and mainland archaeological sites, and they testify to a Greek fascination with the octopus stretching back to antiquity.

The traditional way to kill an octopus is for the fisherman to bite through the nerve center that passes behind the octopus' eyes. Traditionally, too, he tenderizes the octopus by beating it against a rock – 40 times, say some fishermen; as many times as you can stand it, say others! Octopus is usually sold cleaned, and tenderized (tenderizing must be done when the octopus is killed, so don't waste your time trying to pound a tough one to tenderness). Octopus must also be skinned but this is an easy job if you let the cooking do some of the work for you. In this recipe the octopus first braises in its own juices until the moisture has evaporated, at which point it will be almost cooked and the skin will peel off easily. Serve Octopus in Red Wine with other strong flavors of the Greek countryside – *khorta* (see page 221), tiny sweet Elitses olives (see page 2), slices of *feta* or *kephalotyri* cheese, and Country Bread (page 250).

Serves 6

1 (5-to-7-pound) tenderized octopus, with eyes, mouth, and inside of head discarded (see page 117)
1½ cups dry red wine
6 tablespoons extra virgin olive oil
1 pound small boiling onions, about 1 inch in diameter, peeled (see page 132)
6 large ripe tomatoes, skinned, diced, and juices reserved
1 teaspoon honey
4 bay leaves
Freshly ground black pepper, to taste
4 sprigs dried thyme *or rigani* (see page 13)

For serving
1 small bunch flat-leaf parsley, leaves coarsely chopped
1 tablespoon dried thyme *or rigani*
Sea salt, to taste (see Note)

Heat the oven to 300°F. Rinse the octopus well in several changes of water, place in a heavy baking dish with 4 tablespoons red wine, cover tightly, and bake 1 hour. Check once or twice, and add a few tablespoons of water if necessary. Thoroughly rinse, cover tightly, and refrigerate until cold.

Heat half the olive oil over low heat in a large heavy baking dish. Add the onions and gently roll them in the oil for 5 minutes. Meanwhile, cut up the octopus: sever the legs from the body; cut the body (head) lengthways in quarters; and peel off the skin to expose the pale pink flesh – the suckers come off easily with the skin. Cut into 1½-inch pieces and add to the baking dish. Add the tomatoes and their juices, honey, bay leaves, pepper, and the remaining olive oil and red wine. Tie the thyme sprigs into a bundle with kitchen string and add to the baking dish. Bring to a gentle boil, cover tightly, and simmer over very low heat for 2 hours. Stir occasionally; by the end of the cooking time the sauce should be reduced by half.

Discard the thyme sprigs. Chop together the parsley, thyme, and salt, and sprinkle over the octopus. Serve hot.

Note Never rub octopus with salt or add salt to the pot before it is almost cooked, or it will toughen beyond redemption.

Grilled Octopus
Khtapothi sti Skhara

The taste of octopus grilled over the embers of a wood fire always reminds me of beach parties in Greece on balmy starry nights. Guests are greeted with a glass of ouzo or raki and while they chat the charcoal burns down to just the right dull glow and the octopus marinates in olive oil, lemon juice, and *rigani.* Grilling takes just a few minutes and the octopus, cut into small pieces, is served as a *meze,* accompanied by bowls of olives and cheese. Or serve it as a main course with pilaf and Beets Island-Style (page 183), or *khorta* (see page 221).

Serves 6

1 (5-to-7-pound) octopus, tenderized (see page 116)
2 cups dry white wine *or* water
1¼ cups extra virgin olive oil
Juice of 2 lemons
12 sprigs fresh oregano *or* rosemary, leaves stripped from the stems, and
    stems reserved *or* 4 tablespoons dried *rigani* (see page 13)
1 tablespoon coarse-grain sea salt, or to taste
1 tablespoon cracked black pepper

For serving
Lemon wedges
1 large bunch flat-leaf parsley, leaves coarsely chopped

Start preparing the dish one day ahead of serving. First, remove the eyes, mouth, and inside of the head of the octopus if it has not been done already. To remove the head, cut below the eyes at the spot where the tentacles meet; to remove the eyes and mouth, turn the pouch-like head inside out, discard the innards, and cut out the eyes and mouth. Rinse well in several changes of water and place in a large saucepan with the wine, adding water, if necessary, to cover. Bring slowly to a boil, cover, reduce the heat, and simmer 1¼ hours (for a 5-pound octopus) to 1¾ hours (for a 7-pound octopus). Drain, thoroughly rinse, cover tightly, and refrigerate overnight.

Prepare the grill. Meanwhile, cut up the octopus: sever the legs from the body and leave whole; cut the body (head) lengthways in quarters; and peel off the skin to expose the pale pink flesh – the suckers come off easily with the skin.

Whisk together 1 cup of the olive oil, the lemon juice, and *rigani* in a shallow bowl. Add the octopus pieces and turn to coat with the marinade. Set aside.

Set a grill rack 4 inches above hot coals, and brush with olive oil. Throw the herb stems on the fire. Remove the octopus pieces from the marinade, sprinkle with the salt and pepper, and grill a few minutes on either side, until browned, brushing once or twice with the marinade. Arrange on a warm serving plate and garnish with the lemon wedges. Sprinkle with the parsley.

Cuttlefish in Ink Sauce
Soupia me Saltsa Melanis

At any time of year Crete's largest city, Heraklion, boasts a lively market, vibrant with color, bustling with noise, and overflowing with produce from the surrounding villages. In spring and autumn Greek cooks head first for the fishermen's stalls, which are piled high with towers of gleaming cuttlefish. Bargaining with stall-holders, they reject the large cuttlefish and choose instead the small ones. Cuttlefish are the most tender and easily prepared of all cephalopods and a favorite food on the islands, especially when cooked with this creamy ink sauce.

Serves 4

3 pounds cuttlefish, preferably small, of a similar size
5 tablespoons extra virgin olive oil
2 large mild onions, quartered and thinly sliced
1/2 cup dry white wine
3 tablespoons finely chopped flat-leaf parsley
1/2 tablespoon fresh oregano, finely chopped, *or* dried *rigani* (see page 13), crumbled
Coarse-grain sea salt *and* cracked black pepper, to taste

For serving
1 tablespoon finely chopped Preserved Lemons (page 18), *optional*
Lemon wedges

Rinse the cuttlefish. Small ones (4–5 inches) can be left whole. Prepare larger ones as follows: gently pull off the head with the tentacles still attached, then carefully slash the center front of the body with a sharp knife. Remove the 2 small black ink sacs, and check to make sure they contain no sand – try to avoid rinsing them, or they will lose too much ink. Set aside 8 sacs, and discard the rest. Wash any ink off the cuttlefish. Remove the single bone, discard everything else from inside the body, and rub off the brownish outer skin. Rinse again, cut into long 1-inch wide strips, and place in a colander to drain.

Slice off and discard the part of the head that contains the eyes, and rinse the head. Slice it open so it unfolds into a strip, with the tentacles on one side. Discard the beak, and thoroughly rinse and rub the tentacles to remove any sand. Cut into 1-inch pieces and add to the colander.

Heat 4 tablespoons of the olive oil in a large heavy frying pan and sauté the onion over low heat until soft, about 6 minutes. Add the cuttlefish and cook, stirring occasionally, until any liquid has evaporated and the cuttlefish and onion begin to brown, about 15 minutes. Put the ink sacs and ½ cup water into a small bowl and gently rub the sacs to expel all the ink. Strain through a fine strainer into the pan, add the wine, and raise the heat to medium-low. Cook, stirring frequently, until all the liquid has evaporated and the cuttlefish are coated with a creamy sauce, about 15 minutes. Stir in most of the parsley, season with salt and a generous amount of pepper, and cook 1 minute longer.

Chop the Preserved Lemons, remaining parsley, and a large pinch of salt and pepper together to mix. Transfer the cuttlefish to a warm platter, or serve directly from the pan, sprinkled with the lemon mixture and the rest of the olive oil. Serve at once, with the lemon wedges.

CHICKEN AND GAME

Kotopoula ke Kinigi

Sizzling on spits, scented with lemon and fruity olive oil, glistening and golden-roasted – that's how Greeks like chicken best. That's also how the traveler to Greece most often remembers chicken – the pungent aroma of mountain herbs as chicken spit-roasting assails the senses and sets the taste buds racing. Greek chickens may not be as plump as our own but they are invariably free range and have a superb flavor and texture.

Greeks also enjoy a variety of chicken casseroles and baked dishes. These traditional dishes are meant to be baked in the village oven, but they are easily adapted to our ovens and slow cookers. Greek ways to flavor chickens may come as a surprise: many feature the strong use of Eastern spices – Chicken in a Pot (page 122), for example, includes cloves and cinnamon, and just the aroma of this heartening dish envelops you in a comforting warmth of gastronomic expectation. Also spiced, with cumin, allspice, and cloves, is Baked Chicken and Okra (page 123), a colorful dish to make in early summer when this vegetable is at its best. Other chicken dishes are tied to seasonal change – in spring, the clear lemony fragrance of a poached Chicken in Avgolemono Sauce (page 126) and, in autumn, the creamy coriander-and-walnut flavored sauce enrobing a braised chicken (page 125) are delights.

For us chicken is commonplace: for Greeks in rural communities, rabbit, hare, and game birds in season are everyday fare. Simple spit-roasted rabbit or game birds are popular at village feasts and the spicy *stifado*, made with rabbit, hare, or even snails, and sweetened with large quantities of onions, is a favorite winter meal. Greece lies on the migratory path between northern Europe and Africa and from September to November Greek skies are darkened with flocks of birds on their way south. At this time of year "Hunter's Pot" (page 135) may contain quail, woodcock, partridge, or pigeon, gently braised under a covering of grape leaves and fragrant with herbs. Duck, particularly wild duckling from the Macedonian lakes, is a popular spring food – cooked Thessalía-style (see page 138), scented with juniper berries, cloves, and orange zest, it's a dish fit for the gods.

Roast Chicken with Rigani and Garlic

Kotopoulo Riganato

Pungent *rigani* grows in wild abundance on the mountain slopes of Greece. The Greek cook's favorite herb, the flavor is evident in this aromatic roast chicken dish. This is a recipe for garlic lovers too – the amount used is generous! Cook the chicken whole for elegance, or cut into serving-size pieces for speed and convenience.

Serves 4 to 6

One (4-to-5-pound) chicken, whole or cut into serving pieces, skin and
  excess fat removed
Juice of $1\frac{1}{2}$ lemons
$\frac{1}{2}$ cup extra virgin olive oil, or to taste
$\frac{1}{2}$ tablespoon coarse-grain sea salt, or to taste
2 pounds roasting potatoes, cut lengthways into quarters
6 cloves garlic, unpeeled, and lightly crushed
4 tablespoons dried *rigani* (see page 13), crumbled
Cracked black pepper, to taste
6 bay leaves
1 tablespoon unsalted butter
$1\frac{3}{4}$ cups Chicken Stock (page 343)
$\frac{1}{2}$ teaspoon Dijon mustard
1 teaspoon honey

For serving
1 small bunch flat-leaf parsley, leaves coarsely chopped

Heat the oven to 375°F. Rub the chicken with the juice of 1 lemon, 3 tablespoons of the olive oil, and the salt. Place the chicken in a deep heavy baking dish and surround with the potatoes and garlic in a single layer.

Sprinkle the chicken with the *rigani*, pepper, bay leaves, and the remaining olive oil and dot with the butter. Add half the stock, and roast, uncovered, 15 minutes. Reduce the oven temperature to 350°F and continue roasting until tender, about 1 hour longer for a whole chicken, 40 minutes longer for chicken pieces. Baste the chicken and potatoes frequently, adding more stock to the dish if necessary.

Transfer the chicken, potatoes, and garlic to a serving platter and keep warm. Strain the pan juices into a small saucepan, remove the fat with a spoon, and add any remaining stock. If there is more than about $1\frac{1}{2}$ cups of liquid, reduce it by rapid boiling. Combine the mustard, honey, and half the remaining lemon juice and stir into the sauce. Add the salt, pepper, and lemon juice to taste, and heat to warm.

Pour sauce over the chicken and potatoes just to moisten, and sprinkle with the parsley. Serve the remaining sauce separately.

Chicken in a Pot
Kapama Kotopoulo

On a morning stroll through a traditional Greek village visitors are often welcomed by the warm, comforting aromas of *kapamas* wafting from private kitchens or the baker's oven. These are no ordinary stews: they are rich and colorful creations cooked slowly so that flavors blend and the meat becomes so tender that you could eat it with a spoon. *Kapama kotopoulo,* a classic country dish, is flavored with cloves and cinnamon, marjoram and bay leaves, tomatoes, onions, and honey; you can use this recipe to make glorious casseroles of lamb or hare, too. The real secret of these wonderful stews is that the ingredients are packed in closely together and a tight-fitting lid locks in the spicy flavor during baking. Serve with fried eggplant slices, *pilafi,* and grated *kasseri* cheese.

Serves 4 to 5

1 (4-to-5-pound) chicken, cut into serving pieces, skin and excess fat
   removed and giblets reserved
2 tablespoons extra virgin olive oil
1 tablespoon unsalted butter
1 large onion, chopped
8 ripe tomatoes, skinned and diced
1 teaspoon honey
3 bay leaves, broken into pieces
1 tablespoon dried marjoram *or* rosemary, crumbled
4 cloves
1 3-inch cinnamon stick *or* 1 teaspoon ground cinnamon
½ to 1 cup Chicken Stock (page 343) *or* water
1 teaspoon cracked black pepper, or to taste
4 tablespoons all-purpose flour
1 clove garlic, finely chopped
1 teaspoon coarse-grain sea salt, or to taste
³/₈ cup pine nuts
3 tablespoons finely chopped flat-leaf parsley
12 Amfissa *or* Niçoise olives

Heat the oven to 325°F. Discard the chicken liver. Rinse the remaining giblets and trim off the membranes. Heat the olive oil and butter in a heavy frying pan and sauté the chicken and giblets over medium-low heat until lightly browned. Drain between layers of paper towels and transfer to a heavy casserole.

Drain off most of the fat from the pan, add the onions and sauté until soft, about 5 minutes. Add the tomatoes, honey, bay leaves, marjoram, cloves, cinnamon, ½ cup of the stock, and pepper, and simmer 5 minutes. Pour over the chicken.

Mix the flour with a little water to make a thick paste and spread it over the top rim of the casserole and inner rim of the lid. Place the lid in position, smooth the paste to make a good seal, and bake 15 minutes. Reduce the oven temperature to 300°F and bake 2½ hours longer.

Meanwhile, pound the garlic and salt together in a mortar or bowl until blended. Add the pine nuts and half the parsley, pound until well-mixed, and set aside. (You can use a food processor, but process only until the nuts are chopped, not ground.)

Lift off the casserole lid, using a blunt-ended knife (such as a butter knife) to break the seal, and wipe the rim. Transfer the chicken pieces to a serving bowl and keep warm. Strain the sauce into a saucepan, pressing the solids with a wooden spoon to extract as much liquid as possible; discard the solids. Add stock or water if needed to the sauce to make 2 cups. Simmer, adding the parsley mixture and olives, and season to taste; the sauce should be highly flavored.

Pour the sauce over the chicken, sprinkle with the remaining parsley, and serve.

Baked Chicken and Okra

Kotopoulo me Bamies

In summer when okra is at its best, this intriguing dish appears on taverna menus all over Greece. The colorful combination of golden chicken and onions, pale green okra, and vivid red tomatoes, spiced with cumin, cloves, and allspice, makes this a perfect party dish. Adding the okra at the end of cooking time keeps it whole and deliciously juicy. If okra is unavailable, you can substitute green beans, leeks, or artichokes. Potatoes in a Clay Pot (page 207) makes a good side dish.

Serves 4 to 6

1½ pounds okra, trimmed and rinsed
Juice of 2 large lemons
1 tablespoon coarse-grain sea salt

One (4-to-5-pound) chicken, cut into serving pieces and skin and excess fat
   removed *or* 3 whole chicken breasts, skinned and split in half
½ cup extra virgin olive oil, to taste
2 large onions, thinly sliced
1 teaspoon ground allspice
½ tablespoon ground cumin
6 cloves
6 large ripe tomatoes, skinned, seeded, and diced
1 teaspoon honey
1½ tablespoons dried thyme, crumbled
1 cup Chicken Stock (page 343) *or* dry white wine *or* water
1 tablespoon cracked black pepper, or to taste
1 small bunch flat-leaf parsley, leaves coarsely chopped

Spread the okra on a baking tray in a single layer, sprinkle with half the
lemon juice and 2 teaspoons of the salt, and set aside for 1 hour.

Heat the oven to 375°F. Heat 3 tablespoons of the olive oil in a large
heavy frying pan and sauté the chicken over medium-low heat until lightly
browned on all sides. Drain between layers of paper towels and transfer to
a baking dish.

Drain off most of the oil from the pan, reduce the heat to low, and sauté
the onion 10 minutes, until soft. Stir in the allspice, cumin, cloves, and
tomatoes. Raise the heat to medium, bring to a boil, and boil until the
liquid is reduced by one third. Add the honey, thyme, stock, a pinch of salt,
and ½ tablespoon of the pepper. Simmer a few minutes longer and pour
over the chicken. Cover and bake chicken pieces 35 minutes, chicken
breasts 20 minutes.

Meanwhile, rinse the okra and dry with paper towels. Heat 3 tablespoons
of the remaining olive oil in a large heavy sauté pan and sauté the okra over
low heat until it begins to change color, rolling it gently around the pan with
a wooden spoon. Drain between layers of paper towels.

Add the okra to the baking dish; firmly but carefully shake the dish to
combine the ingredients. Bake, uncovered, 15 minutes longer.

Add some or all of the remaining lemon juice to the baking dish; its
flavor should be quite distinct. Add the remaining salt, pepper, olive oil to
taste, and the parsley. Shake gently to mix all the ingredients together and
serve at once.

Chicken with Walnut and Coriander Sauce
Kotopoulo me Saltsa Karythion

I first tasted this unusual dish in a tiny taverna in the mountains of northern Greece, as all around me the villagers gathered the autumn harvest from the ancient walnut trees in the village square.

Freshly gathered walnuts give the best flavor but plump older walnuts (blanched to remove any bitterness) can be substituted. I like the creamy sauce with a slightly coarse nutty texture, but use a food processor to produce a smooth version if you prefer. Serve with *pilafi* and a zucchini dish.

Serves 4 to 6

^{1}/$_2$ cup extra virgin olive oil
1 (4-to-5-pound) chicken, cut into serving pieces and skin and excess fat removed
1 cup dry white wine
3 bay leaves
1^3/$_4$ cups hot Chicken Stock (page 343) *or* water
Sea salt *and* freshly ground black pepper, to taste
^{7}/$_8$ cup walnut halves or pieces (if not freshly gathered, blanch in boiling water for 1 minute)
2 tablespoons coriander seeds, crushed *or* ^{1}/$_2$ tablespoon ground coriander
1 large clove garlic, finely chopped
Pinch of cayenne pepper
Juice of 2 lemons, or to taste
3 large eggs

For serving
5 tablespoons coarsely chopped flat-leaf parsley

Heat the oven to 350°F. Heat half the olive oil in a heavy sauté pan and lightly brown the chicken pieces on all sides. Drain between layers of paper towels and transfer to a heavy baking dish.

Drain off the oil from the pan, add the wine, and boil 1 minute, stirring in the browned bits from the bottom of the pan. Pour over the chicken, and add the bay leaves, stock, and salt and pepper. Cover and bake 45 minutes, until tender.

Meanwhile, in a large wooden mortar or bowl, pound the walnuts, coriander, garlic, and cayenne pepper to a fairly smooth paste. Add the remaining olive oil and half the lemon juice, drop by drop, pounding constantly, until well mixed. (Or you can do this in a food processor, using the pulse switch; do not overprocess.) Season to taste and set aside.

Transfer the chicken to a serving platter and keep warm. Strain the liquid from the baking dish, measure 1¾ cups, and combine it with the walnut sauce. Set aside.

Whisk the eggs in a large bowl with a whisk or an electric mixer until pale and frothy. Gradually add the remaining lemon juice, beating constantly. Stir in the walnut sauce. Transfer to a heavy saucepan and heat slowly, stirring with a wooden spoon, until creamy and a little thickened, about 5 minutes; don't let it boil.

Pour the sauce over the chicken and sprinkle with the parsley. Serve at once.

Chicken in Avgolemono Sauce
Kotopoulo Avgolemono

The taste of this classic springtime dish is fresh and clean, the flavors light and fragrant: zesty lemon, delicate dill, and mild, vitamin-rich lettuce. Serve with Potatoes in a Clay Pot (page 207) or boiled new potatoes, and a dry white wine to enhance the subtle flavor. As a variation try *arnaki fricassé*, a popular version made with boned lamb instead of chicken.

Serves 4

1 (3½-pound) chicken, cut into serving pieces, skin and excess fat removed
2 cups Chicken Stock (page 343) *or* water
2 carrots, cut into large pieces
1 stalk celery, cut into large pieces
3 bay leaves
6 black peppercorns
6 scallions, trimmed, with 2 inches of green left intact
2 tablespoons extra virgin olive oil
2 heads Romaine *or* endive lettuce, trimmed of outer leaves and tough stems and cut into ¼-inch wide ribbons
1 small bunch fresh dill, coarsely chopped
Sea salt *and* freshly ground white pepper, to taste
Juice of 2 large lemons
3 eggs, separated

Combine the chicken, stock, carrots, celery, bay leaves, and peppercorns in a large heavy saucepan. Slowly bring to a boil, cover, reduce the heat, and simmer 40 minutes, until the chicken is tender.

Meanwhile, slice the scallions lengthways in half and cut into 1-inch long pieces. Warm the olive oil in a heavy sauté pan and cook the scallions over low heat until soft, about 2 minutes. Add the lettuce, cover, and cook, stirring once or twice, until wilted, about 2 minutes. Stir in the dill, salt and pepper, and half the lemon juice. Add the cooked chicken to the pan and set aside.

Strain the cooking broth into a bowl. Whisk the egg whites in a large bowl with a whisk or an electric mixer until they hold soft peaks. Add the yolks and whisk 1 minute longer. Slowly add the remaining lemon juice and the broth, whisking constantly. Transfer to a medium saucepan and gently heat over low heat, stirring constantly with a wooden spoon, until creamy and slightly thickened, about 5 minutes; don't let the sauce boil.

Pour the sauce over the chicken, place the sauté pan over low heat, and heat to warm through – do not boil. Season to taste, transfer to a warm serving dish, and serve at once.

Marinated Chicken with Tiny Onions and Vinegar
Kotopoulo Marinato me Xsithi

This ancient recipe brings together traditional ingredients favored by Greek cooks for centuries. Honey and vinegar blend to produce a sweet-and-sour sauce and the piquant theme is repeated in the garnish of capers, parsley, and lemon zest. This delicious dish makes for easy entertaining too – much of the work can be done ahead of time. Serve with Pilaf with Green Lentils (page 229).

Serves 4

1 (3-to-4-pound) chicken, cut into serving pieces, skin and excess fat removed
2 tablespoons extra virgin olive oil
1 tablespoon freshly squeezed lemon juice
1 teaspoon coarse-grain sea salt, or to taste
1 teaspoon freshly ground black pepper, or to taste
2 bay leaves
1 sprig fresh thyme *or* rosemary
2 tablespoons unsalted butter
1 pound tiny boiling onions, peeled (see page 132)
3 tablespoons aged red wine vinegar
1 teaspoon honey diluted with 1 tablespoon hot water
4 large ripe tomatoes, skinned, seeded, and diced
4 tablespoons small dark seedless raisins, soaked in 2 tablespoons hot water for 30 minutes

For serving
3 tablespoons finely chopped flat-leaf parsley
1 tablespoon capers
1 teaspoon grated lemon zest

Rub the chicken with the olive oil, lemon juice, and most of the salt and pepper, and place in a bowl with the bay leaves and thyme. Cover and let marinate for 2 hours in the refrigerator.

Melt the butter in a heavy saucepan and add the chicken, marinade, including the herbs, and onions. Turn the chicken and onions to coat with the butter, cover tightly, and cook 40 minutes over low heat, until the chicken is tender; add 2 tablespoons water if the butter begins to brown. Transfer the chicken to a warm platter, cover, and keep warm.

Pour off the pan juices, remove the fat with a spoon, and reserve; discard the bay leaves and thyme. Add the vinegar to the saucepan, raise the heat to medium high, and reduce to a syrup by rapid boiling. Add the honey and tomatoes and boil gently for 1 minute. Add the raisins, reserved pan juices, and remaining pepper, and reduce the heat.

Chop the parsley, capers, lemon zest, and remaining salt together. Spoon the onions and tomatoes around the chicken, sprinkle with the parsley mixture, and serve.

Bay-Scented Chicken with Figs
Kotopoulo me Dafni ke Sika

Bay trees and bushes flourish in Greece and the leaves are widely used in Greek cooking – a dozen leaves impart a pungent perfume to this dish. The chicken and figs are cooked separately so their individual flavors remain distinct. Serve with Pilaf with Currants and Pine Nuts (page 227).

Serves 4

1 (3-to-4-pound) chicken, cut into serving pieces, skin and excess fat removed
2 tablespoons extra virgin olive oil
1 teaspoon coarse-grain sea salt, or to taste
1 teaspoon freshly ground black pepper, or to taste
1 tablespoon unsalted butter
12 bay leaves
4 ripe figs, rinsed *or* 4 dried figs, soaked in ½ cup dry red wine *or* water for 30 minutes
1½ tablespoons aged red wine vinegar
1 teaspoon honey
4 tablespoons dry red wine

½ cup Chicken Stock (page 343) *or* water
24 Elitses *or* Niçoise olives, rinsed and pitted

For serving
Watercress sprigs

Rub the chicken with the olive oil and half the salt and pepper and place in a bowl. Sprinkle with the bay leaves, cover, and refrigerate for 2–4 hours.

Heat the oven to 325°F. Melt the butter in a flameproof baking dish over low heat. Add the chicken, bay leaves, and 2 tablespoons water. Cover and simmer 2–3 minutes. Transfer to the oven and bake 30–40 minutes, basting occasionally, until the chicken is cooked; if the butter begins to brown, add 2 tablespoons water.

Meanwhile, trim the stems from the figs, cut lengthways in half, and arrange in a baking dish, cut sides up. Add 3 tablespoons water (or the liquid remaining from soaking dried figs) and bake fresh figs 20 minutes, dried figs 10 minutes.

Transfer the chicken to a platter and keep warm. Discard the bay leaves. Add the vinegar to the dish and reduce the cooking liquid to 2 tablespoons by rapid boiling. Add the honey, wine, and stock, and reduce to ½ cup. Add the olives and heat to warm.

Spoon the sauce over the chicken, and garnish it with the figs and watercress sprigs.

Spit-Roasted Chicken
Kotopoulo tis Souvla

Homer relates that Odysseus enjoyed a spit roast or two on his homeward journey after the Trojan War. Modern Greeks have certainly inherited his love of them. Turn a corner in any Greek city and you'll meet with the enticing smell and sight of a turning spit threaded with sizzling golden-brown chickens. For a successful spit roast you need a plump young chicken, a patient cook to baste it constantly, and a good hardwood fire to sear the skin but keep the meat juicy.

Serves 4

2 (2½-to-3-pound) chickens, excess fat removed
Juice of 1 large lemon
½ cup extra virgin olive oil
1 teaspoon sea salt
1 teaspoon freshly ground black pepper
1 tablespoon finely chopped fresh oregano *or* flat-leaf parsley

For serving
1 large bunch watercress, sprigs only
Lemon wedges
24 Elitses *or* 12 Amfissa *or* Niçoise olives
Kephalotyri or mild *feta* cheese, cut into slices

Rub the chickens with the lemon juice and half the olive oil. Set aside for 1 hour.

Prepare the fire.

Fasten the wing tips over the chicken breasts with short metal or wooden skewers. Insert the spit into each chicken to dissect the wishbone and tie the drumsticks and tail together; the chickens will now revolve with the spit.

Brush the chickens with the remaining olive oil, and place the spit about 12–15 inches above the hot coals. Roast 10 minutes, frequently turning the spit, catching the juices in a pan held under the chickens.

Raise the spit 2–3 inches and roast 30–45 minutes longer, turning the spit and basting with the juices, until deep golden brown. The juices will gradually darken and become very aromatic; to prevent them from burning, add a few tablespoons water to the pan. Check if the meat is cooked by piercing the thickest point of one chicken thigh with a skewer or knife; the juices should run clear. Sprinkle the chickens with salt and pepper.

Strain the pan juices into a small saucepan. Heat to warm and stir in the oregano. Carve the chicken into serving pieces.

Line a platter with the watercress, place the chickens on top, and garnish with the lemon wedges. Serve the sauce, olives, and cheese separately.

Spit-Roasted Mountain Rabbit
Kounelli tou Vounou

Mountain villagers in Greece are practiced in the art of creating memorable feasts from simple foods. Spit-roasted rabbit, a variety of salads, olives, cheese, country bread, and wild pears, all washed down with fiery raki, make for splendid – and lively – village celebrations. Eggplant dishes are particularly good with spit-roasted rabbit. If raki is not to your taste, choose a full-bodied red wine.

Serves 4–5

1 (5-pound) rabbit, prepared by the butcher (see Note)
1 tablespoon wine vinegar
Juice of 1 lemon
3 sprigs fresh thyme

2 bay leaves, broken in pieces
2 shallots, thinly sliced
4 juniper berries, lightly crushed
5 tablespoons extra virgin olive oil
½ cup Chicken Stock (page 343) *or* white wine
1 tablespoon Dijon mustard
1 teaspoon cracked black pepper, or to taste
Sea salt, to taste
2 tablespoons finely chopped flat-leaf parsley

Rub the rabbit all over with the vinegar, then rinse it and dry with paper towels. Place in a glass or ceramic dish with the lemon juice, thyme, bay leaves, shallots, juniper berries, and olive oil. Tightly cover and marinate for 12–48 hours in the refrigerator.

Prepare the fire.

Secure the rabbit to the spit and set it 12–15 inches above a medium-hot fire. Set a pan on a rack underneath to catch the juices. Add the stock to the marinade and baste the rabbit with this mixture. Roast, turning and basting, until the rabbit is cooked, about 50 minutes. Check if the meat is cooked by piercing the thickest part of one thigh with a skewer or knife; the juices should run clear.

Strain the pan juices and any remaining marinade into a small saucepan. Add the mustard, pepper, salt, and parsley, and heat to warm. Cut the rabbit into serving pieces, arrange on a warm platter, and pour over just enough sauce to moisten. Serve the remaining sauce separately.

Note This recipe can also be made with rabbit pieces rather than a whole rabbit. Use a hinged grill to hold the pieces and grill over medium-low fire for 15–20 minutes, basting frequently and turning occasionally.

Rabbit Stifado
Kounelli Stifado

Stifado is a favorite family casserole in winter: rich and sustaining, spiced with cumin, cloves, and cinnamon, it's a dish full of character. Although it's traditionally made with wild rabbit, I have made delicious versions with chicken, beef, and pork, and a neighbor on Crete makes a remarkable snail *stifado*. The most important ingredient, however, is onions – large quantities are essential to produce the characteristic rich sweet sauce. Like most stews, *stifado* can be made ahead of time and it tastes even better when reheated.

Serves 6

3 pounds small boiling onions, about 3/4–1 inch in diameter
1 (5-pound) rabbit, cut into 8 serving pieces and excess fat removed
All-purpose flour, for dredging
3/4 cup extra virgin olive oil, or to taste
1/2 cup aged red wine vinegar
2 cloves garlic, finely chopped
6 large tomatoes, skinned, seeded, and diced
1 teaspoon honey
1 2-inch cinnamon stick
1 1/2 tablespoons ground cumin
8 cloves
1 teaspoon ground allspice
4 bay leaves
Zest of 1 orange, removed in large strips and tied together with kitchen string
2 tablespoons tomato paste diluted with 1/2 cup water
1 cup red wine
Sea salt, to taste
1/2 tablespoon cracked black pepper, or to taste

For serving
4 tablespoons finely chopped flat-leaf parsley

Slice the root end off each onion and remove the feathery outside layer of skin. Blanch the onions in boiling water for 5 minutes, drain, and peel. Set aside.

Heat the oven to 350°F. Rinse the rabbit pieces and pat dry with paper towels. Lightly dredge with flour. Heat 4 tablespoons of the olive oil in a large heavy sauté pan and lightly brown the meat on all sides. Drain between layers of paper towels and transfer to an earthenware or enameled cast-iron baking dish.

Add the onions to the pan and sauté 10 minutes, until lightly browned. Transfer to the baking dish.

Drain off the oil from the pan and add the vinegar. Boil 1 minute, scraping up the browned bits from the bottom and sides with a wooden spoon. Add the garlic, tomatoes, honey, cinnamon, cumin, cloves, allspice, bay leaves, and orange zest, and boil 1 minute. Stir in the tomato paste, red wine, and remaining olive oil and season with salt and pepper. Pour over the meat, cover tightly, and bake 20 minutes. Reduce the oven temperature to 300°F and bake 1 1/2 hours longer; if the liquid in the casserole reduces to less than 2 cups, add hot water as necessary.

Discard the orange zest and season to taste. Sprinkle with the parsley and serve hot.

Marinated Hare
with Juniper Berries
Lagos Stifado

This is a wonderful cold-weather dish, strongly spiced and rich in flavor. The marinade can also be used with great success for other meats, such as beef. Serve with a *pilafi* or *macaronia* dish and *khorta* (see page 221) or a green salad.

Serves 6 to 8

1 (7-to-8-pound) hare, skinned, cut into 12–14 serving pieces
   (see page 346), trimmed, and excess fat removed
1³/4 cups aged red wine vinegar
6 cloves garlic
6 juniper berries, lightly crushed
6 whole allspice berries
3 cloves
12 black peppercorns
1 3-inch cinnamon stick, broken into pieces
8 bay leaves
¹/2 cup extra virgin olive oil, or to taste
2 pounds ripe tomatoes, skinned, seeded, and diced
1 tablespoon honey
¹/2 tablespoon cracked black pepper, or more to taste
1 tablespoon paprika
2 tablespoons ground coriander
4 pounds small boiling onions, peeled (see previous recipe)
1 cup robust red wine
1 tablespoon dried thyme *or* winter savory (see page 14)
Sea salt, to taste

For serving
Coarsely chopped fresh cilantro

Rinse the meat and pat dry with paper towels. Place in a ceramic or glass bowl and add the vinegar, garlic, juniper berries, allspice, cloves, peppercorns, cinnamon, and 4 of the bay leaves. Tightly cover and refrigerate for 1–2 days, occasionally turning the meat in the marinade.

Heat the oven to 350°F. Transfer the meat to an earthenware or enameled cast-iron baking dish.

Pour the marinade (and spices) into a small saucepan and reduce to about 3/4 cup by rapid boiling over high heat; strain over the meat and discard the solids. Add half the olive oil, the tomatoes, honey, pepper, paprika, coriander, onions, red wine, and remaining bay leaves to the meat. Cover and bake 20 minutes.

Reduce the oven temperature to 300°F and bake 2½ hours longer; add hot water as necessary if there appears to be less than 2½ cups of liquid in the baking dish.

Add the thyme, salt, and remaining olive oil and bake 15 minutes longer. Season to taste, sprinkle with the fresh cilantro, and serve hot.

Pheasant over a Fire

Fasianos sti Skhara

In Hania on the island of Crete, there is a tiny taverna set into the rock, and the focal point of its one cave-like room is a huge open fire over which plump pheasants are often slowly roasting. The birds are stuffed with a country mixture of bacon, mushrooms, and pine nuts and wrapped in blackberry leaves and pork fat, and the whole room fills with their heavenly aroma.

Serves 4 to 6

4 young pheasants, giblets reserved
Sea salt *and* freshly ground black pepper, to taste
½ cup extra virgin olive oil
2 tablespoons unsalted butter
4 ounces Canadian bacon, cut into tiny cubes
1 pound mushrooms, trimmed and cut into tiny cubes
½ cup pine nuts, chopped
4 tablespoons port *or* sweet red wine
8 thin slices bacon
8 slices whole wheat bread, crusts removed
1 clove garlic, cut into 3 or 4 pieces
2 tablespoons hot water

Prepare the fire. Rub each pheasant inside and out with salt and pepper, half the olive oil, and 1½ tablespoons of the butter. Set aside. Trim and finely chop the giblets.

Heat the remaining butter and 1 tablespoon olive oil in a heavy saucepan and sauté the giblets and bacon pieces 2 minutes over low heat, stirring constantly. Add the mushrooms, pine nuts, and pepper and cook 2 minutes longer. Stir in the port and remove from the heat.

Stuff the pheasants with the mushroom mixture and sew up the openings or fasten with small skewers. Cover the breasts and legs with the bacon slices, securing them with toothpicks.

Secure the pheasants to the spit and set the spit 2 feet above medium-hot coals. Baste with olive oil, catching the juices in a pan held under the pheasants. Roast, turning the spit and basting with the pan juices, until cooked, about 50 minutes. Remove the bacon slices 10 minutes before the pheasants are done, to let them brown. Check if the meat is cooked by piercing the thickest part of one pheasant thigh with a skewer or knife; the juices should run clear.

Meanwhile, heat the remaining olive oil in a large sauté pan and sauté the garlic until it is pale golden and the oil is aromatic. Discard the garlic. Fry the bread until golden on both sides and drain on paper towels. Cut into triangles and keep warm.

Remove the stuffing from the pheasants with a spoon and keep warm. Pour off any juices from the cavities of the pheasants into the pan of roasting juices and add the hot water. Heat over medium-low heat, stir in the browned bits from the bottom and sides of the pan with a wooden spoon, and strain the sauce into a pitcher or gravy boat.

Carve the pheasants and arrange on a warm serving platter. Spread the stuffing on the slices of fried bread and arrange around the pheasants. Serve the sauce separately.

Hunter's Pot
Tsoukali Kinigou

This rich and herb-scented dish is traditionally made with partridge, pigeon, or guinea fowl – the spoils of a day's hunting in ancient times. I have made highly successful versions with game hens and chicken. It is a sweet and fragrant casserole that will fill your kitchen with a warm homely aroma to create a wonderful welcome for family and friends. Serve with Potatoes in a Clay Pot (page 207), fried eggplants, and a robust red wine.

Serves 4

2 large partridges *or* 4 pigeons, giblets reserved
Juice of ½ lemon
7 tablespoons extra virgin olive oil
Sea salt *and* freshly ground black pepper, to taste
4 ounces Canadian bacon, finely diced
1 tablespoon unsalted butter
2 medium carrots, finely diced
1 small onion, finely chopped
3 bay leaves

1 tablespoon fresh rosemary, crumbled
1 tablespoon dried thyme, crumbled
4 cloves garlic
3 tablespoons finely chopped parsley
1³/₄ cups dry white wine *or* Chicken Stock (page 343) *or* a mixture of both
8 fresh *or* brine-preserved grape leaves, rinsed, blanched in boiling water
    for 5 seconds if fresh, 3 seconds if preserved, and drained
¹/₂ cup fresh coarse whole wheat bread crumbs
20 Elitses *or* 10 Niçoise olives, rinsed, pitted, and coarsely chopped

Rub the partridges inside and out with the lemon juice, 3 tablespoons of the olive oil, and salt and pepper. Set aside for 1 hour.

Trim the giblets. Heat 1 tablespoon of the remaining olive oil in a heavy sauté pan and lightly brown the bacon and giblets. With a slotted spoon, transfer to a heavy baking dish. Add the butter to the pan, lightly brown the partridges on all sides over medium-low heat, and transfer to the baking dish.

Heat the oven to 375°F. Add the carrots, onion, bay leaves, rosemary, thyme, garlic, and half the parsley to the pan and reduce the heat to low. Sauté 15–20 minutes, until golden brown, stirring occasionally with a wooden spoon. Transfer to the baking dish.

Add the wine to the pan and bring to a boil, scraping up the browned bits from the bottom and sides of the pan with a wooden spoon. Pour into the baking dish, cover the partridges with the vine leaves, and tightly cover the baking dish. Reduce the oven temperature to 325°F and bake 40–50 minutes.

Meanwhile, heat the remaining 3 tablespoons olive oil in a frying pan. Add the bread crumbs and fry, stirring occasionally, until golden brown. Drain on paper towels.

Transfer the partridges to a warm platter, discarding the grape leaves and giblets, and keep warm. Pour the liquid from the baking dish into a shallow saucepan and reduce to ³/₄ cup by rapid boiling over high heat; add any juices that have accumulated around the partridges. Add the bread crumbs, olives, and remaining parsley to the vegetables in the baking dish, stir just to mix, and return to the oven to heat through. Strain the sauce. Spoon the vegetables around the partridges, pour over the sauce, and serve at once.

Note You can substitute 4 whole game hens or 1 3¹/₂-pound chicken, cut into serving pieces and skin and excess fat removed, for the partridges.

Grilled Quail
Ortikia tis Skhara

Quail is a popular autumn dish in Greece and, in some country tavernas, it is still cooked in a traditional way. Rubbed with olive oil and herbs, the quail is wrapped in red clay and baked until the clay hardens – at the table the pot is cracked open with a dramatic flourish to reveal a perfectly cooked bird. The nearest modern equivalent is baking in parchment paper or in a pot tightly sealed with a flour-and-water paste. Or try this recipe, which gives the tiny birds an exquisite delicate flavor; game hens can be substituted if quail is not available.

Serves 4

4 quail, livers reserved
Juice of 1 large lemon
1 teaspoon freshly ground black pepper, or to taste
1 onion, sliced
6 sprigs parsley
6 bay leaves
3 sprigs of dried *rigani* (see page 13) *or* fresh oregano *or* marjoram
6 tablespoons extra virgin olive oil
4 slices whole wheat bread, crusts removed and cut into triangles
½ tablespoon aromatic honey, such as Hymettus
1 teaspoon Dijon mustard
Fine-grain sea salt, to taste

For serving
Watercress sprigs
Lemon wedges

Using a sharp knife, split the quail along their breastbones, turn over, and flatten by gently pressing on the backbones with the palm of your hand. Combine half the lemon juice, the pepper, and 3 tablespoons of the olive oil in a bowl. Place the quail in this marinade and set aside for 1–2 hours, turning the quail occasionally.

Prepare the grill.

Arrange a grill rack over medium-hot coals and brush the grill with olive oil. Remove the quail from the marinade, leaving all the herbs in the bowl. Grill until lightly browned on both sides, about 15 minutes.

Meanwhile, heat the remaining olive oil and fry the bread crumbs over medium-low heat until golden on both sides. Dip the livers in the marinade and fry them. Mash gently, spread on the fried bread, and keep warm.

Strain the marinade. Combine the honey, mustard, and remaining lemon juice in a saucepan, add the marinade, and heat to warm.

Arrange the quail on a warm platter, season with salt and pepper, pour over the sauce, and garnish with the fried bread, watercress sprigs, and lemon wedges.

Duckling Thessalía-Style
Papaki Thessalias

Highly perfumed lemons are the secret of this sweet roasted duckling. Lemon juice is rubbed inside the duckling, and it is also used in the roasting dish so that the meat absorbs its fragrance throughout the slow cooking. Serve with Beets Island-Style (page 183) or Turnips and Grapes in Aromatic Sauce (page 189).

Serves 4

....

1 (3-pound) duckling, excess fat removed and giblets reserved
1 carrot, scrubbed, and cut into large pieces
1 onion, sliced
3 bay leaves
2 sprigs fresh thyme
Sea salt *and* freshly ground black pepper, to taste
Juice of 1 large lemon
4 tablespoons extra virgin olive oil
4 juniper berries
3 cloves
Zest of ½ orange, removed in thin strips
1 cup fresh coarse whole wheat bread crumbs
3 tablespoons finely chopped flat-leaf parsley
½ cup lightly toasted pine nuts
24 Elitses *or* 12 Niçoise olives, soaked in hot water for 5 seconds, drained, pitted, and coarsely chopped

For serving
Watercress sprigs
Lemon wedges

....

Place all the giblets except the liver in a small saucepan, and add the carrot, onion, 1 bay leaf, 1 sprig thyme, salt and pepper, and 1¾ cups water. Bring to a boil, cover, reduce the heat, and simmer 40 minutes. Strain the broth into a bowl and set aside; discard the solids.

Rub the duckling inside and out with half the lemon juice, the olive oil, and salt and pepper. Set aside.

Heat the oven to 375°F.

Place the remaining 2 bay leaves, 1 sprig thyme, the juniper berries, cloves, and orange zest in the duckling's cavity and sew up the opening or fasten with small skewers. Lay the duckling on its side in a heavy baking dish and add 4 tablespoons water to the dish. Roast, uncovered, for 20 minutes. Remove the fat with a spoon and set aside. Add the remaining lemon juice to the dish and stir in the browned bits (residue) from the bottom and sides of the dish with a wooden spoon. Roast 5 minutes longer to caramelize the juices. Pour the pan juices into a measuring cup and add enough reserved fat to make about 4 tablespoons. Set aside.

Turn the duckling onto its other side, pour over ¾ cup of the reserved broth, and roast 20 minutes longer, basting occasionally. Turn the duckling breast upward and roast until deep golden brown, about 10 minutes.

Meanwhile, heat the reserved pan juices in a heavy frying pan. Add the bread crumbs and cook over low heat until lightly browned and most of the liquid has been absorbed. Stir in the parsley, pine nuts, and olives and heat thoroughly. Keep warm.

Pour off the pan juices from the baking dish and remove the fat with a spoon. Add the spices and any juices from the cavity of the duckling and strain the sauce into a warm serving bowl or gravy boat.

Carve the duckling. Spread the bread crumb mixture on a warm serving plate, arrange the duckling pieces on top, garnish with the watercress sprigs and lemon wedges, and coat with a little sauce. Serve the remaining sauce separately.

MEATS

Kreata

According to Greek mythology, the god Prometheus made mankind from clay and, in opposition to Zeus, the king of the gods, stole fire for his new creation from the forge of the fire god Hephaestus. Fitting, then, that many of the best Greek meat dishes are readily associated with this gift of the ancient gods, with the crackling brilliance of living flame and the soft, lambent glow of red embers.

Spit roasting and grilling over an open fire has been an integral part of Greek life for centuries, and equipment for long-ago barbecues has been found on Minoan archaeological sites. Its popularity is undiminished today, and for anyone who has visited Greece or the islands, the sizzling aroma of herb-perfumed meat roasting outdoors and the scented haze of wispy wood smoke inevitably conjures up myriad images of the country.

Tradition, custom, and experience dictate the preferred aromatics and flavorings for different meats and the types of fuel used for the fire. Pine is said to give an authentic traditional taste, grapevine clippings bring out the fine flavor of game, and hardwoods such as olive, apple, pear, or cherry make perfect embers over which to grill meat to tender succulence. Charcoal, of course, is most convenient; the type made from softwoods like cedar or pine makes a perfect fire for the meats in this chapter, or you can just use charcoal briquets.

Easter, the most important date in the Greek Orthodox calendar, is marked not by a dish of amazing intricacy and complexity, but by a splendidly simple aromatic spit-roasted tender young lamb. Lamb, kid, and suckling pig are all favorites for spit roasting, and for these meats aromatic marinades are important; many of those used today are traditional recipes based on vinegar, wine, yogurt, pomegranate juice, and onion juice. An infinite variety of other meat delicacies also acquire a unique flavor when marinated and grilled, most notably *souvlakia* – small pieces of deliciously tender meat, speared on skewers, and grilled over charcoal – and *sheftalia* – highly-seasoned sausage. All over Greece *souvlakia* (from the Greek word, *souvla*, for spit or skewer), *sheftalia*, and a variety of other sausage snacks are sold from *souvlaki* stands – covered stalls or tiny cafés boasting a fierce grill, a makeshift counter, and, perhaps, a rickety table or two. These stands are everywhere and are never without customers, day or night.

The Greek repertoire also includes versatile oven-baked meat dishes. In the country these dishes are still cooked in the traditional wood-burning *fournos*, and *fournos* cooking does produce a truly delectable and unique flavor, especially if clay pots are used. The meat simmers gently in its own juices, enhanced with herbs, spices, and vegetables; the result is meltingly tender meat covered with a thick aromatic sauce. While the open-air spit roasts and grilled dishes of Greece are inspired by the delicate fragrance of hillside and mountain herbs, the flavors of these oven-baked dishes are stronger and more pungent. They are characterized by heady Eastern spices and a generous use of strong flavorings. The oven-baked dishes in this chapter are traditional recipes adapted for use with modern ovens and enameled cast-iron pots, but if you do possess a partly glazed clay pot, so much the better.

Paschal Lamb
Arnaki Paskalino

After the dark austerity of the Lenten fast comes the abundance and joy of the season of rebirth. All over Greece the centerpiece of the celebratory meal, traditionally cooked by men, is spit-roasted milk-fed lamb. As early as sunrise on Easter Day coils of fragrant smoke begin to rise from pinewood fires in preparation for the midday feast. All morning the whole lamb turns on a long spit and the cooks, using brushes made from rosemary sprigs, lemon leaves, or branches of thyme, baste the meat with olive oil. My memories of this splendid celebration always explode with brilliant color – the burning red of spring poppies, the ecclesiastical purple of wild irises, the paint-box blue skies – and above all, an atmosphere of happiness and rejoicing. Only the finest accompaniments are fit for the Paschal Lamb – spring vegetables, especially young asparagus and fava beans, a salad of romaine lettuce, and, of course, the special Easter Bread (page 261). For this roast you will need a spit about 6 feet long to pass through the whole length of the lamb; for smaller parties this recipe works equally well with a leg of lamb.

Serves 10 to 12

1 lamb (about 22 pounds)
Juice of 2 lemons
2 cups extra virgin olive oil
Coarse-grain sea salt *and* finely cracked black pepper, to taste
10–12 sprigs fresh rosemary tied together to make a basting brush *or*
    1 branch thyme *or* dried *rigani* (see page 13)

For serving
Lemon wedges

Prepare the fire.

Rub the lamb inside and out with the juice of 1 lemon and sew up the stomach using a larding needle. Pierce the skin in a dozen or so places with the point of a sharp knife, and baste liberally with the olive oil.

Secure the lamb to the spit and place it about 2 feet above the glowing embers. Roast 2–2½ hours, slowly moving the spit closer to the embers until the lamb is only 6 inches from the heat, and catching the juices in a pan. Baste liberally at frequent intervals with the pan juices and remaining olive oil; near the end of the roasting time, add the juice of the second lemon to the pan.

To make the sauce, add a few tablespoons of water to the pan juices and stir to mix. Strain into a small saucepan and gently heat to warm. Carve the lamb, arrange on a large warm platter, and sprinkle with salt and pepper. Pour some of the sauce over and garnish with the lemon wedges. Serve the remaining sauce separately.

Spit-Roasted Leg of Lamb
Arnaki tis Souvla

For really tender meat and a rich country flavor let the lamb marinate overnight and be sure to baste it frequently as it roasts. The marinade given here is also very good with kid (see page 144); for a different flavor try the marinade on page 145.

Serves 6

1 (5-to-6-pound) leg of lamb
Red wine vinegar, to rub over the lamb
3 tablespoons coriander seeds, crushed
2 tablespoons fresh rosemary, chopped
½ tablespoon freshly ground black pepper
Sea salt, to taste
Juice of 2 small lemons (reserve 1 juiced lemon half)
½ cup extra virgin olive oil
½ cup dry red wine *or* water, or to taste

For serving
Fresh rosemary sprigs

Trim off any excess fat or tough skin from the lamb and pierce the meat in a dozen places with the point of a sharp knife. Moisten a cloth with the vinegar and wipe the lamb all over to remove any gamy flavor. Combine the coriander, rosemary, pepper, salt, and lemon juice in a bowl, and whisk in the olive oil. Rub this marinade over the lamb, cover loosely, and set aside for 4–6 hours at room temperature, or refrigerate overnight.

Prepare the fire.

Run the spit lengthways through the leg and arrange it so the lamb is about 12 inches above medium-hot coals. Roast 45 minutes to 1 hour, slowly moving the spit closer to the coals, until the lamb is only 6 inches from the heat; pierce the lemon half with a skewer and use it to baste the lamb liberally at frequent intervals with the marinade, catching the juices in a pan.

Strain the pan juices and any remaining marinade into a small saucepan. Add the wine to the pan that held the pan juices, stir in any browned bits from the bottom of the pan, and strain into the saucepan. Heat to warm.

Slice the lamb, arrange on a warm platter, pour over some of the sauce, and garnish with the rosemary sprigs. Serve the remaining sauce separately.

Spit-Roasted Easter Sausages
Kokoretsia

Kokoretsia, made from the offal of the Paschal Lamb, are an integral part of the Easter Day feast, eaten as either a mid-morning snack or a *meze*. The diced variety meats are marinated in herbs and spices, garlic, and lemon juice, wrapped in the lamb's intestine, and roasted over glowing charcoal. The "sausages" are then cut into thick slices and sprinkled with sliced onion, salt, and parsley. *Kokoretsia* are served with lemon wedges, olives, and radishes as a *meze*.

Serves 8 to 10

1 lamb's liver (about ½ pound)
4 lamb's kidneys
2 small lamb's hearts
2 lamb's sweetbreads
Other lamb's variety meats, *optional*
Sea salt
1 tablespoon wine vinegar
Juice of 1 large lemon
½ teaspoon ground cumin
1 teaspoon dried thyme, crumbled
1 tablespoon dried *rigani* (see page 13), crumbled
½ tablespoon cracked black pepper
½ cup extra virgin olive oil, to taste
4 bay leaves
1 large clove garlic, lightly crushed, *optional*

1 small bunch flat-leaf parsley, leaves finely chopped
About 8 ounces prepared sheep's intestine *or* sausage casings (see page 350)
About 6 ounces pork caul fat (see page 350)

For serving
1 small red *or* mild onion, thinly sliced

Trim off and discard all the fat sinew, valves, and membranes from the variety meats. Dissolve 1 tablespoon of salt and the vinegar in a bowl of water, and soak the meats for 30 minutes.

Drain and pat dry with paper towels. Chop the liver, kidneys, and heart into 1/4-inch cubes and the other variety meats into smaller cubes.

Combine the lemon juice, cumin, thyme, *rigani*, pepper, 1 teaspoon of salt, and 4 tablespoons of the olive oil in a large bowl. Add the meats, bay leaves, and garlic, and mix together with your hands. Cover and set aside for 1 hour.

Prepare the fire.

Discard the bay leaves and garlic, and add half the parsley to the meats; mix well. Stuff the intestine or sausage casing to make 1 large or 2 small sausages, and tie at both ends. Carefully spread out 1 or 2 sheets of caul fat and wrap the sausage(s) in it. Insert a skewer the length of the sausage(s).

Add the remaining olive oil to any marinade remaining in the bowl and baste the sausages liberally with this.

Arrange the skewer(s) 12 inches above medium-hot coals. Slowly roast thin sausages 45 minutes, plump sausages 1–11/4 hours, turning and basting frequently, until browned on all sides.

Cut into 1/2-inch slices, sprinkle with the onion, salt, and the remaining parsley, and serve immediately.

Spit-Roasted Kid
Katsiki tis Souvla

Spit roasting is the best way to cook young kid, and a long marinating time produces the most tender, flavorsome meat. The strong marinade in this mountain recipe includes garlic, herbs, bay leaves, orange zest, peppercorns, and juniper berries, and the meat rests in this heady mixture for 36 hours. The finishing touch is the clear sharp flavor of a sauce made from blueberries. Fresh blueberries are seasonally available; blueberries preserved in light syrup are available year-round. Greeks begin a festive meal like this with *mezedes* of olives, cheese, eggplants, and beans; with the kid they enjoy Potatoes in a Clay Pot (page 207), country bread, and a green salad. A full-bodied red wine such as Naoussa is the perfect accompaniment.

Serves 8 to 10

----

1 (6-to-7-pound) leg of kid, prepared by the butcher
4 tablespoons wine vinegar

Marinade
2 onions, sliced
3 carrots, scrubbed, and cut into large pieces
2 cloves garlic, lightly crushed
2 sprigs each fresh thyme *and* rosemary
3 sprigs fresh summer savory, (see page 14), *optional*
6 bay leaves
1 tablespoon chopped dried orange zest (see page 349)
24 black peppercorns
8 juniper berries, lightly crushed
Dry red wine, to cover the meat

1 cup extra virgin olive oil
4 ounces bacon, cut into small cubes
1 tablespoon all-purpose flour
2 cups Light Meat Stock *or* Meat Stock (page 348)
5 tablespoons fresh blueberries *or* 4 tablespoons strained preserved
   blueberries (see Note)
1/2 tablespoon cracked black pepper, or to taste
Sea salt, to taste

For serving
Watercress sprigs

Soak a cloth with the vinegar and rub the meat all over to remove any stall. Rinse and pat dry. Place all the marinade ingredients in a large glass or ceramic bowl, add the meat, cover, and set aside for 36 hours at room temperature.

Remove the meat, onion, and carrots from the marinade and pat dry with paper towels. Trim the meat of all fat and skin, and cut these trimmings into 1-inch pieces. Dice the onion and carrot. Set aside.

Bring the marinade, including all the herbs and spices, to the boil in a large heavy saucepan and reduce to about 2½ cups by rapid boiling. Strain and set aside.

Prepare the fire.

Run the spit lengthways through the legs and arrange it so the kid is about 12 inches above medium-hot coals. Roast 2–2½ hours (20 minutes per pound), basting frequently with the reduced marinade and olive oil and catching the juices in a pan.

Meanwhile, add 2 tablespoons of the olive oil to a heavy saucepan and sauté the bacon and meat trimmings over low heat until browned. Add the diced onion and carrot and lightly brown, stirring frequently. Sprinkle with the flour, stir to mix, and cook 1 minute. Add 1¼ cups of the reduced marinade and the stock, reduce the heat, and simmer until reduced to 2 cups. Strain into another saucepan, add the blueberry syrup (see Note), pepper, and salt, and set aside.

Skim the excess fat from the pan juices and stir the juices into the sauce. Season to taste.

Slice the meat, arrange on a warm platter, garnish with the watercress, and spoon over enough sauce to moisten. Serve the remaining sauce separately.

Note To make blueberry syrup, combine 1¾ cups fresh berries and 2 tablespoons water in a nonreactive saucepan and simmer for 10 minutes. Press through a strainer, preferably plastic, measure the juice, and return to the saucepan. Add an equal amount of sugar and simmer for 10 minutes. Strain and store in airtight jars or bottles for up to 1 month. Preserved blueberries need only to be drained and pressed through a strainer.

The Villagers' Grilled Lamb
Arni Skharas Khoriatiko

Fresh and fragrant country herbs, perfumed lemons, and tender lean meat are the essence of this simple classic dish. Since the cooking is fast, the lamb benefits from the tenderizing and flavoring of a sharp marinade of lemon juice, pepper, and pungent bay leaves. The flavorful pan juices, to which a liberal amount of *rigani* is added, make a delicious sauce and eggplant or bean dishes are the perfect accompaniment.

Serves 4

8 small loin *or* rib lamb chops
Juice of 1 large lemon (reserve 1 juiced lemon half)
Cracked black pepper, to taste
4 bay leaves
4–6 tablespoons extra virgin olive oil, to taste
Coarse-grain sea salt
2 tablespoons dried *rigani* (see page 13), briefly pounded in a mortar *or*
    1 tablespoon dried thyme *or* rosemary, crumbled

For serving
Lemon wedges

Trim off most of the fat from the chops and carefully wipe them to remove any bone splinters. Place in a glass or ceramic bowl. Sprinkle with the lemon juice, pepper, and the bay leaves, cover, and set aside for 3–4 hours, turning the chops occasionally.

Prepare the grill.

Set a grill rack 4 inches above hot coals. Lightly brush the grill and the chops with the olive oil, and add the remaining oil to any marinade left in the bowl. Discard the bay leaves. Pierce the lemon half with a skewer and use this as a baster.

Grill the lamb until browned on both sides, basting frequently with the marinade and catching the juices in a pan. Raise the grill 2 inches and grill about 5 minutes longer for rare meat, 15 minutes longer for well done. A few minutes before the chops are done, add salt, pepper, and half the *rigani* to the marinade, and baste the chops several times.

Add 2 or 3 tablespoons water to the pan juices, stir to mix, and heat; strain this sauce. Arrange the chops on a warm platter and pour over enough sauce to moisten. Sprinkle with salt, pepper, and the remaining *rigani* and garnish with the lemon wedges. Serve the remaining sauce separately.

Marinated Lamb Souvlakia with Pilaf
Arni Souvlakia me Pilafi

This is wonderful party food – preparation can be done well ahead of time and then it takes only minutes to produce succulent *souvlakia*, grilled to a dark crust outside, tender and juicy within. To keep the meat tender, serve *souvlakia* immediately – with bowls of radishes, olives, *feta* cheese, *khorta* (see page 221), and a fresh bean or green salad.

Serves 6

1 2½-pound lean leg of lamb
Juice of 2 lemons
½ cup extra virgin olive oil
Coarse-grain sea salt *and* cracked black pepper, to taste
24 (dry) bay leaves
2 tablespoons dried *rigani* (see page 13)
1 teaspoon dried thyme
Pilaf
4 tablespoons (½ stick) unsalted butter

2 ounces vermicelli, crushed (broken into small pieces)
2 cups long-grain rice
1 teaspoon ground allspice
1 teaspoon sea salt
3³/4 cups Light Lamb Stock (page 347) *or* water

For serving
1 small bunch flat-leaf parsley, leaves coarsely chopped
Finely grated zest of 1 small lemon *or* 1 tablespoon finely chopped
    Preserved Lemons (page 18)
2 small red *or* mild onions, cut into thin rings
3 lemons, cut into wedges

....

Cut the meat into 1-inch cubes and trim off any fat or sinew. (Reserve the bones to make stock.)

Combine the juice of 1¹/2 lemons, 5 tablespoons of the olive oil, and salt and pepper in a glass or ceramic bowl. Add the lamb, mix together with your hands, cover tightly, and refrigerate for 4 hours or overnight.

One hour before grilling, remove the bowl from the refrigerator.

Melt the butter in a heavy saucepan and cook the vermicelli 10 minutes over medium-low heat, until the butter is dark nutty brown. Add the rice and allspice and cook 1 minute, stirring constantly. Add the salt and stock, raise the heat, and boil 8 minutes, until holes appear in the surface of the rice. Turn off the heat, place 2 layers of paper towels over the top of the saucepan, and cover with the lid. Set aside for 30 minutes in a warm place such as the back of the stove.

Meanwhile, prepare the grill.

Remove the meat from the marinade and thread onto 6 lightly oiled skewers, occasionally alternating the pieces with the bay leaves. Brush liberally with the marinade.

Set the grill rack 3 inches above the hot coals and lightly brush with olive oil. Grill the *souvlakia* until browned on all sides, basting frequently with the marinade. Raise the grill 2 inches and grill 8–10 minutes longer, basting, until the meat is dark and crusty outside, juicy and tender inside.

Pound the *rigani* and thyme together in a small mortar until aromatic and add to the remaining marinade along with olive oil (to taste). Continue basting the *souvlakia* with this mixture.

Chop the parsley and lemon zest together until mixed, and combine with the onion, remaining lemon juice, and salt and pepper.

Spread the *pilafi* on a warm platter. Using a fork, push the *souvlakia* off the skewers onto the rice. Sprinkle with the onions, remaining marinade, and salt and pepper, and garnish with the lemon wedges.

Yogurt Lamb Souvlakia with Saffron Rice

Arni Souvlakia Yiaourti

The saffron crocus produces a deep purple flower with feathery red stamens that yield a rich yellow coloring and strong, aromatic flavor. For centuries saffron has been a highly prized commodity; the early Minoan civilization on Crete prospered through the cultivation and export of this sought-after spice. Proof of its importance to the Minoans can still be seen at the reconstructed Cretan Palace of Knossos where a fresco depicts saffron gatherers at work. Greeks now use Macedonian saffron, which has a pungent aroma; here Spanish saffron, which has an excellent flavor and strong color, is the most widely available. Accompanied by Beet Salad with Allspice (page 184) or Beets Island-Style (page 183), this delicious dish is ideal for informal dinner parties.

Serves 6

1 2½-pound lean leg of lamb
Juice of 1 large onion (see page 349), about 5 tablespoons
1½ cups Strained Yogurt (page 7)
1–3 cloves garlic, finely chopped
12 bay leaves
Coarse-grain sea salt, to taste
Extra virgin olive oil, for basting
Cracked black pepper, to taste

Saffron Rice
1 teaspoon saffron threads
3 cups Light Lamb Stock (page 347) *or* water
4 tablespoons extra virgin olive oil
2 cups long-grain rice
1 teaspoon sea salt

For serving
1 large bunch watercress, sprigs only *or* a handful of small arugula leaves, torn in pieces
24 Elitses *or* Niçoise olives, drained
4 tablespoons finely chopped flat-leaf parsley
3 lemons, cut into wedges

Cut the lamb into 1-inch cubes and trim off any fat or tendons. (Reserve the bones to make stock.)

Combine the onion juice, yogurt, garlic, bay leaves, and salt in a glass or ceramic bowl. Add the lamb and mix with your hands. Cover tightly and refrigerate for at least 12 hours, turning the lamb in the marinade 2 or 3 times.

One hour before grilling, remove the bowl from the refrigerator.

Heat the saffron in a small dry frying pan over low heat until aromatic. Crumble the threads into the stock. Heat the olive oil in a heavy saucepan over medium-low heat, add the rice, and cook, stirring, 1 minute. Add the salt and the saffron broth, raise the heat, and boil 8 minutes, until holes appear in the surface of the rice. Turn off the heat, place 2 layers of paper towels over the top of the saucepan, and cover with the lid. Set aside for 30 minutes in a warm place such as the back of the stove.

Meanwhile, prepare the fire.

Remove the meat from the marinade and thread onto 6 lightly oiled skewers. Baste with the marinade, brush liberally with olive oil and dust with the pepper.

Set the grill rack 3 inches above the hot coals and lightly brush with olive oil. Grill the *souvlakia* on all sides until crusty, basting frequently with the marinade and olive oil. Raise the grill 2 inches and grill 8–10 minutes longer, basting, until the meat is dark and crusty outside, juicy and tender inside.

Spread the saffron rice in the center of a warm platter and garnish with the watercress. Using a fork, push the *souvlakia* off the skewers onto the rice. Sprinkle olive oil over the salad greens and the olives and parsley over the *souvlakia*, season with salt and pepper, and surround with the lemon wedges. Serve immediately.

The Baker's Lamb

Arni me Fassolia

In the morning quiet of a Greek village traditionally clad women may be seen hurrying to the village baker with huge covered trays; at midday they return to pay the baker a few drachmas and to collect the now succulent stews that have been simmering in the baker's oven. This aromatic dish of new lamb and young fava beans, cooked with tomatoes and onions and spiced with cumin and *rigani*, is the spring version of a popular Greek dish that is made year-round in an infinite variety of meat, vegetable, and spice combinations. In summer and autumn chicken may be substituted for the lamb; in winter a pork and dried beans version warms and sustains. For best results, make sure the cooking is slow and steady, so that the pungent flavors of the herbs and spices can penetrate the meat and vegetables and develop a rich and highly seasoned sauce.

Serves 6

6 lean lamb chops
5–8 tablespoons extra virgin olive oil, to taste
2 large onions, quartered and thinly sliced
2 pounds ripe tomatoes, skinned and diced, juices reserved
1 teaspoon honey
Sea salt
1 teaspoon cracked black pepper, or to taste
1 tablespoon tomato paste diluted with 2 tablespoons water
½ cup Meat Stock (page 348) *or* water
2 tablespoons ground cumin
3 tablespoons dried *rigani* (see page 13)
2 pounds green beans such as young fava beans (see page 344) *or* string beans, trimmed, strings removed, and cut into 2–3 inch lengths (see Note)
1 large bunch flat-leaf parsley, leaves coarsely chopped
Juice of 1 large lemon, or to taste

For serving
2 tablespoons finely chopped Preserved Lemons (page 18) *or* finely grated lemon zest, blanched in boiling water for 5 seconds
1 large clove garlic, finely chopped

Heat the oven to 325°F. Trim off all fat and sinew from the lamb and carefully wipe the meat to remove any bone splinters.

Heat 3 tablespoons of the olive oil in a large heavy sauté pan and lightly brown the lamb over medium heat. Drain on paper towels and transfer to a deep glazed clay or enameled cast-iron baking dish at least 4 inches deep. Reduce the heat to low and sauté the onion 10 minutes or until soft. Add the tomatoes, honey, salt, and pepper, raise the heat, and boil 3 minutes or until reduced by one third. Add the tomato paste, stock, cumin, and *rigani*, stir to mix, and pour over the meat. Cover, and bake 50 minutes.

Blanch the beans in slightly salted boiling water for 1 minute. Drain and add to the baking dish with the remaining olive oil. Shake gently to mix, cover, and bake 30 minutes longer. There should be about 1½ cups sauce – if there is more, uncover the dish; if less, add a few tablespoons water and cover – bake 15 minutes longer. Reserve 2 tablespoons of the parsley, and stir in the rest. Set aside in a warm place for 5 minutes.

Mix together the Preserved Lemons, garlic, reserved parsley, and a large pinch of salt. Set aside.

Add salt, pepper, and the lemon juice to the baking dish; the sauce should be highly seasoned. Serve straight from the baking dish, or transfer to a warm serving dish. Sprinkle with the parsley mixture and serve.

Note Unless you can find very tender young fava beans, shell them before using.

Variations

♦ Substitute 6 lean bone-in beef steaks for the lamb, and use allspice instead of the cumin, dried thyme instead of the *rigani*.

♦ Substitute lamb shanks for the lamb chops. Popular in eastern Mediterranean countries, lamb shanks produce a rich gelatinous sauce. Have the butcher cut 4 medium shanks into 2 or 3 thick slices each. Substitute 1¹/₂ tablespoons ground cinnamon for the cumin if desired.

♦ Substitute chicken for the lamb. Cut 1 large chicken into 8 serving pieces and remove the skin and excess fat. Lightly brown the pieces in olive oil and bake only 15 minutes before adding the beans.

♦ Substitute large cubes of eggplants, cauliflower florets, small potatoes, baby zucchini, artichoke hearts, slender leeks, or cooked dried beans for the green beans. Fry the eggplant cubes in olive oil until golden brown on all sides before adding to the meat; blanch the fresh vegetables in boiling water for 1 minute before adding. Cooked dried beans need no additional advance preparation.

Cinnamon Lamb with Eggplants
Arni Kanellas

Sweet raisins and honey, spicy perfumed cinnamon, and pungent vinegar and capers – the combination of flavors in this recipe evokes the tastes of medieval Byzantine cooking. Ideal for a lunch or dinner party, this casserole tastes even better if made a day ahead to allow the strong flavors a chance to mellow.

Serves 6

3 large eggplants (about 1¹/₂ pounds total)
Sea salt
¹/₂ cup small dark seedless raisins
5 tablespoons aged red wine vinegar *or* 2 tablespoons balsamic vinegar
    diluted with 2 tablespoons water
3¹/₂ pounds very lean lamb, preferably from the leg
¹/₂ cup extra virgin olive oil
2 large onions, quartered and thinly sliced
2 large cloves garlic, finely chopped
2¹/₄ pounds ripe tomatoes, skinned and diced, juices reserved
1 tablespoon honey
Cracked black pepper, to taste
1 tablespoon ground cinnamon, or to taste

For serving
1 bunch flat-leaf parsley, leaves coarsely chopped
1 tablespoon small capers, rinsed, *optional*

Trim off the ends of the eggplants and cut into 1½-inch cubes. Sprinkle with 2 tablespoons salt and set aside for 30 minutes to "sweat."

Combine the raisins and vinegar in a glass or ceramic bowl and set aside. Trim off all fat and sinew from the lamb and cut into 1½-inch cubes.

Heat the oven to 350°F.

Heat half the olive oil in a large heavy sauté pan and lightly brown half the lamb over medium heat. With a slotted spoon, transfer to a heavy baking dish. Repeat with the remaining lamb.

Reduce the heat under the pan to low and sauté the onion until soft, about 10 minutes. Add the garlic, stir well, and transfer to the casserole.

Dry the eggplants thoroughly with paper towels. Wipe out the pan, set it over medium-low heat, and add half the remaining olive oil. Add half the eggplants and fry until deep golden brown on all sides, about 12 minutes. Drain on paper towels and add to the baking dish. Repeat with the remaining olive oil and eggplants.

Add the tomatoes and their juices, honey, salt, pepper, 1 tablespoon of the cinnamon, and the raisins and vinegar to the casserole. Add 4 tablespoons water, cover, and bake 1 hour.

Season the sauce with salt, pepper, and additional cinnamon to taste. There should be about 1½ cups of sauce – if there is more, leave the casserole uncovered; if less, add a few tablespoons water and cover – bake 30 minutes longer.

Chop the parsley and capers together just to mix. Serve the lamb hot or warm, piled high in a shallow serving bowl, with the parsley mixture sprinkled on top.

Variations
♦ Substitute 1 tablespoon ground allspice for the cinnamon.
♦ Substitute ground cumin for cinnamon, and 6 tablespoons Meat Stock (page 348) for the vinegar and raisins. To serve, sprinkle with a mixture of 3 tablespoons coarsely chopped fresh mint; 1 small bunch flat-leaf parsley, leaves coarsely chopped; and 2 tablespoons finely chopped Preserved Lemons (page 18).

Spring Lamb with Mountain Herbs
Arni me Votana

On spring Sundays the fragrance of this immensely satisfying dish floats on the morning air of many Greek villages. My particular memory of it takes me back to the mountain village of Milia where, on trestle tables set up in a cool whitewashed courtyard, crusty bread, bowls of crisp green salad, and jugs of local rosé wine awaited a gathering of family, friends, and neighbors. At midday our hostess brought out large shallow bowls of this aromatic stew – a complete Sunday lunch in one pot. No haute cuisine meal, I decided, could have tasted more wonderful at that moment.

Serves 6

3 pounds small lamb shoulder chops
½ cup extra virgin olive oil
1 pound small boiling onions, peeled (see page 132)
2 tablespoons all-purpose flour
½ cup dry red wine, *optional*
1–1½ cups Meat Stock (page 348)
6 large tomatoes, skinned and diced, juices reserved
1 tablespoon tomato paste diluted with 2 tablespoons water
1 teaspoon honey
2 tablespoons fresh rosemary, chopped, *or* 3 tablespoons dried rosemary, crumbled
2 tablespoons dried *rigani* (see page 13), crumbled
1 tablespoon dried thyme, crumbled
6 bay leaves
2 large cloves garlic, finely chopped
Coarse-grain sea salt *and* cracked black pepper, to taste
1 pound young carrots, cut into 2 inch-lengths
1 pound small new potatoes, peeled if desired, and cut in half
6 small young turnips, peeled and cut in half
¾ pound green beans such as string beans, trimmed and cut into 1½-inch lengths

For serving
1 small bunch flat-leaf parsley, leaves coarsely chopped

Trim off all the fat from the meat and wipe it to remove any bone splinters. Heat half the olive oil in a large sauté pan and brown half the lamb over medium heat. Transfer to a large heavy saucepan, and repeat with the remaining lamb.

Reduce the heat under the sauté pan, add the remaining olive oil, and cook the onions until lightly browned on all sides, about 10 minutes. Drain between layers of paper towels and transfer to the saucepan.

Drain off most of the olive oil from the sauté pan and sprinkle the pan with the flour. Stir any browned bits into the flour with a wooden spoon and gradually add the wine, stirring vigorously. Bring to a boil, simmer 1 minute, and stir in 1 cup of the stock. Stir in the tomatoes and their juices, tomato paste, honey, rosemary, *rigani*, thyme, bay leaves, garlic, and salt and pepper. Transfer to the saucepan and bring to a boil over medium heat. Cover, reduce the heat, and slowly simmer 1 hour.

Fill a large saucepan with lightly salted water and bring to a boil. Add the carrots and potatoes and lightly boil 4 minutes. Add the turnips and boil 1 minute longer. Drain and add to the lamb. Add more stock or water if necessary to make about 2 cups sauce. Cover, bring to a boil, and simmer 15 minutes longer.

Bring a small saucepan of water to a boil, add the beans, cook 1 minute, and drain. Add the beans to the casserole and shake gently to combine; don't stir or the vegetables may break up. Simmer 15 minutes longer, until the vegetables are just done. Season to taste with salt and pepper.

Sprinkle with the parsley and serve.

Lamb Klephtiko
Arni Klephtiko

In this classic dish thick slices of lamb, larded with slivers of garlic and seasoned with oregano, lemon juice, and olive oil, cook gently in a tight paper parcel from which no juices or tantalizing aromas can escape. The dish probably has as many origins as there are storytellers. Village women have told me that the cooking method was devised to protect food from the hungry marauding bandits who had an unpleasant habit of turning up at mealtimes. Village men say that the meat would be left cooking gently in paper while courageous villagers went off to rout out the bandits. On their return their supper would be tender, aromatic, and cooked to perfection! Traditionally only lamb, goat, and fish are cooked this way, but this wonderfully flavorful method can also be used very successfully with vegetables.

Serves 6

1 (5-to-6-pound) leg of lamb, cut (by the butcher) into 1½-inch slices across the bone *or* 1 boned leg of lamb, cut into 1½-inch slices *or* 6 1-inch thick lean lamb chops

½ cup extra virgin olive oil, or to taste

2 large cloves garlic, cut into large slivers

Sea salt *and* cracked black pepper, to taste

**3 tablespoons coarsely chopped fresh oregano *or* rosemary *or*
2 tablespoons dried *rigani* (see page 13), crumbled**
Juice of 1 large lemon

Trim off any fat from the meat; wipe lamb on-the-bone to remove any tiny bone splinters. Tie a piece of kitchen string around each slice of boned lamb to keep it in shape.

Heat 3 tablespoons of the olive oil in a large sauté pan and brown half the meat over medium-low heat. Drain on paper towels. Repeat with the remaining meat.

Heat the oven to 400°F. Cut out 6 12-inch squares of parchment paper. Fold each piece in half and trim the two outer corners to make 6 folded ovals. Open up the papers and divide the meat between them, placing it in the center of the bottom half of the paper. (Remove the string from the boneless lamb.) Push the garlic into creases in the meat, season generously with salt and pepper, and sprinkle with the oregano, lemon juice, and remaining olive oil. Fold the top halves of the papers over the meat and roll up the edges tightly to make neat parcels that will not leak. Arrange in a large baking pan and bake 10 minutes.

Reduce the oven temperature to 350°F and bake boneless lamb 20 minutes longer, lamb on-the-bone 35–40 minutes longer.

Place the parcels on warm dinner plates. Carefully open each one by cutting the four corners with scissors and pulling back the edges of the paper.

Moussakas

Moussakas

One of the best-known Greek dishes, *moussakas* remains a popular favorite all over Greece and her islands. In tavernas it's usually made in large shallow baking dishes; in a private home you may be presented with *papoutsakia*, "little shoes" of eggplant shells filled with meat sauce and cheese custard, or your own individual *moussaka* cooked in a clay pot. An authentic *moussakas* does take time, but it can be made a day ahead, and it also freezes well.

Serves 8 to 10

4 large eggplants (about 2¼ pounds total)
Sea salt
¾ cup extra virgin olive oil
2 large onions, finely chopped
2 pounds lean lamb *or* 1 pound each of lamb *and* beef, finely ground

1 cup red wine, *optional*
6 large ripe tomatoes, skinned and diced, juices reserved
1 teaspoon honey
1 bunch flat-leaf parsley, leaves finely chopped
1 cup Meat Stock (page 348)
4 tablespoons dried *rigani* (see page 13), crumbled
2 tablespoons ground cinnamon, or to taste
1 teaspoon ground allspice, or to taste
Freshly ground black pepper, to taste
2 cups milk
4 tablespoons (½ stick) unsalted butter
4 tablespoons all-purpose flour
4 ounces small-curd cottage cheese, drained
2 ounces *feta* cheese, grated
4 ounces *graviera or* Gruyère cheese, grated
1 teaspoon grated nutmeg
5 large eggs
2 ounces *kephalotyri or* Parmesan cheese, grated
³/₄ cup fresh fine breadcrumbs

Trim off the ends of the aubergines and cut into ¼-inch slices. Sprinkle with 2 tablespoons salt and set aside in a colander for 1 hour to "sweat."

Heat 3 tablespoons olive oil in a large deep sauté pan and cook the onion over medium-low heat until soft, about 6 minutes. Raise the heat, add the meat, and sauté until lightly browned, breaking up any lumps with a wooden spoon and stirring occasionally to prevent sticking. Add the wine and boil until reduced by half. Add the tomatoes with their juices and the honey, lower the heat, and simmer 10 minutes. Set aside 1 tablespoon of the parsley, and stir in the rest with the stock, *rigani*, cinnamon, allspice, and 1 teaspoon each of salt and pepper. Simmer 30 minutes, until almost all the liquid has evaporated. Season to taste with salt, pepper, and cinnamon. Cover and set aside (or refrigerate overnight).

Heat 3 tablespoons of the remaining olive oil in a large frying pan (or use 2 frying pans for extra speed). Thoroughly dry the eggplant slices with paper towels. Add just enough slices to make a single layer in the pan and fry over medium heat until dark golden brown on both sides. Drain between layers of paper towels. Add 1 tablespoon olive oil to the frying pan and fry another batch of eggplant slices; repeat with the remaining slices. Set aside.

Melt the butter in a heavy saucepan, add the flour, and stir with a wooden spoon until smooth. Cook, stirring, over low heat, 1–2 minutes, until the roux turns pale golden brown. Gradually add the milk, a half cup at a time, stirring until smooth after each addition. Bring to a boil, stirring, and remove from the heat.

Combine the cottage *feta*, *graviera*, and nutmeg, and stir into the white sauce. With a wire whisk or electric mixer, beat the eggs until pale and frothy. Thoroughly stir one third of the beaten eggs into the cheese mixture, then add the remainder all at once. Season to taste and set aside.

Heat the oven to 350°F. Arrange about one quarter of the eggplant slices in the bottom of a large 3–4 inch deep baking dish, cover with one third of the meat sauce, then lightly smooth about 4 tablespoons of the cheese mixture over it. Make 2 more layers of eggplant, meat sauce, and cheese, and top with the remaining eggplant slices. Cover with the remaining cheese mixture, sprinkle with the *kephalotyri* and bread crumbs, and bake uncovered for 1 hour. If the top appears to be browning too quickly, loosely cover with a sheet of aluminium foil. (Do not press down, or you will remove the lovely crust when you take off the foil.)

Sprinkle with the reserved parsley and serve hot or warm.

To make individual casseroles Divide the eggplant slices, meat sauce, and cheese mixture between 8 or 10 individual baking dishes or small soufflé dishes, each about 3 inches deep, layering the ingredients as above. Bake about 40 minutes.

To make papoutsakia Cut 5 large eggplants lengthways in half, sprinkle the cut sides with salt, and "sweat" for 30 minutes. Dry with paper towels. Fry in olive oil until the cut sides are golden brown and the skin is dark and wrinkled, drain between layers of paper towels, and carefully scoop out the flesh from each, leaving a 1/2-inch thick shell. Fill the shells with the meat sauce and cover each with a layer of the cheese mixture. Sprinkle with the *kephalotyri* and bread crumbs and bake 40–45 minutes.

Moussakas with Potatoes

Use only 2 large eggplants and substitute 1 pound small new potatoes, boiled in salted water for 10 minutes and cut in 1/4-inch slices, for the bottom layer of eggplant slices. Or omit the eggplants altogether, and substitute 3 pounds potatoes.

Moussakas with Courgettes

Substitute zucchini for the eggplants: trim 3 pounds zucchini, cut lengthways into 1/4-inch slices, and fry in olive oil until golden brown on both sides. Drain between layers of paper towels, and assemble as above.

Multi-colored Moussakas

Use 1 pound new potatoes, boiled 10 minutes and sliced, as the bottom layer, and 1 pound zucchini and 1 large eggplant, sliced and fried, for the remaining layers. Proceed as directed above.

Grilled Kephtedes

Kephtedes sta Karvouna

Spicy beef and lamb patties are a traditional centerpiece for many outdoor parties and village gatherings. These grilled *kephtedes* are highly flavored but simple food, usually served mounded on a platter with an array of colorful garnishes for an eye-catching presentation. They are good with eggplant dishes, *tsatsiki* (page 54), *khorta* (see page 221), and fried potatoes.

Serves 6

12 ounces lean beef, finely ground
12 ounces lean lamb, finely ground
1 large onion, finely chopped
4 tablespoons finely chopped flat-leaf parsley
2 tablespoons dried *rigani* (see page 13), briefly pounded in a small mortar
1 teaspoon dried thyme, crumbled
1½ cups fresh fine whole wheat bread crumbs
1 tablespoon mustard seeds *or* ½ teaspoon powdered mustard
4 tablespoons dry red wine *or* 2 tablespoons aged red wine vinegar
Coarse-grain sea salt *and* cracked black pepper, to taste
Extra virgin olive oil

For serving
2 small red *or* mild onions, quartered and thinly sliced
1 small bunch flat-leaf parsley, leaves coarsely chopped
3 ripe tomatoes, skinned and cut into small cubes
½ medium cucumber, peeled and cut into small cubes
Juice of ½ lemon
1 tablespoon sumas (see Note) *or* 1 teaspoon paprika *and* a large pinch of cayenne pepper
Watercress sprigs
Lemon wedges

Combine the beef, lamb, onion, parsley, *rigani*, thyme, and bread crumbs in a large bowl. Heat the mustard seeds in a small dry frying pan over low heat until a few pop. Pulverize them in a mortar or spice grinder. Mix this powder with the wine and add to the meat, along with salt and pepper.

Knead the mixture for a few minutes, tightly cover, and refrigerate for 1–4 hours.

Prepare the grill.

Moisten your hands with cold water and shape the meat mixture into 12 balls, flattening each one into a 3/4-inch thick patty.

Oil a grill rack and place it 4–5 inches above the hot coals. Grill the *kephtedes*, basting frequently with olive oil, for about 8 minutes, until browned and crusty on both sides but still moist and pink in the center.

Combine the onion, parsley, tomatoes, cucumber, lemon juice, sumac, and salt and pepper to taste and spread this mixture over a platter. Arrange the *kephtedes* on top, sprinkle with olive oil to taste, and garnish with the watercress and lemon wedges.

Note Sumac, available from Greek and Middle Eastern shops, is the pulverized berry of a piquant herb. It has a coarse texture, pleasantly tangy acid flavor, and a deep auburn color.

Smyrna Sausages
Soudzoukakia

These spicy sausages are the legacy of the Greeks who once lived in Smyrna (now Izmir, Turkey) and brought back to their home country a taste for Eastern flavorings. Here are two versions: In the first, the *soudzoukakia* are browned, then simmered for just a few minutes in a tomato sauce; in the second, they are marinated overnight in the tomato sauce before cooking. Either way they are a simple, tasty, and economical dish.

Serves 6

1 medium onion, grated
2 tablespoons cumin seeds
2 tablespoons aged red wine vinegar
3/4 cup fresh fine bread crumbs
1½ pounds lean lamb, finely ground twice
1 small bunch flat-leaf parsley, leaves finely chopped
1 clove garlic, finely chopped
1 egg, lightly beaten
Sea salt
1 tablespoon cracked black pepper, or to taste
3 tablespoons extra virgin olive oil
4 cups Tomato Sauce made with cumin and parsley (page 321)

Combine the onion and 4 tablespoons water in a small saucepan, bring to a boil, and simmer until the water has evaporated, about 6 minutes. Take care not to let the onion burn. Meanwhile, in a small dry frying pan, gently heat the cumin seeds until aromatic, about 2 minutes. Pulverize them in a small mortar or spice grinder. Sprinkle the vinegar over the bread crumbs and combine with the lamb, half the parsley, the garlic, egg, onion, cumin, and salt and pepper. Knead the mixture for few minutes, cover tightly, and refrigerate for 1 hour.

Moisten your hands with cold water, divide the meat mixture into 18 portions, and shape them into 2-inch long sausages. Flatten them slightly between your palms.

Heat the olive oil in a large heavy frying pan and sauté the sausages until browned on both sides, about 12 minutes. (You can use 2 frying pans for greater speed.) Drain between layers of paper towels.

Bring the Tomato Sauce to a simmer in a shallow saucepan large enough to hold the sausages in a single layer. Add the sausages and simmer 3 minutes, until hot. Season to taste with salt and pepper.

Transfer to a warm serving platter and sprinkle with rest of the parsley.

Marinated Smyrna Sausages
Soudzoukakia Marinata

....

1 onion, grated
1/2 cup red wine
3/4 cup fresh fine bread crumbs
1 1/2 pounds lean lamb, finely ground twice
1 1/2 teaspoons ground cinnamon, or to taste
1/4 teaspoon ground cloves
3 tablespoons finely chopped flat-leaf parsley
1 egg, lightly beaten
Sea salt *and* cracked black pepper, to taste
Olive oil, for frying
4 cups Tomato Sauce made with cinnamon and parsley (page 321)
3 bay leaves

For serving
3 tablespoons finely chopped flat-leaf parsley

....

Make the sausages and fry them as directed above, substituting 4 tablespoons of the wine for the vinegar, the ground cinnamon and cloves for the pulverized cumin.

Bring the Tomato Sauce to a simmer and add the remaining wine and bay leaves.

Place the sausages in a nonreactive bowl and cover with the sauce. Cool, tightly cover, and refrigerate overnight.

To serve, heat the sausages in the sauce and serve warm or hot, sprinkled with the parsley.

Peppery Grilled Liver
Sikotakia Piperato tis Skhara

For this quick and easy popular delicacy tender lamb's liver is marinated in lemon juice, mustard, and olive oil, then dusted with crushed peppercorns and grilled. The secret is to grill just long enough to brown the outside but keep the inside moist and pink.

Serves 3 to 4

1 pound lamb's liver, cut into ¼-inch thick slices
Juice of 2 lemons
½ teaspoon powdered mustard
6 tablespoons extra virgin olive oil
1½ tablespoons cracked black pepper

For serving
Watercress sprigs
1 tablespoon finely chopped Preserved Lemons (page 18) *or* finely grated
    lemon zest of 1 small lemon
4 tablespoons finely chopped flat-leaf parsley
½ teaspoon coarse-grain sea salt, or to taste
1 small red *or* mild onion, cut into thin rings
½ teaspoon paprika
1 lemon, cut into wedges
2 ripe tomatoes, cut into wedges, *or* 8 tiny tomatoes

Trim off any membrane from the liver.

Whisk together the lemon juice, powdered mustard, and the olive oil in a nonreactive bowl. Add the liver, cover tightly, and set aside.

Prepare the grill.

Set a grill rack 3 inches above the hot coals and lightly brush with olive oil. Remove the liver from the marinade, reserving the liquid, and sprinkle with the pepper. Grill until browned on both sides but still pink inside, about 2 minutes.

Meanwhile, mix together the Preserved Lemons, parsley, and salt.

Combine with the onion and paprika.

Arrange the liver in the center of a warm platter and garnish with the watercress and lemon and tomato wedges. Spoon over a few tablespoons of the marinade and scatter over the onion mixture. Serve immediately.

Note Grilled liver is also delicious prepared with the marinade for lamb on page 147 or pork (see page 170).

Piquant Garlic Beef
Sofrito

In this classic recipe strong red wine vinegar, liberal amounts of perfumed mountain herbs, and a generous quantity of garlic turn modest beef stew into an outstanding dish. Richly flavored *sofrito* is an island speciality from Corfu, and in tavernas there it is cooked in tightly sealed individual earthenware pots; at the table the lids are removed to release a wonderful fragrance and reveal meltingly tender beef in a thick, garlicky herb sauce. This special dish takes very little time to prepare. Serve with Eggplant Pilaf with Glazed Tomatoes (page 228), bowls of purple and green olives and *feta* cheese, and Island Green Salad (page 219).

Serves 6

2¼ pounds lean beef (top round *or* rump)
All-purpose flour, for dredging
½ tablespoon cracked black pepper, or to taste
6 tablespoons extra virgin olive oil, or to taste
1 cup aged red wine vinegar
8 bay leaves
3 tablespoons dried thyme, marjoram, *or* rosemary, *or* a mixture
1 cup Meat Stock (page 348) *or* water
Sea salt, to taste
2–3 heads garlic, or to taste, cloves separated and peeled
4 tablespoons all-purpose flour

For serving
Finely chopped flat-leaf parsley
24 Elitses *or* Niçoise olives, drained

Heat the oven to 275°F. Trim the meat of all fat and sinew and cut into 1½-inch cubes. Dredge with flour, shaking off any excess, and sprinkle with the pepper.

Heat half the olive oil in a large heavy sauté pan and lightly brown half the meat over medium-low heat. Drain between layers of paper towels and transfer to a large heavy baking dish. Repeat with the remaining meat.

Drain off any oil from the pan and add the vinegar. Bring to a boil, stirring in any residue from the bottom and sides of the pan with a wooden spoon. Simmer a few minutes to reduce slightly, and pour over the meat. Add the bay leaves, thyme, stock, salt, and the remaining olive oil and shake the dish gently to mix. Add the garlic, pushing it down between the pieces of meat so its flavor will penetrate the dish.

Combine the flour and a few tablespoons water to make a thick paste. Spread it around the top rim of the casserole and the inner edge of the dish's lid. Place the lid in position, smooth the paste to make a good seal, and bake 3 hours.

Insert a blunt-ended knife between the lid and casserole to break the seal. Remove the lid and wipe the rim of the casserole clean. Season to taste with salt and pepper; the dish should be highly seasoned. Sprinkle with the parsley and olives, and serve immediately.

To serve in individual casseroles Divide the *sofrito* equally between 6 individual casseroles, seal them, and bake 2½ hours at 250°F.

Aromatic Beef in Red Wine
Kapamas

This dish is said to be the invention of the nomadic tribes of antiquity who wandered all over Greece and the Balkans. That could explain the rich variety of seasonings used – the flavors of East and West are blended in a supremely aromatic and exotic concoction. After marinating for as long as 18 hours in red wine, the beef is slowly cooked in a tightly sealed pot. Prepared and cooked a day ahead, *kapamas* becomes even more intensely flavored. Serve with Garlic Potatoes with Juniper Berries (page 208), Potatoes in a Clay Pot (page 207), or a vegetable pilaf.

Serves 6

....

3 pounds lean beef (such as rump), in one piece
2 large onions, sliced
1½ tablespoons ground allspice
2 large cloves garlic, each cut into 5 or 6 pieces
8 bay leaves
2 tablespoons dried *rigani* (see page 13)
About 3 cups dry red wine
2 slices Canadian bacon, finely diced
½ cup extra virgin olive oil
1½ pounds small boiling onions, peeled (see page 132)
4 tablespoons all-purpose flour *plus* extra flour for dredging
2 pounds ripe tomatoes, skinned and diced, juices reserved

1 teaspoon honey
1 3-inch cinnamon stick, broken in half
$^1/_2$ cup Meat Stock *or* Light Meat Stock (page 348) *or* water
Sea salt *and* cracked black pepper, to taste
12 Thasos *or* Kalamata olives, rinsed, halved, and pitted

For serving
3 tablespoons finely chopped flat-leaf parsley
2 tablespoons capers, rinsed
1 clove garlic, finely chopped
2 tablespoons finely grated lemon zest

Trim off any fat or sinew from the meat and cut into pieces about 2$^1/_2$-inches square and 1 inch thick. Combine the meat, sliced onion, allspice, garlic, 4 of the bay leaves, 1 tablespoon of the *rigani,* and the red wine in a large nonreactive bowl. Cover and set aside in a cool place for 2–4 hours, or refrigerate for 12–18 hours.

Heat the oven to 275°F. Place a large heavy sauté pan over low heat and fry the bacon in its own fat for 2–3 minutes. Transfer to a large heavy baking dish. Add half the olive oil to the pan and sauté the boiling onions until lightly browned on all sides, about 10 minutes. Drain between layers of paper towels and set aside.

Remove the meat from the marinade, reserving the marinade, and pat dry with paper towels. Lightly dredge with flour, shaking off any excess. Add 3 tablespoons of the remaining olive oil to the pan and sauté half the meat over medium heat until lightly browned on both sides, about 10 minutes. Transfer to the baking dish with a slotted spoon and repeat with the remaining meat.

Meanwhile, transfer the marinade to a saucepan. Bring to a boil, lower the heat, and simmer until reduced by one third. Once the meat is browned, strain the marinade through a sieve into the sauté pan, and discard the solids. Bring to a boil, stirring in all the residue from the bottom and sides with a wooden spoon.

Add the reduced marinade, tomatoes and their juices, honey, cinnamon, stock, salt and pepper, and the remaining 4 bay leaves, and 1 tablespoon *rigani* to the baking dish. Gently shake the dish to mix everything together.

Make a thick paste with the 4 tablespoons flour and a few tablespoons water and spread it round the top rim of the dish and the inner edge of its lid. Place the lid in position, smooth the paste to make a good seal, and bake 2$^1/_2$ hours.

Insert a blunt-ended knife between the lid and dish to break the seal, remove the lid and wipe the rim of the dish clean. Add the onions. If there is more than about 1$^1/_2$ cups sauce, leave the dish uncovered; if less, add a little water or stock and replace the lid. Bake 30 minutes longer.

Bring a small saucepan of water to a boil, add the olives, and remove the saucepan from the heat. Let stand for 5 minutes, then drain and rinse the olives, add to the baking dish, gently shaking to mix, and bake about 5 minutes longer. Season with salt and pepper to taste. Meanwhile, chop the parsley, capers, garlic, and lemon zest together until well mixed.

Arrange the meat and onions on a warm platter and spoon over the sauce. Sprinkle with the parsley mixture and the remaining olive oil and serve hot.

Note If you plan to refrigerate the cooked dish overnight before serving, do not add the olives until reheating.

Beef Stifado
Stifado Moschari

Beef *stifado* is one of the best examples of the wonderful braised dishes to be found in good tavernas throughout Greece. The secret to its fine flavor is long slow cooking, a generous quantity of spices, and a large quantity of onions – the same amount as meat. *Stifado* is traditionally made with wild rabbit (see page 131) or hare (see page 133), but a beef version is a popular city dish and an easy-to-make family favorite. Like most stews, beef *stifado* tastes even better when reheated, so it can be made ahead of time. Very good with Pilaf and Green Lentils (page 229) or crusty Country Bread (page 250).

Serves 6 to 8

2½ pounds lean beef (such as rump *or* any cut suitable for braising)
½ cup extra virgin olive oil, or to taste
2½ pounds small boiling onions, about 1 inch in diameter, peeled (see page 132)
2 cloves garlic, finely chopped
6 large tomatoes, skinned, seeded, and diced
½ tablespoon honey
1 tablespoon tomato paste diluted with 4 tablespoons water
1 cup dry red wine
1 2-inch cinnamon stick
8 cloves
12 whole allspice
8 bay leaves
4 sprigs dried thyme *or rigani* (see page 13)
Zest of 1 orange, removed in large strips and tied together with kitchen string
Sea salt *and* cracked black pepper, to taste

For serving
4 tablespoons finely chopped flat-leaf parsley

Trim off any fat or sinew from the meat and cut into pieces about 1½ inches square and ½ inch thick.

Heat the oven to 300°F. Heat half the olive oil in a heavy frying pan and lightly brown half the meat over low heat. Drain between layers of paper towels and transfer to a heavy baking dish. Repeat with the remaining meat.

Add the onions to the pan and gently roll them around over low heat until a pale golden brown, about 10 minutes; transfer to the baking dish. Add the garlic to the pan, heat until aromatic, then add the tomatoes and their juices, and the honey, and simmer gently for 2 minutes. Add the tomato paste, red wine, cinnamon stick, cloves, allspice, bay leaves, thyme sprigs, orange zest, and salt and pepper. Stir to mix and simmer 3 minutes. Transfer the tomato sauce to the baking dish, add the remaining olive oil, and gently shake to mix everything together. Cover with a tight fitting lid and bake 2 hours, until the meat is meltingly tender and the sauce is thick; check once or twice during baking and add water if necessary.

Discard the thyme sprigs and orange zest and check the seasonings. Sprinkle with parsley and serve hot.

Country Beef
Brizoles

Popular country food, these spicy steaks are ideal for large parties. Delicious, attractive, and colorful, this is such an easy dish you'll find yourself making it often. Bone-in steaks are essential for flavor and juiciness; try the variations with lamb or pork.

Serves 6
....

6 small beef steaks on-the-bone (about ½ pound each)
Juice of 1 lemon
2 tablespoons ground coriander
¼ teaspoon grated nutmeg *or* ground mace
1 tablespoon dried *rigani* (see page 13)
½ tablespoon dried marjoram
1 teaspoon coarse-grain sea salt
1 tablespoon cracked black pepper
6 large ripe tomatoes, cut in half
1 teaspoon sugar
8 medium potatoes, peeled if desired, and cut lengthways in half or into quarters
6 large cloves garlic, each cut into 2 or 3 pieces
1 cup extra virgin olive oil

For serving
4 tablespoons finely chopped flat-leaf parsley

Trim off all fat from the meat and wipe it to remove any bone splinters. Place in a nonreactive bowl and pour over the lemon juice. Set aside.

Gently heat the coriander and nutmeg in a dry frying pan until aromatic, and transfer to a small mortar. Add the *rigani,* marjoram, salt and pepper, and pound until well mixed and slightly crushed. Rub the steaks all over with this mixture.

Heat the oven to 350°F.

Lay the steaks in a single layer in a large baking dish, spaced well apart. Sprinkle the tomatoes with the sugar and place them between the steaks, cut sides up. Add the potatoes, arranging them so each piece is touching a steak. Press the garlic down between the meat and potatoes. Pour over any remaining marinating liquid, sprinkle with the olive oil, and add ½ cup water to the dish. Bake uncovered, basting the beef and potatoes occasionally with the pan juices, for 1 hour, until the meat is very tender and the tomatoes are almost falling apart.

Season to taste with salt and pepper and sprinkle with the parsley. Serve hot.

Variations
♦ Substitute 12 small lamb chops or 6 small shanks, trimmed of fat, for the beef, 3 tablespoons chopped fresh rosemary for the coriander, nutmeg, and marjoram, and vinegar for the lemon juice. Omit the tomatoes and leave the garlic cloves whole and unpeeled – your guests can spread the softened garlic on the cooked meat at the table.
♦ Substitute pork chops, trimmed of fat, for the beef and 1 teaspoon ground cumin for the nutmeg. Cut 3 small eggplants in half, sauté them in 4 tablespoons olive oil, and add to the baking dish with the potatoes and tomatoes. Allow an additional 15 minutes baking time.

Spit-Roasted Suckling Pig

Gourounopoulo tis Souvla

The ancient Greeks worked hard to keep their gods happy and, when the occasion demanded it, a sacrifice was the best way to enlist divine help or give thanks for favors rendered – and the best sacrifice of all was a succulent pig! It's still a favorite celebration dish in Greece today, especially in late summer and early autumn. A true suckling pig weighs around 10–14 pounds and has a soft, pliant skin and mild gamy flavor. Greeks spit roast the meat without stuffing (a few bay leaves in the cavity are enough to lend a delicate fragrance) and baste it during cooking with a flavorful marinade so that the skin becomes crisp, brown, and sweetly scented. Serve in thick slices accompanied by Potatoes in a Clay Pot (page 207) and Beet Salad with Allspice (page 184) or an eggplant dish.

Serves 8 to 12

1 (10-to-14-pound) suckling pig, prepared by the butcher
Wine vinegar, to rub over the pig
Coarse-grain sea salt
6 bay leaves
Juice of 3 lemons
½ tablespoon cracked black pepper
1 tablespoon honey
1 cup extra virgin olive oil, to taste
1 tablespoon dried thyme, crumbled
1 teaspoon dried summer savory (see page 14), crumbled

For serving
Watercress sprigs
Elitses *or* Niçoise olives
Slices of aged *myzithra* cheese

Prepare the fire.

Scrub the pig's skin with a stiff brush and lightly wipe the pig inside and out with vinegar and then with salt. Place the bay leaves in the stomach cavity and sew up the cavity using a trussing needle.

Combine the lemon juice, pepper, ½ teaspoon salt, honey, and olive oil, and set this marinade aside. Tie the forelegs and hind legs of the pig together and secure it to the spit. Pierce the skin in a dozen places, baste liberally with the marinade, and place the spit 2 feet above the hot coals. Roast, rotating the spit and basting the pig frequently, for 1¼–2¼ hours (depending on the size of the pig); catch the juices in a pan. Gradually bring the spit closer to the coals; after about an hour of roasting, add the thyme and savory to the marinade and continue basting. Check if the meat is cooked by inserting a sharp knife into the thickest part of the pig; the juices should run clear.

Carve into serving pieces and arrange on a warm platter. Pour off as much fat as possible from the pan juices, strain the remaining liquid, and pour over the pork. Garnish with the watercress, olives, and cheese.

The Winemaker's Pork
Khirino Einopiou

In country districts the family pig is traditionally slaughtered on the day after the first autumn rain, and the Greek pork-eating season generally runs from September to late February. Legend has it that, because it is a source of formidable strength, pork is the food for warriors, and a neighbor of mine on Crete always serves this dish to the men who trample her grapes for wine-making – a job that calls for great perseverance and stamina. The flavors are indeed assertive – strong garlic, scented bay leaves, the bouquet of parsley and thyme, spicy coriander and mustard. Serve this pork and mushroom dish with potatoes and a green salad.

Serves 4

4 thick pork chops, 6–7 ounces each after boning, trimmed of fat
2 cloves garlic, crushed
4 bay leaves, broken in half
6 sprigs parsley
2 tablespoons coriander seeds *or* 1 tablespoon fennel seeds
1 tablespoon dried thyme, crumbled
About 3 cups dry red wine
1 tablespoon mustard seeds *or* 1/2 teaspoon powdered mustard
Coarse-grain sea salt
1/2 tablespoon cracked black pepper, or to taste
1 tablespoon aged red wine vinegar
5 tablespoons extra virgin olive oil
12 large white mushrooms, cut into quarters

For serving
24 Elitses *or* Niçoise olives, drained
Coarsely chopped flat-leaf parsley *or* cilantro

Place the chops between 2 sheets of waxed paper. With a kitchen mallet or the side of a heavy knife, pound until an even 1/2 inch thick. Combine the pork, garlic, bay leaves, parsley sprigs, half the coriander, the thyme, and enough red wine to cover the pork in a nonreactive bowl. Cover and set aside.

Prepare the grill.

Heat the mustard seeds in a small dry frying pan until a few pop. Pound the mustard seeds and remaining coriander with salt and pepper in a small mortar until pulverized. Whisk the vinegar and olive oil together in a small bowl and whisk in the pulverized spices. Remove the pork from the marinade, dry with paper towels, and brush liberally with the spiced olive oil. Reduce the marinade to ¾ cup by rapid boiling in a saucepan over high heat, and strain.

Set a grill rack 4 inches above the hot coals and brush with olive oil. Grill the pork until lightly browned on both sides, basting frequently with the oil and catching the juices in a pan. Raise the grill 2 inches and grill 10–12 minutes longer. (For an attractive appearance, "square" the chops: give them a 45-degree turn on each side halfway through the cooking time to give them "grill marks.") Meanwhile, brush the mushrooms liberally with the spiced oil and grill for 2–3 minutes, turning once.

Arrange the pork and mushrooms on a warm platter. Drain off the fat from the pan juices and add the juices to the marinade. Stir in the olives and the remaining spiced olive oil, and heat through. Pour over the pork and mushrooms, sprinkle with the parsley, and serve.

Mani Pork Souvlaki
Khirino Souvlakia Manis

During the period when Greece was part of the Ottoman Empire the Muslim occupation naturally discouraged the eating of pork. This did not, however, deter the rebellious inhabitants of the isolated and mountainous Mani region at the southern tip of the Peloponnese, who continued to raise pigs throughout the centuries of occupation and developed a long tradition of cooking pork. This is a simple and easy-to-prepare dish but, what it lacks in sophistication, it more than makes up for in flavor. The meat is marinated in a blend of coriander, juniper berries, and mustard, grilled with perfumed bay leaves, and garnished with cilantro. Serve with *pilafi* and Beets Island-Style (page 183) or *tsatsiki* (page 54).

Serves 6

2½ pounds boneless lean pork from the tenderloin *or* leg
1 tablespoon coriander seeds
6 juniper berries
3 tablespoons aged red wine vinegar
½ teaspoon powdered mustard
½ cup extra virgin olive oil
18 bay leaves, each broken in half
1 tablespoon honey
Cracked black pepper *and* coarse-grain sea salt, to taste

For serving
Coarsely chopped cilantro *or* watercress *or* purslane
Lemon wedges

Cut the meat into 1-inch cubes and trim off any fat and sinew. Pound the coriander seeds and juniper berries in a small mortar until crushed and well mixed. Combine with the vinegar and mustard in a small bowl, and whisk in the olive oil. Combine the meat and marinade in a nonreactive bowl, mix together with your hands, and cover. Set aside 2–3 hours.

Prepare the grill.

Remove the meat from the marinade and thread alternatively with the bay leaves onto 6 skewers. Whisk the honey into the marinade and baste the meat liberally with this sauce, then sprinkle it with pepper.

Set a grill rack 4 inches above the hot coals and lightly brush with olive oil. Grill the *souvlakia* until lightly browned on all sides, then raise the grill 2 inches. Grill 10–15 minutes longer, basting frequently, or until the *souvlakia* are cooked.

Arrange on a warm platter, sprinkle with salt, pepper, and fresh coriander, and garnish with the lemon wedges.

Traditional Pork and Bean Casserole

Khirino Khoriatiko

Robust flavors dominate this warming winter country dish; although similar to the comforting cassoulet of the Languedoc region of France, this casserole almost certainly predates it. The preparation is time-consuming, so it's best to assemble it one day, final cooking the next. It's ideal to serve at a supper party, so the quantities given here are large. Pork and smoked ham are cooked with onions, garlic, red wine, and hillside herbs and tangy Eastern spices, then layered in a casserole with country sausages and dried lima beans that absorb all the rich flavors, and baked. Serve with olives, *feta* cheese, radishes, and country bread, accompanied by a red wine such as Nemea or Naousa.

Serves 10–12

1½ pounds dried lima beans, soaked overnight in water to cover, cooked and drained; canned beans are unsuitable for this recipe

1 3-pound boneless lean pork shoulder

½ cup extra virgin olive oil, or to taste

3 heaping tablespoons finely diced *pastourmas* ham (see page 349) *or* pancetta *or* bacon

3 large onions, chopped

3 large cloves garlic, finely chopped

1 cup red wine, *optional*

2 pounds tomatoes, skinned and diced, juices reserved

1 teaspoon honey

4 tablespoons dried *rigani* (see page 13)
1 tablespoon dried marjoram
1 tablespoon dried winter savory (see page 14) *or* thyme
2 tablespoons ground coriander
5 cloves
4 juniper berries
1 small bunch flat-leaf parsley, leaves finely chopped
Sea salt, to taste
1 tablespoon cracked black pepper, or to taste
1–1½ cups Meat Stock (page 348)
½ pound homemade (see page 179) *or* commercial country sausages, grilled *or* sautéed
1 cup fresh whole wheat bread crumbs
4 tablespoons grated *kasseri or* Parmesan cheese
Juice of ½ lemon

Trim off any fat from the meat and cut into 1-inch cubes. Heat 3 tablespoons of the olive oil in a heavy sauté pan and lightly brown half the meat over medium heat. Drain between layers of paper towels, and repeat with the remaining meat.

Drain off any fat from the pan, add the ham, and sauté 2–3 minutes. Add the onion and sauté, stirring occasionally, until light golden brown, about 15 minutes. Add the garlic, cook 1 minute longer, and add the red wine. Bring to a boil and boil a minute or two, then stir in the tomatoes with their juices, honey, *rigani*, marjoram, savory, coriander, cloves, juniper berries, parsley, salt, and pepper. Simmer until the liquid is reduced by half. Add 1 cup of the stock and simmer 5 minutes longer.

Add the meat, cover, reduce the heat, and simmer 30 minutes longer; add stock or water if there appears to be less than 2 cups of sauce. Season to taste with salt, pepper, and/or additional herbs; the sauce should be highly flavored.

Heat the oven to 325°F. Slice the sausage into ½-inch thick slices and combine with the beans.

Sprinkle 2 tablespoons olive oil over the bottom of a heavy baking dish and cover with one third of the sausages and beans. Cover with a layer of half the meat mixture, then half the remaining beans, then the remaining meat. Top with a layer of the remaining beans and sprinkle with the bread crumbs and cheese. With the back of a wooden spoon, gently press down on the beans so some of the sauce rises to the surface.

Sprinkle with the lemon juice and the remaining olive oil, cover, and bake 45 minutes. Reduce the oven temperature to 300°F and bake 1–1½ hours longer, until a golden crust has formed. Remove the dish's lid and bake 10 minutes or until the crust is deep golden brown. Serve hot.

Pork Cretan-Style
Khirino Kritiko

An autumn and winter speciality on the island of Crete, this hearty dish makes the most of winter savory, a lovely mountain herb that has a particular affinity with pork. In rural communities, this popular Sunday dinner dish is still cooked in the traditional way – baked very slowly overnight in the village *fournos*. A crisp Purslane Salad (page 220) or Wild Greens Salad (page 222) provides a refreshing complement to the richness of the pork.

Serves 6

6 thick pork loin chops, on-the-bone (about ½ pound each) *or* boneless (6–7 ounces each)
Juice of 3 lemons
2 medium eggplants
2 tablespoons coarse-grain sea salt, or to taste
2 tablespoons coriander seeds, lightly crushed
1 tablespoon cumin seeds
1½ tablespoons cracked black pepper, or to taste
2 tablespoons dried winter savory (see page 14) *or* thyme
1 tablespoon dried *rigani* (see page 13)
8 juniper berries
½–1 cup extra virgin olive oil, or to taste
4 large potatoes, peeled and cut lengthways in half or into quarters
6 large tomatoes, skinned and cut in half
1 teaspoon sugar
6 large cloves garlic, feathery outer skins rubbed off
12 bay leaves

For serving
1 small bunch flat-leaf parsley, leaves finely chopped

Trim off any fat from the pork and wipe chops on-the-bone to remove any bone splinters. Combine the pork and lemon juice in a nonreactive bowl, cover, and set aside for 3 hours to marinate.

Slice off the stem ends of the eggplants. Cut lengthways in half and sprinkle the cut sides with 1 tablespoon of the salt. Set aside for 1 hour to "sweat."

Heat the oven to 325°F. Heat the coriander and cumin seeds in a small dry frying pan over low heat until aromatic, about 1 minute. Combine the cumin, coriander, pepper, savory, *rigani*, juniper berries, and remaining salt in a mortar and pound until slightly pulverized. Remove the pork from the marinade, reserving any juices, and rub all over with this mixture. Arrange the pork chops in a large baking dish, spaced well apart. Set aside.

Heat 3 tablespoons of the olive oil in a large heavy frying pan. Thoroughly dry the eggplants with paper towels, fry until the cut sides are golden brown, about 6 minutes, and drain between layers of paper towels.

Add the potatoes to the baking dish, arranging them so that each one is touching a piece of meat. Sprinkle the tomatoes with the sugar and add to the dish, cut sides up. Add the eggplants, skin sides down, and place the garlic cloves between the pieces of meat.

Pour over the remaining olive oil and the reserved marinade and sprinkle with the bay leaves and any remaining herb mixture. Add 1 cup water to the dish and bake boneless pork 30 minutes, pork on-the-bone 45 minutes, basting the meat several times with the pan juices; if the liquid evaporates, add a little more water. Reduce the oven temperature to 300°F and bake 15 minutes longer, until the pork is cooked.

Spoon the pan juices over the pork and sprinkle with the parsley.

Variation

♦ Substitute a 2½-pound boneless pork loin roast for the pork chops. Marinate for 3 hours in the lemon juice, turning the pork occasionally. Rub all over with the herb and spice mixture, place in the center of the baking dish, and pour over ½ cup of the olive oil. Surround with the vegetables and garlic and sprinkle with bay leaves and remaining marinating liquid including any spice mixture. Bake 1 hour at 325°F, basting frequently with the remaining olive oil. Bake 30 minutes longer at 300°F, or until done; do not baste again.

Slice the pork, arrange in the center of a warm platter, and surround with the vegetables. Spoon over the pan juices.

Pork Cutlets with Mustard Sauce
Khirino me Saltsa Moustarthas

Pork cutlets served with a tangy mustard sauce sharpened and spiced with lemon juice, garlic, and cumin are a popular autumn and winter lunch dish. Serve with Wild Greens Salad (page 222) and vegetable *pilafi*.

Serves 4

4 pork loin chops (about 6 ounces each after boning), trimmed of all fat
Sea salt *and* freshly ground black pepper, to taste
6 tablespoons extra virgin olive oil
3 tablespoons aged red wine vinegar *and* 2 tablespoons water *or* 5
    tablespoons Mavrodaphne wine *or* other heavy sweet wine
Juice of 1 small lemon

2 hard-boiled egg yolks, pressed through a sieve
1½ tablespoon Dijon mustard
½ tablespoon honey
½ teaspoon ground cumin
1 large clove garlic, finely chopped
3 tablespoons finely chopped flat-leaf parsley
1 tablespoon dried *rigani* (see page 13), briefly pounded in a mortar

Sprinkle the pork chops with salt and pepper and place between 2 sheets of waxed paper. With a kitchen mallet or the back of a wooden spoon, pound until an even ½-inch thick. Measure half the olive oil into a small bowl and set aside in a warm spot.

Heat the remaining olive oil in a heavy frying pan and sauté the cutlets over medium-low heat until lightly browned on both sides. Drain off any oil and add the vinegar and water. Cover, reduce the heat, and cook for 15 minutes, until the cutlets are evenly pale all the way through.

Meanwhile, whisk together the lemon juice, egg yolks, mustard, honey, cumin, garlic, and salt and pepper and press through a fine sieve into a bowl. Add the warm olive oil, pan juices, parsley, and *rigani* and briefly whisk to mix. Arrange the pork on a warm platter and pour over the sauce.

Souvlaki Sausages
Sheftalia

These delectable, highly seasoned sausages are popular street food all over Greece, and they are the perfect spicy snack at any time of the day. Meaty parcels of ground beef and pork mixed with onions, mint, parsley, and cumin are wrapped in caul fat and threaded onto skewers – in Greece double skewers, joined at one end, are sold for just this purpose. During grilling the fat melts to reveal the moist and tasty sausages inside. Perfect with *toursi* pickles, yogurt, or *tsatsiki*, and pita, *sheftalia* can be served as a main course or a *meze*.

Serves 4 as a main course, 12 as a *meze*

1½ pound lean pork *or* ¾ pound lean beef *and* lean pork, finely ground twice
1 large onion, grated
2 tablespoons fresh mint leaves, finely chopped *or* 1 tablespoon dried mint, crumbled
1 small bunch flat-leaf parsley, leaves finely chopped
1 teaspoon ground cumin *or* ½ teaspoon ground allspice
2 tablespoons aged red wine vinegar

Coarse-grain sea salt, to taste
1/2 tablespoon cracked black pepper, or to taste
Extra virgin olive oil, for grilling
1/2 pound pork caul fat (see page 350)

For serving
1 small bunch flat-leaf parsley, leaves coarsely chopped
2 small red *or* mild onions, quartered and thinly sliced
2 lemons, cut into wedges
3 ripe tomatoes, cut into thin wedges

Combine the meat, onion, mint, parsley, cumin, 1 tablespoon of the vinegar, salt, and pepper in a large bowl. Knead for a few minutes, cover, and refrigerate for 1–2 hours.

Prepare the grill.

Add the remaining vinegar to a bowl of warm water and soak the caul fat in it for 3 minutes. Separate the pieces, lay flat, and pat dry. With scissors or a sharp knife, cut into pieces approximately 4x3 inches.

Divide the meat mixture into 12 portions. Moisten your hands with cold water and shape 1 portion into a 2 1/2-inch long sausage. Lay it across a narrow end of a piece of caul fat, fold over the edge and sides, and roll up to make a firm parcel. Press down on the sausage firmly but gently to flatten it slightly; take care not to let the caul casing burst. Repeat with the remaining meat and caul fat.

Lightly brush 8 skewers with olive oil. Thread 3 sausages onto 1 skewer, running the skewer through a little off-center; do not pack them closely together. Carefully insert a second skewer through the sausages, parallel to the first one, to keep the *sheftalia* balanced during grilling. Thread the remaining sausage the same way.

Set a grill rack 4–5 inches above low coals and lightly brush with olive oil. Grill the sausages 10–15 minutes, turning them carefully so they brown evenly.

Using a fork, push the sausages off the skewers onto a warm platter. Sprinkle with some of the parsley and onion and garnish with the lemon wedges. Serve the remaining parsley and onion and the tomatoes separately.

Spicy Sausages with Mustard Sauce
Loukhanika me Yefsi Pastourma

Highly spiced with cumin, cayenne pepper, and juniper berries and scented with rosemary and thyme, these sausages, which can be boiled or smoked, are exceptionally good. Although similar in flavor to the Greek delicacy *pastourmas* (spicy preserved veal or pork tenderloin), they are traditionally made with beef. The simple mustard sauce accompanying them is superb, and sets off the spicy sausages to perfection. Serve as a light lunch or supper dish with potatoes or *pilafi*. Or thinly slice the sausages and serve with olives and cheese as a *meze*.

Makes 10 to 12 sausages

....

³/₄ cup fresh whole wheat bread crumbs (for boiled sausages only)

¹/₂ cup (for boiled sausages) to 1 cup (for smoked sausages) red wine *or* \ Meat Stock (page 348)

1¹/₂ tablespoons cumin seeds *or* 1 tablespoon ground coriander

6 juniper berries

1 teaspoon fresh rosemary

1 teaspoon dried savory (see page 14) *or* thyme

¹/₂ teaspoon cayenne pepper, or to taste

2 pounds lean beef *or* 1 pound lean beef *and* 1 pound pork, finely ground twice, *or* 2 pounds lean pork, very finely chopped

¹/₂ pound (for boiled sausages) to 1 pound (for smoked sausages) bacon,\ finely diced or ground

1 clove garlic, crushed

1 tablespoon each of coarse-grain sea salt *and* cracked black pepper, or to taste

¹/₂ pound sausage casings *or* 1 prepared sheep's intestine (for a smoked sausage, see page 350)

Extra virgin olive oil, for cooking the sausages

Mustard Sauce

2 tablespoons mustard seeds

1 tablespoon aged red wine vinegar

1 hard-boiled egg yolk, pressed through a strainer

1 teaspoon honey

2 tablespoons finely chopped flat-leaf parsley

1 tablespoon yogurt, preferably homemade (see page 7) *or* extra virgin olive oil

Sea salt *and* cracked black pepper, to taste

....

Soak the breadcrumbs in the ¹/₂ cup of wine for 30 minutes.

Heat the cumin seeds in a small dry frying pan until aromatic. Pound the

Opposite: Marinated Lamb Souvlakia, Tint Cracked Potatoes, Tsatsiki

juniper berries, rosemary, savory, and cayenne pepper together in a small mortar until pulverized; or grind in a spice grinder. Combine the meat, bacon, bread crumbs (or 1 cup wine), garlic, and salt and pepper in a large bowl. Sprinkle with the herb and spice mixture, knead for a few minutes, cover, and set aside for 1 hour.

With the sausage attachment on an electric mixer, or by hand, fill the casings and tie to make 4-to-5-inch sausages. If they are to be boiled, pierce each sausage in several places.

To make one long sausage for smoking, tie a knot in one end of the intestine and carefully fill with the sausage mixture. Secure with a second knot and tie the two knotted ends together. Pierce in a dozen places. Cover with a clean dish towel, then with a board, and place weights (such as canned fruit) on top. Leave to drain for at least 4 hours.

To boil the sausages Bring a large saucepan of water to a boil, add the sausages, reduce the heat, and simmer 1–1¼ hours, until cooked through. To check if the sausages are cooked, pierce one with a skewer; the meat should be an even color all the way through.

To smoke the sausage(s) Follow the manufacturer's instructions for your particular type of smoker, using Mediterranean pine or lemon leaves or a mixture of both if possible. After smoking, hang the sausage(s) until needed.

To serve, lightly brush the boiled sausages with olive oil and bake 30 minutes at 350°F, turning them once. Or split the sausages lengthways, brush with olive oil, and grill until lightly browned on both sides. Smoked sausages need no cooking, but frying them in olive oil gives an even better flavor.

To make the mustard sauce Gently heat the mustard seeds in a dry heavy frying pan until they begin to pop, about 4 minutes. Pulverize them in a mortar or spice grinder and transfer the powder to a bowl. Add the vinegar, egg yolk, honey, parsley, yogurt, and salt and pepper, and mix until smooth with a wooden spoon.

The sauce can be served immediately or made ahead and refrigerated for up to 2 hours.

Note For a *meze* or to add to an omelet, slice boiled sausages into ½-inch pieces and fry in a little olive oil.

Country Sausages
Loukhanika Khoriatika

Sausages are as much part of the Greek diet today as they were two thousand years ago. They have long added variety to family meals, provided an effective way of preserving meat, and given the cook a chance to create novel mixtures of herbs, spices, and meats. Traditionalists say that

Opposite: **Traditional Pork and Bean Casserole**

meat for sausages should be chopped by hand (to preserve the moisture in the meat). Each different region has its own favored ingredients and cooking methods, and speciality restaurants, called *kapnisteria*, cater for the popular taste in sausages and smoked meats. In this recipe the pork and beef mixture is strongly flavored with herbs, spices, and orange zest, and pine nuts add a crunchy country texture. These are good thinly sliced as a *meze*, cooked in omelets (page 74) or in vegetable dishes, or just grilled and served with crusty bread and salad.

Makes 12 to 14 sausages

1 teaspoon dried thyme
2 tablespoons fennel seeds *or* ½ teaspoon ground allspice
1 teaspoon ground coriander
1 bay leaf, ground
2 pounds lean pork, finely diced *or* 1 pound lean pork, finely diced, *and* 1 pound lean beef, finely ground twice
½ pound bacon
1 tablespoon cracked black pepper
1 tablespoon coarse-grain sea salt, or to taste
1 2-inch strip of orange zest, blanched *or* dried (see page 349), finely chopped
4 tablespoons lightly toasted pine nuts, coarsely ground
½ cup fresh whole wheat bread crumbs, *optional*
1 clove garlic, crushed
3 tablespoons finely chopped flat-leaf parsley
¼–½ cup red wine *or* Meat Stock (page 348), to moisten
½ pound sausage casings (see page 350)
Extra virgin olive oil, for cooking the sausages

For serving
Lemon wedges
Coarsely chopped flat-leaf parsley

Pound the thyme, fennel seeds, coriander, and bay leaf in a small mortar until well mixed and the fennel seeds are lightly pulverized.

Combine the meat, bacon, pepper, salt, orange zest, pine nuts, bread crumbs, garlic, parsley, and spice mixture in a large bowl. Knead for a few minutes and add enough wine to moisten. Cover and set aside for 30 minutes.

With the sausage attachment on an electric mixer or by hand, fill the casings and tie to make 4-to-5-inch sausages. Pierce each sausage in several places.

To cook the sausages, heat 4 tablespoons olive oil in a heavy frying pan and fry the sausages over medium-low heat, turning them occasionally, until deep golden brown on all sides. Or brush the sausages with the olive oil and grill until browned on all sides.

To serve, garnish with the lemon wedges and sprinkle with the parsley.

VEGETABLES AND SALADS

Lakhanika ke Salates

On taverna menus and at Greek family meals vegetables are often the main focus of attention. This relish for the variety and versatility of fresh vegetables, coupled with the national flair for creating exciting dishes with them, makes Greece a paradise for vegetable lovers.

At the height of the growing season Greek vegetable markets are ablaze with color – mountains of shiny multi-hued eggplants, piles of zucchini, baskets of red and green peppers, leafy bunches of purple beets, fronds of salad greens in infinite variety, mounds of tiny carrots, pyramids of huge red tomatoes, creamy sheaves of fresh celery and fennel, and banks of beans in red, pink, white, and purple. From this cornucopia the cook selects the best vegetables for a range of flavorful dishes: asparagus and new potatoes, or peas, carrots, and artichokes, to serve bathed in a delicate *avgolemono* sauce, or cucumbers, beets, or zucchini to turn into sweet and spicy salads. Perhaps carrots, onions, mushrooms, celery, or cauliflower are the best choice for succulent vegetable dishes à la grecque – juicy tomatoes, zucchini, and eggplants to stuff or to bake in aromatic casseroles.

Beans of all sorts appear on Greek family tables at least once a week. In summer bean dishes are made from the fresh varieties available in the market, in winter many of the same dishes are made from dried beans. These range from delicate purees and simple salads for *mezedes* to baked dishes that make substantial main courses.

The cooking method used has a great influence on the flavors of Greek vegetable cooking. Grills and griddles give the special smoky flavor essential to many eggplant dishes; *fournos* cooking produces a glorious texture in vegetables of all kinds, especially beans; and cooking in clay pots lends a unique earthy-sweet taste to potatoes and beets. The curious lemon astringency of grape leaves deserves special mention. Tender young leaves are stuffed with a rice mixture, while tougher leaves impart a subtle, enigmatic flavor to a wide range of grilled and baked dishes. Simply boiled or steamed vegetables are rare in Greece; most often they are served with traditional sauces such as the lemony *latholemono* and *avgolemono*, flavored vinegar sauces, or intriguing concoctions based on pine nuts, walnuts, or almonds. Many of the recipes in this chapter make perfect first courses or light lunches and suppers, as well as delicious side dishes.

Marinated Asparagus

Sparangia Latholemono

This superbly flavored seasonal dish requires little work but it does demand top-quality ingredients: tender young asparagus with a fresh bright color; a good fruity olive oil, and the juice of a plump fresh lemon. Choose asparagus of a similar thickness for even cooking. The dish can be prepared several hours ahead – the longer the asparagus rests in the marinade, the more mellow the flavor. Serve plenty of crusty bread for your guests to mop up the sauce.

Serves 3 to 4

2 pounds asparagus
Coarse-grain sea salt, to taste
Juice of 1 large lemon
4 shallots, finely chopped
1 teaspoon dried *rigani* (see page 13)
1 small bunch flat-leaf parsley, leaves coarsely chopped
1 teaspoon cracked black pepper
³/₄ cup extra virgin olive oil, or to taste

Break off the tough ends of the asparagus at the point where they snap easily and discard. Add 2 inches of water and salt to taste to a shallow saucepan large enough to hold the asparagus in a double layer. Bring to a boil and add the asparagus. Simmer 3–5 minutes, until barely tender. Drain, and spread on paper towels to dry. (Or steam the asparagus as directed on pages 187 to 188.)

Whisk together the lemon juice, shallots, *rigani,* parsley, pepper, salt, and olive oil in a large shallow bowl. Add the asparagus and toss gently to coat. Cover and set aside at room temperature for up to 1 hour, or refrigerate for up to 4 hours, but remove from the refrigerator 15 minutes before serving.

To serve, carefully toss the asparagus with the marinade once more and transfer to a platter. Season to taste with salt and pepper and serve.

Note Artichoke hearts, cauliflower florets, slender leeks, green beans, beets, and zucchini can all be prepared the same way.

Beets Island-Style

Panzaria Nisiotika

For this ancient dish island cooks choose small young beets, each purple-red globe nestling in glossy green leaves. Crisp leaves are a good indication of freshness but, even more important, they're packed with vitamins and minerals – so the Greeks make them an integral part of the dish. Clay-pot cooking gives the beets the best flavor but they can also be oven-baked or boiled. An appetizing light lunch or a good side dish for grilled or roasted pork or chicken, Beets Island-Style is an attractive addition to a *meze* table with Fried Cheese (page 38), olives, and Lamb's Liver with Lemon Juice and Rigani (page 35).

Serves 6 as a *meze*, 3 as a vegetable dish or for a light lunch

6 small beets (about 2 inches in diameter) with their leaves
1 small red *or* mild onion, cut into thin rings
Strained juice of 1 large lemon
Coarse-grain sea salt *and* cracked black pepper, to taste
1 teaspoon dried *rigani* (see page 13)
½ cup extra virgin olive oil, to taste

Trim the stalks and root ends from the beets. Set aside the green leaves and scrub the beets with a stiff brush under cold running water. Bake in a clay pot or baking dish (see page 207), or boil 15 minutes in boiling (salted) water, until just tender when pierced with the point of a knife. Drain, and when cool enough to handle, remove the skins with a small paring knife.

Place the onion in a glass or ceramic bowl and sprinkle with half the lemon juice, salt and pepper, and *rigani*. Toss to mix, cover, and set aside.

Remove the tough stalks from the beet greens and discard any leaves that are not fresh and glossy; leave thin tender stalks intact but trim to 2 inches. Thoroughly rinse, tear into pieces, and place in a saucepan. Add 4 tablespoons boiling water, cover, and cook 2–3 minutes over low heat, until just tender; do not overcook. Drain in a colander set over a bowl, pressing the greens against the colander with the back of a wooden spoon. (Reserve the mineral-rich cooking liquid for soup stock.)

While the beets are still warm, cut lengthways into quarters (the traditional shape) or into 1½-inch matchstick strips. Combine with half the olive oil and half the remaining lemon juice and salt and pepper in a nonreactive bowl and toss to coat. Arrange the beets on one side of a platter and the greens on the other side. Sprinkle with the remaining olive oil and lemon juice and a generous amount of salt and pepper and scatter the onion over the beets. Serve warm or at room temperature.

Variations

♦ Coarsely chop the cooked greens. Combine with the quartered beets and add the lemon juice, olive oil and salt and pepper; omit the onion and *rigani*.

♦ To serve taverna-style, use only the beets; save the greens for Beet Greens Salad (page 223). Cut the cooked beets into matchstick strips. Add the lemon juice, olive oil, salt and pepper, and 1 tablespoon crushed coriander seeds; omit the *rigani*. Immediately before serving, add 6 sprigs fresh mint leaves torn into small pieces or 4 tablespoons coarsely chopped flat leaf parsley to the beets, gently toss together, and garnish with the onion.

Beet Salad with Allspice
Panzaria Kritika

Allspice features often in Cretan cooking, and this easy-to-make salad comes from a most unlikely source – a monastery on the island, where, on a quiet summer's day, I enjoyed a simple but delightful lunch. With typically Cretan hospitality the monks set before us large platters of this excellent salad, bowls of creamy fresh goat's cheese, and trays of grilled fish. You can prepare the dish up to 24 hours ahead; try it with egg dishes or grilled meats, or with cheese and fish.

Serves 4

6 small beets, about 2 inches in diameter
½ tablespoon ground allspice
Coarse-grain sea salt *and* cracked black pepper, to taste
5 tablespoons extra virgin olive oil
Strained juice of 1 lemon

For serving
2 tablespoons fresh mint leaves *or* coarsely chopped fresh dill, *optional*
1 small red *or* mild onion, cut in half and thinly sliced
4 tablespoons coarsely chopped flat-leaf parsley
12 Elitses *or* 8 Niçoise olives, drained

Heat the oven to 325°F. Trim the stalks and root ends from the beets and scrub them under cold running water with a stiff brush. Line a heavy baking dish with aluminium foil (to prevent the beets from discoloring the dish), add the beets and 4 tablespoons water, and bake uncovered for 40 minutes, until just tender; add more water to the dish if necessary. (Or wrap each beet in aluminium foil and bake; allow an extra 30 minutes baking time.)

Peel the beets with a small paring knife and cut into 1½-inch matchstick strips. Place in a nonreactive bowl with the allspice, salt and pepper, olive oil, and half the lemon juice, gently toss together, cover, and set aside.

Just before serving, tear the mint leaves into small pieces. Combine the onion with the parsley, mint, remaining lemon juice, and salt.

Transfer the beets to a serving dish and sprinkle with the onion mixture, any marinade remaining from the beets and onion, and salt and pepper to taste. Scatter the olives over the beets and serve.

Artichokes City-Style
Aginares a la Polita

This fresh-tasting spring vegetable dish dates from the days of the Byzantine Empire, and the "city" in question is thought to be Constantinople (now Istanbul), the glittering empire's capital. Artichokes, new potatoes, carrots, small onions, and fava beans cook slowly in a tightly closed baking dish from which none of the delectable flavor can escape. The dish takes some time to prepare, but it can be made a day ahead for convenience.

Serves 6

2 lemons
12 small *or* 6 medium artichokes, preferably with 2 inches of stem intact
1 tablespoon all-purpose flour
Sea salt
6 small new potatoes, peeled if desired
6 small young carrots
12 boiling onions, about 1 inch in diameter, peeled (see page 132)
2½ pounds young fava beans, shelled
Freshly ground white pepper, to taste
4 sprigs fresh dill
½ cup extra virgin olive oil, or to taste

For serving
Lemon wedges

Fill a large nonreactive saucepan with water and bring to a boil. Meanwhile, squeeze the juice from the lemons, set the juice aside, and add 2 of the lemon halves to a large bowl of ice water; whisk in the flour and 1 teaspoon salt. (Flour and salt help prevent the artichokes from discoloring.) Remove the outer leaves of the artichokes, leaving only the tender light green ones. With a sharp knife, slice off the top third of each artichoke, and scoop out the fuzzy choke with a small spoon. Peel the tough outer skin from the stems. Cut medium artichokes in half lengthways. Rinse, rub with a lemon half, and add to the bowl of ice water.

Cut potatoes larger than 1 inch in diameter in half, and cut the carrots into 1/2x2-inch sticks.

Drain the artichokes and add to the boiling water with the potatoes and onions. Boil 2 minutes, add the carrots, and boil 2 minutes longer, then add the fava beans and cook 1 minute longer. Drain, reserving 1½ cups of the cooking liquid.

Transfer the vegetables to a heavy saucepan large enough to accommodate them in a single layer, arranging the artichokes bottoms up. Add salt, pepper, most of the dill, and enough of the reserved cooking liquid to come halfway up the sides of the artichokes.

Whisk together the olive oil and two thirds of the reserved lemon juice and pour this *latholemono* sauce over the vegetables. Cut a piece of waxed paper to fit the saucepan, making a hole in the center for the steam to escape. Gently press the paper down on top of the vegetables (to prevent the artichokes from discoloring) and cover the saucepan.

Set over medium heat and bring just to a simmer. Immediately reduce the heat to very low and simmer 25 minutes, until the vegetables are just tender; there should always be about 1 cup of liquid in the pan – add more of the reserved cooking liquid if necessary. Season the sauce to taste with the remaining lemon juice and olive oil, salt, and/or pepper. If there is more than 1 cup sauce, pour into a small saucepan and reduce to 1 cup by rapid boiling.

Place the artichokes bottoms up in the center of a warm platter and surround with the other vegetables. Spoon over the sauce and garnish with the remaining dill. Serve hot, warm, or at room temperature, with bowls of lemon wedges.

Note To make ahead, transfer the vegetables and sauce to a nonreactive bowl, let cool, cover, and refrigerate. Heat gently to warm or bring to room temperature before serving. Season the sauce to taste with salt, pepper, and/or lemon juice and serve.

Variations
♦ Add 3 skinned, seeded, and diced ripe tomatoes and 1/2 teaspoon sugar to the saucepan with the drained vegetables. Do not add lemon juice to the cooking liquid, but sprinkle the vegetables with 2 tablespoons lemon juice to serve.
♦ Serve with *avgolemono* sauce instead of *latholemono*. Add only 4 tablespoons olive oil and 2 tablespoons lemon juice to the vegetables. Just before the vegetables are cooked, whisk 2 egg yolks for 1 minute, whisk in the remaining lemon juice, and whisk 1 minute longer. When the vegetables are cooked, remove 1 cup cooking liquid and cover the vegetables to keep

warm. Gradually whisk the cooking liquid into the egg and lemon juice mixture, whisking 1 minute longer, and transfer to the top of a double boiler set over hot water. Cook over low heat, stirring constantly with a wooden spoon, until the sauce thickens enough to lightly coat the back of the spoon, about 1 minute. Arrange the vegetables on a warm platter, pour over the sauce, garnish with the dill, and serve at once.

Asparagus and New Potatoes Avgolemono

Sparangia me Patates ke Avgolemono

This is a spring dish of subtle delicacy and exquisite flavor. The gentle cooking method allows the potatoes to absorb a muted asparagus flavor; the vegetables are lightly coated with the classic *avgolemono* sauce. Serve as an elegant first course or lunch or as an accompaniment to grilled or roasted meats.

Serves 4

16 small new potatoes (about 1½ pounds total), peeled if desired and cut in half or into quarters
1½ pounds asparagus
2 large eggs
Strained juice of 2 lemons
Sea salt *and* freshly ground white pepper, to taste

For serving
Chervil *or* flat-leaf parsley sprigs

Fill an asparagus steamer or large 2-handled saucepan two-thirds full with lightly salted water and bring to a boil. Add the potatoes, cover, and boil for 15 minutes, until barely tender.

Meanwhile, break off the tough ends of the stalks at the point where they snap easily. Rinse the asparagus and tie in 2 bundles with kitchen string, leaving enough string on each to loop over the handles of the saucepan.

When the potatoes are almost cooked, balance the asparagus in the saucepan, the stalks immersed in boiling water. Loop the string firmly around the handles so the asparagus tips remain above the surface to steam. Cover and cook 4 minutes.

While the asparagus cooks, beat the eggs with a hand whisk or electric mixer until pale and frothy, about 2 minutes. Gradually add the lemon juice and whisk 1 minute longer. Drain the vegetables in a colander set over a bowl and keep warm. Gradually whisk ¾ cup of the cooking liquid into the egg mixture. Transfer to the top of a double boiler set over hot water and cook over low heat, stirring with a wooden spoon, until the sauce thickens enough to lightly coat the back of the spoon, about 1 minute.

Arrange the vegetables on a warm platter and sprinkle with salt and pepper. Pour over the sauce, garnish with the chervil, and serve at once.

Peas, Carrots, and Artichokes Avgolemono

Pizelia, Karotta, ke Aginares me Avgolemono

Excellent as a side dish with spring lamb, this is also a popular lunch dish in Greece – light but satisfying, and full of taste. With the green and orange color combination and a dressing of billowy lemon sauce, it looks marvelous.

Serves 4

8 small artichokes *or* 4 medium artichokes, quartered
1 pound small young carrots
1½ cups Chicken Stock (page 343) *or* water
½ teaspoon sugar
½ teaspoon sea salt
1½ pounds young peas in the pod, shelled
2 large eggs
Strained juice of 1 large lemon

For serving
Freshly ground black pepper
Finely chopped flat-leaf parsley

Trim the artichokes as directed on page 186, cutting large artichokes into quarters, and cook in lightly salted boiling water until tender, about 8 minutes.

Cut larger carrots into 1½x½-inch sticks; trim small carrots and leave whole. Bring the stock, sugar, and salt to a boil in a large heavy saucepan. Add the carrots, cover, reduce the heat, and simmer 10 minutes. Add the peas and simmer 6 minutes longer, until the vegetables are barely tender. Add the artichokes and simmer 2–3 minutes.

While the artichokes simmer, beat the eggs with a hand whisk or electric mixer until light and frothy, about 2 minutes. Gradually add the lemon juice and whisk 1 minute longer. Drain the vegetables in a colander set over a bowl and keep warm. Gradually whisk ¾ cup of the cooking liquid into the egg mixture, and transfer the sauce to the top of a double boiler set over hot water. Cook over low heat, stirring with a wooden spoon using a figure-8 motion, until it thickens enough to lightly coat the back of the spoon, 1–2 minutes.

Arrange the vegetables in a warm serving dish, pour over the sauce, and sprinkle with the pepper and parsley. Serve at once.

Turnips and Grapes in Aromatic Sauce
Gogglia ke Stafili Aromatika

Delicious with game, roasted or grilled chicken, or lamb, this unusual dish teams the vigorous earthy flavor of young turnips with sweet pepper, grapes, and currants, and a honeyed ginger sauce.

Serves 4

6–8 small turnips (about 1½ pounds total)
4–6 tablespoons extra virgin olive oil, or to taste
1 small red bell pepper, cored, seeded, and cut into very thin strips
Coarse-grain sea salt *and* freshly ground black pepper, to taste
¾ cup small seedless white grapes
¼ cup currants *or* small seedless raisins
2 tablespoons aromatic honey
½ teaspoon ground ginger
1 tablespoon dried rosemary
3 tablespoons aged red wine vinegar diluted with 3 tablespoons boiling water

Fill a medium saucepan with lightly salted water and bring to a boil. Trim the stalks and root ends from the turnips, peel, and cut lengthways into quarters. Boil 4 minutes, until barely soft when pierced with the point of a knife. Drain and set aside.

Heat the olive oil in a heavy sauté pan large enough to hold the turnips in a single layer and sauté the pepper strips over medium-low heat until slightly softened, about 1 minute. Add the turnips and salt and pepper and sauté until very pale golden brown on all sides, about 5 minutes; take care not to break up the turnips when stirring. Add the grapes and currants and heat to warm through.

Combine the honey, ginger, rosemary, and vinegar, add to the pan, and simmer until the sauce is slightly syrupy, about 2 minutes. Serve immediately.

Sweet and Sour Zucchini

Kolokithaki Glykoxsino

The dominant flavor in this easy dish is cinnamon, but the sprinkling of lemon juice lends just the right hint of tartness to balance the sweetness of the sauce. Serve it with grilled chicken, pork, or swordfish.

Serves 6

2 pounds zucchini, (each preferably about 2 inches long)
Coarse-grain sea salt, to taste
1/3 cup small dark seedless raisins
3/8 cup aged red wine vinegar
5 tablespoons extra virgin olive oil
1 tablespoon ground cinnamon, or to taste
2 tablespoons aromatic honey diluted with 4 tablespoons hot water
1 teaspoon cracked black pepper, or to taste

For serving
1 small bunch flat-leaf parsley, leaves coarsely chopped
1 tablespoon dried *rigani* (see page 13), briefly pounded in a mortar

Trim the zucchini and rub with a clean dish towel to remove any fuzz. If large, cut into pieces 2 inches long and 1 inch thick; if smaller than 2 inches leave whole. Pat dry with paper towels and sprinkle lightly with salt. Combine the raisins and vinegar in a small nonreactive bowl.

Warm the olive oil in a heavy sauté pan large enough to hold the zucchini in a single layer and sauté the zucchini over low heat until just tender, about 8 minutes; stir occasionally with a wooden spoon so they cook evenly. Sprinkle the zucchini with cinnamon and add the raisins and vinegar, honey and water, and pepper. Gently shake the pan to mix, and cook until the sauce becomes slightly syrupy, about 3 minutes.

Transfer the zucchini to a serving dish, pour over the sauce, and sprinkle with the parsley, *rigani,* and salt and pepper to taste. Serve hot, warm, or cold.

Cucumber Salad with Honey Vinegar Sauce

Angouri Salata

Along with more dramatic treasures, archaeologists working on Minoan sites have also found cucumber seeds – remnants of sumptuous royal feasts or frugal family suppers long ago. This simple salad is based on a classic recipe and features ingredients that have been accessible to Greek cooks for centuries – good olive oil, aged red wine vinegar, and aromatic honey. Serve it with grilled meats or fish.

Serves 4

1 large cucumber, peeled
Coarse-grain sea salt
4 tablespoons aged red wine vinegar
2 tablespoons aromatic honey, such as Hymettus
$1/2$ teaspoon cracked black pepper, or to taste
2 tablespoons extra virgin olive oil
4 tablespoons fresh chervil, dill, *or* flat-leaf parsley, coarsely chopped

For serving
12 Elitses *or* 6 Niçoise olives

Slice the cucumber paper-thin with a mandoline or knife, or cut into matchstick strips. Place in a bowl, sprinkle with 1 tablespoon salt, and toss to mix. Cover and set aside for 1 hour.

Combine the vinegar, honey, pepper, and a pinch of salt in a nonreactive bowl. Whisk in the olive oil. Gently squeeze the cucumber slices, a handful at a time, between paper towels, to remove as much moisture as possible. Add the cucumber and chervil to the vinegar sauce and mix well.

Transfer to a shallow bowl or platter, scatter the olives over, and serve.

Carrots and Tiny Onions à la Grecque

Karotta ke Kremithi Mikri Khoriatiko

Tiny delicately-sweet carrots are ideal for this spicy dish, but if they are not available buy the best fresh young carrots you can find. When you make this be sure to give the flavors time to mellow and mature. Serve as part of a buffet, as a first course, or as a side dish. Celery and cauliflower are also good prepared à la grecque (see the variations following this recipe).

Serves 8 as a first course, 4 as a vegetable dish or as part of a buffet

3/4 pound slender young carrots, cut into 2-inch lengths
4 tablespoons extra virgin olive oil
2 tablespoons dried coriander seeds, lightly crushed
1 pound small boiling onions, peeled (see page 132)
2 cups dry white wine
1/2 teaspoon ground mace
3 bay leaves
1/2 tablespoon aromatic honey, such as Hymettus
1 tablespoon cracked black pepper
Coarse-grain sea salt, to taste

For serving
3 tablespoons coarsely chopped cilantro *or* finely chopped flat-leaf parsley
    or 1 1/2 tablespoons chopped fresh oregano *or* thyme
1 tablespoon finely grated lemon zest
Lemon wedges

Blanch the carrots in lightly salted boiling water for 1 minute, drain, rinse, and set aside.

Heat the olive oil in a large heavy saucepan over low heat. Add the coriander seeds and the vegetables in a single layer and stir with a wooden spoon to coat with the oil. Add the wine, mace, bay leaves, honey, pepper, and salt. Bring just to a boil, cover, reduce the heat, and simmer gently 20 minutes, until tender.

Transfer the vegetables to a nonreactive bowl and measure the liquid. If there is more than 1 1/2 cups, return it to the saucepan and reduce by rapid boiling over high heat. Pour over the vegetables and set aside until cool. Cover the bowl and shake it gently to redistribute the vegetables in the marinade, and set aside in a cool spot for 1–2 hours before serving.

To serve, taste the marinade; if more salt is needed, combine it with the cilantro. Choop the cilantro, lemon zest, and salt together just until mixed.

Transfer the vegetables to a shallow serving bowl and pour over most of the marinade (strain it first if you prefer). Sprinkle with the cilantro mixture and serve with the lemon wedges.

Celery à la Grecque
Selino Khoriatiko

Substitute 1 head of celery for the carrots and onions and 1 tablespoon caraway seeds for the mace. Slice off the root end of the celery and rinse the sticks well. Remove the tough strings with a small sharp knife and cut the stalks on the diagonal into 2-inch lengths. Blanch 2 minutes in lightly salted boiling water, drain, and dry on paper towels.

Cauliflower à la Grecque
Kounoupithi Khoriatiko

Substitute 1 medium head of cauliflower, broken into florets, for the celery and use parsley as the garnish. Trim as much stalk as possible from the florets and cut an "X" in the base of each with a small sharp knife. Blanch 1 minute in lightly salted boiling water and drain. Simmer in the marinade for only 6 minutes, until barely soft.

Mushrooms à la Grecque
Manitaria Khoriatika

There are many versions of this popular dish, but most are pale imitations of the original Greek creation, with little of the rich mix of spicy and earthy flavors that are its hallmark. The intensity of flavor can be adjusted according to taste – for a lightly spiced dish prepare only 2 hours ahead; for a more mellow taste and texture leave overnight in the marinade; the dominant cinnamon tones can be similarly exploited or subdued.

Serves 6 as a first course, 3 as a vegetable dish

1 pound small white mushrooms
2–3 tablespoons extra virgin olive oil, or to taste
1 3-inch cinnamon stick, broken in half
2 bay leaves
1 tablespoon coriander seeds, lightly crushed
1½ cups dry white wine
Coarse-grain sea salt, to taste
1 teaspoon cracked black pepper, or to taste

For serving
Chopped fresh thyme, oregano *or* cilantro
Lemon wedges

Trim the mushroom stalks and brush or wipe the mushrooms.

Combine the olive oil, cinnamon stick, bay leaves, and coriander seeds in a heavy sauté pan large enough to hold the mushrooms in a single layer, and heat over low heat. Add the mushrooms, cover, and sweat 5 minutes, or until they have released most of their liquid and are slightly darkened and aromatic; don't let them become soft.

Bring the wine to a boil in a small nonreactive pan over high heat and reduce to 1 cup by rapid boiling. Add to the mushrooms along with the salt and pepper. Bring to a boil, then transfer to a nonreactive bowl, and set aside to cool. Cover and set aside for 2 hours in a cool place or refrigerate overnight.

To serve, transfer the mushrooms to a shallow bowl and pour (or strain) over the marinade. Season to taste with salt and pepper. Sprinkle with the thyme and serve with lemon wedges.

Note Slender leeks, green beans, or artichoke hearts, all blanched 2 minutes, or quartered cooked beets, can be prepared the same way for multi-colored variations.

Fava Beans in Grape Leaves
Fassoulakia sto Fourno

Young grape leaves appear in Crete's lively markets at the same time as fava beans, and this is the dish Cretan cooks make with the pick of the new spring crop. Since grape leaves and fava beans generally do not appear simultaneously in our own markets, brine-preserved grape leaves and green beans such as young limas make good substitutes. The leaves are not wrapped around the beans, but used to line the bottom of the baking dish and as a protective covering, they act as a flavoring agent. This dish is delicious with grilled or roasted meat or chicken.

Serves 4 to 6

....

2 pounds very young fava beans in the pod *or* young lima beans *or* other
   similar beans
About 30 fresh *or* brine-preserved grape leaves, rinsed
½ cup extra virgin olive oil, to taste
Juice of 2 small lemons
Coarse-grain sea salt *and* freshly ground black pepper, to taste

For serving
4 tablespoons finely chopped flat-leaf parsley

....

Heat the oven to 325°F. With a small paring knife, trim the ends of the beans. Remove a thin slice from each side of the fava beans, or remove the strings from limas or other beans (see **Note**). Blanch in lightly salted boiling water for 1 minute, remove with a slotted spoon, and set aside in a colander to drain. Add 6 or so grape leaves to the boiling water and blanch 5 seconds if fresh, 3 seconds if preserved; with a slotted spoon, transfer to paper towels to drain. Repeat with the remaining leaves.

Cover the bottom of a deep heavy baking dish, large enough to hold the beans in a double layer, with half the grape leaves, glossy sides down. Spread the beans over the leaves and add 4 tablespoons of the olive oil, half the lemon juice, and 1 cup water. Sprinkle with salt and pepper and lay the remaining leaves on top, glossy sides up. Bake 50 minutes, until soft; test with a sharp knife, making sure to insert the point through a bean as well as the pod. Bake 15–30 minutes longer if necessary, and sprinkle with an additional 4–8 tablespoons water if the dish seems in danger of drying out.

Discard the top layer of leaves and transfer the beans to a warm serving dish. Sprinkle with the remaining lemon juice and olive oil and cooking liquid to taste. Season with salt and pepper and sprinkle with parsley. Serve hot, warm, or at room temperature.

Variations

♦ Substitute 1½ pounds white mushrooms or 2 pounds waxy potatoes for the beans, or a mixture of both. Trim the mushroom stalks to ½ inch. Peel the potatoes if desired, cut into bite-size pieces, and cook 5 minutes in lightly salted boiling water. Bake mushrooms 25 minutes, potatoes or potatoes and mushrooms 40 minutes, until tender.

Note Small young tender beans need only the ends trimmed off; larger beans have tough strings down the sides that should be removed. To do this quickly, hold a small paring knife firmly in one hand and trim the stem end of the bean from its outside curve nearly through to the inner side; the string will come away with the stem.

Stuffed Grape Leaves with Latholemono Sauce
Dolmades me Latholemono

Dolmades – little rolls of savory rice in grape leaves – are popular all over Greece and there are endless variations on the theme. Tiny versions, called *dolmadakia*, are served as a *meze*, while the larger *dolmades* can be first or main courses. Sometimes the filling is simply rice flavored with allspice or cinnamon; sometimes it includes meat, pine nuts, currants, and fragrant herbs. *Dolmades* are not difficult to make but they do take time, so it's worth knowing that they freeze well (freeze before cooking).

Serves 8 as a first course, 4 as a main course

½ cup extra virgin olive oil, or to taste
6 scallions, trimmed, with best green parts left intact, and finely chopped
1⅓ cups long-grain rice
1 teaspoon ground cinnamon

Sea salt

1 bay leaf

2 cups Chicken Stock (page 343) *or* water

½ cup pine nuts

½ cup currants *or* small dark seedless raisins

32 medium grape leaves *or* 40 smaller leaves, fresh *or* brine-preserved, *plus* extra leaves to make 1 layer in the baking dish

1 small bunch fresh dill, coarsely chopped *or* 8 sprigs fresh mint, leaves torn into small pieces

4 tablespoons finely chopped flat-leaf parsley

Cracked black pepper, to taste

Juice of 2 large lemons

For serving
Lemon wedges

Heat 2 tablespoons of the olive oil in a heavy saucepan and sauté the scallions over low heat until soft, about 5 minutes. Add the cinnamon and rice and stir well with a wooden spoon. Add salt to taste, the bay leaf, and stock. Raise the heat and boil uncovered until the liquid has disappeared and holes appear in the surface of the rice, about 8 minutes. Stir in the pine nuts and currants with a fork and cover the saucepan with 2 layers of paper towels and a tight-fitting lid. Set aside for 15 minutes in a warm spot such as the back of the stove.

Fill a large saucepan with water and bring to a boil. Trim off the stalks from the 32 medium or 40 smaller grape leaves and set aside.

Add the remaining leaves to the boiling water, 5 or 6 at a time, and blanch 3 seconds if preserved, 5 seconds if fresh. Remove with a slotted spoon, spread between layers of paper towels, and blot dry. Line a heavy shallow nonreactive and flameproof dish or sauté pan, large enough to hold the *dolmades* in a single tightly packed layer, with these leaves, glossy sides facing down. Blanch the reserved leaves, drain, and blot dry.

Remove the bay leaf from the rice and, with a fork, stir in most of the dill, the parsley, the juice of half a lemon, and salt and pepper to taste.

Place a grape leaf on a clean work surface, glossy side down and stalk end toward your wrist. Use 1 heaping teaspoon of filling each for first course *dolmas*, 1 tablespoon filling for main course *dolmas*. Place the filling in the center of the leaf at its widest part, pull the stalk end over, and fold in both sides. Firmly roll up the package toward the point of the leaf. Repeat with the remaining leaves and rice; as you finish each *dolmas*, place it in the dish pressing tightly against the next one.

Pour over 2 tablespoons of the remaining olive oil and the juice of another half lemon and add enough water to barely reach the top of the *dolmades*.

Cover with a plate slightly smaller than the dish and place a weight (such as a large can of fruit) on top. Set the dish over medium-low heat and bring just to a boil, reduce the heat, and simmer small *dolmades* 25 minutes, larger ones 30 minutes. There should always be some liquid in the dish; if necessary add more water to barely reach the top of the *dolmades*.

Remove from the heat and, with the plate and weight still in place, set aside for 5 minutes if serving warm, or let cool.

Transfer the *dolmades* to a platter or individual plates and sprinkle with the remaining olive oil and lemon juice. Surround with the lemon wedges, or arrange them between the *dolmades,* and garnish with the remaining dill.

Note For a Cretan touch, substitute Green Grape Sauce (page 319) for half the water used to cook the *dolmades*. The sauce tenderizes the grape leaves to make lovely velvety *dolmades*.

Stuffed Grape Leaves with Avgolemono Sauce

Dolmades me Avgolemono

These *dolmades* are more substantial than the previous version, filled with lamb and rice and flavored with allspice and fresh fennel. They are especially good with a rich *avgolemono* sauce, but try them as well with the simpler *latholemono* sauce (see page 347).

Serves 8 as a first course, 4 as a main course

4 tablespoons extra virgin olive oil
1 large onion, finely chopped
½ pound lean lamb, finely ground
1 teaspoon ground allspice
Sea salt *and* freshly ground black pepper, to taste
1 cup long-grain rice
1¼ cups Light Meat Stock (page 348) *or* water
32 medium grape leaves *or* 40 smaller leaves, fresh *or* brine-preserved, *plus* extra leaves to make 1 layer in the baking dish
2 tablespoons finely chopped fresh fennel leaves *or* 2 tablespoons fresh mint leaves, torn into small pieces
1 small handful flat-leaf parsley, leaves finely chopped
Juice of 2 large lemons
2 egg yolks

Heat half the olive oil in a heavy saucepan and sauté the onion over low heat until soft, about 8 minutes. Add the meat, raise the heat, and sauté until lightly browned, breaking up any lumps with a wooden spoon. Add the allspice, salt and pepper, and rice, and cook 1 minute, stirring. Add the stock and boil uncovered until the liquid has disappeared and holes appear in the surface of the rice, about 8 minutes. Cover the saucepan with 2 layers of paper towels and a tight-fitting lid and set aside for 20–25 minutes in a warm spot such as the back of the stove.

Prepare the grape leaves and line a dish as directed on page 196.

With a fork, stir the fennel, most of the parsley, half the lemon juice, and salt and pepper into the rice. Make the *dolmades* as directed on page 196. Pour the remaining olive oil and lemon juice over the *dolmades* and add enough water to barely cover them. Cover with a plate slightly smaller than the dish and place a weight on top. Set the dish over medium-low heat and bring to a boil, reduce the heat, and simmer small *dolmades* 25 minutes, larger ones 30 minutes. There should always be enough liquid to reach the top of the *dolmades;* add more water if necessary.

Pour off 1¼ cups of the cooking liquid and strain it. Replace the plate and weight and set the dish aside in a warm spot.

Beat the egg yolks with a hand whisk or electric mixer until pale and frothy. Gradually add the remaining lemon juice and whisk 1 minute longer. Slowly add the strained cooking liquid, whisking constantly. Transfer to the top of a double boiler set over hot water and stir over low heat, using a figure-8 motion, until the sauce is thick enough to lightly coat the back of the spoon, about 6 minutes.

Arrange the *dolmades* on a warm platter or individual plates and pour over the sauce. Sprinkle with the remaining parsley and serve immediately.

Stuffed Grape Leaves and Squash Blossoms
Dolmades Kolokithokorfathes

A delight of late spring in Greece is a beautiful platter of stuffed grape leaves and stuffed squash blossoms, garnished with fresh fennel and wedges of lemon. Both are designed as tiny treats, small enough to be eaten in one mouthful, and stuffed with an aromatic flavored rice. Stuffed squash blossoms may sound a trifle exotic but do try them – they're delicious and well worth the effort. Serve these as part of a buffet or a picnic.

Serves 8

½ cup extra virgin olive oil
12 scallions, trimmed, with best green parts left intact, and finely chopped

4 tablespoons coarsely chopped fresh fennel leaves *or* 1 tablespoon ground
  fennel seed
1⅓ cups long-grain rice
Sea salt, to taste
2 cups Chicken Stock (page 343) *or* water
24 small grape leaves (each one no more than 3 inches across at its widest
  point), fresh *or* brine-preserved, *plus* extra leaves to make 1 layer in the
  baking dish
16 squash blossoms *or* additional grape leaves
1 small handful flat-leaf parsley, leaves finely chopped
Strained juice of 2 large lemons
Freshly ground black pepper, to taste

For serving
Fresh fennel sprigs, *optional*
Lemon wedges

Heat 2 tablespoons of the olive oil in a heavy saucepan and sauté the
scallions over low heat until soft, about 5 minutes. Stir in the fennel and
cook 1 minute. Add the rice, stirring with a wooden spoon to coat with the
oil. Add salt to taste and the stock, raise the heat, and boil uncovered until
the liquid has disappeared and holes appear in the surface of the rice,
about 8 minutes. Cover the saucepan with 2 layers of paper towels and a
tight-fitting lid and set aside for 20 minutes in a warm spot such as the
back of the stove.

Prepare the grape leaves and line a dish as directed on page 196 (trim
the 25 small leaves before blanching).

To prepare the squash blossoms, gently pull out the stamens, trim the
stems, and rinse them by dipping in a bowl of cold water. Shake off the
excess water and carefully wrap in a clean dish towel or use paper towels to
pat dry.

With a fork, stir the parsley, the juice of half a lemon, salt, and pepper into
the rice to make a highly-seasoned mixture with a distinct flavor of fennel.

Make the *dolmades* as directed on page 196. To fill a squash blossom,
hold it in the palm of one hand and, with your thumb, gently push 1
heaping teaspoon of stuffing inside, taking care not to break the flower.
Fold 1 petal over the stuffing, then fold in the other petals to make a secure
little parcel. Arrange in the dish with the stuffed grape leaves.

Sprinkle all the *dolmades* with 2 tablespoons of the remaining olive oil
and the juice of half a lemon and add water to barely reach the top of the
dolmades. Place a plate slightly smaller than the dish on top of the
dolmades and set a weight (such as a large can of fruit) on the plate. Place
the dish over medium-low heat and bring to a boil, reduce the heat to low,

and simmer 25 minutes. There should always be liquid in the dish; add a little more water if necessary to barely reach the top of the *dolmades*. Remove from the heat and, with the plate and weight still in place, set aside to cool at room temperature.

To serve, arrange the *dolmades* on a platter and sprinkle with the remaining olive oil and lemon juice, and salt and pepper to taste. Garnish with the fennel sprigs and the lemon wedges.

Note To store, let cool, transfer the *dolmades* to a nonreactive airtight container, and refrigerate for up to 2 days. Serve at room temperature.

Baked Eggplants with Tomatoes and Feta Cheese
Melitzanes me Feta

A slightly sweet, nutty flavor is the hallmark of this dish, and the secret lies in the quantity of olive oil used and in the preliminary cooking of the eggplant. An ideal buffet dish served hot or cold, especially with barbecued meats, this can easily be prepared for large numbers of people.

Serves 8

4 large aubergines (2–2½ pounds total)
Sea salt
¾–1 cup extra virgin olive oil, or to taste
¾ pound *feta* cheese, cut into 8 slices
½ tablespoon cracked black pepper, or to taste
4 large ripe tomatoes, skinned, seeded, and diced, juices reserved
2 tablespoons tomato paste diluted with 4 tablespoons water
1 teaspoon honey
8 bay leaves

For serving
1 small bunch flat-leaf parsley, leaves coarsely chopped

Trim the ends from the eggplants and cut lengthways in half. Sprinkle with 2 tablespoons salt and set aside for 30 minutes to "sweat."

Heat the oven to 350°F. Set a large heavy frying pan over medium heat and add 4 tablespoons of the olive oil. Thoroughly dry the eggplant with paper towels and fry half of them until the cut sides are dark golden brown and the skin is shriveled and darkened, about 12 minutes. Drain between layers of paper towels. Heat 2 tablespoons of the remaining olive oil in the frying pan and fry the remaining eggplant. Drain.

Arrange the eggplants, cut sides up, in a heavy baking dish just large enough to hold them in a single layer. Sprinkle with the pepper and place a slice of *feta* on top of each one.

Combine the tomatoes and their juices, tomato paste, honey, and remaining olive oil and spoon over the *feta* and eggplants. Place a bay leaf on top of each and add just enough water to the dish to cover the bottom. Bake uncovered for 30–40 minutes, until the eggplant is very soft. There should be about 2 cups of sauce in the dish; add more water if necessary.

Serve directly from the baking dish, leaving the bay leaves in place as garnish. Sprinkle with the lemon juice, parsley, and salt and pepper to taste. Serve hot or warm.

Note To grill eggplants, trim them, cut in half, and "sweat." Set a grill rack about 4 inches above hot coals and brush both eggplants and grill with olive oil. Grill on both sides until dark golden brown and soft. Meanwhile, heat the oven and make the tomato sauce. Drain the eggplants on paper towels, arrange in the baking dish as directed, and bake.

Baked Summer Vegetables
Briami Mystras

Magnificent baked vegetable casseroles have been part of Greek life for centuries. The ingredients may vary from season to season, but they always have a rich, satisfying character and fresh flavor. Here the vegetables are slowly baked in an onion and tomato sauce until they have absorbed most of the spicy sauce; a cheesy bread crumb topping adds a golden crusty finish. Serve with country bread, a green salad, and slices of mild *feta* cheese. It's also a perfect accompaniment to grilled meat and fish.

Serves 6

2 medium eggplants (about ³/₄ pound total)
Sea salt
2 green bell peppers, roasted and skinned (see page 343)
1 large onion, cut into quarters and thinly sliced
1 large clove garlic, finely chopped
6 large ripe tomatoes, skinned and diced, juices reserved
1 tablespoon honey
1 tablespoon ground cumin
3 tablespoons dried *rigani* (see page 13)
5 tablespoons coarsely chopped flat-leaf parsley
Freshly ground black pepper, to taste
1 pound new potatoes
1 pound zucchini, cut into ¹/₄-inch slices

5 tablespoons hot water
3/4 cup lightly toasted fresh bread crumbs
2 ounces grated *kasseri or* Parmesan cheese

For serving
Juice of 1 large lemon

....

Trim the ends from the eggplants and cut into 1 1/2-inch cubes. Sprinkle with 1 tablespoon salt and set aside in a colander to "sweat" for 30 minutes. Slice the tops off the peppers, discard the cores and seeds, rinse off any remaining seeds, and cut lengthways into 1/4-inch strips.

Heat 4 tablespoons of the olive oil in a large heavy sauté pan and cook the onion over medium-low heat until soft, about 8 minutes. Add the garlic, tomatoes and their juices, honey, cumin, *rigani,* half the parsley, salt, and pepper. Raise the heat, bring to a boil, and simmer 10 minutes, until reduced by about one third, stirring occasionally with a wooden spoon.

Heat the oven to 375°F. Place a second large heavy sauté pan over medium heat and add 4 tablespoons of the remaining olive oil. Thoroughly dry the eggplant with paper towels and fry until golden brown on all sides, about 10 minutes. Drain between layers of paper towels.

Peel the potatoes and cut into 1/4-inch slices. Arrange them in the bottom of a deep heavy baking dish. Combine the eggplant, pepper, and zucchini and spread over the potatoes. Pour over the sauce, remaining olive oil, and the hot water, firmly shake the dish to distribute the sauce, cover, and bake 15 minutes. Reduce the oven temperature to 350°F and bake 20 minutes longer. Stir the vegetables, taking care not to break the potatoes, and bake uncovered 25 minutes longer or until the potatoes are just tender.

Taste the sauce and add salt and pepper if desired. Combine the bread crumbs and cheese and sprinkle over the vegetables; with the back of a spoon gently press down on the vegetables so a little of the juices reaches the bread crumbs. Bake, uncovered, 15 minutes longer or until golden brown.

Sprinkle with the lemon juice, pepper, and the remaining parsley. Serve hot, warm, or at room temperature.

Note To make individual casseroles, divide the ingredients between 6 small casseroles. Bake covered at 375°F for 15 minutes, uncovered at 350°F for about 25 minutes.

Sweet Sour Okra with Olive Oil
Bamies Psimenes

It is thought that this beautiful little vegetable was first brought to Greece from ancient Egypt, where it had arrived via the slave routes from central Africa. Today, its distinctive, slightly sour, flavor and exquisite shape, makes okra a popular vegetable in stews and an attractive side dish to grilled fish and meats. Choose okra with care – each pod should be small, firm, and a bright pale green. Greek cooks like okra to retain its color, shape, and juices in cooking so the pods are first sprinkled with wine vinegar or lemon juice and then left in the sun for a few hours, to shrivel slightly. Serve hot, with grilled meat or fish, or with eggs, or cold, as a *meze* or side dish.

Serves 3 to 4

1 pound small young okra, rinsed
3 tablespoons freshly squeezed lemon juice
4–6 tablespoons extra virgin olive oil, or to taste
1 tablespoon light honey *or* sugar
Coarse-grain sea salt *and* freshly ground black pepper, to taste

For serving
Finely chopped flat-leaf parsley

With a paring knife, trim off the okra stems; take care not to pierce the pods or they will disintegrate in cooking.

Spread the okra on a large ceramic or glass plate and sprinkle with half the lemon juice. Set aside 2 hours, preferably in the sun.

Heat 3 tablespoons of the olive oil in a heavy sauté pan, large enough to hold the okra in a single layer. Add the okra and gently cook for 6 minutes or until the pods are very lightly browned; stir carefully once or twice. Drizzle over the honey, sprinkle with salt and pepper, and the remaining lemon juice, and add ¾ cup water to the pan. Cover and simmer 20 minutes or until the okra is tender; add a little more water to the pan if it is in danger of drying out, but do not disturb the okra.

Carefully transfer the okra and pan juices to a shallow serving dish and sprinkle with the parsley, salt, and pepper to taste, and the remaining olive oil. Serve hot, warm, or cold.

Okra and Onions in Tomato Sauce
Bamies Ladera

The secret to the magnificent taste and texture of the stove-top stews (*ladera*) of the Greek taverna kitchen is slow cooking, seasonal flavor, and plenty of olive oil. Okra, a favorite ingredient in *ladera* dishes because of its sharp flavor and great affinity with olive oil, is perfect with chicken (see page 123) or beef, or with a rich tomato sauce. The only real care needed in preparing this dish is in the preparation of the okra, to ensure it remains whole during the cooking and doesn't disintegrate into a glutinous mass. Serve warm, with country cheese, olives, and crusty bread, or cold, as a side dish to grilled meat or fish.

Serves 4

1¼ pounds fresh okra, rinsed and trimmed (see page 203)
2 tablespoons white wine vinegar
4–6 tablespoons extra virgin olive oil, or to taste
½ pound pearl onions, peeled (see page 132) *or* 1 large mild onion, quartered and thinly sliced
1 clove garlic, finely chopped
½–1 teaspoon ground coriander, to taste, *optional*
1 pound ripe tomatoes, skinned and diced, juices reserved
1 teaspoon honey *or* sugar
Coarse-grain sea salt *and* cracked black pepper, to taste
Juice of ½ small lemon

For serving
1 small bunch flat-leaf parsley, leaves coarsely chopped

Spread the okra on a glass or ceramic plate and sprinkle with the vinegar. Set aside for 2 hours, preferably in the sun.

Warm 3 tablespoons of the olive oil in a large heavy frying pan and sauté the onions over low heat until soft, about 10 minutes. Add the garlic and coriander and heat until aromatic. Add the tomatoes and their juices, honey, salt, and pepper, and bring to a low boil. Reduce the heat and simmer, uncovered, for 10 minutes, until the sauce is slightly thickened. Meanwhile, rinse the okra and pat dry with paper towels. Add to the pan with the remaining olive oil and gently simmer, uncovered, for 30 minutes or until the okra is tender but not disintegrating and most of the liquid has evaporated. Sprinkle with the lemon juice and most of the parsley and continue cooking for 10 minutes.

Leave in the pan to cool slightly. Transfer to a shallow serving dish, sprinkle with the remaining parsley, and salt and pepper to taste. Serve warm or cold.

Honey-Glazed Onions
Kremithia sto Fourno

Baked in a honey and wine mixture aromatized with pungent cloves, these onions emerge from the oven beautifully glazed in a light sauce. Meltingly soft and sweetly spicy, they are delicious with grilled or roasted meats and game.

Serves 4

1½ pounds boiling onions (about 1 inch in diameter), peeled (see Note)
2 tablespoons unsalted butter
2 tablespoons extra virgin olive oil
1 cup Mavrodaphne *or* Madeira wine *and* 1 tablespoon honey, preferably Hymettus, *or* 1 cup Chicken Stock (page 343) *and* 2 tablespoons honey, preferably Hymettus
4 cloves
Sea salt *and* freshly ground black pepper, to taste
1 small bunch flat-leaf parsley, leaves coarsely chopped
1 tablespoon finely chopped Preserved Lemons (page 18) *or* 1 tablespoon finely grated lemon zest

Heat the oven to 325°F. Arrange the onions in a heavy baking dish large enough to hold them in a single layer and dot with the butter and olive oil. Combine the wine and honey, ½ cup water, cloves, salt, and pepper in a small saucepan. Bring to a boil over medium-low heat and pour over the onions. Cover and bake 1 hour, until there is about ½ cup of light syrupy sauce and the onions are very soft.

Chop the parsley, Preserved Lemons, a pinch of salt, and a generous amount of pepper together to mix. With a wooden spoon, gently roll the onions around in the sauce to glaze, and transfer to a warm platter, discarding the cloves. Pour over any remaining sauce and sprinkle with the parsley mixture. Serve hot or warm.

Note Peeling small onions is easier if they are blanched first: Slice the root end off each onion and remove the feathery outside layer of skin. Blanch the onions in boiling water for 5 minutes, drain, and peel.

Zucchini with Olive Oil and Herbs

Kolokithaki me Elaiolatho

When preparing this as a side dish for grilled or roasted meat or fish, I often bake a few extra zucchini – the next day they provide an instant *meze* or salad or make an unusual omelet filling for a quick and tasty lunch.

Serves 4

1½ pounds small zucchini (2–3 inches long)
4 tablespoons extra virgin olive oil, or to taste
Juice of 2 lemons
Sea salt *and* freshly ground black pepper, to taste
4 tablespoons finely chopped flat-leaf parsley
1 tablespoon dried *rigani* (see page 13), briefly pounded in a mortar

Heat the oven to 350°F.

Trim the zucchini and rub with a clean dish towel to remove any fuzz. Arrange in a heavy shallow baking dish large enough to hold them in a single layer. Pour over the olive oil and half the lemon juice and add ½ cup water. Sprinkle with salt and pepper and bake uncovered for 10 minutes. Roll the zucchini around in the cooking liquid to coat, reduce the oven temperature to 300°F, and bake 40 minutes longer, until the zucchini are barely soft. Roll them around in the cooking liquid once or twice during baking, and add a few tablespoons water if needed – there should always be at least 4 tablespoons liquid in the dish.

Transfer the zucchini to a warm platter and sprinkle with a few tablespoons of the cooking liquid, the remaining lemon juice, the parsley, *rigani,* and olive oil, salt, and pepper to taste. Serve hot, warm, or cold.

Note To serve as a *meze* or salad, refrigerate the zucchini in the cooking liquid, covered, in a nonreactive container for up to 24 hours. Remove from the liquid and cut into ½-inch slices. Sprinkle with lemon juice, olive oil, coarse-grain sea salt, cracked black pepper, a generous amount of finely chopped parsley, and *rigani.*

To use as a filling for an omelet, remove the zucchini from the cooking liquid, cut into thin slices, and drain on paper towels. Add to a barely set omelet, with a little finely chopped parsley, dried basil, freshly ground pepper, and a few tablespoons grated *feta* cheese.

Potatoes in a Clay Pot
Patates sto Fourno

The tradition of cooking in unglazed cooking pots dates from the Minoan period, the earliest Western civilization, but it thrives in modern Greece, and with good reason. Vegetables cooked this way need only to be scrubbed, no special care is needed in baking them, and they not only acquire a unique earthy flavor but also retain almost all their vitamins and minerals. Potatoes cooked in a clay pot develop a delightful slightly sweet flavor, making them especially good in salads or as a side dish for a delicately flavored main course such as Baked Sole in Grape Leaves (page 102). This cooking method is also excellent for beets – during baking their natural crimson color deepens to a rich dark purple and the texture turns velvety smooth.

Serves 4

1½ pounds small new potatoes of a similar size

For serving
Coarse-grain sea salt *and* cracked black pepper, to taste
Freshly squeezed lemon juice
1–2 tablespoons extra virgin olive oil *or* unsalted butter
Finely chopped flat-leaf parsley, *optional*

Prepare the pot following the manufacturer's instructions or immerse it for 5 minutes in warm water. Pour out the water, add the potatoes, and cover with the lid.

Place in a cold oven and set the oven temperature to 325°F. Bake 1¼–1¾ hours or until the potatoes are tender.

Transfer to a warm bowl and sprinkle with the salt and pepper, lemon juice, olive oil, and parsley.

Note You can bake the potatoes at a higher heat (425°F) for a shorter time (50 minutes) or at a lower heat (250°F) for a longer time (2 hours) if necessary, but always start with a cold oven. For easier cleaning, immerse the pot in hot water as soon as you remove the potatoes from it.

Beets in a Clay Pot
Panzaria sto Fourno

Prepare the pot as directed on page 207. Trim the stem and root ends from 6 small beets, about 2 inches in diameter. Scrub with a stiff brush under cold running water, taking care not to break the skins. Add to the pot, cover, and place in a cold oven. Set the temperature to 325°F and bake 1½ hours or until the beets are tender.

When cool enough to handle, peel the beets and cut into quarters or slices. Sprinkle with sea salt and cracked pepper, the juice of 1 small lemon, extra virgin olive oil to taste, 1 tablespoon fresh oregano or dried *rigani,* and finely chopped flat-leaf parsley. These are delicious with *pilafi, feta* cheese, or grilled swordfish.

Note If you are using the beets in a salad, season while they are still warm.

Garlic Potatoes with Juniper Berries
Patates Skorthou

This is a dish for those who like strong flavors – the taste of these tiny baked potatoes is anything but subtle. The finished dish has a bold expressive character and it's perfect with herbed roast chicken (see page 121) or pork dishes. Real garlic lovers can press out the soft centers of the baked cloves and spread them on the potatoes or on toasted bread.

Serves 4

3 tablespoons extra virgin olive oil
2 tablespoons dried juniper berries, lightly crushed
8 large cloves garlic
1½ pounds small new potatoes

For serving
Juice of 1 small lemon
Coarse-grain sea salt *and* cracked black pepper, to taste
Finely chopped fresh oregano *or* dried *rigani* (see page 13)
Triangles of toasted whole wheat bread, *optional*

Heat the oven to 350°F.

Pour the olive oil into a heavy shallow baking dish large enough to hold the potatoes in a single layer. Sprinkle the juniper berries over the oil and place the dish in the oven for a few minutes to warm. Trim off the stem ends of the garlic cloves and rub off any feathery outer skin. Place the potatoes and garlic in the warm dish and roll them in the olive oil to lightly coat. Bake 10 minutes and roll the potatoes and garlic in the olive oil once more. Reduce the oven temperature to 300°F and bake uncovered for 50 minutes or until the potatoes are just tender.

Roll the potatoes in the olive oil to coat once more and transfer to a warm platter. Sprinkle with the lemon juice, salt and pepper, and oregano. Serve hot or warm, with toast, if desired.

Fava Bean Salad with Fennel and Black Olives
Fassoulakia Salata me Elies

Sweet young fava beans and fresh fennel usually appear in the markets at the same time and their very individual flavors complement each other well. This enticing salad is particularly good with sausages, egg dishes, or cold roast pork.

Serves 3 to 4

3 pounds fava beans in the pod
Juice of 1 large lemon, or to taste
³/₈ cup extra virgin olive oil, or to taste
Coarse-grain sea salt, to taste
1 teaspoon cracked black pepper, or to taste
12 Amfissa *or* other mild black olives, cut in half and pitted
1 small red *or* mild onion, quartered and thinly sliced
5 tablespoons coarsely chopped fresh fennel *or* flat-leaf parsley

Shell the beans and reserve 2 tender pods. Blanch the pods and beans in lightly salted boiling water for 5 minutes, drain, discard the pods, and rinse the beans. Remove the skins from the beans and place the beans in a nonreactive bowl. Add the lemon juice, olive oil, salt, and pepper, and gently stir to mix. Cover and set aside for 1–2 hours.

To serve, add most of the olives, onion, and fennel to the beans and season to taste with salt, pepper, lemon juice, and/or olive oil. Transfer to a platter, and garnish with the remaining olives, onion, and fennel.

Note Although it is not necessary to remove the skins of very young fava beans, Greek cooks prefer to remove the opaque skins to reveal the pretty shade of green within. Without their skins, fava beans also are easier to digest and have a subtly different flavor.

Variation

♦ Substitute 1½ pounds green beans, such as string beans, for the fava beans. Trim both ends of the beans and, if necessary, with a small paring knife remove the strings along both sides. Cut into 1½-inch pieces, blanch in lightly salted boiling water for 5 minutes or until barely tender, and rinse. Proceed as directed above.

Green Lentil Salad

Fakes Salata

The ancient Greeks believed that the benign influence of green lentils could greatly improve a grouchy temper – I cannot verify this claim, but I have seen smiles of pleasure creep over the faces of my guests when they try this salad! Cumin, parsley, mint, and garlic enhance the rustic tones of the humble lentil and a *latholemono* dressing deepens all the flavors.

Serves 8 to 10 as a *meze*, 4 as a salad

10 ounces dried green lentils, picked over and rinsed
1 tablespoon cumin seeds, lightly pounded in a small mortar
1 small red *or* mild onion, cut into thin rings
Juice of 1 lemon
Coarse-grain sea salt *and* cracked black pepper, to taste
1 small bunch flat-leaf parsley, leaves coarsely chopped
2 tablespoons fresh mint leaves *or* 1 teaspoon dried mint
1 large clove garlic, minced
4 tablespoons finely chopped Preserved Lemons (page 18)
4 tablespoons extra virgin olive oil
2 tablespoons Strained Yogurt (page 7)

For serving
Large pinch of sumac, cayenne pepper, *or* paprika

Place the lentils in a large saucepan and add cold water to cover by 3 inches. Bring to a boil, cover, reduce the heat, and simmer until soft but not disintegrating, about 30 minutes. Drain, gently shake the colander once or twice, and set aside to dry. Warm the cumin seeds in a small dry frying pan over low heat until aromatic, about 1 minute.

Combine the onion, half the lemon juice and cumin, and a large pinch of salt in a nonreactive bowl. Chop 1 tablespoon of the parsley and the mint leaves together just to mix; add to the onion. Set aside.

Mix together the garlic, most of the Preserved Lemons, the remaining cumin, half the remaining parsley, and a pinch of salt. Combine with the lentils, remaining parsley and lemon juice, the olive oil, and salt and pepper

Opposite: **Baked Summer Vegetables**

to taste. Carefully stir to mix.

Transfer to a platter and sprinkle with the onion and its marinade. Spoon the yogurt over the center and sprinkle with the remaining Preserved Lemons and parsley and the sumac. Serve at room temperature.

Note The lentils can be cooked and combined with their flavorings a day ahead, but do not marinate the onion until a few minutes before serving.

Black-Eyed Peas with Capers
Fassolia me Kapari

A taverna favorite, this highly flavored dish is eaten as a quick snack, a *meze*, or a side dish with grilled meats. The beans are mixed with a lovely sweet-sour sauce, piquant with plump capers, and a bed of arugula leaves supplies a refreshing complement. This dish can be prepared several hours ahead.

Serves 8 as a *meze*, 4 as a vegetable dish

½ pound dried black-eyed peas, soaked for 6–8 hours in cold water to cover
1 tablespoon aromatic honey, such as Hymettus
3 tablespoons aged red wine vinegar, or to taste
Coarse-grain sea salt *and* cracked black pepper, to taste
5 tablespoons extra virgin olive oil, or to taste
3 tablespoons capers, rinsed and coarsely chopped if large
4 tablespoons finely chopped flat-leaf parsley

For serving
1 small bunch arugula leaves, torn into bite-size pieces *or* 1 small bunch watercress, sprigs only
1 small red *or* mild onion, cut into thin rings
1 cup Strained Yogurt (page 7)

Place the beans in a saucepan with cold water to cover. Bring to a boil, drain, and rinse out the saucepan. Return the beans to the pan, add cold water to cover by 3 inches, and bring to a boil. Cover, reduce the heat, and simmer 20–30 minutes or until tender; take care not to overcook. Drain and set aside in a colander for a few minutes to dry.

Combine the honey, vinegar, and salt and pepper in a large bowl and gradually whisk in the olive oil. Add the beans, capers, and parsley, and mix with a spoon. Season with vinegar, olive oil, salt and/or pepper.

Line the edges of a platter or shallow bowl with the arugula leaves and place the beans in the center. Scatter over the onion and serve the yogurt separately.

Opposite: **Macaronia with Chicken and Wild Greens**

Summer Bean Salad
Kalokherini Salata Fassolion

In Greece dried beans and peas are not limited to winter dishes, but appear year-round in various guises – and there's a very good reason for this. At the height of the Greek summer the daytime temperatures are such that slaving over a hot stove is not an activity undertaken with enthusiasm. This is the time to take maximum advantage of the communal village oven. Food preparation can be done in the cool early morning and the main meal of the day taken to the *fournos* for baking; it's common practice to take to the oven not just a meat dish, but also a pot of beans to be baked alongside it. If the beans are not eaten that day they make a lovely cold salad for the next. In this recipe the country flavor of the beans is complemented by the sweet freshness of juicy ripe tomatoes, peppery watercress or purslane, and the perfume of bay leaves, thyme, and parsley. Serve this pretty dish as a *meze*, with crusty bread as a light lunch, or as a side dish for grilled meat, chicken, or liver.

Serves 12 as a *meze*, 6 to 8 as a salad or vegetable dish

10 ounces dried cannellini *or* white haricot beans, soaked for 6–12 hours in cold water to cover
1 onion, peeled and stuck with 2 cloves
1 small carrot, cut into 3 pieces
1 stick celery, cut into 3 pieces
2 bay leaves
2 large sprigs parsley
Juice of 1 large lemon
½ cup extra virgin olive oil
Coarse-grain sea salt *and* cracked black pepper, to taste
4 large ripe tomatoes, skinned and diced
Large pinch of sugar
1 large clove garlic, finely chopped
2 tablespoons fresh thyme, finely chopped *or* 1 tablespoon dried thyme, crumbled
1 small bunch watercress, leaves only, *or* 24 small sprigs purslane

For serving
1 small red *or* mild onion, cut into thin rings
24 Elitses *or* 12 Niçoise olives, drained

Place the beans in a saucepan and add cold water to cover. Bring to a boil, drain, and rinse out the saucepan. Return the beans to the saucepan along with the onion, carrot, celery, bay leaves, parsley, and water to cover by 4 inches. Bring to a boil, cover, reduce the heat, and simmer 50 minutes or until the beans are tender but not disintegrating. Drain and set aside in a colander for a few minutes to dry.

Combine the beans, half the lemon juice and olive oil, a large pinch of salt, and 1 teaspoon pepper in a large bowl. Stir to mix, taking care not to break up the beans. Cover and set aside for up to 1 hour.

Place the tomatoes in a strainer over a bowl and sprinkle with the sugar and a pinch of salt. Set aside.

Whisk together the remaining lemon juice, garlic, thyme, a large pinch of salt, and pepper to taste in a small nonreactive bowl. Add the remaining olive oil in a thin steady stream, whisking constantly. Add to the beans along with the watercress and tomatoes, and season to taste.

Transfer to a platter and sprinkle with the onion and olives. Serve at room temperature.

Note To bake, soak the beans for 6–12 hours in cold water to cover, drain, and place in a large saucepan with cold water to cover. Bring to a boil, drain, and transfer to a large deep baking dish. Add the onion, carrot, celery, bay leaves, parsley, and water to cover by 4 inches. Cover and bake 3–4 hours at 250°F or 2 hours at 350°F (the temperature can be varied to suit your oven schedule). Or, to reduce the baking time by 30 minutes, bring to a boil before placing the baking dish in the oven.

Country Salad
Khoriatiki Salata

No Greek table is complete without a salad; unfortunately, the "Greek salads" served to tourists often fall very short of the real thing. *Khoriatiki salata* is authentic, and it changes with the seasons. In summer the main ingredients are tomatoes, cucumbers, salad greens, and bell peppers; in winter thinly shredded cabbage is dominant. To these are added crumbly *feta* cheese, local black olives, capers, perfumed *rigani,* and a well-flavored olive oil. Present this salad on a good-sized platter and provide warm bread for your guests to dip into the flavorful juices.

Serves 6 to 8

1 large cucumber

4 large ripe tomatoes, skinned if desired

1/2 teaspoon sugar

Coarse-grain sea salt, to taste

1 small green bell pepper, roasted and skinned (see page 343), seeds wiped off, and cut lengthways into thin strips

1 large handful salad greens, such as watercress *or* purslane sprigs *or* bite-
   size pieces of arugula leaves, endive, *or* romaine lettuce
1 small red *or* mild onion, cut into thin rings
12–16 Kalamata olives, drained
8 *toursi* peppers, homemade (see page 326), bottled, *or* drained, *optional*
1/2 pound *feta* cheese, drained and crumbled into large pieces
2 tablespoons small capers, drained
3 tablespoons dried *rigani* (see page 13)
4 tablespoons finely chopped flat-leaf parsley
1/2 cup extra virgin olive oil, or to taste
Strained juice of 1 small lemon, *optional*
Cracked black pepper, to taste

Trim and peel the cucumber. Cut in half lengthways, then into 1/2-inch slices to make half moons. Core the tomatoes and cut into wedges. Sprinkle with the sugar and salt and set aside for 15 minutes. Spread the pepper strips on paper towels to dry.

Arrange the greens around the edge of a platter or shallow serving bowl. Make a circle of tomatoes on the inner part of this border of greens, and arrange a circle of the cucumbers inside it. Sprinkle over the bell pepper, onion, olives, and *toursi* peppers. Pile the cheese in the center and sprinkle with the capers. Chop the *rigani* and parsley together to mix, and sprinkle over the salad, along with the olive oil, lemon juice, and pepper.

Note For a winter salad substitute 1 small head of white or green cabbage (about 1 pound) for the tomatoes and cucumber. Core and rinse the cabbage, then slice very thinly or shred with a large-holed grater. Lightly mix together the cabbage and salad greens and arrange on a platter. Serve as described above.

Traditional Tomato Salad
Domata Salata Patroparadoti

Thick wedges of sweet juicy tomatoes, crumbly *feta* cheese, richly flavored olives, fruity olive oil, and aromatic hillside herbs make a distinctively Greek combination. This salad, the centerpiece of every taverna table in summer, is the first dish I order each time I enter Greece – just to prove to myself that I'm really there.

Serves 4

6 large ripe tomatoes, skinned if desired
Coarse-grain sea salt *and* cracked black pepper, to taste
1/2 teaspoon sugar

6 scallions, trimmed, with the best green parts left intact, and thinly sliced
1 small bunch flat-leaf parsley, leaves coarsely chopped
12 Kalamata olives, drained
2/3 cup crumbled *feta* cheese
2 tablespoons dried *rigani* (see page 13), briefly pounded in a small mortar,
  or 3 tablespoons fresh oregano leaves
6 tablespoons extra virgin olive oil, or to taste
1/2 tablespoon freshly squeezed lemon juice, *optional*

Core the tomatoes, cut into wedges, and arrange on a platter. Sprinkle with salt and pepper and the sugar, loosely cover, and set aside for 1 hour.

To serve, sprinkle the scallions, parsley, olives, and *feta* over the tomatoes. Sprinkle the *rigani*, olive oil, and lemon juice over the salad, add olive oil and/or pepper to taste, and serve at once.

Tomato Salad with Arugula and Tiny Olives
Domatosalata me Rokka ke Elies

Arugula (*rokka*), said to be a native of the Greek islands, is mentioned frequently in myth and legend and still grows wild in the Greek countryside. Be sure to choose arugula that's crisp and bright green. With its slightly bitter, mustardy flavor, arugula has a wonderful affinity with tomatoes, amply demonstrated by this summer salad. It's especially good with cheese dishes.

Serves 4

4–6 large ripe tomatoes, skinned if desired
Coarse-grain sea salt *and* cracked black pepper, to taste
1/2 teaspoon sugar
1 small bunch arugula, leaves trimmed and torn into large pieces
1 small red onion, cut into thin rings
24 Elitses *or* Niçoise olives, drained
1/2 tablespoon freshly squeezed lemon juice, *optional*
6 tablespoons extra virgin olive oil, or to taste

Core the tomatoes, cut into wedges, and sprinkle with salt and pepper and the sugar. Cover and set aside for 1 hour.

To serve, spread the arugula on a platter and arrange the tomatoes on top. Scatter over the onion and olives and sprinkle with the lemon juice, olive oil, and pepper. Serve immediately.

Orange Salad Cretan-Style
Salata Kritiki

Folklore has it that the Lasithi plateau on the island of Crete is the birthplace of watercress, and the Cretans certainly are very fond of its peppery bite. Watercress appears in a variety of classic recipes, including this vibrantly colorful traditional favorite.

Serves 6

....

4 small beets, cooked in a clay pot (see page 208), peeled, and cut into
  matchstick strips
Juice of 1 small lemon
6 tablespoons extra virgin olive oil, or to taste
Coarse-grain sea salt *and* cracked black pepper, to taste
3 large navel oranges
1 large bunch watercress, sprigs only
½ pound *feta* cheese, drained and cut into ½-inch cubes
12 Elitses *or* Niçoise olives, drained
2 tablespoons dried *rigani* (see page 13), briefly pounded in a small mortar

....

Combine the beets, most of the lemon juice, 2 tablespoons of the olive oil, and salt and pepper in a nonreactive bowl. Cover and set aside.

Peel the oranges and remove any white pith with a sharp knife. Cut the oranges crosswise into ¼-inch slices. Remove the pithy centers with the point of a knife. Spread the slices on a plate, tightly cover, and refrigerate until chilled.

To serve, line the edges of a chilled serving platter with the watercress and lay the orange slices in a single overlapping layer on the inside edge of this border. Make a circle of the beets inside the oranges and drizzle their marinade over. Place the *feta* in the center of the platter. Sprinkle the oranges with a little salt, and the beets and cheese with the *rigani* and olives. Sprinkle the remaining lemon juice and olive oil and pepper over the salad and serve at once.

Green Salads
Prasines Salatikes

Contrary to popular opinion, a green salad course did not originate with the French or the Italians but with the ancient Greeks. It was the custom to end a great feast with a simple salad, to refresh the palate after the excesses of a rich and heavy meal and, it was believed, to induce drowsiness (although we might suspect that the drowsiness had more to do with the copious quantities of wine consumed).

When Greeks order a green salad they expect to be served a traditional bowl of either romaine lettuce or one of a variety of wild greens such as purslane, watercress, chicory, or young dandelions. With the exception of those composed of the delicately sweet romaine lettuce, Greek salads have in common an earthy, slightly bitter, flavor that's much appreciated by the peoples of the eastern Mediterranean. This special flavor derives from the particular character of the soil of the region and cannot really be reproduced here. But in our markets we can occasionally find purslane, dandelion, and several varieties of chicory and, more frequently, arugula and watercress. Romaine lettuce is usually available year-round: In the spring, when it is at its best, use the whole head of lettuce for these salads; in other seasons select just the tender sweet heart. The natural astringency of these greens finds perfect partners in the mellow richness of olive oil and the simple flavors of freshly squeezed lemon juice or red wine vinegar and sea salt.

Green Salad with Feta Cheese and Olives
Salatika me Feta

A refreshing and popular salad, perfect for a simple lunch or a side dish. When a variety of greens is available I like to make it with hearts of romaine lettuce, escarole lettuce, watercress, rocket, and tender young spinach leaves in about equal proportions. Be sure to use good-quality mild *feta* cheese or firm and crumbly goat's cheese.

Serves 6 to 8
....

2 small heads romaine lettuce *or* 2 hearts of larger heads *or* 3 handfuls of a
    mixture of young spinach leaves, watercress sprigs, curly endive, young
    sorrel, escarole lettuce, arugula, and young dandelion leaves

Strained juice of 1 small lemon, or to taste

Coarse-grain sea salt *and* cracked black pepper, to taste

5 tablespoons extra virgin olive oil, or to taste

1 small bunch flat-leaf parsley, leaves coarsely chopped

18 Kalamata olives *or* other Greek black *or* purple olives

½ pound mild *feta* cheese, cut into ½-inch cubes

6 scallions, trimmed, the best green parts left intact, and thinly sliced, *or* 1
    small red onion, quartered and thinly sliced

3 tablespoons dried *rigani* (see page 13)
....

Prepare the greens (see recipe below).

Combine the lemon juice and salt and pepper in a nonreactive bowl. Whisk in the olive oil in a thin steady stream. Combine the greens, parsley, olives, *feta,* and scallions in a serving bowl and pour over the dressing. Toss with a wooden spoon and fork, taking care to break up the cheese as little as possible. Sprinkle with the *rigani* and serve.

Easter Green Salad with Latholemono Sauce
Salatika Paskhalina

A classic salad of mixed greens, scallions, and Preserved Lemons, scented with fresh dill and parsley and tossed in an olive oil and lemon juice dressing. This is one of the salads on the traditional Easter table.

Serves 4

2 small heads of romaine lettuce *or* 2 handfuls of curly endive, escarole lettuce, young dandelion leaves, young spinach, young sorrel, arugula, *and/or* watercress *or* purslane sprigs (see page 220)

6 scallions, trimmed, the best green parts left intact

Strained juice of ½ small lemon, or more to taste

1 small handful fresh dill, coarsely chopped *or* 1 teaspoon dill seeds (soaked for a few minutes in the lemon juice)

Coarse-grain sea salt *and* freshly ground black pepper, to taste

4 tablespoons extra virgin olive oil, or to taste

1 small bunch flat-leaf parsley, leaves coarsely chopped

2 tablespoons finely chopped Preserved Lemons (page 18) *or* ½ tablespoon finely grated lemon zest, blanched in boiling water for 5 seconds and drained

Discard any stalks and imperfect leaves from the greens, rinse well, and tear into large bite-size pieces. Spin dry in a salad spinner or shake off any excess water and loosely wrap in a clean dish towel. Refrigerate for up to 12 hours.

To serve, cut the scallions lengthways into quarters, then into 1-inch lengths. Combine the lemon juice (and dill seeds) and salt and pepper in a nonreactive bowl and gradually whisk in the olive oil. Combine the greens, scallions, fresh dill, parsley, and Preserved Lemons in a serving bowl, and pour the *latholemono* sauce over. Toss with a wooden spoon and fork and add lemon juice, salt, and/or pepper to taste. Serve immediately.

Note Greek cooks take pride in slicing romaine lettuce as thinly as possible. This does indeed produce a sophisticated salad but also results in the loss of much vitamin C contained in the leaves. I prefer to tear the green leaves, minimizing the loss of this delicate vitamin.

Island Green Salad
Salatika Nisiotika

Escarole is now sometimes available in our stores, and its flavor is very similar to that of the wild greens popular throughout Greece and the islands. Its tender, mildly astringent inner leaves are a delicious addition to a green salad. If you cannot find these bitter greens add a finely sliced Belgian endive or a few beautiful deep crimson radicchio leaves to give your salad an intriguing bite and lift it out of the ordinary. Choose Belgian endives with tightly closed heads, and buy the freshest escarole greens you can find – the flavor changes to an unpleasant bitterness once they're past their peak. For this popular island salad choose several contrasting types of salad greens. Freshly squeezed lemon juice is the perfect dressing – as a general rule, the more bitter the greens, the more lemon juice you'll need.

Serves 6 to 8

3 handfuls watercress, escarole, young spinach leaves, curly endive, young
    dandelion, young sorrel, radicchio, purslane, romaine lettuce, *and/or*
    arugula
2 slices whole wheat bread, crusts removed and cut into $\frac{1}{2}$-inch cubes
Coarse-grain sea salt *and* freshly ground black pepper, to taste
4 tablespoons extra virgin olive oil, or to taste
1 large clove garlic, cut into 2 or 3 pieces
2 tablespoons finely chopped Preserved Lemons (page 18) *plus* 2
    tablespoons of their oil (see Note)
Juice of $\frac{1}{2}$ small lemon, or to taste
1 small bunch flat-leaf parsley, leaves coarsely chopped
24 Elitses *or* Niçoise olives, drained
1 small red onion, quartered and thinly sliced
3 tablespoons fresh herbs such as marjoram, basil, *or* oregano *or* 2
    tablespoons dried *rigani* (see page 13)

Prepare the greens (see page 218).

Sprinkle the bread cubes with salt and a generous amount of pepper. Warm half the olive oil in a large heavy frying pan and sauté the garlic over low heat until it becomes aromatic, 2–3 minutes. Remove with a slotted spoon and discard. Raise the heat to medium and fry the bread cubes until golden brown on all sides. Drain between layers of paper towels.

Combine the Preserved Lemons and their oil, lemon juice, and pepper to taste, in a nonreactive bowl, and gradually whisk in the remaining olive oil.

Combine the greens, parsley, olives, onion, herbs, and croutons in a serving bowl. Pour over the dressing and toss with a wooden spoon and fork. Add salt and pepper, olive oil, and/or lemon juice to taste and serve at once.

Note You can substitute the juice of 1 whole lemon plus 2 tablespoons extra virgin olive oil for the Preserved Lemons, oil, and juice of ½ a lemon if necessary.

Purslane Salad
Salatika Glistritha

If you have a garden, purslane is very easy to grow and it can be made into a wonderfully refreshing salad, either on its own or with other salad greens for variety in taste and texture. Or try adding other vegetables to the greens, such as beets, potatoes, young fava beans, tomatoes, or chickpeas and other dried beans.

Serves 4

....

2 large handfuls purslane, sprigs only *or* 1 small handful purslane, sprigs only *and* 2 handfuls arugula, escarole, romaine lettuce, *and/or* young spinach leaves
2 scallion, trimmed, the best green parts left intact, and thinly sliced, *optional*
Coarse-grain sea salt *and* cracked black pepper, to taste
Strained juice of 1 lemon, or to taste
5 tablespoons extra virgin olive oil, or to taste

....

Thoroughly rinse the purslane and remove the small fleshy leaves in clusters (the stalks are easily broken with your thumbnail). Prepare the greens (see page 218).

Combine the greens and scallions in a salad bowl and sprinkle with salt and pepper, lemon juice, and olive oil. Toss using a wooden spoon and fork and add salt, pepper, and/or lemon juice to taste. Serve immediately.

Purslane and Young Beets
Salatika Glistritha ke Panzaria

Sweet young beets and crunchy peppery purslane make an appealing combination. With its pretty crimson-green contrast, this is an attractive side dish for grilled meat, chicken, or fish and egg dishes. Other Mediterranean greens such as arugula, watercress, young dandelion leaves, or escarole can be substituted for the purslane.

Serves 4

3 medium young beets, baked in a clay pot (see page 208) or boiled, and
  peeled
Generous pinch of ground cloves
Coarse-grain sea salt *and* cracked black pepper, to taste
Strained juice of 1 large lemon
6 tablespoons extra virgin olive oil, or to taste
2 handfuls of purslane
2 scallions, white parts only, thinly sliced

Cut the beets into matchstick strips. Place in a nonreactive bowl,
sprinkle with the cloves, salt and pepper, and half the lemon juice and olive
oil. Gently toss together, taking care not to break the beets. Cover and set
aside for 1 hour or refrigerate for up to 4 hours.

Thoroughly rinse the purslane and remove the small fleshy leaves in
clusters.

Combine the beets, purslane, and remaining lemon juice and olive oil in
a salad bowl. Add salt and pepper to taste, sprinkle with the scallions, and
serve immediately.

Wild Greens
Agria Khorta

To Greeks *khorta* means green vegetables or wild greens, sometimes even
including grass; to compound the confusion wild greens are occasionally
called wild herbs, and all these may be called *salatika*! For the sake of
clarity, here the term refers only to wild leaf greens such as mustard,
dandelions, and chicory, and green leafy vegetables (such as beets and
turnip greens and radish tops).

Young tender leaves may be used in green salads but the most popular
method of preparing *khorta* is to boil the greens and serve as a vegetable,
warm or at room temperature, dressed with olive oil and vinegar. Crusty
bread, yogurt, country cheeses, and olives are traditional accompaniments.
Khorta is also a favorite filling for pies and a delicious addition to
casseroles.

After the first autumn rains wild greens grow in abundance on the
hillsides and in the fields and the sight of village women picking their
favorites for the family meal is common; during the season Greek markets
also stock many different varieties of *khorta*. Among them is tender *vlita*,
known here as amaranth greens and sometimes available in speciality stores
and markets. Some Asian markets offer purple or water spinach, which has
a similar sweet/sour flavor and makes a delicious substitute for spinach in
Cretan pies (see page 59). Purslane, dandelion greens, radish tops, turnip

greens, beet greens, ruby chard, and sprouting broccoli are all occasionally available.

Wild greens continue to grow in Greece throughout the winter and short spring. Wild chicory (*radiki*), in particular, is at its best in March and April, just before its clear blue flowers appear, and a bowl of this bitter green has pride of place as an accompaniment to the Paschal Lamb on the traditional Easter table. Come early summer, however, the dry season and a shortage of water means the absence of the traditional and healthy *khorta* dishes from Greek tables until the autumn.

Wild Greens Salad
Khorta Salatika

The combination of bitter greens, mustard, vinegar, olive oil, and sea salt creates a delicious explosion of flavors in this salad. Choose only fresh young tender leaves and tear them into pieces, rather than chopping, to preserve as much vitamin C as possible. Cast-iron pots produce an unpleasant flavor in *khorta* and also reduce the valuable vitamin content, so always cook them in a stainless steel or enameled saucepan; wild greens do not shrink in cooking as much as cultivated greens.

Serves 4

1¼ pounds wild greens such as turnip greens, radish tops, amaranth
    greens, water spinach, ruby chard, *or* mustard greens
½ teaspoon Dijon mustard
2–3 tablespoons aged red wine vinegar, to taste, *or* juice of 1 small lemon
5 tablespoons extra virgin olive oil, or to taste
Coarse-grain sea salt *and* cracked black pepper, to taste

Rinse the greens in several changes of cold water. Remove any tough stalks from the turnip greens and radish tops and tear the leaves into bite-size pieces. Break off the tender sprigs of leaves from the amaranth greens, water spinach, or mustard greens and discard any tougher stalks.

Steam the greens, or place in a saucepan, add 4 tablespoons boiling water, and cook, stirring once or twice with a fork: Amaranth greens and young ruby chard take only 1–2 minutes, turnip greens and radish tops take 3–4 minutes, and water spinach and mustard around 5 minutes – take care not to overcook. Drain well in a colander, pressing the greens against the sides with a wooden spoon.

To serve, combine the Dijon mustard and vinegar and whisk in the olive oil. Pour over the greens and sprinkle with a generous amount of salt and pepper. Serve warm or at room temperature.

Beet Greens Salad
Salatika Panzaria

Village cooks would not dream of throwing away the crisp green leaves of young beets. Instead they cook them (reserving the vitamin-rich cooking liquid for soup) and turn them into this nutrient-packed salad.

Serves 3

Fresh green leaves from 6 young beets
4 tablespoons boiling water
Juice of 1 small lemon *or* 2 tablespoons aged red wine vinegar
4 tablespoons extra virgin olive oil, or to taste
1 teaspoon dried *rigani* (see page 13), briefly pounded in a small mortar
$\frac{1}{2}$ teaspoon coarse-grain sea salt, or to taste
Cracked black pepper, to taste

Remove the thicker stalks from the beet greens but leave tender thin stalks intact. Rinse well, and tear into bite-size pieces.

Place in a stainless steel or enameled saucepan, add the boiling water, cover, and boil until barely tender, about 2 minutes. Drain in a colander, pressing the greens against the sides with a wooden spoon to extract as much moisture as possible.

Transfer to a platter and gently separate the leaves with a fork. Sprinkle with the lemon juice, olive oil, *rigani,* salt, and pepper. Serve warm or at room temperature.

Dandelion Greens Salad
Radiki Salatika

Most Greek markets boast several varieties of dandelion greens and those snapped up the most quickly are always the wild ones. Our own garden dandelions are often tough and not usually suitable for cooking, but some speciality shops sell cultivated dandelion greens in season and they make a delicious *khorta.*

Serves 4

1 pound young dandelion leaves
$\frac{1}{2}$ cup boiling water
1 small clove garlic, finely chopped
Juice of 1 small lemon, or to taste
4 tablespoons extra virgin olive oil

Coarse-grain sea salt *and* cracked black pepper, to taste

Discard the coarse dandelion stalks, thoroughly rinse the leaves, and tear the leaves into 2-to-3-inch pieces.

Place in a stainless steel or enameled saucepan, and add the boiling water. Cover, and boil 1–2 minutes. Drain well in a colander, pressing the greens against the sides with a wooden spoon.

Transfer to a platter and gently separate the leaves with a fork. Whisk together the garlic, lemon juice, and olive oil and pour over the greens. Sprinkle generously with salt and pepper and serve warm or at room temperature.

Note If you use wild dandelion leaves, blanch them in boiling water for 1 minute to remove bitterness and drain before boiling a second time.

PILAFS AND PASTAS

Pilafi ke Macaronia

Savory rice dishes are known in Greece as *pilafi*. The rice is always cooked according to a basic method; to it are added meat, vegetables, or fish and one of a range of aromatic sauces to create any number of variations.

For any pilaf dish good-quality long-grain rice, such as Carolina, is essential. This is first cooked in olive oil or butter and then all the stock or water is added at once. The rice is removed from the heat and left in a warm spot while the grains absorb the liquid. For a successful pilaf, therefore, both rice and stock must be carefully measured; the amount of stock should be exactly double the quantity of rice.

In a properly made pilaf the rice grains are dry, firm, and separate and have a pleasantly mild and nutty flavor. The simple instructions for the *pilafi* included should produce perfect results every time. *Pilafi* is the ideal accompaniment to casseroles and stews, and vegetable pilaf is the perfect one-dish meal.

There are two types of Greek *macaronia,* or pasta. One made with unbleached all-purpose flour, is used to make thin flat strips like noodles or tagliatelle or shapes like ravioli, and cooked while fresh. The second type is made from durum flour and is dried and stored. Because of its high gluten content and an ability to retain its shape during cooking, this type is ideal for baked dishes such as *youvetsi* (spiced meat and *macaronia*) and *pastitsio* (page 238). Many of these *macaronia* are simple to make at home and their delicate flavor and ability to absorb aromatics makes them a perfect foil for sauces.

One unusual *macaronia* still made in villages, though difficult to duplicate here, deserves special mention. *Trahanas* is made from stiff dough of hard-wheat flour, eggs, and yogurt or soured milk. The dough is rolled out, spread out to dry in the sun for a day or two, then forced through a special strainer to make an oatmeal-textured pasta. *Trahanas* is sometimes served as a pasta course but more often appears in a soup flavored with lemon juice, wine, egg yolks, or tomatoes.

Greek grocery shops sometimes sell fine-ground *farina* (semolina), a durum flour particularly suited to *macaronia*. *Macaronia* made with *farina* have a deliciously authentic country flavor and are ideal for use in oven-baked dishes such as Stuffed Macaronia in Country Broth (page 242). However making *macaronia* with *farina* is not easy, and a machine is necessary to work the dough to the right texture. Greek grocery stores are also the place to find the long thin rolling pin needed to stretch the dough out and the special rolling pin covered with indented squares for cutting macaronia squares for Macedonian Pie (page 240).

As wheat was cultivated in Greece well before classical times, it's highly probable that macaronia has been produced there since antiquity – and there is indeed archaeological evidence to point in that direction. That being so, the simple and flavorsome recipes included here, popular all over Greece and the islands in regional variations, are based on a rich and ancient culinary tradition.

Rice Dishes
Pilafi

Perfect Pilaf
Pilafi

This simple bay leaf-scented pilaf is excellent with casseroles and grilled dishes. A good fruity olive oil and a well-flavored stock produce the best results and a last minute sprinkling of parsley and paprika adds a touch of color. (If necessary, it can be reheated over a heat diffuser plate or in a double boiler.)

Serves 4

2 tablespoons extra virgin olive oil
2 cups long-grain rice
3 bay leaves
1 tablespoon sea salt, or to taste
3 cups hot Chicken *or* Light Meat Stock (page 343 or page 348) *or* water

For serving
Juice of ½ lemon
Finely chopped flat-leaf parsley
Pinch of paprika
Cracked black pepper, to taste

Heat the olive oil in a heavy saucepan and stir the rice over low heat until the grains whiten, about 2 minutes. Add the bay leaves, salt, and stock, raise the heat to medium, and boil uncovered, without stirring, until the liquid has disappeared and holes appear in the surface of the rice, about 10 minutes. Remove from the heat, cover with a clean dish towel and a tight-fitting lid, and set aside for 30–40 minutes in a warm spot such as the back of the stove. The grains will become firm, dry, and separated.

Transfer the rice to a warm platter or bowl and lightly separate the grains with a fork. Discard the bay leaves and sprinkle the pilaf with the lemon juice, parsley, paprika, and pepper. Serve hot or warm.

Pilaf with Currants and Pine Nuts
Pilafi me Stafili Korinthiako

The strong clove, fresh ginger root, and orange zest flavorings reveal the Eastern influences behind this spicy pilaf. Currants and pine nuts are traditional additions sometimes cooked with the rice, sometimes added at the last minute. Adding them after the rice has absorbed all the liquid seems the best way to preserve their textures and distinctive flavors. Always served cold, this is especially good with game.

Serves 4

4 tablespoons extra virgin olive oil, or to taste
2 cups long-grain rice
4 cloves
1 1-inch piece of fresh ginger root, peeled
1 bouquet garni (2 bay leaves, 3 sprigs parsley, *and* 1 sprig thyme, tied together)
1 2-inch strip of orange zest
3 cups hot Chicken Stock (page 343) *or* water
1 teaspoon sea salt, or to taste
2/3 cup currants, soaked in 2 tablespoons Mavrodaphne wine *or* warm water for 1 hour
1/2 cup lightly toasted pine nuts *or* coarsely chopped walnuts

For serving
Juice of 1 small lemon
1/2 small red onion, thinly sliced
2 tablespoons finely chopped flat-leaf parsley *or* coarsely chopped cilantro
1 tablespoon finely chopped Preserved Lemons (page 18), *optional*
Cracked black pepper, to taste

Heat half the olive oil in a heavy saucepan, add the rice, and stir over low heat until the grains whiten, about 2 minutes. Add the cloves, fresh ginger root, bouquet garni, orange zest, stock, and salt. Raise the heat to medium and boil uncovered, without stirring, until the liquid has disappeared and holes appear in the surface of the rice, about 10 minutes. Stir in the currants and pine nuts with a fork and remove from the heat. Cover with a clean dish towel and a tight-fitting lid and set aside 30–40 minutes in a warm spot such as the back of the stove.

Discard the ginger root, bouquet garni, and orange zest, and turn the pilaf out onto a platter. Lightly separate the grains with a fork and set aside to cool.

To serve, sprinkle with the lemon juice, onion, parsley, Preserved Lemons, salt, pepper, and remaining olive oil.

Eggplant Pilaf with Glazed Tomatoes
Pilafi me Melitzanes ke Domates

Serve this flavorful pilaf, garnished with thin strips of smoky grilled peppers and caramelized tomatoes, as a side dish for grilled meats or chicken, *souvlakia,* or sausages. For vegetable lovers it makes a satisfying lunch or supper.

Serves 4

2 medium eggplants
Coarse-grain sea salt
4 tablespoons extra virgin olive oil
1½ tablespoons unsalted butter
1 ounce *fides* (vermicelli), broken into small pieces
1 small onion, finely chopped
1⅔ cups long-grain rice
4 cloves
2 bay leaves
2½ cups hot Chicken *or* Light Meat Stock (page 343 or page 348) *or* water
⅔ cup lightly toasted almonds *or* walnuts, coarsely chopped
⅓ cup currants *or* small dark seedless raisins
12 large cherry tomatoes *or* tiny tomatoes (about 1 inch in diameter)
½ teaspoon sugar, or to taste
Cracked black pepper, to taste
2 medium green *or* yellow bell peppers

For serving
Juice of ½ lemon
4 tablespoons coarsely chopped flat-leaf parsley
Strained Yogurt (page 7)

Trim the ends from the eggplants and cut into ¾-inch cubes. Sprinkle with ½ tablespoon salt and set aside for 30 minutes to "sweat."

Dry the eggplants with paper towels. Heat 3 tablespoons of the olive oil in a large heavy frying pan and lightly brown the eggplants on all sides over medium heat. Drain between layers of paper towels and set aside.

Melt the butter in a heavy saucepan and cook the vermicelli over low heat until the butter turns a deep golden brown, about 6 minutes; take care not to burn the butter. Add the onion and cook 5 minutes. Stir in the rice, cloves and bay leaves and cook, stirring, until the grains whiten, about 2 minutes. Add the stock and salt to taste, raise the heat to medium, and boil uncovered, without stirring, until the liquid has disappeared, and holes appear in the surface of the rice, about 10 minutes. Stir in the eggplants, almonds, and currants with a fork. Remove from the heat, cover with a clean dish towel and tight-fitting lid, and set aside for 30–40 minutes in a warm spot such as the back of the stove.

Fifteen minutes before you are ready to serve, heat the broiler. With a sharp knife, slash open the top of each tomato and sprinkle the insides with a pinch of salt, the sugar, and a generous amount of pepper. Arrange the peppers on a broiling pan and broil 2 inches from the heat, turning, until the skin is shriveled and darkened. Remove from the pan and arrange the tomatoes on the pan. Brush with the remaining olive oil and grill until the tops are darkened and slightly caramelized. While the tomatoes are cooking, remove the cores and seeds from the peppers. Rub off the skin and any remaining seeds with your fingers, dry with paper towels, and cut into thin strips. Turn the pilaf out onto a warm platter. Arrange the peppers on top, garnish with the tomatoes, and sprinkle with the lemon juice and parsley. Serve hot or warm, with bowls of yogurt.

Pilaf with Green Lentils
Pilafi me Fakes

Those who are fond of the flavor of good olive oil will appreciate this dish. Coriander, allspice, and bay leaves perfume the lentils and rice, and when they are cooked, a sweet-and-sour honey, vinegar, and olive oil sauce is poured over them. The result is a highly seasoned pilaf with an unusual combination of flavors. Fava Bean and Sweet Carrot Pilaf (page 230) is the spring version of this winter dish.

Serves 4

....

4 ounces green lentils, picked over, rinsed, and soaked for 2 hours in cold water to cover

5 tablespoons extra virgin olive oil

1 medium onion, cut into quarters and thinly sliced

1½ tablespoons dried coriander seeds, crushed *or* 1 tablespoon ground
coriander
½ teaspoon ground allspice
3 bay leaves
¾ pound carrots, halved or quartered lengthways and cut into 1-inch
lengths
1 cup long-grain rice
2 cups hot Chicken *or* Light Meat Stock (page 343 or page 348) *or* water
1 teaspoon sea salt, or to taste
1 tablespoon aromatic honey, such as Hymettus
1 tablespoon aged red wine vinegar
3 tablespoons finely chopped flat-leaf parsley
1 tablespoon dried *rigani* (see page 13), crumbled
½ teaspoon cracked black pepper, or to taste

For serving
Strained Yogurt (page 7)

Drain the lentils and place in a saucepan with water to cover. Bring to a
boil, drain, rinse, and set aside.

Heat 2 tablespoons of the olive oil in a heavy saucepan and sauté the
onion over low heat until soft, about 6 minutes. Stir in the coriander,
allspice, and bay leaves, add the carrots, and cook, stirring occasionally, 5
minutes longer. Stir in the rice and cook, stirring, until the grains whiten,
about 2 minutes. Add the lentils, stock, and salt to taste. Raise the heat to
medium and boil uncovered, without stirring, until the liquid has
disappeared and holes appear in the surface of the rice, about 10 minutes.
Remove from the heat, cover with a clean dish towel and tight-fitting lid,
and set aside for 30 minutes in a warm spot such as the back of the stove.

Combine the honey and vinegar in a small saucepan, stir in the
remaining olive oil, and heat to warm. Stir in the parsley, *rigani,* pepper,
and salt to taste. Turn the pilaf out onto a warm platter and pour over the
honey sauce. Serve hot with bowls of yogurt.

Fava Bean and Sweet Carrot Pilaf
Pilafi me Fava ke Karotta

When the first fava beans and tender young carrots appear in the market
this popular spring dish is served in homes throughout Greece. The carrots
cook to a sweet velvety texture with the rice, the crunchy beans are added
at the last minute. Served warm or cold, with a bowl of yogurt and a green
salad or wild greens dish, this is a satisfying meal on its own. It's also a
perfect complement to grilled lamb.

Serves 4

3 tablespoons extra virgin olive oil
2 shallots, finely chopped
1 pound young carrots, halved or quartered lengthways and cut
    into 1-inch lengths
1 cup long-grain rice
1 teaspoon sea salt, or to taste
1 teaspoon honey
2 bay leaves
3/4 cup hot Chicken Stock (page 343) *or* water
3/4 cup hot water
1 1/2 pounds fava beans in the pod, shelled
Juice of 1 lemon
Cracked black pepper, to taste

For serving
Handful of small sprigs fresh dill *or* young mint, torn into small pieces just
    before using

Heat 2 tablespoons of the olive oil in a heavy saucepan and sauté the
shallots over low heat until soft, about 5 minutes. Add the carrots and cook
2–3 minutes, stirring with a wooden spoon. Add the rice and cook, stirring,
until the grains whiten, about 2 minutes. Add 3/4 teaspoon of the salt, the
honey, bay leaves, stock, and water. Raise the heat to medium and boil
uncovered, without stirring, until the liquid has disappeared, and holes
appear in the surface of the rice, about 10 minutes. Remove from the heat,
cover with a clean dish towel and tight-fitting lid, and set aside for 30–40
minutes in a warm spot such as the back of the stove.

Peel the skins from the fava beans (see **Note,** page 209). Heat the
remaining olive oil in a small saucepan, add the beans, cover, and cook 4
minutes over low heat to soften. Add half the lemon juice, the remaining
salt, and pepper.

Stir the beans and cooking juices into the pilaf with a fork and turn out
onto a warm platter. Sprinkle with the remaining lemon juice and the dill.

Spinach Pilaf
Spanakorizo

In traditional kitchens this classic country dish is made in a heavy,
round-bottomed pan so that the pilaf can be turned out to make an
attractive mound. Serve *spanakorizo* as a simple lunch or supper dish, with
olives and slices of *feta* cheese, or as an accompaniment to grilled meats.

Serves 4

2 medium leeks
5 tablespoons extra virgin olive oil, or to taste
1 clove garlic, finely chopped, *optional*
Large pinch of ground cumin
2 pounds tender fresh spinach, rinsed twice and stalks discarded
6 sprigs fresh dill, chopped, *optional*
Coarse-grain sea salt *and* freshly ground black pepper, to taste
1 cup long-grain rice
1½ cups Chicken Stock (page 343) *or* water

For serving
Juice of ½ lemon

Slice off the roots and green tops of the leeks. Cut a slit lengthways halfway through each leek, keeping the original shape intact. Hold upright under running water and gently pull the layers apart, one at a time, to wash out any grit or dirt. Shake off any excess water and blot dry with paper towels.

Heat 3 tablespoons of the olive oil in a large heavy saucepan or baking dish. Thinly slice the leeks, add to the pan, and sauté over low heat, stirring occasionally, until soft, about 10 minutes. Add the garlic and cumin, stir to mix, and continue cooking until aromatic.

Slice the spinach into ½-inch ribbons and add to the pan with the dill, 1 teaspoon salt (or to taste), and pepper. Stir with a wooden spoon and cook until the spinach has reduced in bulk by half, about 1 minute. Add the rice, stir once, then add the stock. Raise the heat to medium and boil uncovered, without stirring, until the liquid has disappeared, and holes appear in the surface of the rice, about 10 minutes. Remove from the heat, cover with a clean dish towel and tight-fitting lid, and set aside for 30–40 minutes in a warm spot such as the back of the stove.

To serve, hold the serving dish over the top of the pan and, using both hands, invert the pan to turn out the pilaf onto the dish. Whisk together the lemon juice and remaining olive oil and pour over the pilaf. Sprinkle with salt and pepper to taste and serve hot, warm, or at room temperature.

Variations
♦ Substitute 1½ pounds young beet greens or ruby chard for the spinach and omit the dill.
♦ Substitute ¾ pound young arugula leaves, torn into pieces, or small clusters of watercress or purslane, or turnip greens or mustard greens, torn into small pieces, for the spinach, and omit the dill. Add the greens to the pan *after* the rice has absorbed the liquid; fork the greens into the rice.

Cover the pan and set aside in a warm spot as described. For serving, substitute 1/2 tablespoon (or to taste) aged red wine vinegar for the lemon juice and be generous with the salt and pepper.

Saffron Rice with Mussels
Mythia me Risi

On the last day of one of the cooking courses I ran on the island of Crete a large basket was delivered to one of my students. Inside was a marine treasure trove – sea urchins, baby squid, mussels, shrimp, cuttlefish, razor clams, and sea anemones. Using this generous gift, we made a lovely saffron pilaf. Here is a simpler version of that delightful dish – try it also with baby squid, cuttlefish, shrimp, or a combination of seafood.

Serves 4

1 teaspoon saffron threads
32–40 mussels
3 tablespoons extra virgin olive oil
3 shallots, finely chopped
12/3 cups long-grain rice
2 bay leaves
2 cups hot water
1/2 cup lightly toasted pine nuts
1/3 cup currants *or* small dark seedless raisins
4 tablespoons chopped flat-leaf parsley
Sea salt *and* cracked black pepper, to taste
Juice of 1/2 lemon

For serving
Lemon wedges

Heat the saffron in a small dry frying pan until aromatic, about 1 minute. Set aside.

Discard any open mussels and those with broken shells. With a stiff brush, thoroughly scrub the mussels under cold running water and pull off their "beards." Place in a large saucepan, cover, and set over medium-high heat. Holding the lid firmly in place, shake the saucepan once or twice. After a minute or two all the mussels should have opened; discard any that do not open. Pour the mussel broth into a small bowl, crumble in the saffron, and set aside. Remove all but 8 mussels from their shells, reserving the juices, and set aside.

Heat half of the olive oil in a heavy saucepan and sauté half the shallots over medium-low heat until pale golden, about 5 minutes. Stir in the rice, and cook, until the grains whiten, about 2 minutes. Strain the saffron broth and add to the rice with the bay leaves and hot water. Raise the heat to medium and boil uncovered, without stirring, until all the liquid has disappeared and holes appear in the surface of the rice, about 10 minutes. Stir in the pine nuts and currants with a fork. Remove from the heat, cover with a clean dish towel and tight-fitting lid, and set aside for 30 minutes in a warm spot such as the back of the stove.

Five minutes before you are ready to serve, heat the remaining olive oil in a small frying pan and sauté the remaining shallots over low heat until soft, about 3 minutes. Add the parsley, salt and pepper, and half the lemon juice and heat to warm. Add the shelled mussels, cover, and heat 1 minute over very low heat.

Stir the mussel and parsley mixture into the pilaf with a fork, turn out onto a warm platter, and sprinkle with the remaining lemon juice and reserved mussel juices. Garnish with the lemon wedges and the mussels in their shells and serve at once.

Spiced Shrimp Pilaf
Pilafi Aromatiko me Garithes

Although this island pilaf is simple to make, it looks splendidly exotic and colorful, with its coriander- and turmeric-flavored rice, sweet tomato and shrimp sauce, and garnish of yogurt, parsley, and piquant capers. Although saffron is popular for coloring and flavoring *pilafi*, the Greeks use it only in dishes made with a very light stock, which preserves its delicate fragrance and color. As this pilaf is cooked in a heavier stock, the preferred aromatic is the less subtle (less expensive) turmeric.

Serves 4

1½ pounds medium shrimp in the shell
4 tablespoons extra virgin olive oil
1 large onion, chopped
1 stick celery, chopped
3 bay leaves
2 shallots, finely chopped
1 teaspoon ground coriander
½ teaspoon turmeric
1²/₃ cups long-grain rice
½ teaspoon sea salt, or to taste
3 ripe medium tomatoes, skinned, seeded, and diced
Pinch of sugar

½ teaspoon cracked black pepper, or to taste
1 teaspoon dried *rigani* (see page 13), crumbled

For serving
5 tablespoons Strained Yogurt (page 7)
2 tablespoons finely chopped flat-leaf parsley
1 tablespoon capers, rinsed and coarsely chopped

Rinse the shrimp, and shell all but 4, reserving the shells. Devein all the shrimp, cover, and refrigerate.

Heat 1½ tablespoons of the olive oil in a heavy saucepan, and sauté the onion and celery over low heat until golden, about 15 minutes. Add the shrimp shells (or 2 shelled shrimp), 1 of the bay leaves broken into 2 pieces, and 2 cups water. Bring to a boil over medium heat, cover, reduce the heat, and simmer 40 minutes. Strain the stock through a fine strainer into a bowl, pressing the solids against the sides of the strainer with the back of a wooden spoon. Add water if necessary to make 2½ cups and set aside.

Heat 1 tablespoon of the remaining olive oil in a heavy saucepan and sauté the shallots over low heat until pale golden, about 6 minutes. Stir in the coriander, turmeric, rice, and remaining 2 bay leaves. Cook, stirring, until the rice whitens, about 2 minutes. Add the shrimp stock and salt, raise the heat to medium, and boil uncovered, without stirring, until the liquid has disappeared, and holes appear in the surface of the rice, about 10 minutes. Remove from the heat, cover with a clean dish towel and tight-fitting lid, and set aside for 30 minutes in a warm spot such as the back of the stove.

Heat the remaining olive oil in a heavy sauté pan. Lightly toss the shrimp in their shells 2 minutes over medium-low heat and add the shelled shrimp. Cook, stirring occasionally, until pink and opaque all the way through, 3–5 minutes. Remove with a slotted spoon and keep warm. Add the tomatoes, sugar, and pepper to the pan. Cook 1 minute, add the *rigani*, and return the shelled shrimp to the pan. Lower the heat, simmer 1 minute longer, and season to taste. Warm the yogurt in a small saucepan over low heat.

Turn the pilaf out onto a warm platter, pour over the tomato and shrimp sauce, and spoon the yogurt on top. Sprinkle with the parsley and capers and garnish with the shrimp in the shell. Serve at once.

Pasta
Macaronia

Although you can use a pasta machine to do some of the work in making *macaronia*, I usually prefer to roll out the dough by hand.

Macaronia cut in ¼-inch wide strips (what the Italians call tagliatelle) are easy to produce without a machine. For a soft and pliant dough all the ingredients should be at room temperature and the dough should be well kneaded.

Serves 4 (Makes approximately 1 pound dough)

2¼ cups all-purpose flour *or* semolina (*farina,* see page 344)
3 large eggs

Mound 2 cups of the flour on a large clean work surface and make a deep hollow in the center. Break the eggs into the hollow and lightly beat them with a fork. Little by little draw in the flour with your fingers and mix it with the eggs. Continue until you have incorporated all the flour; add some or all of the remaining flour if the dough feels sticky. Knead the dough for at least 5 minutes, until the dough leaves the work surface clean, adding a little more flour if necessary. Tightly wrap the dough in plastic wrap and set aside for 10–30 minutes; do not refrigerate.

Lightly dust a rolling pin and a clean work surface with flour. Divide the dough into 6 portions and roll out each as thin as possible without tearing. Use the rolling pin to push, rather than press, the dough into a large rectangular shape. Trim the sides of each sheet and loosely roll it up into a cylinder. With a sharp knife, cut each cylinder crosswise into strips of desired width. Separate the strips, and spread them on clean dish towels or a pasta drying rack to dry slightly, about 15 minutes, before cooking. They are ready to cook when they are no longer sticky but are not so dry that they would crack if folded.

Macaronia with Olive, Anchovy, and Sweet Tomato Sauce
Macaronia me Elies ke Saltsa Domatas

Strong flavors and bold color contrasts make this simple dish exceptionally attractive and appetizing. The cooked *macaronia* is coated with an anchovy-garlic paste, and then a sweet tomato sauce is poured over it. Interestingly enough, although basil is seen growing in pots all over Greece, this is one of the few basil-flavored Greek dishes I know.

Serves 4

....

3 whole salted anchovies (see page 343), filleted, *or* 6 salted anchovy fillets
½ cup extra virgin olive oil, or more to taste
2 cloves garlic, thinly sliced
12 Nafplion *or* other Greek green olives, blanched in boiling water for
   3 seconds, patted dry, pitted, and coarsely chopped
6 large ripe tomatoes, skinned
1 teaspoon honey
½ teaspoon cracked black pepper, or to taste
Sea salt, to taste
2 tablespoons fresh basil *or* 1 tablespoon chopped fresh thyme *or* oregano
1 recipe *macaronia* (page 236, about 1 pound), cut into ¼-inch strips and
   dried for 15 minutes

....

Soak the anchovy fillets in cold water for 5 minutes. Rinse, pat dry, and
cut into small pieces. Place in a small bowl with 2 tablespoons of the olive
oil and set aside.

Fill a large saucepan with lightly salted water and bring to a boil.
Meanwhile, heat 2 tablespoons of the remaining olive oil in a small heavy
frying pan and sauté the garlic over a low heat until aromatic; do not let it
brown. Transfer the garlic and oil to a wooden mortar or bowl, add the
anchovies and their oil, and pound together until mixed but not smooth.
Return the mixture to the frying pan, add the olives, and heat to warm.

Cut the tomatoes in half, squeeze out the seeds, and slice into thin
wedges. Heat 1 tablespoon of the remaining olive oil in a second small
frying pan over medium heat and add the tomatoes, honey, salt, and
pepper. Cook just until the tomatoes begin to lose their shape, about 1
minute. Tear the basil leaves into small pieces and stir into the tomatoes.
Add the *macaronia* to the boiling water and cook until they rise to the
surface, about 3 minutes; drain immediately.

Combine the *macaronia* and olive sauce in a warm shallow bowl. Pour
over the tomatoes, sprinkle with the remaining olive oil, and serve at once.

Macaronia with Chicken and Wild Greens

Macaronia me Kotopoulo ke Khorta

This popular dish is simple and quick to prepare but it does require
high-quality ingredients. Be sure to use a well-flavored olive oil, plump
olives, and the freshest young beet or dandelion greens you can find.

Serves 4

....

8 ounces thin 1-inch long strips of cooked chicken

2 tablespoons aged red wine vinegar *or* 1 tablespoon balsamic vinegar

Freshly ground black pepper, to taste

4 tablespoons extra virgin olive oil

1 clove garlic, cut into 2 or 3 pieces

1 large handful tender young beet greens *or* dandelion greens, tough stalks removed and leaves torn into small pieces

4 tablespoons boiling water

½ cup lightly toasted pine nuts

24 Elitses *or* 12 Niçoise olives, drained, pitted, and coarsely chopped

1 recipe *macaronia* (page 236, about 1 pound), cut into ¼-inch strips and dried for 15 minutes

Sea salt, to taste

For serving

Grated aged *myzithra, halloumi, or kasseri* cheese

....

Combine the chicken, vinegar, pepper, and 1 tablespoon of the olive oil in a bowl, toss to mix and set aside.

Heat most of the remaining olive oil in a large heavy frying pan and sauté the garlic over low heat until pale golden; don't let it burn. Discard the garlic and set aside the pan.

Fill a large saucepan with lightly salted water and bring to a boil. Meanwhile, place the greens in a heavy saucepan, add the boiling water, cover, and gently boil 1 minute. Drain well, spread between layers of paper towels, and blot dry.

Return the frying pan to low heat and add the chicken, pine nuts, and olives. Cook 3 minutes, stirring occasionally with a fork. Add the greens and heat through. Add the *macaronia* to the boiling water and cook only until they rise to the surface, about 3 minutes; drain.

Combine the chicken mixture and *macaronia* in a warm earthenware bowl and toss to mix. Sprinkle with the remaining olive oil and salt and pepper to taste. Serve at once, with bowls of cheese.

Macaronia and Spicy Meat in a Pie
Pastitsio

This traditional dish, composed of layers of *macaronia,* in a sweet and spicy meat sauce, and a creamy cheese sauce, makes no pretensions to elegance but its heady aroma, beautiful bubbling and golden-crusted appearance, and utterly delicious taste are pleasure enough. It needs only the simplest of accompaniments – Wild Greens Salad (page 222) is ideal.

Serves 8

5 tablespoons extra virgin olive oil
2 large onions, finely chopped
1 1/2 pounds lean beef *or* lamb *or* a mixture of both, ground
1/2 cup red wine *or* 2 tablespoons aged red wine vinegar
6 large ripe tomatoes, skinned, seeded, and diced, juices reserved
1 1/2–2 tablespoons ground cinnamon
Large pinch of cayenne pepper
1 tablespoon dried marjoram, crumbled
1 small handful flat-leaf parsley, leaves finely chopped
Sea salt *and* cracked black pepper, to taste

White Sauce
4 tablespoons (1/2 stick) unsalted butter
4 tablespoons all-purpose flour
3 3/4 cups warm milk
1/2 teaspoon grated nutmeg
3 eggs, separated
2 egg yolks

1 1/2 pounds macaroni *or* penne

4 ounces small-curd cottage cheese, drained
1/2 cup grated *feta* cheese
2 tablespoons unsalted butter, melted
1 1/2 cups fresh fine bread crumbs, dried 5 minutes in a low oven
1/3 cup grated *kasseri or* Parmesan cheese
8 Elitses *or* Niçoise olives, drained, pitted, and each cut in half

Warm half of the olive oil in a heavy frying pan and sauté the onion over medium-low heat until pale golden, about 5 minutes. Add the meat, raise the heat, and cook, stirring and breaking up any lumps with a spoon, until lightly browned, about 6 minutes. Add the red wine and boil until reduced by half. Add the tomatoes and their juices, 1 tablespoon of the cinnamon, and the cayenne pepper, and cook until the liquid is reduced by half. Add the marjoram, half the parsley, a pinch of salt, and a generous amount of pepper. Simmer 5 minutes longer and add cinnamon, salt and pepper to taste; the sauce should be highly flavored.

Fill a large saucepan with lightly salted water and bring to a boil. Meanwhile, melt the butter in a heavy saucepan and stir in the flour with a wooden spoon to make a roux. Cook, stirring, over low heat until the roux is smooth and light and gold in color. Stir in the milk 1/2 cup at a time, adding more only when the sauce is smooth. Cook, stirring, until the sauce comes to a low boil. Remove from the heat, stir in the nutmeg and 5 egg yolks, and set aside.

Arrange a rack in the center of the oven and heat the oven 350°F.

Cook the macaroni in the boiling water until barely soft, about 10 minutes. Drain and rinse briefly under cold running water. Shake the colander once or twice and set aside to dry.

Stir the cottage cheese, most of the *feta* cheese, and a little pepper into the white sauce. Whisk the egg whites until they hold soft peaks and fold half of them into the white sauce. Combine the remaining egg whites and *feta* cheese, the parsley, 1 cup of the white sauce, a pinch of cinnamon, and the macaroni in a large bowl.

Brush a baking dish with half the melted butter and 1 tablespoon of the remaining olive oil, and sprinkle with half the bread crumbs. Spread one third of the macaroni mixture over the bottom of the dish and cover with half the meat filling. Spread a thin layer of macaroni over the meat, cover with the remaining filling and then the remaining macaroni. Cover with the white sauce, lightly smooth the top with a spatula, and sprinkle with the remaining bread crumbs and the *kasseri* cheese. Set 2 olive halves, cut sides down, in the center of each of which will be 8 serving portions and sprinkle with the remaining olive oil and melted butter.

Bake 40 minutes, until a deep golden brown. Let rest for 10 minutes before cutting into serving portions.

Macedonian Pie
Laganes

I once spent a week in a Macedonian village where the inhabitants seemed to exist solely on this glorious dish. *Laganes* (from which the Italian word *lasagna* derives) is an extravagant pie of thin *macaronia* squares, layered with three sauces, spicy sausages, and wild greens, and topped with *kasseri* cheese and bread crumbs. Freshly baked, with each component in perfect balance, this dish is a triumphant success.

Serves 10

3 cups all-purpose flour *or* semolina (*farina,* see page 344) *or* a mixture of both
4 large eggs

Meat Sauce
2 tablespoons extra virgin olive oil
1 large onion, finely chopped
1 pound lean beef, finely ground
4 tablespoons finely chopped flat-leaf parsley

1 tablespoon dried *rigani* (see page 13), crumbled
1 teaspoon ground allspice
1/2 cup dry white wine
1 2-inch strip of orange zest
3 bay leaves
Sea salt *and* cracked black pepper, to taste

Sausage Filling
2 4-to-5-inch sausages (pages 176, 178, and 179), casings discarded, cubed
   or 1 cup finely diced lean prosciutto ham
1 tablespoon extra virgin olive oil
Fresh leaves from 6 young beets, cooked, drained, and chopped (see page
   223) *or* 1/2 pound fresh spinach, chopped

White Sauce
3 cups milk
3 tablespoons unsalted butter
3 tablespoons all-purpose flour
1/2 teaspoon grated nutmeg
3 egg yolks
1 cup grated *graviera or* Gruyère cheese

2 tablespoons unsalted butter, melted
3 tablespoons extra virgin olive oil
2 cups fresh fine bread crumbs, briefly dried in a low oven
4 ounces small-curd cottage cheese, drained
1/2 cup grated *feta* cheese

3 cups Tomato Sauce (page 321), made with cinnamon and parsley
2 tablespoons grated *kasseri or* Parmesan cheese

Make a dough with the 3 cups flour and 4 eggs, as directed on page
236. Wrap the dough in plastic wrap and set aside.

To make the meat sauce, heat the olive oil in a heavy frying pan and
sauté the onion over medium-low heat until pale golden, about 8 minutes.
Add the meat, raise the heat, stirring with a wooden spoon to break up any
lumps, and cook, until lightly browned, about 5 minutes. Add the parsley,
rigani, allspice, wine, orange zest, bay leaves, and salt and pepper, and
simmer until most of the liquid has evaporated. Set aside.

To make the sausage filling, heat the olive oil in a second frying pan and
lightly brown the cubed sausage. Drain on paper towels, combine with the
beet greens and set aside.

Divide the dough into 6 portions. Dust a rolling pin and a clean work
surface with flour. Roll out each portion as thin as possible into a 6-inch

wide strip. Trim the edges and cut in half lengthways, then into 3-inch squares. Lightly dust with flour and spread on clean dish towels for a few minutes to dry. Fill a large saucepan with lightly salted water and bring to a boil.

Meanwhile, to make the white sauce, heat the milk just to a simmer and remove from the heat. Melt the butter in a heavy saucepan and stir in the flour with a wooden spoon. Cook, stirring, over low heat until smooth and light gold in color. Briskly stir in the milk a half cup at a time, adding more only when the sauce is smooth. Cook, stirring, until the sauce comes to a low boil. Remove from the heat, stir in the nutmeg, egg yolks, and *graviera* cheese, and set aside.

Add the *macaronia* squares to the boiling water, 4 or 5 at a time, and cook until they rise to the surface, about 4 minutes. Drain on paper towels.

Arrange a rack in the center of the oven and heat the oven to 375°F. Brush a large heavy baking dish, at least 2½-inches deep, with half the melted butter and 2 tablespoons of the olive oil and sprinkle with half the bread crumbs. Cover the bottom of the dish with a single layer of *macaronia*. Remove the orange zest and bay leaves from the meat sauce and spoon half the meat sauce over the *macaronia*. Combine the cottage cheese, *feta* cheese, and ½ teaspoon pepper, and spoon half of this mixture over the meat. Spoon over ½ cup white sauce and cover with a third of the remaining *macaronia*. Spread the sausage filling over the *macaronia,* cover with half the tomato sauce, and then with half the remaining *macaronia*. Spoon over the remaining meat sauce and cottage cheese mixture, and then 4 fl oz of the white sauce. Cover with the remaining *macaronia,* tomato sauce, and, finally, the white sauce. Sprinkle with the remaining bread crumbs, the *kasseri,* and remaining olive oil and melted butter.

Bake 30 minutes, until golden brown and aromatic. Let rest 10 minutes before cutting into serving portions.

Stuffed Macaronia in Country Broth
Macaronia Yemista

These stuffed *macaronia* are traditionally served at celebrations, and I first sampled them at a country wedding on the island of Crete. Squares of *macaronia* are stuffed with a spicy meat or chicken mixture, baked until golden brown, and served in large shallow bowls with broth to moisten and plump the *macaronia,* and a sprinkling of olive oil. Bowls of cheese, warm yogurt, or tomato sauce and the Wild Greens Salad (page 222) are traditional accompaniments.

Serves 4

3/8 cup extra virgin olive oil, or more to taste
1 large onion, finely chopped
3/4 pound lean beef *or* lamb, finely ground twice
5 cups Light Meat *or* Chicken Stock (page 348 or page 343) *or* Meat Stock
(page 348)
1 teaspoon ground cinnamon, or to taste
Sea salt *and* freshly ground black pepper, to taste
1 tablespoon dried *rigani* (see page 13), crumbled
4 tablespoons finely chopped flat-leaf parsley
2 1/4 cups all-purpose flour *or* semolina (*farina,* see page 344) *or* a mixture
of both
3 large eggs

For serving
Grated aged *myzithra, or kasseri, or* Parmesan cheese, *or* 3 cups Strained
Yogurt (page 7), *or* Tomato Sauce (page 321 and page 322), made with
rigani or parsley, warmed

Heat 2 tablespoons of the olive oil in a heavy frying pan and sauté the
onion over medium-low heat until golden, about 12 minutes, stirring
frequently. Add the meat and cook, stirring to break up any lumps, until
lightly browned and any meat juices have evaporated. Spread on paper
towels to drain, drain off the fat from the pan, and wipe it out. Return the
meat and onion mixture to the pan, add 1/2 cup of the stock, the cinnamon,
salt and pepper, *rigani,* and parsley. Simmer 5 minutes over low heat and
set aside.

Make a dough with the flour and 3 eggs as directed on page 236.

Divide into 6 portions and let rest for 10 minutes. Dust a rolling pin and
clean work surface with flour and stretch and roll out each as thin as
possible without tearing. Trim the edges and cut into 2-inch strips, then 2-
inch squares. You should have 40 squares.

Heat the oven to 375°F. Place 1 teaspoon of filling in the center of each
square and, with lightly dampened forefinger and thumb, gently pull 2
opposite corners of each square up and together. Repeat with the other 2
corners so they all meet in the center to make a neat packet.

Brush a heavy baking dish, at least 2-inches deep and large enough to
hold all the *macaronia* in a single layer, with olive oil. Arrange the
macaronia in it and brush them with olive oil. Bake 10 minutes, then
reduce the oven temperature to 350°F and bake 10–15 minutes longer, until
light golden brown. Season the remaining stock to taste and pour into the
dish. Bake 15–20 minutes longer, until the *macaronia* are tender; taste one
to test.

Divide the *macaronia* and stock between individual shallow bowls, sprinkle with the remaining olive oil, and serve with bowls of the cheese, yogurt, or Tomato Sauce.

Variations
♦ Cooked chicken cut into tiny cubes can be substituted for the meat, or substitute the filling for Baked Cheese and Spinach Pies (page 58). Use 1/2 cup white wine and 4 cups homemade Chicken Stock (page 343) instead of Light Meat Stock.

Stuffed Macaronia with Tomato Sauce
Macaronia Yemista me Saltsa Domatas

This is the Greek version of ravioli – *macaronia* stuffed with a nutmeg-spiced chicken and cheese mixture.

Serves 4

2 1/4 cups all-purpose flour
4 large eggs
8 3/4 cups Chicken Stock (page 343) *or* water
1/2 cup finely diced cooked chicken
2 tablespoons finely chopped flat-leaf parsley
2 egg yolks
2 tablespoons minced shallots
1/4 teaspoon grated nutmeg
2 ounces *feta or kasseri* cheese
3 ounces small-curd cottage cheese, drained
Sea salt *and* cracked black pepper, to taste

For serving
2 cups Roasted Tomato Sauce (page 323)
1/2 cup Rich Chicken Stock (page 344)
Extra virgin olive oil, to taste
Grated aged *myzithra or feta* cheese

Make a dough with the flour and 3 of the eggs, as directed on page 236. Divide into 6 portions and let rest for 10 minutes. Lightly dust a rolling pin and clean work surface with flour and roll out the dough as thin as possible without tearing. Trim the edges, cut into strips 2 1/2-inches wide, then into 2 1/2-inch squares; you should have at least 24. Spread them out to dry for a few minutes. Bring the chicken stock to a low boil.

Meanwhile, combine the chicken, parsley, egg yolks, shallots, nutmeg, *feta*, cottage cheese and salt and pepper. Beat the remaining egg with a little water. Place 1 tablespoon of the filling in the center of each *macaronia* square, lightly brush the edges of each square with the beaten egg, and fold over to form a triangle. Trim into half-moons with a pastry wheel, firmly pressing the edges together to seal.

Add half the *macaronia* to the stock and cook until they rise to the surface, about 6 minutes. Drain, keep warm, and cook the remaining *macaronia*.

To serve, combine the Roasted Tomato Sauce and Rich Chicken Stock in a saucepan, season to taste, and heat to warm; do not boil. Transfer the *macaronia* to a warm earthenware bowl and pour over the tomato sauce and olive oil. Gently toss together and serve at once, with bowls of the cheese.

Variations
♦ Substitute a cheese (see page 57), cheese and spinach (see page 58), wild greens (see page 59), or meat (see page 62) filling for the chicken filling; you will need only half the quantity of filling those recipes make.

Kritharaki with Brown Butter and Cheese
Kritharaki me Voutiro ke Tyri

Archaeological evidence suggests that *kritharaki* may have been an early "convenience food," sold in the marketplaces of ancient Greece. The tiniest grains of *kritharaki* are no larger than pearl rice, the largest are the size of cantaloupe seeds; you can find it in Greek or Middle Eastern shops – it is also called *manestra* or *orza*. Goat's butter is the traditional flavoring but brown butter and lemon juice makes a fine substitute. Be generous with the cheese and fresh herbs.

Serves 4 to 6
....
2 cups medium-size *kritharaki*
3³/₄ cups homemade Light Meat *or* Chicken Stock (page 348 or page 343),
   Meat Stock (page 348), *or* water
6 tablespoons unsalted butter
Juice of 1 large lemon, or to taste
1¹/₃ cups finely grated aged *myzithra or kasseri* cheese
1 small handful fresh herbs, leaves only, snipped or finely chopped
1 small handful flat-leaf parsley, leaves coarsely chopped
6 scallions, best green parts only, finely sliced
Coarse-grain sea salt *and* cracked black pepper, to taste
....

Bring the stock to a boil in a large saucepan. Add the *kritharaki* and simmer until barely tender, about 10 minutes. Drain, and briefly refresh under cold running water. Rinse out the saucepan.

Meanwhile, heat the butter in a small heavy saucepan over a very low heat until deep golden brown, about 10 minutes. (Keep the heat very low or the solids in the butter will burn.) Strain through 2 layers of cheesecloth into a bowl and add most of the lemon juice.

Return the *kritharaki* to the rinsed-out saucepan. Add the butter mixture, the cheese, herbs, parsley, scallions, salt and pepper, and remaining lemon juice. Stir just to mix, heat to warm, and transfer to a warm serving bowl. Serve at once.

Note Your choice of herbs to flavor *kritharaki* depends on what is available and the dish it is to be served with. The quantity of herbs you use depends on their strength. Fresh oregano, chervil, thyme, borage, or cilantro are all good choices. Herbs with a mild flavor, such as chervil, are simply snipped into small pieces, but stronger herbs, such as oregano, must be finely chopped.

BREADS

Psomia

Bread is a fundamental part of Greek life – it appears in some form at every meal and special festive breads are of great significance in religious festivals and family celebrations. Greek bakeries, piled high with breads of every conceivable size and shape, have a special magic. In rural communities bread is still baked in the *fournos* and the village baker supplies a range of breads, from the basic everyday loaf to wonderful crusty whole wheat, barley, or stone-ground breads, as well as one or two savory or fruit breads.

Savory breads are seasonal and vary from region to region and baker to baker. The one essential common ingredient is a good fruity olive oil, which results in a wonderfully supple dough with an appealing aroma and the characteristic flavor and texture of all Greek breads. Flavored with cheese, olives, fennel, or herbs these savory breads invariably appear as round loaves but you may prefer to make the dough into rolls. And if you have savory bread left over, just sprinkle slices of the bread with olive oil and toast them in a low oven; dipped into red wine and accompanied by fresh cheese and olives, they are a delectable, traditional, and quickly made snack.

Sweet breads, such as Currant Bread (page 264), are enjoyable all year and *paximathi*, a sweet anise-flavored hard bread, is a universal treat with coffee. The flavorings used in sweet breads hint at their ancient origins – mastic (see page 13), *petimezi* (see page 307), cinnamon, allspice, vanilla, and nutmeg are all traditional.

Both sweet and savory breads play a central role in Greek religious life, as part of Orthodox ritual and as celebration food. The women of each church congregation make a dense-textured bread for the celebration of the Eucharist, and a special bread flavored with mastic is made for Saints' days. These church breads are known as *artos*, the ancient Greek word for bread. A flat sesame seed bread called *lagana* is baked to mark the first day of Lent; later, this important fast is broken by the sharing of the rich Easter Bread (page 261). At Christmas and New Year's, more festive sweet breads (page 262 and page 263) appear – ornately decorated or shaped and gleaming with sugary glaze. And throughout the year, for any celebration – an engagement, a wedding, the birth of a child – there is the all-purpose Festive Bread called *tsoureki* (page 259).

Many of these breads are not difficult to make at home, although they do take a little extra time. Most can be frozen very successfully, so you can make extra loaves or rolls to serve with Greek meals later, and they also keep extremely well.

Notes on
Successful Bread Making

Making bread is wonderfully satisfying and not at all difficult if you follow some simple guidelines. These tips should help you succeed in making a variety of delicious breads, both savory and sweet.

Equipment you will need

- Large mixing bowl
- Dough scraper
- Scales and measuring spoons; heavy baking trays
- Oven thermometer; clean dish towels; plastic wrap; an uncluttered, clean work area
- Draught-free warm spot
- Loaf pans are useful but not essential

Ingredients

Flour: These recipes use whole wheat flour, pastry flour, and all-purpose flour. Other flours, such as stone-ground, can be substituted; you will usually need to use less of them and to knead the dough for a longer time. Flour measurements are approximate; the important thing is to add enough flour to make the dough the required texture. I use organic flour whenever possible.

Salt: Salt serves two primary functions in bread making: It helps retain moisture in the dough and acts as a flavor enhancer. Use only sea salt – the taste of the chemical additives in other salts is intensified in bread. Salt must be dissolved before it is incorporated into the dough; fine-grain sea salt dissolves the most quickly.

Olive oil: The "secret" ingredient in Mediterranean breads, it makes a pliant, easy-to-handle dough. Pungent extra virgin olive oil gives the most authentic taste, but use less-expensive refined olive oil, if you prefer.

Yeast: For convenience, these recipes use active dry yeast. However, do use fresh yeast if you can find it since it gives a better flavor; one small cake is equivalent to one tablespoon active dry yeast. Dissolve in liquid heated to 85–90°F instead of 110°F.

Techniques

Temperature: Temperature is an important factor during all stages of bread making. Yeast is a living organism; it weakens and dies if overheated, refuses to work if too cold. It is activated only at specific temperatures, and once activated, will die if left too long (usually more than about 12 minutes) without a "host" (the flour). Mixing bowls should be lukewarm. Kneading warms the dough so that it will rise. The oven must be hot enough for a quick rise, but not too hot or the dough may collapse. After 10 minutes or so the temperature is usually reduced so that the loaf cooks through. Oven temperatures must be exact – use an oven thermometer.

Kneading dough: Use a lightly floured board or work surface for kneading dough, and press into the dough with your knuckles each time you fold it over. Kneading enables the dough to rise. A few minutes practice is all you need to become competent, and it is a very satisfying culinary skill but, if you prefer, you can use the dough hook attachment on an electric mixer.

Rising: To rise properly, bread dough needs warmth and contact with the yeast microorganisms that exist in the air. High humidity can cause bread to rise faster so be prepared to reduce the rising time if the atmosphere is humid. Cold will slow down the rising process: if you have to leave the dough for more than 2 or 3 hours, refrigerate it to prevent it over-rising and breaking. If it should over-rise and collapse, knead again and bake immediately.

Flavor: In addition to the type of flour used and any added flavorings, the taste of bread is also affected by:
Yeast – too much adversely flavors the dough
Salt – without it the bread, whether savory or sweet, will be flat-tasting
Water – any unpleasant flavors in treated water are intensified in bread; use bottled water for best results
Rising – the longer the rise, the greater the flavor – cover the dough or bowl with plastic wrap to minimize contact with the air and slow down the rising

Making a good crust: A simple way to create a good bread crust is to spray the dough with water once or twice during baking. Slashing the top of the dough with a clean razor blade or very sharp knife gives the bread an attractive appearance; this can be done either before the second rise, in which case the crust will separate quite dramatically during baking, or just before baking. Wet doughs (such as that for Spinach Bread, page 258) cannot be slashed, nor can over-risen dough. Greek bakers usually slash only round loaves; a traditional design is two or three parallel lines cut diagonally across the center.

Country Bread
Khoriatiko Psomi

This is the flavorful bread that appears daily on village tables. It's easy to make, has an excellent crumb, and a good strong flavor enhanced with honey and olive oil.

Makes 2 loaves

2 tablespoons active dry yeast
1 cup warm (110°F) water
2 tablespoons honey
2 teaspoons fine-grain sea salt
1 egg, lightly beaten
²/₃ cup milk, warmed (110°F)
2 tablespoons olive oil
2 tablespoons unsalted butter, melted
3³/₄ cups whole wheat flour *or* 2 cups *plus* 2 tablespoons whole wheat flour *and* 1¹/₂–2 cups graham flour (available in health food shops)

Sprinkle the yeast over 4 tablespoons of the warm water and set aside in a warm spot for 10 minutes, until foamy.

Combine the honey, salt, egg, milk, remaining water, 1 tablespoon of the olive oil, and half the butter in a bowl. Sift 2 cups of the flour into a large mixing bowl, make a well in the center, and stir in the yeast and honey mixtures. Knead for 10 minutes, gradually adding enough of the remaining flour to make a firm, smooth, and elastic dough. Tightly cover the bowl and set aside in a warm draft-free spot for 1¹/₂ hours, until doubled in bulk.

Lightly oil a heavy baking sheet. Knead the dough 1 minute. Form into 2 round loaves and place well apart on the baking sheet. Cover with a clean dish towel and set aside for 1 hour in a warm spot to rise.

Heat the oven to 375°F.

Brush the loaves with the remaining olive oil and butter and bake 40 minutes, or until lightly browned and, when tapped on the bottom, sound hollow. Cool on a rack.

Shepherd's Bread
Artos Voskou

This strongly flavored, densely-textured bread is sometimes made into a large round loaf, often with a hole in the center, sometimes into long or round rolls. Greeks have been baking tasty country bread like this for centuries; originally made with oat bran and barley meal it's now more commonly made with oat and wheat brans and stone-ground flour. This bread is delicious served with grilled meats, salads, and sheep's or goat's cheeses or just dipped in olive oil or red wine. Try making it with fresh sheep's milk instead of water, as the ancient Greeks did.

Makes 2 round loaves or 10 rolls

2 tablespoons honey
3 teaspoons sea salt
5 tablespoons olive oil
1 cup wheat bran
1 cup oat bran
2 cups lukewarm water *or* sheep's *or* goat's milk
2½–3 cups whole wheat flour

Combine the honey, salt, 3 tablespoons olive oil, the wheat bran, oat bran, and water in a large jar. Tightly cover and set aside for 18–22 hours in a warm draft-free spot to ferment. After about 12 hours the mixture should begin to give off an aroma rather like that of fresh beer; let ferment longer. Don't worry if it takes a few hours longer to give off the characteristic aroma.

Sift ⅝ cup flour, mix it into the fermenting bran mixture with a wooden spoon, replace the lid, and set aside for 4 hours longer in the same warm spot. The dough will have developed a sponge-like texture.

Sift ⅞ cup of the remaining flour into a large mixing bowl, make a well in the center, and pour in the bran mixture. Knead thoroughly for at least 5 minutes, adding additional flour if necessary to make a firm dough – it will never feel as smooth or as elastic as dough made with yeast.

Lightly brush a heavy baking tray with some of the olive oil. Form the dough into 2 round loaves or 10 round or long rolls and arrange on the tray, spaced well apart. Cover with plastic wrap and set aside for 2–3 hours in a warm draft-free place to rise. The dough will increase in bulk by only about one third.

Heat the oven to 350°F.

Brush the loaves or rolls with the remaining olive oil and bake 15 minutes, then reduce the oven temperature to 325°F. Bake loaves 50 minutes longer, rolls 30 minutes longer, until they sound hollow when lightly tapped on the bottom. Cool on a rack.

Store Cupboard Bread
Paximathi me Salata

Bread quickly becomes stale in hot climates, and this bread is a country solution to the problem. Baked until it becomes hard and dry, it can be stored almost indefinitely. Then, when it is needed, it is soaked in wine, olive oil, or water and almost magically regains its dense and delicious texture. A village neighbor spreads chopped sweet tomatoes over the bread and sprinkles them with pungent herbs, making a simple and delicious summer lunch. Serve with Purslane Salad (page 220) and bowls of olives and cheese.

The Greeks also double-bake rolls and thick slices of bread, but the method works only with coarse or densely textured bread; softer, loose-textured loaves just become soggy if revived in the same way.

Serves 4 to 6

1 round loaf Shepherd's Bread (page 250), cut in half horizontally
½ cup water
Juice of 1 lemon
6 large ripe tomatoes, skinned, seeded if desired, and diced
½ teaspoon sugar
1 teaspoon coarse-grain sea salt, or to taste
1–2 teaspoons cracked black pepper, or to taste
1 cup extra virgin olive oil to taste
1 small red *or* mild onion, cut into thin rings
4 tablespoons finely chopped flat-leaf parsley
2 tablespoons dried *rigani* (see page 13) *or* 1 tablespoon dried thyme, crumbled

Heat the oven to 225°F.

Place the bread, cut sides up, on a heavy baking tray, and bake 30 minutes, until hard, turning once. Cool on a rack.

Place the bread on a plate and sprinkle the water and lemon juice evenly over it. Set aside for 30 minutes, or until the liquids are absorbed. Sprinkle the tomatoes with the sugar, salt, and pepper, and set aside.

Pour ½ cup of the olive oil over the bread, set aside for a few minutes, then spoon over the tomatoes. Scatter the onion over the tomatoes and sprinkle with the parsley, *rigani*, and remaining olive oil. Serve at once.

Pita Bread
Pita

The perfect bread to accompany *souvlakia* and other grilled meats, *pita* is soft-textured and mildly sweet. It's also straightforward to prepare and well worth making since the flavor of homemade *pita* is far superior to that of the bland commercial product. It keeps well for a few days and can be frozen. There are a surprising number of ways to make it, but the following is the one I find works the best.

Makes 6 medium pita breads

1 teaspoon light honey
3/4–1 cup warm (110°F) water
1 tablespoon active dry yeast
1 teaspoon fine-grain sea salt
3 tablespoons olive oil
1 cup whole wheat flour
1 cup all-purpose flour

Combine the honey and 4 tablespoons warm water in a bowl and sprinkle the yeast over. Set aside for 10 minutes in a warm spot. Dissolve the salt in the remaining warm water and add 1½ tablespoons of the olive oil.

Sift the whole wheat flour and ½ cup all-purpose flour into a large bowl, make a well in the center, and pour in the yeast and salt mixtures. Mix with your hands, adding up to 4 tablespoons additional water or up to ½ cup additional all-purpose flour if necessary to make a moist but firm dough. Transfer to a lightly floured surface and knead 10 to 15 minutes, until smooth and elastic. Transfer to a lightly oiled bowl, and brush with olive oil. (The oil keeps the dough moist while rising.) Cover the bowl with a slightly damp clean dish towel and set aside in a warm draft-free spot for 2 hours, or until at least doubled in bulk.

Arrange 1 rack close to the bottom of the oven, 1 to the top, and heat the oven to 425°F.

Knead the dough 2 minutes and divide into 6 portions. Set aside for 10 minutes in a warm spot to rest, then flatten each portion with your palm. Lightly flour a work surface and roll the dough into ¼-inch thick rounds or ovals. Brush a heavy baking sheet with the remaining olive oil and slide the pita rounds onto it, spacing them at least 4 inches apart. (Don't brush the pitas or they will not rise properly.)

Place the baking sheet on the lower oven rack and bake 3 minutes. Quickly transfer to the top rack and bake 3 or 4 minutes longer, until the pitas are puffy but not even lightly browned. They should still be soft. (If your oven is small and you need to use 2 baking sheets or more, place the second sheet in the oven when you move the first to the top rack.)

Stack between warm and very slightly damp clean dish towels and set aside in a draft-free spot until cool. Seal in plastic bags to store.

Olive Bread
Eliopsomo

This aromatic bread changes its character with the seasons. In spring it's gently perfumed with fresh rosemary or fennel; in winter dried thyme or mint gives it a more pungent but less subtle flavor. Olive bread has a long-standing tradition in Greek life and is believed to have appeared on Minoan tables three thousand years before the birth of Christ. This is a modern version of an ancient recipe, made with added yeast, but it retains all the rustic simplicity and taste of the original. Cut it into thin slices and serve with *mezedes,* sausages, or omelets.

Makes 1 large round loaf or 2 small ones

1 teaspoon honey
1 cup warm (110°F) water
1½ tablespoons active dry yeast
½ cup extra virgin olive oil
1 teaspoon fine-grain sea salt
2½–3 cups whole wheat flour
12 plump Greek *or* other oil-cured olives, pitted
1 large onion, finely chopped
1 tablespoon fresh rosemary *or* fennel leaves, finely chopped *or*
    1 tablespoon dried thyme *or* mint, crumbled

Dissolve the honey in the water in a small bowl and sprinkle the yeast over. Set aside in a warm place until foamy, about 10 minutes. Whisk in 3 tablespoons of the olive oil and the salt.

Sift 1½ cups of the flour into a large mixing bowl, make a well in the center, and add the yeast mixture. Knead 10 minutes, adding enough of the remaining flour to make a firm but elastic dough. Set aside in a warm draft-free place for 2 hours, until at least doubled in bulk.

Heat 3 tablespoons of the remaining olive oil in a heavy frying pan and sauté the onion over low heat until pale golden, about 10 minutes. Set aside.

Blanch the olives in boiling water for 1 second; drain and dry with paper towels. Cut 5 of the olives into small pieces and finely chop the rest. Add the olives and rosemary to the onions and stir to mix. Add to the dough and knead 1 minute.

Brush a heavy baking sheet with olive oil. Form the dough into 1 or 2 slightly flattened round loaves on the sheet, spaced well apart. Cover with a clean dish towel and set aside for 1 hour in a warm draft-free spot.

Heat the oven to 375°F.

Bake the bread 10 minutes, reduce the oven temperature to 350°F, brush with the remaining olive oil and bake 25–35 minutes longer, until the bread is deep golden brown and sounds hollow when tapped on the bottom.

Note Also try plump fleshy Amfissa olives instead of the more pungent oil-cured ones.

Cheese Mint Bread

Tyropsomo Thiosmou

The characteristic, rather musty, flavor of *halloumi* cheese is particularly suited to bread made with olive oil. If it is unavailable, *feta* cheese makes a perfectly good substitute, but it should be drained well before using. This densely textured bread, fragrant with mint, is traditionally made in small loaves, ideal for picnics or to serve with salads.

Makes 3 small loaves

About 1/2 cup warm (110°F) water
1 tablespoon active dry yeast
5 tablespoons extra virgin olive oil
1 teaspoon fine-grain sea salt
2 1/4 cups whole wheat flour
2 tablespoons dried mint, finely crumbled
Scant 1/2 pound *halloumi or feta* cheese, cut or crumbled into small pieces
1 tablespoon freshly squeezed lemon juice

Pour 3/8 cup of the water into a small bowl and sprinkle the yeast over. Set aside in a warm place until foamy, about 10 minutes. Whisk in 4 tablespoons of the olive oil and the salt.

Sift the flour into a large mixing bowl, make a well in the center, and pour in the yeast mixture. Knead 10 minutes, adding some, or all, of the additional water if necessary to make a firm elastic dough. Transfer to a lightly oiled bowl, and brush the dough with olive oil. Tightly cover the bowl with plastic wrap and set aside for 2 1/2 hours in a warm draft-free spot. It will not quite double in bulk, but the long resting time produces a well-flavored bread.

Knead in the mint. Divide the dough into 3 portions. Form each into a ball, then flatten on a board to a thickness of 3/4 inch. Place one third of the cheese in the center of each and bring up the edges of the dough to barely enclose the cheese, but do not seal. Transfer to a lightly oiled heavy baking sheet, cover with a clean dish towel, and set aside for 1 hour in a warm draft-free spot.

Heat the oven to 350°F.

Combine the remaining olive oil and the lemon juice and lightly brush the loaves with this mixture. Bake 10 minutes, reduce the oven temperature to 325°F, and bake 40 minutes longer or until golden brown.

Rigani Cheese Bread

Tryopsomo Riganato

I first tasted this delicious bread at a picnic high in the Pindus mountains – an appropriate setting for a bread heavily scented with mountain herbs. The great round loaf, with its glistening olive oil glaze and rich cheese flavor, was the delicious centerpiece of the outdoor feast; around it were spread olives, *kephtedakia* (page 31), Smoked Fish Salad (page 29), and *mezedes* of eggplant and other vegetables.

Makes 1 large round loaf

1 tablespoon active dry yeast
1 cup warm (110°F) water
3 tablespoons olive oil
1/2 teaspoon fine-grain sea salt
2 1/4–3 cups whole wheat flour
2 tablespoons dried *rigani* (see page 13), crumbled
1/2 tablespoon dried mint, finely crumbled
3/4 pound *feta* cheese, well drained and finely crumbled
1 egg yolk beaten with 2 tablespoons warm water

Sprinkle the yeast over the water and set aside in a warm place until foamy, about 10 minutes. Whisk in 2 tablespoons of the olive oil and the salt.

Sift 2 1/4 cups of the flour into a large mixing bowl, make a well in the center, and pour in the yeast mixture. Knead 10 minutes, adding the remaining flour if necessary to make a firm, elastic dough. Transfer to a lightly oiled bowl, tightly cover with plastic wrap, and set aside for 2 hours in a warm draft-free spot.

Knead in the *rigani*, mint, and *feta* until evenly distributed throughout the dough. Lightly oil a heavy baking sheet and place the dough in the center. Form into a round loaf and flatten to a thickness of 2 inches.

Cover with a clean dish towel and set aside for 1 hour in a warm draft-free spot. The dough will rise only slightly.

Heat the oven to 350°F.

With a sharp thin blade, slash the top of the loaf diagonally in 2 or 3 parallel lines, brush with the remaining olive oil, and bake 25 minutes. Brush with the beaten egg yolk and bake 15 minutes longer, until the bread is deep golden brown and sounds hollow when tapped on the bottom.

Fennel Bread
Marathopsomo

Fennel bread changes its character during the year, according to the type of fennel used to flavor it. The finest-flavored loaves appear on Greek tables in early spring when succulent young fennel is at its best. Later in the season finely chopped larger fennel sprigs are used, and, for the rest of the year, the bread is made with pulverized fennel seeds. This exquisite bread is the perfect complement to a light meal of Beets Island-Style (page 183), olives, and *myzithra* cheese (see page 10). Its distinctive flavor is also superb with grilled fish, chicken, or pork.

Makes 1 large or 2 smaller loaves

1 tablespoon active dry yeast
1 cup warm (110°F) water
5 tablespoons extra virgin olive oil
1 teaspoon fine-grain sea salt, or to taste
2¼–3 cups whole wheat flour
1 large handful fennel sprigs *or* 3 tablespoons fennel seeds
2 medium onions, finely chopped
Juice of 1 large lemon
4 ounces *feta* cheese, well-drained and finely crumbled
1 teaspoon coarse-grain sea salt, or to taste
6 Elitses *or* Niçoise olives, blanched in boiling water for 5 seconds, drained, pitted, and halved

Sprinkle the yeast over the water and set aside in a warm place until foamy, about 10 minutes. Whisk in 2 tablespoons of the olive oil and ½ teaspoon of the fine-grain sea salt.

Sift 2¼ cups of the flour into a large bowl, make a well in the center, and pour in the yeast mixture. Knead 10 minutes, adding the remaining flour if necessary to make a firm elastic dough. Transfer to a lightly oiled bowl, brush the dough with olive oil, tightly cover with plastic wrap, and set aside for 2 hours in a warm draft-free spot. The dough will not quite double in bulk.

Blanch fresh fennel in boiling water for 5 seconds, pat dry with paper towels, and chop finely. (Or pound fennel seed and the remaining fine-grain salt in a mortar, or grind in a coffee grinder until almost pulverized, just before the seeds become a powder.) Combine the fresh fennel and remaining fine-grain salt (or the pounded fennel), onion, most of the lemon juice, and 2 tablespoons olive oil, and knead into the dough along with the cheese.

Lightly oil a baking sheet. Form the dough into 1 or 2 round loaves and flatten to 2 inches. With a clean thin blade, slash 2 parallel lines diagonally across the top of the loaf(ves), and set aside for 1 hour in a warm draft-free spot. The slashes will open as the dough rises.

Heat the oven to 350°F.

Sprinkle the coarse-grain salt inside the slashes and gently press the olives into the tops of the loaf(ves), cut sides down. Brush with the remaining olive oil and lemon juice and bake smaller loaves 35 minutes, 1 large loaf 50 minutes, until browned and the bread sounds hollow when tapped on the bottom.

Spinach Bread

Spanakopsomo

Traditionally this bread is made with wild greens. Spinach gives a smoother, lighter bread (and is easier to find), but you may like to try the ancient khorta version too. This flattish, chewy bread with its distinctive flavor is perfect with salads, egg dishes, and cheese and olives.

Makes 1 large round loaf or 2 smaller ones

1 teaspoon honey
2 teaspoons fine-grain sea salt
3/4 cup warm (110°F) water
1 tablespoon active dry yeast
5 tablespoons olive oil
3 cups whole wheat or spelt flour (available in health food shops)
2 pounds fresh spinach
2 large mild onions, finely chopped
1 large clove garlic, finely chopped
1½ tablespoons cumin seeds or 1 tablespoon ground cumin
Juice of 1 lemon

Combine the water, honey, and 1 teaspoon salt in a medium bowl and sprinkle the yeast over. Set aside in a warm place until foamy, about 10 minutes. Whisk in 2 tablespoons of the olive oil, then sift in 2/3 cup flour and stir to mix. Set aside in a warm draft-free spot for 1 hour, until sponge-like in texture.

Meanwhile, rinse the spinach in several changes of cold water, remove the tough stalks and leaves, and cut tender leaves into 1/4-inch strips. Set aside. Heat 2 1/2 tablespoons of the olive oil in a large heavy frying pan and sauté the onion over a low heat until pale golden, about 15 minutes. Heat the cumin in a small dry frying pan until aromatic, and pulverize it in a mortar or grinder. Add the cumin, garlic, and remaining salt to the onion. Stir in the spinach and cook 5 minutes, stirring frequently, until soft. Sprinkle with the lemon juice and drain in a colander set over a bowl. Set aside, reserving the cooking liquid.

Sift 1 3/4 cups of the remaining flour into a large bowl, make a well in the center, and pour in the yeast sponge. Knead 10 minutes, adding enough of the reserved cooking liquid to make a firm but elastic dough. Transfer to a lightly oiled bowl, tightly cover with plastic wrap, and set aside for 2 hours in a warm draft-free place.

Add the *feta* to the dough and knead 1 minute. Add the spinach mixture, sprinkle with the remaining flour, and quickly mix together – the dough will be quite moist and loose; do not knead it again.

Brush a baking sheet with olive oil and place the dough on it. Form into 1 large round loaf or 2 smaller ones spaced well apart. Cover with a clean dish towel and set aside for 1 hour in a warm draft-free spot.

Heat the oven to 375°F.

Bake the bread 20 minutes, reduce the oven temperature to 350°F, brush with the remaining olive oil, and bake 20–30 minutes longer, until golden brown.

Festive Bread
Tsoureki

During any major religious festival, this shiny glazed celebration bread is attractively displayed in every Greek cake shop and coffeehouse window, and laden baskets of the loaves hang from the ceiling of every bakery.

However, many Greeks still prefer to make their own *tsoureki*, and every family has a favorite flavoring – orange, lemon, mastic, vanilla, allspice, or cloves and bay are the most popular. The traditional shape is a braided or round loaf, but forming the dough into long loaves makes it easier to store and cut. It makes delicious toast, and it keeps for well up to 1 week.

Makes 2 braided loaves or 3 long loaves

3/4 cup light brown sugar
1/2 cup warm (110°F) water
2 tablespoons active dry yeast
2 1/2 cups all-purpose flour

2½–2¾ cups pastry flour

½ cup *plus* 2 tablespoons milk, warmed (110°F)

2 tablespoons olive oil

5 eggs

Juice of ½ orange

2 tablespoons finely grated orange zest, briefly dried in a low oven and pulverized in a mortar *with* ½ teaspoon sugar, *or* 1½ tablespoons orange extract

½ teaspoon vanilla extract

1 teaspoon ground allspice *or* 1 teaspoon mastic granules (see page 13) pulverized in a mortar *with* ½ teaspoon sugar

1 teaspoon fine-grain sea salt, or to taste

4 tablespoons (½ stick) unsalted butter, melted

1 egg yolk

1 tablespoon honey

4 tablespoons sesame seeds *or* blanched slivered almonds

Dissolve 1 teaspoon brown sugar in the water and sprinkle the yeast over. Set aside in a warm place until foamy, about 10 minutes.

Sift 1⅔ cups of the all-purpose flour into a large bowl, make a well in the center, and pour in the yeast mixture. Knead and gradually add the ½ cup milk, remaining all-purpose flour, and 1½ cups of the pastry flour, or enough to make a light, smooth, and elastic dough. Turn onto a lightly floured surface and knead 10 minutes. Transfer to a lightly oiled bowl, and brush with olive oil. Cover with a warm damp dish towel and set aside in a warm draft-free place for 1 hour, until at least doubled in bulk.

Beat the eggs in a large bowl until light and frothy and beat in the remaining brown sugar, the orange juice, orange zest, vanilla, allspice, and salt. Add to the dough with 3 tablespoons melted butter and knead in enough of the remaining pastry flour to make a soft dough. Transfer to a lightly floured surface and knead 3 minutes.

Divide the dough into 6 portions. With the palms of your hands, roll each into a 9-inch rope, slightly fatter in the middle and with pointed ends. Brush a large heavy baking tray with the remaining melted butter. Lay 3 ropes on it side by side, loosely braid, and tuck the pointed ends underneath so the loaf ends are rounded. Repeat with the remaining 3 ropes, spacing the 2 braided loaves well apart. To make long loaves, either form the dough into loaves on the baking sheet or place in buttered loaf pans. Loosely cover with plastic wrap and set aside in a warm draft-free place for 2 hours, until doubled in bulk.

Heat the oven to 400°F.

Whisk together the egg yolk, honey, and the 2 tablespoons milk and brush the loaves with this mixture. Sprinkle with sesame seeds and bake 10 minutes.

Reduce the oven temperature to 350°F and bake 20 minutes longer, until a beautiful honey brown. Transfer to racks to cool.

Easter Bread
Lambropsomo

The almond-topped bread that breaks the Lenten fast has pride of place on the Easter Sunday table. Rich in eggs and butter (foods forbidden during Lent), these shinny loaves display all the baker's artistry with their splendid decorations of spring flowers, leaves, or berries shaped in dough. Many of these Easter breads are so beautifully crafted that they are used as wall decorations throughout the year. Red eggs, signifying both rebirth and the blood of Christ, are an important part of the decoration – they delight the children but, unlike our traditional Easter eggs, are never eaten.

Makes 2 braided or large round loaves

6 white eggs, at room temperature
2 teaspoons red food coloring
Few drops blue food coloring
1 tablespoon olive oil
1 recipe Festive Bread dough (page 259), made without allspice or mastic
²/₃ cup blanched slivered almonds

Half fill a stainless steel saucepan with water, bring to a boil, and add the food colorings. Gently boil the eggs 20 minutes; add a little more coloring if necessary to produce deep crimson-colored eggs.

Let the eggs cool in the water, remove them, and set aside to dry. Dip a paper towel in the olive oil, and rub each egg all over with it.

Form the dough into 2 braided (see page 260) or round loaves on buttered baking sheets; if making round loaves reserve a little of the dough for decoration. Roll the reserved dough into thin ropes with the palms of your hands and break off small pieces to make into spring symbols, such as flowers, leaves, or berries. Decorate the tops of the round loaves with these shapes. Set the loaves aside for 2 hours in a warm draft-free spot to rise.

Heat the oven to 400°F.

Place the eggs either around the centers of the round loaves or between the decorations, or arrange the eggs between the braids. Brush with the egg and honey glaze, sprinkle with the almonds, and bake 10 minutes. Reduce the oven temperature to 350°F and bake 20 minutes longer, until golden brown, and transfer to racks to cool.

Discard the eggs once the bread is cut.

Christmas Bread

Christopsomo

This enticingly festive bread is the focal point of a strong religious tradition. After midnight mass on Christmas Eve, each family gathers together to share the loaf, in great anticipation of who will find the lucky coin baked inside. The head of the household first breaks off a piece and sets it aside "for Christ"; then pieces are given to guests sharing the celebration. The next two pieces are for himself and the female head of the household, and finally the remainder is shared between the others at the table, men first, then women and, lastly, the children. Whoever finds the coin will be blessed with good luck; if it is found in the piece reserved for Christ, the money is given to the church or to charity. For a traditional Christmas table the bread is baked in the shape of any "blessing" the family would like to give thanks for, such as livestock or produce of the fields, and many city-dwelling cooks still shape their Christmas breads into these ancient symbols of good fortune.

Makes 2 shaped or round loaves

1 recipe Saint Basil's Bread (page 263), substituting:
3 cloves, 2 bay leaves *and* 1 2-inch cinnamon stick for the aniseed;
2 tablespoons lemon zest *or* lemon extract for the orange zest, *optional;*
    and ²/₃ cup blanched slivered almonds for the sesame seeds
2 egg whites
¹/₃ cup *plus* 1 tablespoon superfine sugar
Pinch of salt
12 small walnut halves
¹/₃ cup candied fruit, cut into tiny cubes

Form the dough into 2 loaves on a buttered baking sheet and let it rise a second time (see page 263).

Heat the oven to 375°F.

Whisk the egg whites until thick but not stiff, then whisk in the sugar and salt. Brush the loaves generously with this glaze. Arrange the walnut halves on top, gently pushing them onto the dough, then sprinkle over the candied fruit. Lightly brush with the remaining glaze and bake 40–50 minutes, until deep chestnut brown. Cool on a rack.

Saint Basil's Bread

Vasilopitta

Named for a founding father of the Orthodox church, this is the traditional New Year's bread and, like Christmas Bread, has a lucky coin baked inside. At the last chime of midnight on New Year's Eve the head of the family breaks the bread and divides it between those gathered for the celebration. Appropriately, for a bread made in honor of a Byzantine saint, the Eastern spice *mahlepi* is a favorite flavoring, but aniseed is also popular and whole aniseed gives the bread an interesting texture and a pungent festive aroma. This delectable loaf is a year-round favorite in nontraditional households. The traditional shape is a very large round loaf with a smaller loaf on top, but it's easier to store if you make it into two long loaves or rolls. It keeps well and can also be frozen.

Makes 1 large round loaf, 2 long loaves, or 18 rolls

2 tablespoons whole aniseed *or* 1 tablespoon *mahlepi* seeds (available in Greek or Middle Eastern shops), lightly crushed

2 tablespoons active dry yeast

1 cup *plus* 2 tablespoons milk, warmed (110°F)

2½ cups all-purpose flour *and* 2¼–3 cups whole wheat *or* spelt flour, *or* about 5 cups all-purpose flour

7 eggs

⅔ cup honey

1 teaspoon fine-grain sea salt, or to taste

⅔ cup *plus* 2 teaspoons superfine sugar

¾ cup unsalted butter, melted

5 tablespoons light olive oil

2 tablespoons finely grated orange zest, briefly dried in a low oven and pulverized in a mortar *with* 1 teaspoon sugar, *or* 2 tablespoons orange extract

¾ cup sesame seeds

Combine the aniseed and ½ cup water in a small saucepan, bring to a boil, and simmer 1 minute. Set aside to cool. Strain and set aside the liquid (or set aside both seeds and liquid).

Pour 1 cup milk into a medium bowl, sprinkle the yeast over, and set aside for 10 minutes in a warm spot, until foamy. Stir 1 cup of the all-purpose flour into the yeast with a wooden spoon, tightly cover, and set aside in a warm draft-free spot for 1 hour, until it has become sponge-like in texture.

With a wire whisk or electric mixer, beat 6 of the eggs, the honey, salt, and all but 2 teaspoons of the sugar in a large bowl until light and frothy.

Sift the remaining all-purpose flour and 1¹¹/₂ cups of the whole wheat flour into another large bowl, make a well in the center, and pour in the yeast sponge, aniseed liquid (and seeds if desired), about ½ cup of the butter, 4 tablespoons olive oil, the orange zest, and the egg mixture. Knead 5 minutes, transfer to a lightly floured surface, and knead 10 minutes longer, adding enough of the remaining flour to make a soft smooth dough.

Transfer to a lightly oiled bowl and brush the dough with the remaining olive oil. Tightly cover and set aside in a warm draft-free spot for 2 hours, until at least doubled in bulk.

Transfer to a lightly floured surface and knead 5 minutes. Divide into 2 portions, one twice as large as the other. Liberally butter a baking sheet with the remaining butter and place the larger portion on the sheet. Form it into a round loaf about 2 inches thick, and flatten the top slightly with your palm. Form the smaller portion into a round loaf about 1 inch thick, flattening it on the bottom, and center it on top of the larger one. (To make long loaves, either form into loaves on the baking sheet or place in buttered loaf pans. To make rolls, divide the dough into 18 portions and form into round or long rolls on a buttered baking sheet, spaced at least 3 inches apart.) With a wooden skewer or equivalent, write the year on top for New Year's bread or make a simple design. Loosely cover with plastic wrap and set aside for 30 minutes in a warm draft-free spot.

Heat the oven to 375°F.

Beat the remaining egg with the reserved 2 teaspoons sugar and the 2 tablespoons milk and liberally brush the dough with this glaze. Sprinkle over the sesame seeds and bake 40–50 minutes, until deep chestnut brown. Cool on a rack.

Currant Bread

Stafithopsomo

With a more refreshing and lighter flavor than the familiar sweet raisin bread, this currant loaf is easy to make and has an attractive country character. It can be shaped into loaves or rolls and it makes perfect breakfast bread with yogurt, honey, and fresh fruit. Or try it toasted, with jam or preserves.

Makes 2 medium loaves or 12 rolls

¹/₃ cup *plus* 2 tablespoons honey
2 tablespoons unsalted butter, melted
1¹/₂ teaspoons fine-grain sea salt, or to taste
1¹/₄ cups milk, warmed (110°F)
2 tablespoons active dry yeast

3 cups whole wheat flour
1 cup all-purpose flour
½ teaspoon ground cloves
2 eggs, lightly beaten
1 tablespoon light olive oil
1⅓ cups currants

With a whisk, combine ⅓ cup plus 1 tablespoon honey, half the butter, the salt, and 1 cup of the milk in a small bowl. Sprinkle the yeast over and set aside in a warm place until foamy, about 10 minutes.

Sift both flours and the ground cloves into a large mixing bowl; remove and set aside 1 cup. Make a well in the center of the remaining flour, and stir in the yeast mixture and the eggs. Turn out onto a floured work surface and knead 4–5 minutes, until the dough is light, smooth, and elastic. Transfer to a lightly oiled bowl, brush the dough with the remaining olive oil, tightly cover with plastic wrap, and set aside in a warm draft-free place for 30 minutes, until increased in bulk by one third.

Sprinkle the currants and half the reserved flour mixture over the dough, and knead 5 minutes, adding some or all of the remaining flour, if necessary, to make a firm elastic dough. Cover the bowl and set aside in a warm draught-free place for 2 hours, or until doubled in bulk.

To make loaves Divide the dough into 2 portions. Lightly brush two 9x5-inch loaf pans with the remaining melted butter. Place 1 piece of dough in the center of each, or roll each piece into a 9x12-inch rectangle. Starting with a shorter side, roll up each rectangle to make a 9-inch loaf.

To make rolls Divide the dough into 12 portions and shape into rolls. Brush a heavy baking sheet with the remaining melted butter and set the rolls on it, spaced well apart.

Cover the loaves or rolls with a clean dish towel and set aside for 1 hour in a warm draft-free place, to rise.

Heat the oven to 375°F.

Whisk together the 1 tablespoon honey and the remaining milk and lightly brush the top of the dough to glaze. Bake loaves 1 hour, rolls 25 minutes, until they sound hollow when tapped on the bottom. Transfer to a rack to cool.

PIES, PASTRIES, CAKES, AND COOKIES

Glykes, Pittes, Tartes, ke Biscotakia

Greeks have a great fondness for syrup-drenched pastries, pies, and cakes, but they rarely end a meal with them. Fresh fruit is the usual dessert and the Greek sweet tooth is satisfied between meals, most often at a pastry shop. Every village has at least one of these *zacharoplastia*, and in large cities the visitor is tempted at every turn by ornate examples of sculptured sweetness.

The skill of the *zacharoplastis* ("sugar sculptor") elevates cake and pastry making to fine art and the range of these sugary concoctions is breathtaking. Gloriously honeyed pastries such as *baklava*, syrup-laden *kataifi* (page 270), and creamy Phyllo Custard Pie (page 268) are displayed alongside regional specialities such as the wonderful lemon pie from the island of Kos.

To mark historic occasions the pastrymaker bakes special celebration cakes; for festivals he bakes traditional sweet breads (pages 259 to 265), Tiny Sweet Phyllo Pies (page 272), and a variety of fragrant Honey Cakes (page 283), just as Greek bakers have done since ancient times.

Many of these traditional pastries and cakes are known as *glyka tou tapsiou*, meaning "sweets from the baking pan." After baking they are drenched in honey or syrup perfumed with orange-flower water or rose water or an aromatic spice. These, and the other pastries included here, are ambrosial. Serve them as snacks or dessert and, in the Greek fashion, provide Greek coffee (see page 335) and tall glasses of ice-cold water – perfect complements to the richness of these sweets.

Phyllo
Phyllo

The golden pies in the windows of Greek pastry shops owe their crisp beauty to phyllo pastry. Paper-thin sheets of phyllo are difficult to make at home, but excellent phyllo is available ready-made, fresh, or frozen. It is generally sold in 1-pound packages, each containing between 16 and 26 sheets of pastry, measuring 12x18 inches. Frozen phyllo must be allowed to thaw slowly in the refrigerator or it will become soggy. Unopened commercial phyllo can be refrigerated for up to five days but, once opened, it should be used within 24 hours.

Working with phyllo is straightforward if you bear in mind that, since it contains little oil, it must be kept moist or it will dry out and become impossible to manipulate. So cover it first with plastic wrap, then with a slightly damp clean dish towel (if the pastry touches the towel it will disintegrate). You can also protect the phyllo by working quickly but carefully.

If you would like to make your own phyllo you will need a large smooth tabletop or marble slab, a long thin rolling pin – and patience. Phyllo pastry must be stretched as thin as possible. In some small Greek villages, making phyllo is a group effort, requiring four people: One stands at each corner of the rolled-out dough and each helps to pull and stretch out the pastry until it is paper-thin.

Makes 1 pound pastry

2½ cups all-purpose flour
1 teaspoon fine-grain sea salt
¾–1 cup cold water
2 tablespoons olive oil

Sift 2 cups of the flour and the salt into a large mixing bowl and gradually add enough of the water to make a firm but moist dough. Transfer to a floured work surface and knead 15 minutes, until smooth and elastic. Sprinkle with half the olive oil and continue kneading, then sprinkle with the remaining olive oil and knead until it has all been incorporated. Tightly wrap in plastic wrap and refrigerate 1 hour to firm.

Lightly flour a tabletop or marble slab. Break off an egg-sized piece of dough and roll it out, rolling first in one direction, then turning the pastry and rolling again. Lightly flour the board as necessary. As the sheet becomes larger and thinner, use the rolling pin to help turn the pastry, or use a broom handle if the rolling pin is too short. When the pastry is paper-thin, trim the edges, cut into rectangles about 12x18 inches, and stack between lightly floured clean dish towels. Set aside to dry for 10 minutes before using or storing. Repeat with the remaining dough.

To freeze, stack half the phyllo on waxed paper, cover with another sheet of waxed paper, and roll up loosely. Repeat with the remaining phyllo, wrap each roll in plastic wrap, and store in sealed freezer bags for up to 3 months.

Phyllo Custard Pie
Galaktoboureko

This magnificent syrupy pie is best eaten very fresh. The light custard filling is scented with vanilla and lemon; the syrup, poured hot over the baked pie, is sharpened with lemon and orange – or, often, perfumed with cloves and rose water (see page 350). Be sure to use unsalted butter, which is essential to the subtle and fragrant flavor.

Serves 12 to 15

5 cups milk

5 large eggs, separated

1 cup *plus* 2 tablespoons vanilla sugar (see page 15) *or* 1 cup superfine sugar *and* 1 teaspoon vanilla extract

1½ cups semolina (*farina, see* page 344)

1 tablespoon unsalted butter

1 (1-pound) package phyllo pastry *or* homemade phyllo (see page 266)

1 cup clarified butter (see page 11) *or* unsalted butter, melted

Syrup

1 cup honey

1 cup *plus* 2 tablespoons superfine sugar

Zest of 1 orange, removed in thin strips

Juice of 1 small lemon

3 tablespoons orange-flower water, or to taste

For serving

confectioners' sugar, sifted

Ground cinnamon

Heat the milk to just below a boil. Remove from the heat and set aside. With an electric mixer or whisk, beat the egg yolks and sugar (and vanilla) in a large bowl until pale and creamy. Beat in the semolina and gradually beat in the hot milk. Rinse out the saucepan and return the custard mixture to low heat. Cook, stirring constantly in a figure-8 motion with a wooden spoon, until the custard is firm enough to come away from the sides of the pan, about 6 minutes. Transfer to a bowl. Secure the butter on the tip of a knife and rub it over the surface of the custard; the butter will immediately melt to make a thin oily layer, preventing a skin from forming. Lightly press waxed paper on top and set aside to cool.

Arrange a rack in the center of the oven and heat the oven to 375°F.

Remove the package of phyllo pastry from the refrigerator and set aside unopened.

With a wire whisk, beat the custard until smooth. Whisk the egg whites in a copper or other mixing bowl until they hold stiff peaks. Stir one third of the whites into the custard to lighten it, then quickly fold in the remainder.

Divide the phyllo into 2 portions. Rewrap 1 and refrigerate. Lightly brush a 9x13-inch cake pan, at least 2^1/$_2$ inches deep, with melted butter. Line with 1 pastry sheet, carefully pushing it up the sides with your knuckle (fingernails tear phyllo). Lightly brush with butter and lay another sheet on top. Repeat with the remaining unrefrigerated phyllo, but do not brush the last sheet. Pour the custard into the pan, taking care not to disturb the phyllo lining the sides. Lightly smooth with a spatula and gently fold over any phyllo extending beyond the edges of the pan.

Remove the second portion of the phyllo from the refrigerator. Lay 1 sheet on top of the custard letting it hang over the sides of the pan and lightly brush with butter. Repeat with the remaining phyllo, but do not butter the last sheet. Ease the fingers of one hand down between the edge of the pie and sides of the pan. Gently pull the bottom edges of the pie slightly toward the center and lightly tuck the top sheets in around the bottom of the pie. Liberally butter the top sheet. With a thin sharp knife, score the top 2 sheets into 3-inch squares or into diamonds with 2-inch long sides.

Reduce the oven temperature to 350°F. Bake for 40 minutes, until the pastry is a deep golden brown and the custard is set: Gently shake the pie – it should sway only slightly; loosely cover with aluminium foil if it seems to be browning too quickly.

Meanwhile, combine the honey, sugar, orange zest, and 2 cups of water in a syrup pan or heavy saucepan. Bring slowly to a boil and simmer 10 minutes, until the syrup lightly coats the back of a metal spoon. Set aside.

As soon as you remove the pie from the oven, immediately cut through the score marks to the bottom of the pan. Add the lemon juice and orange-flower water to the syrup, strain, reserving the zest, and pour over the hot pie. Cover the pan with a clean dish towel, making sure the towel does not touch the top of the pastry, and set aside; the trapped steam softens the top layers of phyllo. Refrigerate if serving time is more than 2 hours away.

To serve, cut through the score marks once more to loosen the pieces. Liberally sprinkle with the icing sugar, lightly sprinkle with the cinnamon, and scatter the reserved orange zest over. Spoon over any syrup remaining in the pan, or serve the syrup separately if you prefer.

Kataifi Nut Rolls with Caramel Syrup

Kataifi Bourekakia

Aromatic nut-filled pastries made from very thin strands of vermicelli-like pastry, *kataifi* are sumptuous honey-sweet treats. The pastry, also called *kataifi*, is available frozen in Greek and Middle Eastern shops, and the preparation, although it sounds complicated, is really not difficult. For best results make these a day ahead and pour on the hot syrup as soon as you remove the cake pan from the oven: The *kataifi* will be sticky-sweet underneath but will remain crisp and golden on top. My favorite filling is made with pistachio nuts but almonds or walnuts are also good. For a dish of unashamed extravagance serve with Rich Cream (page 310).

Makes approximately 24 pastries

---

3 cups finely chopped unsalted skinned (see page 304) pistachio nuts, walnuts, *or* blanched almonds
1 egg white
1 pound honey
1 teaspoon ground cinnamon, or more to taste
1¼ cups clarified butter (see page 11) *or* unsalted butter, melted
1 (1-pound) package *kataifi*
1 cup sugar
Strained juice of ½ lemon

Heat the oven to 350°F.

Whisk the egg white in a small bowl until it holds stiff peaks. Stir in the nuts, 4 tablespoons of the honey, the cinnamon, egg white, and 2 tablespoons of the butter and set aside.

Loosen the strands of *kataifi*: Place the *kataifi* in the center of a clean work surface, pull off a small amount, and gently squeeze it in one hand. With your other hand pull apart the strands, but avoid tearing them. Repeat with all the pastry, but work fast (don't spend more than 1 minute doing this – *kataifi* dries out very quickly).

Lay a small handful in the palm of one hand and form into a rectangular shape. Place 1 tablespoon filling in the center, fold over the edges, and roll up toward your fingertips to make a parcel. As you finish each pastry, arrange it in 10-inch round or 9x13-inch cake pan in tight concentric circles (round pan) or lines (rectangular pan). Spoon the remaining butter evenly over the pastries and bake 40 minutes, until crisp and deep golden brown.

Meanwhile, melt the sugar in a syrup pan or small heavy saucepan and cook over a low heat until a deep gold (light caramel). While the sugar cooks, combine the remaining honey with 1¼ cups water in a heavy saucepan, slowly bring to a boil, and simmer 6 minutes, until the honey syrup lightly coats the back of a metal spoon. Wrap your hand in a clean dish towel and carefully spoon the honey syrup into the caramel – don't pour: Caramel can spit and burn. Stir in the lemon juice.

As soon as you remove the pastries from the oven, pour the hot syrup over them. Cover the pan with a clean dish towel, making sure it does not touch the pastries, and set aside to cool. Serve the pastries directly from the cake pan or piled high on a platter.

Kataifi Custard Pie in Rose Water Syrup
Kataifi me Krema

This easy-to-make pie is composed of layers of crisp golden *kataifi* and smooth rich custard. The *kataifi* are saturated with an exotic perfumed syrup of honey, cloves, lemon juice, and rose water and the result is mouth-watering. Serve with Rich Cream (page 310) and Greek Coffee (page 336).

Serves 16 to 20
....

½ cup rice flour
1 cup *plus* 2 tablespoons superfine sugar
3 cups pints milk
5 egg yolks
1 teaspoon vanilla extract
1 (1-pound) package *kataifi* (page 270)
1¼ cups clarified butter (see page 11) *or* unsalted butter, melted and
    strained through cheesecloth
1 pound aromatic honey (see page 17)
6 cloves
Strained juice of 1 small lemon
3 tablespoons rose water, or to taste

For serving
Kaymaki rolls (page 310), *optional*
....

Combine the rice flour with ¼ cup sugar and enough of the milk to make a smooth paste. Warm the remaining milk over low heat and whisk it into the paste. Rinse out the saucepan, return the milk mixture to the pan, and slowly bring to a boil, stirring constantly with a wooden spoon.

Reduce the heat to very low and simmer, stirring, 3 minutes or until smooth and thick. Beat together the egg yolks and vanilla, and briskly whisk into the milk mixture. Cook, stirring, 1 minute longer; don't let the custard boil. Set aside to cool.

Heat the oven to 350°F. Loosen the strands of *kataifi* as directed on page 270 and place in a large bowl. Brush 2 9-inch or 10-inch cake pans, one at least 3 inches deep, with melted butter and add the remaining butter to the *kataifi*. With your fingers, quickly coat the strands with butter, divide between the pans, and spread evenly. Bake 30–40 minutes, until crisp and a deep golden brown. Set aside to cool in the pans.

While the *kataifi* is baking, combine the honey, cloves, remaining sugar, and 1½ cups water in a heavy saucepan. Bring to a boil, then gently boil 10 minutes, until the syrup coats the back of a metal spoon. Set aside to cool slightly.

Discard the cloves and stir the lemon juice and rose water into the syrup. Pour two thirds of the warm syrup over the cooled *kataifi* in the deeper pan. Set aside for 5 minutes, until the syrup is absorbed by the pastry.

Cover the syrup-drenched *kataifi* with the custard and place the second *kataifi* layer on top. Gently press down on it and spoon over the remaining syrup. Cover the pan with a clean dish towel and set aside for at least 1 hour. Cut into slices and serve.

Tiny Sweet Phyllo Pies
Bourekakia

Traditionally shaped into triangles, squares, rectangles, cigars, or coils, these crisp golden glazed pastries are stuffed with a range of delectable fillings. Pistachio nuts, almonds, or walnuts are favorites, combined with honey and cinnamon, custard, or fresh cheese. For a spectacular display on a buffet table make them in a variety of shapes and with a choice of fillings. For this recipe, you can either make one of the two fillings given below or one of the fillings detailed on pages 270, 276, and 277.

Makes approximately 24 pastries

Nut filling
1¼ cup finely chopped walnuts
⅔ cup finely chopped blanched almonds
⅓ cup aromatic honey (see page 17)
1 teaspoon finely grated lemon zest
1 teaspoon ground cinnamon
1 egg, lightly beaten

Custard filling
2½ cups milk
4 large eggs, separated
½ cup vanilla sugar (see page 15) *or* ½ cup superfine sugar *and* ½
  teaspoon vanilla extract
¾ cup semolina (see *farina*, page 344)
1 tablespoon unsalted butter

1¼ cup clarified butter (see page 11) *or* unsalted butter, melted
1 (1-pound) package phyllo pastry (see page 266)

Syrup
⅞ cup aromatic honey (see page 17)
½ cup superfine sugar
Zest of 1 lemon, removed in thin strips
Juice of ½ lemon
2 tablespoons rose water *or* orange-flower water, *optional*

For serving
confectioners' sugar, sifted
1 cup finely chopped unsalted pistachio nuts, walnuts, *or* blanched
  almonds

To make the nut filling, combine the ingredients in a large bowl.

To make the custard filling, heat the milk to just below a boil. Remove
from the heat and set aside. With an electric mixer or whisk, beat the egg
yolks and sugar (and vanilla) in a large bowl until pale and creamy. Beat in
the semolina and gradually beat in the hot milk. Rinse out the saucepan
and return the custard mixture to low heat. Cook, stirring constantly in a
figure-8 motion with a wooden spoon, until firm enough to come away
from the sides of the saucepan, about 5 minutes. Transfer to a bowl. Secure
the butter on the tip of a knife and rub it over the surface of the custard.
Lightly press waxed paper on the top of the custard and set aside to cool.

Heat the oven to 350°F. Brush 2 baking sheets with some of the melted
butter.

Divide the phyllo into 2 portions. Rewrap 1 and refrigerate. Fold half
the remaining sheets in half, loosely cover with plastic wrap and then a
slightly damp clean dish towel, and set aside. Lay the remaining sheets,
stacked on top of each other, on the table, with the shorter side facing you.

To make triangles Cut the phyllo sheets lengthways into 4 strips and
stack the strips on top of each other. Lightly brush the top strip with
melted butter and carefully remove from the pile, then lightly butter a
second strip and place it on top of the first. Place 1 tablespoon nut filling
or 2 tablespoons custard filling on the bottom end of the buttered strips.

Take the bottom right corner of both strips between finger and thumb and fold over to the left side to make a triangle. Gently pull up the bottom left corner and fold up to make a second triangle. Continue folding until you reach the top. Place seam side down on the baking sheet. Repeat with the remaining phyllo and filling.

To make rolls Cut the phyllo sheets lengthways into 3 strips and stack on top of each other. Lightly brush the top strip with melted butter and carefully remove from the pile, then lightly butter a second strip and place it on the first. Spread 1½ tablespoons nut filling or 3 tablespoons custard filling along the bottom of the strip, leaving a ¾-inch border along the lower edge and the sides. Fold the lower edges of the strips over the filling and roll over twice, then bring both sides over the filling, lightly brush with butter, and roll up the strip. Place seam down on the baking sheet.

Cigars are small, thin rolls; rectangles and squares are made similarly but folded up, not rolled. If you prefer, all can be made with 1 phyllo strip instead of 2.

To make coils Cut the phyllo sheets lengthways into 3 strips and stack on top of each other. Lightly brush the top strip with melted butter and carefully remove from the pile. Spread 1 tablespoon nut filling or 2 tablespoons custard filling along the bottom, leaving a ¾-inch border along the lower edge and the sides. Fold the lower edge over the filling and fold over both sides. Firmly roll up, and lightly brush with butter. Place a finger on one end of the cylinder and, with the other hand, wrap it around to make a tight coil. Tuck the outside end in and under, and set it seam side down on the baking sheet.

Brush the pastries with the remaining melted butter and bake 20–25 minutes, until crisp and golden.

While the pies are baking, combine the honey, sugar, lemon zest, and 1 cup water in a syrup pan or a small heavy saucepan. Bring to a boil and simmer 10 minutes, until the syrup lightly coats the back of a metal spoon. Set aside to cool slightly, then add the lemon juice and rose water.

Dip the hot pastries in the warm syrup a few at a time and pile on a platter. Sprinkle with the confectioners' sugar and nuts, and serve warm or cold. Serve any remaining syrup in a bowl.

Nut Pastries in Fragrant Honey Syrup
Floyeres

With regional variations these crisp nut pastries are made throughout Greece and the islands. Sometimes they are baked, sometimes fried, and they may be shaped into half-moons, small circles, or squares. The filling given here is heady with cinnamon and cloves; these can also be made with the filling for Sweet Cheese Pastries (page 276) or any of those suggested for Tiny Sweet Phyllo Pies (page 272), and honey can be substituted for the syrup.

Makes approximately 24 pastries

Pastry
2 cups all-purpose flour
Pinch of salt
2 tablespoons confectioners' sugar
2 tablespoons unsalted butter, melted
2 tablespoons olive oil
2 egg yolks, lightly beaten
1 tablespoon finely grated orange zest, briefly dried in a low oven and
    pulverized in a mortar *with* 1 teaspoon sugar, *or* 1 teaspoon orange
    extract
Juice of 1 small orange

Filling
2 egg whites
2½ cups unsalted skinned (see page 304) pistachio nuts, walnuts, *or*
    blanched almonds, chopped
½ teaspoon ground cloves
1 teaspoon ground cinnamon
⅓ cup aromatic honey, such as Hymettus

⅝ cup unsalted butter, melted
2 egg yolks, lightly beaten with 2 tablespoons water

Syrup
⅞ cup aromatic honey, such as Hymettus
1 3-inch cinnamon stick, broken in half
4 cloves
Zest of 1 lemon, removed in thin strips
3 tablespoons orange-flower water, or to taste

For serving
½ cup unsalted skinned pistachio nuts, walnuts, *or* blanched almonds,
chopped
Confectioner's sugar, sifted

To make the pastry, sift the flour, salt, and sugar into a large bowl. Add the butter, olive oil, egg yolks, orange zest, and orange juice, and knead well for 5 minutes. Add cold water if necessary to make a smooth dough.

Tightly cover with plastic wrap and refrigerate for 1 hour.

To make the filling, beat the egg whites until they just hold soft peaks. Combine the nuts, cloves, cinnamon, honey, and egg whites, and set aside.

Heat the oven to 350°F. Lightly brush 2 baking sheets with melted butter.

Divide the dough in half, rewrap 1 portion, and refrigerate it. Lightly flour a clean work surface. Roll out the dough as thin as possible and cut into 3-inch circles with a cookie cutter or inverted glass or into 2-inch squares with a knife. Place 1 tablespoon filling in the center of half the circles or all the squares. Dip your forefinger in water and lightly dampen the pastry edges. Place a second circle on top of the first, or pull the corners of each square almost into the center to make a smaller square with a little filling exposed, and lightly press the edges together. Seal each circle by pressing the edge with the prongs of a fork or pastry wheel, or pinch the edge at ½-inch intervals to make a decorative border. Set the pastries 1 inch apart on the baking sheets, and repeat with the remaining dough and filling.

Brush with the remaining butter and bake 15 minutes, until the pastry is set. Brush with the beaten egg yolks and bake 10 minutes longer, until a deep golden brown. Transfer to a rack to cool.

Combine the honey, 1½ cups water, cinnamon stick, cloves, and lemon zest in a syrup pan or a heavy saucepan. Bring to a boil and simmer 5 minutes. Add the orange-flower water and keep the syrup hot over low heat. Dip the warm pastries in the syrup a few at a time and pile high on a warm platter. Sprinkle with the nuts and confectioners' sugar, and serve warm.

Sweet Cheese Pastries
Skaltsounakia

A speciality of the island of Crete, *skaltsounakia* are made with a lemon-scented pastry and filled with a sweetened mixture of *myzithra* and *feta* cheeses. Serve with bowls of warm Hymettus honey or syrup fragrant with orange-flower water (see page 17 or page 19).

Makes approximately 24 pastries

Pastry
2 cups all-purpose flour
Pinch of salt
1 tablespoon finely grated lemon zest, briefly dried in a low oven and pulverized in a mortar *with* 1 teaspoon sugar
½ cup (1 stick) unsalted butter, cold, cut into small pieces
2 egg whites

1 teaspoon vanilla extract
1–3 tablespoons cold milk *or* water
Filling
12 ounces fresh *myzithra* cheese (see page 10) *or* drained small-curd
    cottage cheese, pressed through a fine sieve
¼ cup grated *feta* cheese
2 egg yolks, lightly beaten
⅓ cup aromatic honey, such as Hymettus
1 teaspoon vanilla extract
2 tablespoons brandy, *optional*
1 teaspoon ground cinnamon, or to taste

4 tablespoons unsalted butter, melted
2 egg yolks, lightly beaten

For serving
Ground cinnamon *or* orange flower water
Confectioners' sugar, sifted

To make the pastry, sift the flour into a large bowl. Stir in the salt and lemon zest, add the butter, and lightly rub the mixture together with your fingers until it resembles coarse bread crumbs. Whisk the egg whites until they just hold soft peaks. Add the whites and vanilla to the flour and knead well, adding milk or water if necessary to make a smooth and elastic dough. Tightly cover with plastic wrap and refrigerate for 1 hour.

To make the filling, lightly mash the *myzithra* in a bowl. Add all the remaining filling ingredients and mash lightly with a fork until well mixed but not smooth. Set aside.

Heat the oven to 350°F. Lightly brush 2 baking sheets with melted butter.

Divide the dough in half, rewrap 1 portion, and refrigerate it. Lightly flour a clean work surface. Roll out the dough as thin as possible and cut into 4-inch circles with a cookie cutter or inverted glass or into 4-inch squares with a knife. Place 1 heaping tablespoon filling in the center of each. Dip your forefinger in water and lightly dampen the pastry edges. Fold over circles to make half-moons and seal by gently pressing the edges together with a pastry wheel or the prongs of a fork; or pull the corners of each square almost into the center to make a smaller square with a little filling exposed, and lightly press the edges together. Set the pastries 1 inch apart on the baking sheets, and repeat with the remaining dough and filling.

Brush with the remaining butter and bake 15 minutes, until the pastry is set. Brush with the beaten egg yolks and bake 10 minutes longer, until golden brown. Cool on a rack.

Sprinkle with the cinnamon (or orange-flower water) and sugar, and serve warm or at room temperature, with bowls of honey or a syrup of your choice.

Kos Lemon Pie

Lemonopitta tou Ko

A strong refreshing lemon flavor is the hallmark of this easy-to-make island speciality. For best results use whole blanched almonds and grind them yourself. And use a light touch when making the dough; the essence of this pie is its melt-in-the-mouth pastry and the perfect blend of the fresh natural ingredients. Serve this attractive midsummer dessert surrounded by lemon leaves if available.

Serves 10 to 12

Pastry
1 cup all-purpose flour
4 tablespoons confectioners' sugar
½ tablespoon finely grated lemon zest
Pinch of salt
½ cup (1 stick) unsalted butter, cold, cut into small pieces
2 egg yolks
1 teaspoon vanilla extract

Filling
½ cup (1 stick) unsalted butter, at room temperature
⅓ cup honey
5 egg yolks
2 cups finely ground blanched almonds
Strained juice of 2 lemons
4 tablespoons smooth Rich Cream (without crust, page 310) *or* heavy cream
½ cup superfine sugar
Zest of 2 lemons, removed in thin strips
Juice of 1 lemon

For serving
Confectioners' sugar, sifted

To make the pastry, sift the flour and confectioners' sugar into a large cold bowl, stir in the lemon zest and salt, and add the butter. Quickly and lightly rub the mixture together with your fingers until it resembles coarse bread crumbs. Beat the egg yolks and vanilla together and stir into the flour mixture. Pull the dough together into a ball with your fingers, adding cold water only if necessary to make a soft dough. Tightly cover with plastic wrap and refrigerate for 30 minutes.

Set a rack in the center of the oven and heat the oven to 375°F.

Lightly flour a work surface and roll out the pastry to fit a 9-inch or 10-inch tart pan with a removable bottom. To transfer the pastry, wrap it around the rolling pin, lift above the pan, and unroll over the rim. With your thumb or knuckle, gently press the pastry into the tart pan, then roll the rolling pin over the rim to trim the edges. Line with aluminium foil and bake 6–8 minutes or until just set. Set aside, and lower the oven temperature to 325°F.

To make the filling, beat the butter and honey with an electric mixer or by hand until pale and creamy. Beat in the egg yolks one at a time. Then stir in the almonds, the juice of 2 lemons, and the cream. Pour into the pastry shell and lightly smooth the top with a spatula. Bake 30–40 minutes, until golden brown and set.

Meanwhile, combine the sugar, lemon zest, and ½ cup water in a syrup pan or small heavy saucepan. Slowly bring to a boil, then simmer 6 minutes or until the syrup lightly coats the back of a metal spoon. Set aside to cool slightly.

Add the lemon juice to the barely warm syrup and strain, reserving the zest. Pour the syrup over the warm pie, remove from the pan, and liberally sprinkle with confectioners' sugar and the reserved zest. Serve immediately.

Note To make the pastry in the food processor, chill the processor container and metal blade in the refrigerator for 1 hour. Working very quickly, process the flour, sugar, lemon zest, and butter until the mixture resembles coarse bread crumbs. Add the egg yolks and vanilla and pulse just to mix. (It is unlikely that you will need to add water.) Wrap and refrigerate.

Sticky Yogurt Cake
Yiaourtopitta Glykisma

When the occasion calls for a really sticky cake, with lashings of syrupy sweetness, this is the treat to make. It's one of the best examples of the Greek tradition of *glyka tou tapsiou*, meaning "sweets from the baking pan." In a traditional version there would be even more of the sticky lemon syrup. Increase the amount of syrup if you like, but it's quite sweet as it is. This cake can be made in advance and in fact tastes even better if the flavors are allowed to mellow for a day. Serve, cut into slices, with Greek Coffee (page 336).

Serves 14 to 18

1¼ pounds aromatic honey, such as Hymettus *or* orange blossom
Zest of 1 lemon, removed in thin strips

³/4 cup superfine sugar
6 tablespoons unsalted butter, melted
4 eggs, separated
2 cups all-purpose flour
2 teaspoons baking powder
1⁷/8 cups Strained Yogurt (page 7), beaten until smooth
Juice of ½ lemon

Combine the honey, lemon zest, 2 tablespoons of the sugar, and 2 cups water in a syrup pan or heavy saucepan. Bring to a boil and simmer 10 minutes, until the syrup lightly coats the back of a metal spoon. Set aside to cool.

Meanwhile, remove the zest from the cooled syrup and stir in the lemon juice.

Set a rack in the center of the oven and heat the oven to 375°F. Brush a round 9-inch cake pan at least 2½ inches deep with 1 tablespoon of the melted butter and place on a baking sheet.

With an electric mixer, beat the egg yolks and remaining sugar together until pale and thick. Sift in 1½ cups of the flour and the baking powder and stir to mix. Stir in the remaining butter and the yogurt. Sift in enough of the remaining flour to make a dough stiff enough to come away from the sides of the bowl. (The consistency of the yogurt affects the quantity of flour needed.)

Whisk the egg whites until they hold stiff peaks and stir one third of the whites into the flour mixture. Fold in the remaining whites and pour into the cake pan. Bake 35 minutes, until golden brown and a cake tester is clean when removed.

As soon as you remove the cake from the oven, spoon the syrup over the top, letting it run down the sides. Cover the pan with a clean dish towel and set aside until cool.

Note For a traditional version of this cake, increase the quantity of syrup by half: Use 2 pounds honey, zest of 1½ lemons, ½ cup sugar, 2 cups water, and the juice of 1 small lemon.

Almond Cake in Honey Syrup

Revani

This cake has a pleasant almond and yogurt flavor and the syrupy coating can be orange- or lemon-scented, according to your taste. It will keep for up to one week in an airtight container, but it is likely to magically disappear long before that. Serve it cut into squares or diamond shapes, with *kaymaki* rolls (page 310) and Greek Coffee (page 336).

Serves 15 to 20

1 pound aromatic honey (see page 17)
1²/₃ cups superfine sugar
Zest of 1 large navel orange *or* 2 lemons, removed in thin strips
1½ tablespoons unsalted butter, melted
6 eggs, separated
2 cups fine-grain semolina (see *farina,* page 344)
3 oz blanched almonds, coarsely ground
1 cup Strained Yogurt (page 7), beaten until smooth
1 cup chopped blanched almonds
Strained juice of 1 large navel orange *or* 2 lemons
2 tablespoons orange-flower water, or to taste

Combine the honey, ½ cup of the sugar, the zest, and 1½ cups water in a syrup pan or heavy saucepan. Bring to a boil, and simmer 10 minutes or until the syrup lightly coats the back of a metal spoon. Let cool.

Heat the oven to 350°F. Brush a 9 inch-square cake pan, at least 2½ inches deep, with the melted butter.

With an electric mixer or by hand, beat the remaining sugar and the egg yolks together until pale and thick, about 5 minutes. Stir in the semolina, ground almonds, and yogurt. Whisk the egg whites until they form stiff peaks and stir one third into the semolina mixture. Fold in the remaining whites, pour into the cake pan, and sprinkle with the chopped almonds. Bake 40–45 minutes, until golden brown.

Meanwhile, stir the orange juice and orange-flower water into the cooled syrup.

As soon as you remove the cake from the oven, spoon the syrup and zest over the top, letting it run down the sides. Cover the pan with a clean dish towel and set aside for at least 2 hours before serving.

Honey Puffs
Loukoumades

Tucked away in the back streets of many Greek towns are tiny cafés that serve only these light fluffy puffs of yeast batter bathed in a velvety honey and cinnamon syrup. The pastries are made to order and served with a glass of ice water to cleanse the palate after the sweetness.

Make the batter at least 2 hours ahead. It should be of a pouring consistency but only just. As a *loukoumades* cook once explained to me, the batter is right "when the dough needs a little help to leave the hand or the spoon." Then fry the pastries when your guests are ready to eat – and not a minute before.

Makes about 36 pastries

2 teaspoons active dry yeast
3 tablespoons *plus* 1 teaspoon superfine sugar
3/4–11/4 cups warm (110°F) water
2 cups all-purpose flour
Pinch of salt
2 tablespoons olive oil
Peanut *or* corn oil, for deep-fat frying
11/4 pounds aromatic honey, such as Hymettus
2 tablespoons freshly squeezed lemon juice
2 tablespoons rosewater, or to taste, *optional*

For serving
11/2 tablespoons ground cinnamon

Dissolve the yeast and 1 teaspoon of the sugar in 4 tablespoons of the warm water and set aside until foamy, about 10 minutes.

Sift the flour and the salt into a large bowl and add the yeast mixture, olive oil, and 1/2 cup of the warm water. Beat with a wooden spoon or an electric mixer to make a soft dough, adding more warm water if necessary to make it just firm enough to need scooping off a spoon. Tightly cover and set aside in a warm draft-free spot for 2–3 hours to rise. The dough is ready when the surface bubbles and blisters; if the batter seems thin, beat in a little more sifted flour. Knead 2 minutes and set aside.

Heat the oil to 375°F (or until a little batter dropped in sizzles immediately) in a large saucepan or deep-fat fryer. Dip a spoon in the hot oil, then scoop up about 1 tablespoon of dough, and use a second spoon to push it off into the oil. Don't hold the spoons too high above the oil or you will be splashed. Fry 5 or 6 *loukoumades* at a time until deep golden brown on all sides, about 3 minutes. Remove with a slotted spoon and drain on paper towels.

Combine the honey and 1 cup water in a heavy saucepan, bring to a boil, and simmer 3 minutes. Stir in the lemon juice and rose water. Remove from the heat. Dip the *loukoumades* in the syrup a few at a time and heap on a warm platter or individual plates (5–6 per person). Mix the cinnamon with the remaining sugar and sprinkle over the pastries. Drizzle over a few threads of syrup and serve immediately.

Honey Cakes

Melomacarona (Finikia)

These light and crumbly cakes, Phoenician in origin, are offered to all visitors at Christmas and New Year's gatherings. The dough is shaped into small flat ovals and marked with a criss-cross design; after baking, each cake is dipped into a sweet syrup and sprinkled with nuts, cinnamon, and sugar for an attractive finishing touch. *Melomacarona* can be kept for up to 1 week in an airtight container.

Makes 24 small cakes

¹/₂ cup (1 stick) unsalted butter, melted
¹/₂–³/₄ cup olive oil
1¹/₂ cups fine-grain semolina (see *farina*, page 344)
5 tablespoons superfine sugar
2 tablespoons brandy, *optional*
1 tablespoon finely grated orange zest, briefly dried in a low oven and pulverized in a mortar *with* 1 teaspoon sugar, *or* ¹/₂ tablespoon orange extract
1¹/₄ pounds aromatic honey, such as Hymettus
1–1¹/₂ cups all-purpose flour
1 teaspoon baking powder
¹/₄ teaspoon grated nutmeg
¹/₂ teaspoon ground cloves
Strained juice of ¹/₂ lemon
Strained juice of 1 small orange *or* 2 tablespoons orange-flower water

For serving
⁵/₈ cup finely chopped walnuts *or* blanched almonds
1 teaspoon ground cinnamon

Combine 6 tablespoons of the butter and ¹/₂ cup of the olive oil in a large bowl. Gradually stir in the semolina, 2 tablespoons of the sugar, the brandy, orange zest, and ¹/₂ cup of the honey. Sift together the flour, baking powder, nutmeg, and cloves, and stir into the semolina mixture. Turn out onto a lightly floured surface and knead 10 minutes, until soft and pliant. If it seems stiff, add a little more oil; if thin, more flour.

Heat the oven to 350°F. Brush 2 baking sheets with the remaining melted butter.

Form the dough into egg-sized ovals and set them 2 inches apart on the baking sheets. With the back of a fork, lightly press down twice on top of each oval to make a criss-cross design, slightly flattening them at the same time. Bake 20 minutes, until lightly browned. Transfer to a rack to cool.

While the cakes are cooling, bring the remaining honey and 1½ cups water to boil in a saucepan and simmer 4 minutes. Remove from the heat and add the lemon and orange juices. With a spoon, place the barely warm cakes in the hot syrup a few at a time. Leave them in the syrup 1 minute, and transfer to paper or foil baking cups or a serving platter.

Combine the nuts, cinnamon, and remaining sugar, and sprinkle over the cakes.

Shortcakes
Kourabiethes

No festive table in Greece would be complete without a large platter piled high with these snowy white, sugar-dusted shortcakes. Scented with cloves and rose water, these buttery treats are perfect with fruit desserts and spoon sweets. Their flavor improves with age – store them at room temperature in an airtight container with confectioners' sugar sprinkled over each layer, and dust with fresh sugar before serving. A variation of these can be made with blanched almonds (see below).

Makes approximately 36 shortcakes

1 pound unsalted butter, at room temperature
½ cup superfine sugar
1 teaspoon vanilla extract
2 egg yolks
2 tablespoons brandy, *optional*
3–3½ cups all-purpose flour
1 teaspoon baking powder
2 tablespoons unsalted butter, melted
12–36 cloves, as desired

For serving
3 tablespoons rose water
2 cups confectioners' sugar

With an electric mixer or by hand, beat the room-temperature butter in a large bowl until light and fluffy. Beat in the sugar, vanilla, egg yolks, and brandy. Sift in 2 cups of the flour and the baking powder and beat to mix. Gradually stir in enough of the remaining flour to make a soft dough. (Traditional cooks use their fingers to do this; it is easier to judge the right moment to stop.) Tightly cover and refrigerate for 1 hour.

Heat the oven to 325°F. Lightly brush 2 baking sheets with the melted butter and dust them with flour.

Break off pieces of dough the size of very small eggs and shape into balls, ovals, pears, S-shapes, or crescents. Set 2 inches apart on the baking sheets.

Press 1 clove into each of 12 of the shortcakes or into every one if you prefer. Bake 15 minutes, until firm and very pale gold. Transfer to racks to cool.

Sprinkle the shortcakes with the rose water. Spread half the confectioners' sugar on a plate and arrange the shortcakes side by side on the sugar. Liberally dust with the remaining sugar.

Variations
♦ Substitute 1⅓ cups finely ground lightly toasted blanched almonds for 1 cup of the flour.
♦ In a small mortar, pulverize 1 teaspoon mastic granules (see page 13) with 1 tablespoon sugar, and add with the eggs. Omit the brandy and the cloves.

Hazelnut Cookies
Foundoukia Biscotakia

The perfect accompaniment to fruit desserts and cream desserts, these sweet and spicy mouthfuls are easy to make – and they are irresistible!

Makes 30 to 36 cookies

2 tablespoons unsalted butter, melted
2 tablespoons all-purpose flour
1 cup (2 sticks) unsalted butter, at room temperature
¼ cup superfine sugar
⅓ cup aromatic honey, such as Hymettus *or* orange blossom
3 eggs
3 cups hazelnuts *or* walnuts, finely ground
½ teaspoon ground cloves
1 teaspoon ground cinnamon

For serving
1½ cups confectioners' sugar

Heat the oven to 325°F. Lightly brush 2 baking sheets with the melted butter and dust with flour.

Beat the room-temperature butter and the sugar in a bowl of an electric mixer or a large mixing bowl until pale and creamy, about 5 minutes. Beat in the honey, then beat in the eggs 1 at a time. Stir in half of the hazelnuts, the cloves, and the cinnamon. Add some or all of the remaining hazelnuts to make a mixture just stiff enough to hold its shape.

Place heaping tablespoons of the mixture 2 inches apart on the baking sheets, and use your fingers to pull each gently up into a cone shape. Bake 20–25 minutes or until firm but not hard. Transfer to racks to cool.

Liberally dust with the confectioners' sugar and pile high on a platter.

FRUIT DESSERTS AND OTHER SWEETS

Frouta, Krema, ke Glykisma

For most Greeks, after a meal, juicy refreshing fruit is the dessert of choice. Fruits of all kinds appear on Greek tables in various seasons – although it's said that modern Greeks have nowhere near the choice of fruits that were available to their classical ancestors: For example, it is believed that there were over one hundred varieties of pear in ancient Greece.

The fruits most commonly associated with Greece are the grape and the fig. Legend has it that Hercules ate vast quantities of figs and that, on one campaign, Alexander the Great's army survived for a time on only figs, so it's not surprising that even modern Greeks believe figs to be a source of strength and stamina. The wild figs of the Greek countryside are usually small and often seedless but filled with the most heavenly sweet nectar. In the early 1900s Greek immigrants took cuttings of Smyrna figs, a particularly luscious variety, to California, where they now produce magnificently plump and juicy Calimyrna figs, a lovely green-amber fruit perfect for drying. Also available is the deep rich purple Turkish fig. Either of the figs is perfect for the sweets included here. Grapes, in contrast, are a relative newcomer to Greek dessert tables. Until recent years, they were grown only for wine making or drying.

Also based on fruits (although young vegetables and nuts can be used) are spoon sweets, *glyka tou koutaliou*, a very Greek speciality. Preserving ripe fruits and nuts in honey was a technique much favored by both the Minoans and the ancient Greeks. These honey-coated delicacies are a fundamental part of the Greek expression of friendship and welcome, and every guest entering a Greek house is offered a lace-covered tray holding small silver bowls of spoon sweets along with a glass of ice water, a small cup of thick strong coffee, and a small glass of liqueur. The rims of the bowls are indented to hold long-handled spoons with which the visitor scoops up the mellifluous treat. In this ritual the sweet offering is a traditional symbol of hospitality: It is extremely impolite to refuse it.

Spoon sweets are probably best described as a cross between a jam and a preserve. Almost any fruit can be used to make them, but those made with tiny whole fruits are the most treasured of all. Spoon sweets made from sour cherries and fragrant citrus blossoms are especially delectable. All of these sweets are excellent with ice cream, pancakes, and, surprising as it may sound, with pungent goat's or sheep's cheeses.

Puddings, custards, ice creams, and sweetmeats are rarely eaten straight after a meal in Greece but instead at various times throughout the day or night – whenever the need for something sweet overwhelms. In summer the whole family may go out to the pastry shop or café late in the evening to enjoy ice creams, sweetmeats, velvety smooth rice puddings, custards made from pistachios or almonds, and elaborate honeyed pastries. Many of these sweet treats have been enjoyed by generations of Greeks since antiquity – the chewy Honey Sesame Sweetmeats called *pasteli,* for example, were presented to victorious athletes at the classical Olympic games. And many other custards, puddings, sweetmeats, and spoon sweets are based on ancient flavors and fragrances. With their unusual tastes, textures, and aromas they are unmistakably Greek.

Platter of Fresh Fruits
Freska Frouta

Magnificent platters of prepared fresh fruit must have been one of the earliest Greek desserts. Use only fruit in perfect condition and keep the arrangement simple but colorful. Since most fruits discolor very quickly, prepare them just a few minutes before serving. Allow half a dozen pieces of fruit per person.

Serves 4

Choose from any of the following:

½ small sweet melon such as honeydew *or* Persian
¼ small watermelon
1 crisp sweet apple, cored and cut into 8 wedges
1 ripe pear, cored and cut into quarters
½ pound large sweet grapes, cut into 4 clusters
1 large prickly pear, peeled (see page 299) and cut into quarters
8 strawberries, with their stems if possible
16 cherries, with their stems if possible
4 ripe figs, halved
2 peaches *or* nectarines, peeled, pitted, and cut into quarters

For serving
Green leaves such as those of the fig, strawberry, lemon, or apple, rinsed
    and patted dry
12 ounces *myzithra* cheese, cut into 8 slices
Hymettus *or* other aromatic honey

Remove the seeds from the honeydew melon, cut it into 4 slices, and cut off the rind. Cut the watermelon flesh into 4 or 8 chunks.

Line a serving plate with the leaves and arrange the fruit attractively on the leaves. Serve with a plate of the sliced cheese and small bowls of the honey.

Note Mulberries, apricots, plums, and quince are other traditional Greek fruits. For breakfast, serve with Strained Yogurt (page 7), honey, and Currant Bread (page 264).

Fruits in Sweet Wine and Honey
Frouta Glykisma

At summer tables today it is still traditional to dip fresh fruit into a glass of sweet wine before eating it, but the fruit can also be poached in wine. For this versatile, not-too-sweet dish you can use a variety of fruits, including peaches, nectarines, plums, apricots, cherries, figs, pears, apples, and quinces or melons. The fruit should be ripe but it does not have to be perfect to produce a special dessert. Here the flavoring for the poaching syrup is vanilla, coriander, and lemon but you can also try cinnamon, cloves, or orange (see below). For a particularly delicate flavor add the pits of fruits such as apricots to the poaching liquid. Serve poached fruit on its own or with cookies, Rich Cream (page 310), and chilled Samos wine.

Serves 6

2 cups sweet Samos wine *or* 1 cup Mavrodaphne wine
1/3 cup aromatic honey, such as Hymettus
1 2-inch piece of vanilla bean *or* 1 teaspoon vanilla extract
24 coriander seeds
Zest of 1/2 small lemon, removed in thin strips
6 portions of any of the fruits mentioned above

Combine the wine, honey, vanilla, coriander seeds, and lemon zest, and enough water to cover the fruit in a large saucepan, slowly bring to a boil, and simmer 5 minutes.

Meanwhile, remove the stems from the fruit (or trim those of figs), and remove any pits carefully so the fruit does not lose its shape. Use a pitter for cherries and a small paring knife for plums and apricots. Cut melon into bite-size pieces. Peel apples, pears, and quinces and cut into slices. If you are poaching apricots, crack a few pits with a nutcracker, remove the kernels, and add to the poaching liquid.

Add the fruit to the poaching liquid in small batches, slightly raise the heat, and return to a gentle simmer. Poach until barely tender: figs, grapes, or melons 1–2 minutes, apricots or gooseberries about 4 minutes, plums or cherries about 6 minutes, and apple, pear, or quince slices about 8 minutes. Transfer to paper towels to drain and place in a serving bowl.

Raise the heat and boil the poaching liquid until it is slightly syrupy and lightly coats the back of a metal spoon. Let cool slightly, strain, and pour over the fruit. Set aside for up to 2 hours, or cover and refrigerate for up to 24 hours. Serve at room temperature.

Note Strawberries, other soft berries, and citrus fruit segments need no poaching; just macerate them in a little honey or sugar before pouring the warm syrup over them.

Peaches in Sweet Wine and Honey
Glykisma me Rodakina

Choose 6 small or 3 large ripe peaches with no bruise marks or soft spots, and handle them carefully; do not peel until after poaching so the fruit retains flavor and color. Substitute 3 cloves and 1 3-inch cinnamon stick for the vanilla and coriander seeds. Cut larger peaches in half and discard the pits; to pit a small peach, hold it firmly, insert the point of a paring knife into its stem end, carefully loosen the pit, and then push it out from the other end. Poach small peaches or peach halves 5 minutes, larger whole peaches 8 minutes.

Note Nectarines can be substituted for the peaches.

Fragrant Apricot Ice Cream
Verikoka Pagota Aromatika

Apricots, said to originate in China, are thought to have been brought to Greece by the Phoenicians. In those days they were probably made into sweetmeats, but modern Greeks are more likely to use this ancient flavor in ice creams. Make this rich ice cream in early summer when apricots are ripe and sweet. Serve it prettily garnished with toasted almonds and small colorful flowers, and accompanied by glasses of sweet Samos liqueur.

Serves 6

2 pounds fresh apricots
1 teaspoon vanilla extract
1/3 cup aromatic honey, such as Hymettus, or to taste
3 eggs, separated
1/3 cup Rich Cream (without crust, page 310) *or* 3/4 cup heavy cream
2 tablespoons Samos liqueur *or* apricot ratafia, *optional*

For serving

Toasted slivered almonds

Handful citrus blossoms *or* **borage flowers** *or* **other fragrant, decorative (non-poisonous) flowers**

Fill a large saucepan with water and bring to a boil. Drop the apricots into the boiling water, remove the saucepan from the heat, count to 3, then carefully remove the apricots with a slotted spoon. Peel with a small paring knife, cut each in half, and discard the pits. If they are not quite ripe, bring about ½ cup water to boil in a heavy saucepan, add the apricots, and simmer 5 minutes. Drain and reserve the cooking liquid. Process the apricots until smooth in a food processor fitted with the plastic blade. Add the vanilla and most of the honey. Add the remaining honey to taste, and add some of the reserved cooking liquid if necessary to produce a mixture the consistency of heavy cream.

Place 1 cup of this puree in a nonreactive bowl, tightly cover, and refrigerate. Whisk the egg yolks until thick and pale and gradually add the remaining puree, whisking constantly. Transfer to a small heavy saucepan or the top of a double boiler set over hot water. Heat over low heat, stirring constantly, until thick enough to lightly coat the back of the spoon, about 5 minutes. Immediately transfer to a bowl. Let cool.

Stir the Rich Cream until smooth (or whisk heavy cream until slightly thickened), and lightly whisk in the cooled custard. Transfer to an ice cream machine and freeze according to the manufacturer's instructions. When the mixture is almost frozen, whisk the egg whites until they hold soft peaks, fold into the custard, and freeze until firm.

Add the liqueur to the reserved puree. Stir in honey to taste if desired and add some of the reserved juice or water if necessary to give a pouring consistency.

To serve, spoon the sauce onto chilled plates, place small scoops of ice cream in the center of the sauce, and sprinkle with the toasted almonds and blossoms. Serve immediately.

Note You can also freeze this ice cream in the freezer. Pour the cooled custard into metal pans and freeze, stirring occasionally, until almost firm. Whisk the egg whites until they hold firm peaks and fold them into the custard until thoroughly combined. Freeze until firm.

Honey Ice Cream with Fresh Fig Compote

Pagoto me Sika ke Khimo Rothion

In early autumn tall glasses of honeyed ice cream topped with a syrupy compote of figs and pomegranate juice are served in pastry shops throughout Greece. It's an elegant and refreshing dessert, rich with the deep, luscious flavors of the two best fruits of the season. Serve it with Shortcakes (page 284) or Hazelnut Cookies (page 285).

Serves 6

2 large ripe pomegranates
1 tablespoon freshly squeezed lemon juice
1/3 cup honey, preferably Hymettus
1 pound fresh figs, peeled, and each cut into 4 or 6 wedges
1 cup milk
1 2-inch piece vanilla bean, split *or* 1 teaspoon vanilla extract
4 egg yolks
1 tablespoon superfine sugar
3/4 cup Rich Cream (without crust, page 310) *or* 1 cup heavy cream

Scoop out the flesh and seeds from the pomegranates and place in a food processor bowl fitted with the plastic blade. Blend at low speed just until the flesh is separated from the seeds, about 15 seconds. (A gentle touch is essential or the juice will be tannin-flavored, a result of working the membranes too vigorously.) Strain the juice through 2 layers of cheesecloth into a nonreactive bowl. Stir in the lemon juice and 2 tablespoons of the honey, then add the figs. Tightly cover and refrigerate for 2–3 hours, shaking the bowl occasionally, to redistribute the figs in the sauce.

Place the milk and vanilla bean in a heavy saucepan and heat over low heat until very hot, but not boiling. Remove from the heat. With a hand whisk or electric mixer, whisk the egg yolks and sugar until pale and frothy, about 2 minutes. Gradually add the hot milk, whisking constantly, until it lightly coats the back of a spoon. Transfer to a bowl and set aside to cool.

Remove the vanilla bean from the custard and discard. Add the remaining honey to taste. Whisk the Rich Cream until smooth (whisk the heavy cream until thick), and stir into the custard. Transfer to an ice cream machine and freeze according to the manufacturer's instructions, or pour into metal pans and freeze until firm, stirring occasionally.

To serve, place 2 or 3 small scoops of ice cream in tall parfait glasses and spoon over the fig and pomegranate compote.

Fresh Fig Custard
Freska Sika Afrothi

This fluffy custard is perfect for figs that are too battered to serve on their own. You can use any variety of fig, although deep purple figs will give the custard the most spectacular color. Adding the optional egg white will produce a custard somewhat like a soufflé although it will not rise very high. You can make this in a large soufflé dish or individual dishes, and it can be served hot or at room temperature.

Serves 6

3/4 cup superfine sugar
1 pound figs, preferably purple, peeled, and each cut into 4 or 6 wedges
1/2 cup (1 stick) unsalted butter
3 tablespoons all-purpose flour
3/4 cup milk
1 2-inch piece vanilla bean *or* 1 teaspoon vanilla extract
4 large eggs separated
1 egg white, *optional*

For serving
confectioners' sugar, sifted

Heat the oven to 425°F. Combine 1/2 cup of the sugar and 4 tablespoons water in a syrup pan or a heavy saucepan and bring to a boil over low heat. Raise the heat and boil rapidly for 3–4 minutes, until the syrup lightly coats the back of a metal spoon. Add the figs, gently shake the saucepan to coat the figs, and reduce the heat to very low. Simmer 6–8 minutes, until the figs darken a little. Set aside.

Melt half the butter in a heavy saucepan over low heat. Stir in the flour with a wooden spoon and cook, stirring, 2 minutes longer or until the roux turns a medium gold. Meanwhile combine the milk, 1 tablespoon of the remaining sugar, and the vanilla in another saucepan and heat to just under a boil. Whisk the milk into the roux and cook, whisking constantly, until the custard reaches a low boil. Reduce the heat, simmer a few minutes longer, and remove from the heat.

Brush a 1 quart soufflé dish with the remaining butter and sprinkle with the remaining sugar. Invert over the sink and tap sharply to remove excess sugar.

Remove the vanilla bean from the custard and stir in the egg yolks one at a time. Stir in the figs and their syrup just to combine. With a hand whisk or an electric mixer, whisk the egg whites until they hold stiff peaks.

Stir one third of the whites into the fig custard, then lightly fold in the remaining whites and transfer to the soufflé dish. Reduce the oven temperature to 375°F and bake 30 minutes. Gently shake the dish – it should wobble only slightly. Bake another 5–10 minutes if necessary.

Dust the custard with the confectioners' sugar and serve immediately. Or let cool, dust with the sugar, and serve warm or at room temperature.

To make individual custards Butter small (1 cup) soufflé or other ovenproof dishes, sprinkle with sugar, and divide the custard equally between them. Bake 20–25 minutes at 350°F.

Variation
♦ Double the quantity of vanilla and add 3 ounces *myzithra* cheese (see page 10) or 4 tablespoons Rich Cream (page 310) to the custard after the egg yolks. Bake at 350°F and increase the baking time by 5–10 minutes; if the custard browns too quickly, loosely cover with aluminium foil. This custard is especially good warm.

Sweet-Baked Figs

Sika sto Fourno

Firm but not under-ripe figs are the kind to choose for this dish. They are baked whole in a honeyed orange juice syrup until they are soft, sweet, and shiny. Arranged on a white serving platter, sprinkled with syrup and fragrant orange-flower water, they make an elegant and delicious dessert. Also try baking figs in Mavrodaphne or Samos wine instead of orange juice. Fresh *myzithra* (see page 10) is the traditional accompaniment.

Serves 4

....

12–16 small fresh figs *or* 8 large figs
4–5 tablespoons honey, preferably Hymettus *or* superfine sugar, or to taste
1/2 teaspoon vanilla extract
Strained juice of 1 large navel orange *or* 1/2 cup Mavrodaphne *or* sweet
  Samos wine

For serving
2 tablespoons orange-flower water, *optional*

....

Heat the oven to 325°F. Rinse the figs and trim the stems. Arrange in a single layer, stem ends up, in a heavy baking dish.

Combine the honey, vanilla, and orange juice in a small saucepan and gently heat until the honey has dissolved. Pour over the figs, and add enough water to cover the bottom of the dish. Bake, uncovered, 15 minutes and baste the figs with the juices in the dish. Bake small figs 40 minutes longer, large figs 1 hour longer, basting occasionally; add a few tablespoons water if necessary so there is always some liquid in the dish.

Transfer the figs to a platter, spoon over the syrup, sprinkle with the orange-flower water, and serve.

Anoula's Dried Figs
Sika Xsera

This recipe comes from my neighbor on Crete, Anoula. Each year she dries hundreds of figs, first laying them out in the sun for 3 days on a bamboo frame covered with dried grass, then completely drying them in a low oven. The most attractive figs from this abundance are packed into wooden boxes to be given as gifts; others are threaded on long grass strings and hung from storage room rafters, to serve later as a *meze;* and still others are kept for spicy sweet desserts like this one.

Serves 6

18 plump dried figs, preferably organic Greek
6 bay leaves
1 2-inch cinnamon stick
1 1-inch piece lemon zest
3 cups Mavrodaphne wine *or* strong freshly brewed tea, strained
1/2–1 cup sugar
18 lightly toasted blanched almonds

For serving
2 tablespoons freshly squeezed lemon juice *or* orange-flower water

Rinse the figs, trim the stems, and combine the figs, bay leaves, cinnamon stick, lemon zest, and wine in a nonreactive bowl. Cover and set aside overnight.

Transfer to a heavy saucepan and slowly bring to a boil. Simmer 10 minutes, then transfer the figs with a slotted spoon to paper towels to drain. Measure the cooking liquid, return it to the saucepan, and add half as much sugar as measured liquid. Raise the heat and boil 10 minutes, until the syrup lightly coats the back of a metal spoon. Strain and set aside.

With a small knife, make an incision in each fig just below the stem. Insert an almond into each fig, leaving the tip exposed. Place the figs in a bowl and pour over the syrup. Let cool, tightly cover, and set aside for 2–6 hours.

To serve, arrange the figs on a platter with the almonds upward, pour over any remaining syrup, and sprinkle with the lemon juice.

Dried Apricots with Sweet Samos Wine
Verikoka Xsera me Krasi Samiotiko

Substitute sun-dried apricots for the figs and sweet Samos wine for the Mavrodaphne. Omit the bay leaves and cinnamon. Simmer only 2 minutes.

Minoan Dates and Prunes
Mourmathes Xsera ke Damaskina

Dried prunes were exported to Egypt by the Minoans; dates imported from Egypt by the same route. This ancient dish remains a favorite of Cretan islanders. An attractive dessert, it is easy to prepare. When choosing the fruit, select large California prunes and dates if possible (avoid sticky shiny dates, which are too sweet for this recipe).

Serves 6

12 large prunes, soaked in 2 cups Mavrodaphne wine *or* strong freshly brewed tea for 4–12 hours
$1/3$–$1/2$ cup sugar
12 large dates, preferably Medjool
1 cup Rich Cream (without crust, page 310) *or* $3/4$ cup mascarpone cheese
12 toasted blanched almonds, coarsely chopped

Transfer the prunes and their liquid to a heavy saucepan and slowly bring to a boil. Simmer 2 minutes, then, using a slotted spoon, transfer the prunes to paper towels to drain. Measure the cooking liquid, return it to the saucepan, and add half as much sugar as the measured liquid. Raise the heat and boil 10 minutes, until the syrup lightly coats the back of a metal spoon. Set aside.

Make a lengthways incision in each fruit and carefully remove the pits. For a neat appearance, tuck in the sides of the prune incisions with the point of a small knife. Arrange the prunes and dates on a platter.

Beat the Rich Cream until firm enough to hold its shape and divide in half. Using one half, place a spoonful of cream in each date. Whisk 3 tablespoons of the remaining syrup into the remaining cream and whisk until stiff. Fill each prune with a spoonful of this mixture.

Sprinkle the almonds over the prunes, and sprinkle with some or all of the remaining syrup if desired. (Dates need no added sweetness.) Serve immediately.

Morello Cherry Preserves
Vissino

Morello cherries are much loved by Greeks and have been popular since classical times. The delicious summer fruit is eaten both fresh from the tree, juicy and sharp, or as a preserve, mellowed by sugar and brandy. Dried cherries are eaten with strong country cheese as a simple *meze,* cherry juice is fermented into liqueur, and plump and luscious cherries are made into this delicious spoon sweet. Morello cherries are seldom found fresh in our markets; sweet cherries are not a perfect substitute, but they too can be made into a satisfactory spoon sweet (recipe follows). The perfect accompaniment for both versions is *myzithra* cheese (see page 10).

Makes approximately 3 pints preserves

2 pounds Morello cherries *or* other sour cherries
5 cups sugar
1 teaspoon vanilla extract
2 tablespoons freshly squeezed lemon juice

Thoroughly wash and sterilize six ½-pint jars and set aside in a warm spot.

Working over a bowl to catch any juices, remove the pits from the cherries with a cherry-pitter or small paring knife. Reserve the juice. Crack 12 of the pits and remove the kernels. Wrap these in a small square of cheesecloth, tying up the edges to make a bag. Set aside.

Combine the sugar, any reserved juices, and 4 tablespoons water in a large heavy saucepan and melt the sugar over very low heat. Raise the heat to medium-low and boil 1 minute, stirring vigorously. Add the cherries and bag of kernels and boil 12 minutes. Remove any froth with a slotted spoon, taking care not to stir into the syrup. With the slotted spoon, transfer the cherries to paper towels to drain, leaving as much syrup as possible in the pan. Discard the bag of kernels. Add the vanilla to the syrup, raise the heat, and boil rapidly until the syrup reaches 235–240°F on a candy thermometer (or a little syrup dropped into a glass of cold water immediately forms a soft ball). Add the lemon juice, and set aside to cool slightly.

Divide the cherries between the sterilized jars and add enough syrup to cover. (Use any remaining syrup for drinks or to pour over ice cream.) Let cool, tightly cover, and store at room temperature for up to 6 months.

Sweet Cherry Preserves
Kerasi

Use 2¹/₂ pounds small ripe but firm sweet cherries, 2 pounds sugar,
2 teaspoons vanilla extract, and the juice of 1 small lemon. Boil the
cherries in the syrup for 10–15 minutes or until they are plump and a little
translucent. Drain and proceed as directed on page 296.

Fresh Fig and Honeydew Preserves
Sika ke Peponi Glyko

Perfectly ripe melons and figs need no adornment and are deliciously
refreshing to eat just as they are. But bruised or less-than-perfect fruits can
be made into this ancient spoon sweet, an ideal way to enjoy all their juicy
flavor.

Makes approximately 3 pints preserves

1 (2-pound) honeydew *or* other sweet melon
1 pound fresh figs, trimmed, peeled, and cut into 6–8 wedges
Strained juice of 2 large lemons
3¹/₂–4¹/₂ cups sugar

Thoroughly wash and sterilize six ¹/₂-pint jars. Cut the melon in half,
remove the seeds, and finely chop the flesh. Place the figs, melon, and
lemon juice in a large heavy saucepan and simmer 20–30 minutes, until the
fruit is soft. Transfer to a nonreactive sieve set over a bowl and press the
fruit through with a wooden spoon.

Measure the puree, return it to the rinsed-out pan, and add exactly the
same quantity of sugar. Slowly bring to a boil to dissolve the sugar, then
raise the heat. Boil rapidly, stirring occasionally to prevent sticking or
burning, until the syrup reaches 235–240°F on a candy thermometer (or a
little syrup dropped into a glass of cold water immediately forms a soft
ball), about 20 minutes. The mixture will be thick and a deep reddish
brown. Let it cool slightly.

Fill the jars, let cool completely, and cover tightly. Store at room
temperature for up to 4 months.

Lemon Blossom Preserves
Glyko Lemonanthos

The perfumed blossoms of rose, orange, grapefruit, jasmine, and honeysuckle can all be made into delectable preserves, but the most exquisitely fragrant of them all is made from lemon blossom. For this recipe you need the flower petals only, so enlist a friend's help to gather them. One of you holds a bag under a blossom-laden branch while the other gently shakes the flowers so that the petals fall into the bag. (Be sure to leave some blossom on the tree so that, in a few months' time, you can gather a harvest of perfumed juicy lemons.)

Makes approximately 1 1/2 pints preserves

6 ounces lemon petals
2 1/4 cups sugar
Juice of 1 lemon

Thoroughly wash and sterilize three 1/2-pint jars.

Combine the petals with the sugar and set aside, uncovered, for 4–6 hours. With your fingers, toss the petals occasionally, gently rubbing them together so they bruise lightly. Your kitchen will smell wonderful.

Slowly bring 1/2 cup water and half the lemon juice to a boil in a large heavy nonreactive saucepan. Add the petals and sugar, reduce the heat to very low, and cook until the sugar has dissolved. Raise the heat, gently boil 20 minutes, and set aside to cool.

Strain through a strainer, preferably plastic, set over a bowl and discard the solids. Return the syrup to the rinsed-out pan, add the remaining lemon juice, and boil until the syrup reaches 235°F on a sugar thermometer (or a little syrup dropped into a glass of cold water immediately forms a soft ball). Let cool slightly.

Fill the jars, let cool completely, and cover tightly. Store at room temperature for up to 3 months.

Prickly Pear Preserves
Glyko Frangosika

The large prickly pear bush (also known as cactus pear) is a common sight all around the eastern Mediterranean. Its sweet ruby-red fruits, occasionally available here in the autumn, taste wonderful chilled, with a little lemon juice sprinkled over them. Or choose tender prickly pears to make this colorful spoon sweet, especially good with *myzithra* (see page 10) or pungent *kephalotyri* cheese (see page 9).

Makes approximately 3 pints preserves

8 medium to large prickly pears (about 3 pounds total)
1²/₃–2¹/₄ cups sugar
Strained juice of 1 small lemon

Thoroughly wash and sterilize six ¹/₂-pint jars and set aside in a warm spot.

Without touching it – or your hand will be covered with tiny hair-like spines – secure 1 prickly pear with a fork and slice off each end with a sharp knife. Make 4 or 5 lengthways incisions through the skin, and lift it off. Without letting the exposed fruit touch the work surface (to avoid the spines), transfer it to a clean cutting board and cut into small pieces. Repeat with the remaining fruit.

Place the fruit, including the seeds, in a large heavy saucepan and simmer until tender, about 10 minutes. Transfer to a strainer, preferably plastic, set over a bowl, and press the fruit through it. Discard the seeds. Measure the puree, return it to the rinsed-out pan, and add the lemon juice and ³/₄ cup sugar for every 1 cup puree. Slowly bring to a boil over medium-low heat. Raise the heat and rapidly boil, stirring occasionally to prevent sticking or burning, until the puree reaches 235–240°F on a candy thermometer (or a little puree dropped onto a cold plate retains its shape). Let cool slightly.

Fill the jars, let cool completely, and cover tightly. Store at room temperature for up to 3 months.

Vanilla Rice Pudding
Risogalo me Vanillia

The enticing moist and creamy rice puddings of Greece, never thick or overly sweet, bear no resemblance to any versions remembered from childhood. Greeks enjoy them as a snack as well as a satisfying end to a meal and this vanilla-flavored pudding is one of the most popular. Other traditional flavorings are mastic (see page 13), lemon (see page 17), and orange (see page 18).

Serves 6

³/₄ cup pudding *or* short-grain rice
3 cups milk
¹/₃ cup *plus* 1 tablespoon superfine sugar *or* vanilla sugar (see page 15), or more to taste
1¹/₂-inch strip of orange zest

Pinch of salt
1 tablespoon unsalted butter
1 egg
½ teaspoon vanilla extract, or to taste
1 tablespoon freshly squeezed lemon juice, or more to taste
⅓ cup Rich Cream (without crust, page 310) *or* ½ cup heavy cream

For serving
Ground cinnamon
Confectioners' sugar, sifted

Place the rice in boiling water and leave for 5 seconds; drain, and rinse. Bring the milk almost to a boil in a heavy saucepan, and stir in the rice, the ⅓ cup sugar, the orange zest, salt, and butter. Reduce the heat to very low and simmer uncovered, stirring occasionally to prevent sticking, for 1 hour, until thick and creamy. Remove from the heat and set aside.

Whisk together the egg, vanilla, lemon juice, and remaining 1 tablespoon sugar until pale and thick, about 2 minutes. Remove the orange zest from the rice mixture and stir half the rice into the egg mixture. Return this to the saucepan and stir to combine. Gently cook over low heat, stirring well, for 2 minutes. Stir in the Rich Cream and add more sugar or lemon juice if desired. (If using heavy cream, beat until slightly thickened, then stir into rice mixture.) Divide between individual dishes and chill.

To serve, liberally dust with the cinnamon and confectioners' sugar.

Aromatic Rice Pudding
Risogalo Aromatiko

Mastic, the resin of the mastic tree, was greatly valued by the ancient gourmets as a flavoring for puddings, spoon sweets, and bread.

There is no substitute for the strong, rather mysterious taste and perfume of mastic – look for small packets of the granules in Greek and Middle Eastern shops. It is particularly good combined with other flavors of antiquity such as those of Sweet-Baked Figs (page 293), Glazed Sweet Chestnuts (page 306), or the preserves (pages 296 to 298). Serve small quantities of this delectable pudding, since the flavors are strong and too much can be overpowering.

Serves 6

½ cup pudding *or* short-grain rice
3¾ cups milk
Pinch of salt
1 tablespoon unsalted butter

¼ cup vanilla sugar (see page 15) *or* ¼ cup superfine sugar *and* ½
 teaspoon vanilla extract, or more sugar to taste
1 tablespoon mastic granules
1 tablespoon freshly squeezed lemon juice

For serving
Confectioners' sugar, sifted
Finely chopped toasted almonds

....

Place the rice in boiling water and leave for 5 seconds; drain, and rinse.
Bring the milk almost to a boil in a heavy saucepan, and add the rice, salt,
butter, all but 1 tablespoon of the sugar, and the vanilla. Reduce the heat to
very low and simmer uncovered, stirring occasionally to prevent sticking,
for 1 hour, until soft and creamy. Remove from the heat before all the
liquid evaporates; the mixture thickens on cooling. Set aside.

Pound the mastic in a mortar with the remaining sugar to a fine powder
(or grind in a clean coffee grinder). Stir this powder, the lemon juice, and
more sugar if desired into the warm rice. Divide between individual dishes,
let cool, cover, and chill.

To serve, dust with the confectioners' sugar and sprinkle with the
almonds.

Lemon Rice Pudding

Risogalo me Lemoni

These refreshing, meltingly creamy puddings can be served on their own,
or with Lemon Blossom Preserves (page 298). With their golden brown
topping of caramelized sugar, they look extremely pretty.

Serves 6
....

¾ cup pudding *or* short-grain rice
Finely grated zest of 1 lemon
3 cups milk
½ cup superfine sugar, or to taste
Pinch of salt
1 tablespoon unsalted butter
3 eggs, separated
½ teaspoon vanilla extract
Strained juice of 1 lemon, or to taste
⅜ cup heavy cream

For serving
Confectioners' sugar, sifted

....

Place the rice with the lemon zest in boiling water and leave for 5 seconds; drain, and rinse. Bring the milk nearly to a boil in a heavy saucepan and stir in the rice and lemon zest, half the sugar, the salt, and the butter. Reduce the heat to very low and simmer uncovered, stirring occasionally to prevent sticking, for 1 hour, until thick and creamy. Set aside.

Set a rack in the center of the oven and heat the oven to 350°F. Whisk together the egg yolks, vanilla, most of the remaining sugar, and most of the lemon juice until pale and creamy; lightly beat the cream until slightly thickened. Add this mixture to the rice, and add sugar and the remaining lemon juice to taste. Whisk the egg whites in a large copper or mixing bowl until they hold stiff peaks. Stir one third of the whites into the rice, and lightly fold in the remainder. Divide between 6 dishes and smooth the tops.

Place in shallow baking dishes and add water to come 1 inch up the sides of the dishes. Bake 25 minutes, until barely set.

Meanwhile, heat the broiler. Place the puddings in a broiling tray and sprinkle with the remaining 2 tablespoons sugar. Broil 3–4 inches from the heat source until caramelized and golden brown, about 2 minutes.

Serve warm, at room temperature, or chilled, lightly dusted with the confectioners' sugar.

Orange Rice Pudding
Risogalo me Portokali

Substitute the juice of 2 sweet oranges and the finely grated zest of 1 sweet orange for the lemon juice and lemon zest.

Remove the zest of the second orange with a stripper or zester. Combine an additional ½ cup sugar and ½ cup water and boil to a light syrup, about 8 minutes. Add the orange zest and simmer 5 minutes longer. Remove the zest with a slotted spoon, drain on paper towels, and coarsely chop. Reserve the syrup.

To serve, sprinkle the puddings with chopped orange zest, some of the syrup, and orange-flower water if desired. Dust with confectioners' sugar and a pinch of cinnamon.

Almond Creams
Krema Amigdalou

The perfect dinner party dessert after a rich main course, these light creams have a delicate sweet almond flavor enhanced with a subtle hint of mace. Garnished with a scattering of honeyed almonds and fresh or crystallized flowers, they have an elegant appearance and an unusual exotic

taste. The almond cream must be prepared at least 6 hours before serving
to allow the flavors to develop.

Serves 6

3 tablespoons cornstarch
2 tablespoons ground rice
2 cups milk
4 tablespoons aromatic honey, such as Hymettus
1 egg yolk
1/2 cup freshly ground blanched almonds
1/4 teaspoon ground mace

For serving
Confectioners' sugar, sifted
About 1 cup honeyed blanched almonds (see Note), lightly crushed *or*
    toasted blanched almonds, finely chopped
Fresh *or* crystallized violets *or* rose petals, *optional*

Combine the cornstarch and ground rice with 4 tablespoons of the milk
and stir until smooth. Warm the remaining milk in a large saucepan and
whisk it into the cornstarch mixture. Return it to the rinsed-out saucepan
and slowly bring to a boil, stirring. Simmer 1 minute, stirring, then transfer
to a nonreactive bowl. Stir in the honey, egg yolk, almonds, and mace.
Let cool, cover, and refrigerate for at least 6 hours, or overnight.

Set a strainer, preferably plastic, over a bowl and press the almond
cream through with a wooden spoon. Divide between individual bowls,
lightly dust with the confectioners' sugar, and sprinkle with the almonds.
Serve cold, garnished with the flowers.

Note To make honeyed almonds, heat the oven to 300°F. Toast 24 whole
blanched almonds, turning once so they brown evenly, until pale golden
brown, about 10 minutes. Combine with enough honey to coat (about 3–4
tablespoons) and spread on a lightly buttered baking sheet. Bake 8 minutes,
or until the honey coating hardens. Cool on the baking sheet, and store in
an airtight jar between layers of waxed paper.

Pistachio Creams
Krema Fistikiou

The aromatic flavor of pistachio nuts in this beautiful pale green cream
is enhanced with fragrant honey and vanilla. For an elegant and
sophisticated dessert, serve with a bowl of perfectly ripe pears.

Serves 6

1½ cups unsalted pistachio nuts
2 tablespoons cornstarch
2 tablespoons semolina (see *farina,* page 344)
2 cups milk
4–8 tablespoons aromatic honey, such as Hymettus, or to taste
1 2-inch piece vanilla bean *or* 1 teaspoon vanilla extract
2 egg yolks

For serving
Confectioners' sugar, sifted

Wrap the pistachio nuts in a clean dish towel, rub briskly, and remove the loosened skins with your forefinger and thumb. Coarsely chop about 6 nuts and set aside for garnish. Finely chop the remaining nuts and set aside.

Combine the cornstarch and semolina with 4 tablespoons of the milk and stir until smooth. Warm the remaining milk in a large saucepan and whisk it into the cornstarch mixture. Return it to the rinsed-out saucepan and slowly bring to a boil, stirring well. Add the honey and vanilla and simmer 2 minutes, stirring. Transfer to a nonreactive bowl, and stir in the egg yolks and finely chopped nuts. Let cool, cover, and refrigerate for at least 6 hours or overnight.

Set a strainer, preferably plastic, over a bowl and press the pistachio cream through with a wooden spoon. Discard the vanilla bean. Divide between individual bowls, lightly dust with the confectioners' sugar, and sprinkle with the reserved nuts. Serve cold.

Sweet Chestnuts and Lemon Cheese
Kastana Glykisma me Kaymaki

The chestnut season is always anticipated with relish in Greece and, for a few weeks in the autumn, small braziers appear at every street corner and the debris of roasted chestnuts cover the pavements. Syrupy chestnut desserts are popular, especially this treat, based on thick and mellow *kaymaki* cream, perfumed with lemon, vanilla, and cloves. You can use heavy cream instead of *kaymaki* with no great loss of character to the dish, but make the lemon cheese at least 4 hours in advance for the richest flavor and texture.

Serves 8

Lemon cheese
2 cups Rich Cream (without crust, page 310) *or* heavy cream
Finely grated zest of 1 lemon
Strained juice of 1 lemon
1/2 cup superfine sugar
3 egg whites

1 1/2 pounds chestnuts, shelled and skinned (see page 306)
1/4 cup vanilla sugar (see page 15) *or* 1/4 cup superfine sugar *and* 1/2
    teaspoon vanilla extract
1 cup milk
3 cloves

For serving
3/4 cup unsalted pistachio nuts, shelled, skinned (see page 304), and
    coarsely chopped

To make the lemon cheese, line a strainer, preferably plastic, with a
single layer of damp cheesecloth large enough to hang over the sides, and
set over a bowl.

Whisk together the Rich Cream, lemon zest, lemon juice, and sugar in a
bowl until the mixture is just stiff enough to hold its shape. Take care – it
will curdle if overworked. Whisk the egg whites until they hold stiff peaks
and fold quickly and lightly into the cream. Transfer to the sieve, pull the
corners of the cheesecloth up and together, and tie with string to make a
bag. Hang the bag over the bowl or the sink, away from heat or direct
sunlight, and let drain 4 hours, occasionally giving the bag a firm squeeze
to remove as much moisture as possible. Set aside, or refrigerate in the
cheesecloth bag for up to 4 hours.

Prepare the chestnuts no more than 2 hours before serving. Combine the
chestnuts, sugar, vanilla, milk, and cloves in a heavy saucepan and simmer
until all the milk is absorbed, about 15 minutes. Discard the cloves. Fit a
food mill with the medium disc and pass the chestnuts through into a
bowl.

Lightly spoon one third of the chestnut mixture into a glass serving
bowl. Don't flatten the top – that would spoil its airy texture. Gently
smooth half the cheese over the top, then carefully add half of the
remaining chestnut mixture. Add another layer of cheese, reserving a little
for decoration, and finish with a layer of the remaining chestnut mixture.
Garnish with the reserved cheese and the pistachio nuts. Serve immediately,
or refrigerate for up to 6 hours.

Glazed Sweet Chestnuts

Zakharota Kastana Glykisma

During the long slow baking of this sweet and spicy dish the fruity aromatic Mavrodaphne wine permeates the chestnuts and glazes them with a deep red syrup. Easy to make, this dessert is ideal for dinner parties since it can be made a day ahead. It is equally delicious warm or cold and is traditionally accompanied by fresh *myzithra* cheese (see page 10), Rich Cream (page 310), or lemon cheese (see page 305).

Serves 4

16 fresh plump chestnuts (see Note)
4 tablespoons honey *or* superfine sugar
1/4 teaspoon ground allspice
1 1/2 cups Mavrodaphne wine

Heat the oven to 300°F. Fill a medium saucepan with water and bring to a boil.

Using a small knife with a strong blade (or a special chestnut knife), make an incision around the middle of each chestnut shell, beginning and ending on the flat side; take care not to cut into the chestnut. Add to the boiling water, and boil 10 minutes; then turn off the heat. Remove 2 or 3 chestnuts at a time and, as soon as they are cool enough to handle, carefully peel off the shells and inner skins, leaving the chestnuts whole. Work quickly – warm chestnuts are much easier to peel. Arrange in a single layer in a heavy baking dish just large enough to hold them.

Combine the honey, allspice, and wine, and pour over the chestnuts. Bake uncovered 1 1/2 hours, gently turning the chestnuts in the syrup about every 20 minutes. Handle the chestnuts with care; they break easily. At the end of the baking time there should be about 6 tablespoons syrup: add a little more wine or water if necessary, or bake 15–30 minutes longer to reduce the syrup.

Cool in the dish, then gently roll the chestnuts in the syrup. Transfer to a shallow serving dish or individual dishes and pour over any remaining syrup. Serve at room temperature or cold.

Note To use canned chestnuts, rinse, drain, and dry with paper towels. Bring the wine, honey, and allspice to a boil in a large saucepan, add the chestnuts, and gently simmer 5 minutes. With a slotted spoon, transfer the chestnuts to paper towels to drain. Rapidly boil the cooking liquid until it is syrupy and coats the back of a metal spoon, about 8 minutes. Transfer the chestnuts to a serving dish and pour the syrup over. Let cool and serve.

Moustalevria Sweetmeats

Moustalevria Glykisma

This jelly-like sweet, made from grape must and flour, was probably one of the very first sweetmeats. It was a popular sweet in ancient Greece and down through the centuries Greeks have had a special fondness for its unusual flavor. In the villages *moustalevria* is still made in the traditional way: The grapes are trodden by women (men tread the grapes for wine) and the must is first clarified with wood ash from the *fournos,* then boiled until it forms a light syrup called *petimezi.* This is then thickened with flour, semolina, or cornstarch to make the sweetmeat.

The exact moment for removing the sweetmeat from the heat is judged in dramatic fashion by slipping a piece of flaming charcoal into the mixture – if the flame stays alive it is ready. For this recipe, you need to prepare the grape juice a day or two before making *petimezi,* a true must is grape juice that is just beginning to ferment. However, *petimezi* can be prepared ahead and stored for up to 3 months. Use it to flavor fruit salads, cookies, breads, cakes, and Moustalevria Pudding (page 308) as well as these sweetmeats.

Makes approximately 18 pieces

5 pounds large sweet grapes
2 tablespoons wood ash
6 tablespoons honey
6–8 level tablespoons sifted all-purpose flour
Few drops olive oil
Ground cinnamon
About 1/3 cup lightly toasted sesame seeds

Fill a large saucepan with water and bring to a boil. Stem the grapes and add them all at once to the boiling water. Count to 5 and drain.

Peel the grapes with your fingernails or a small paring knife and, with a wooden spoon, press them through a strainer, preferably plastic, set over a bowl. Strain the juice through cheesecloth into a saucepan and discard the pulp. There should be about 6½ cups juice.

Cut out a 6-inch square of a double layer of cheesecloth, place the wood ash in it, and tie up the edges to make a bag. Add to the juice, bring to a boil, and simmer 10 minutes. Discard the bag of ash and pour the juice into a nonreactive bowl. Cover and set aside for 1–2 days.

Line a strainer with 2 layers of cheesecloth and set over a saucepan. Strain the must into the saucepan, add the honey, and boil until it reaches 225–230°F on a candy thermometer, the light thread stage. To test, dip the tip of a pair of scissors into the syrup. Remove them and open them – if the syrup (*petimezi*) forms a thread between the blades, it is ready. Set aside to cool. Measure the *petimezi,* and place 2 level tablespoons flour for each 1 cup *petimezi* in a bowl. Add enough *petimezi* to make a thin paste, and bring the remaining *petimezi* to a boil in a large saucepan. Whisk the boiling *petimezi* into the paste, and return it to the rinsed-out saucepan. Simmer over low heat, stirring frequently with a wooden spoon, until it reaches the soft ball stage on a candy thermometer (235–240°F), or test by dropping a small amount of the *moustalevria* onto a cold plate: It should keep its shape. Lightly wipe a baking sheet with the olive oil and carefully pour on the *moustalevria* to make a ½-inch layer. Set aside to cool.

Sprinkle the cinnamon on a plate and sesame seeds on another. Cut the *moustalevria* into 1-inch squares and gently roll them first in the cinnamon, then in the sesame seeds. Store in an airtight container between layers of waxed paper for up to 1 month.

Moustalevria Pudding
Moustalevria

A variation of the mixture used for making *moustalevria* sweetmeats makes an unusual pudding. Here raisin juice is used for a quicker and easier version of *moustalevria.* Do not be tempted to use grape juice – it is not a successful substitute and produces an unpleasant flavor in this pudding.

Serves 4
....
2 cups small dark seedless raisins soaked in ½ cup Mavrodaphne wine *and*
    ½ cup hot water for 2 hours *or*
    1½ cups *petimezi* (see page 307)
³⁄₄ cup semolina (see *farina,* page 344)
1 tablespoon honey

For serving
Finely chopped walnuts *or* blanched almonds *or* lightly toasted sesame
    seeds
Ground cinnamon
....

Fit a food mill with the fine disc and pass the raisins and their liquid through into a bowl. (Or process in a blender or food processor.) Set a strainer over a bowl and press the mixture through with a wooden spoon. Add water if necessary to make 1½ cups liquid.

Combine the semolina, honey, and 4 tablespoons of the raisin juice to make a paste, then stir in the remaining juice. Transfer to a heavy saucepan and slowly bring to a boil. Simmer over very low heat until the mixture comes away from the sides of the saucepan, about 4 minutes, stirring constantly with a wooden spoon; take care not to let it burn.

Divide between small bowls and let cool. Cover tightly and refrigerate until chilled, or up to 2 days.

To serve, sprinkle with the nuts and cinnamon.

Honey Sesame Sweetmeats
Pasteli

In summer the cry of the *pasteli* vendor is a familiar sound in every Greek village and town and he has no lack of customers for this traditional sweet, rich, and nourishing sweetmeat. It is also very good crushed and sprinkled over ice cream.

Makes 16 pieces

1⅓ cups sesame seeds
1⅓ cups aromatic honey, such as Hymettus *or* orange blossom
2 tablespoons freshly squeezed lemon juice
1½ tablespoons unsalted butter, melted
1 tablespoon orange-flower water, *optional*

Heat the oven to 350°F. Line a 8x4-inch bread loaf pan with waxed paper. Spread the sesame seeds on a baking sheet and bake 5 minutes to toast lightly. Set aside.

Combine the honey and 4 tablespoons water in a small saucepan and slowly bring to a boil. Add the lemon juice and sesame seeds and gently boil until the mixture reaches the soft ball stage (235–240°F) on a candy thermometer, or a small amount forms a slightly misshapen ball when dropped into a glass of cold water.

Brush the prepared pan with the melted butter and pour in the honey and sesame seed mixture. Sprinkle with the orange-flower water and set aside to cool.

Turn out, peel off the paper, and, with a sharp knife, cut into pieces about ¾x2 inches. Store up to 1 month between layers of waxed paper in an airtight container.

Rich Cream
Kaymaki

Thick rich eastern Mediterranean *kaymaki* (literally, "frothy cream") is unique, but two more readily available products have a similar flavor and texture. Clotted (Devon) cream, and imported Italian mascarpone cheese both make good substitutes, or you can make your own. Make this when you plan to be in the kitchen for a couple of hours – for an even, smooth texture and a thick crust you need to stir the hot cream at regular intervals. Be sure to use meticulously clean utensils and keep the cooking heat very low (or use a heat diffuser plate). *Kaymaki* should be made at least 18 hours before you need it; it can be stored for up to one week.

Makes about 1 cup cream (plus the crust)

1 quart heavy cream

Slowly bring the cream almost to a boil in a heavy saucepan, stirring occasionally with a wooden spoon. Reduce the heat to as low as possible, or place the saucepan on a heat diffuser plate. Lift a ladleful of cream about 12 inches above the saucepan, and pour it back in a thin steady stream; repeat 2 or 3 times. Repeat this procedure every 10 minutes or so over the next 1½ hours, and stir the cream occasionally to make sure it does not stick.

Leave the cream undisturbed over the lowest heat for 30 minutes longer; it will have reduced by at least two thirds. Remove the saucepan from the heat and let it cool.

Loosely cover with a clean dish towel and set aside for 2 hours.

Remove the towel, tightly cover, and refrigerate for at least 12 hours, or overnight.

Cut the crust on top of the cream into 1 inch-wide strips. Gently fold one end of a strip over the handle of a wooden spoon and roll it up (cut in half if the roll becomes too thick or unwieldy), and slide off onto a plate. Repeat with the remaining strips. The remaining *kaymaki* will have the texture of thick airless cream. It can be refrigerated in a tightly covered container for up to 1 week; refrigerate the rolls for up to 3 days.

Note Serve *kaymaki* rolls on their own or with desserts such as Kataifi Nut Rolls with Caramel Syrup (page 270) or Almond Cake in Honey Syrup (page 280). *Kaymaki* cream can be added to ice cream (see page 289) or rice pudding (see page 300) for an especially good flavor. Or whisk it together with a little sweet wine or lemon juice for a perfect accompaniment to fresh or poached fruit or sweet pastries.

SAUCES

Saltses

The philosopher Plato believed that, although anyone can grill food, only a skilled chef could flavor a sauce. It may be impudent to disagree with the great man but if that were true most of us would immediately abandon any attempt at sauce making.

Greek sauces are generally not awesomely complex – the ubiquitous *latholemono* (lemon juice and olive oil) and *lathoxsitho* (wine vinegar and olive oil) do not even require recipes since they are simple mixtures of oil and an acid, blended and seasoned to taste. The sauces in this chapter are those the visitor to Greece is likely to encounter most often. They range from two contrasting mayonnaises and the famous *avgolemono* and *skordalia* to creamy sauces based on walnuts, almonds, or pine nuts, a piquant anchovy sauce, and several very different tomato sauces. Throughout the book, of course, there are many more unusual sauce recipes detailed in individual recipes.

Many of the sauces have ancient origins and would traditionally be made with a wooden mortar and pestle. For modern cooks food processors and blenders now make speedy work of many of them and produce excellent results with fine flavors and textures.

A good sauce harmonizes all the flavors of a dish and brings out the essential character of the individual ingredients. These versatile sauces will add verve and vivacity to your Greek meals.

Avgolemono Sauce
Avgolemono

Avgolemono seems to add the perfect finishing touch to practically any dish, except those containing tomatoes or garlic. Its delicate flavor is ideally suited to fish dishes, turns a simple chicken dish into one of elegant subtlety, marries well with lamb or pork, enhances pungent grape leaves, and lifts plain vegetables into the luxury class.

Avgolemono is simply a mixture of eggs, lemon juice, and broth. For a rich deep-yellow sauce, suited to vegetables and roast meats, yolks alone are used. For casseroles and soups Greeks prefer a lighter sauce, made with whole eggs.

The key to successful *avgolemono* is to use gentle heat, as high temperatures will cause the sauce to curdle, and to make it just before serving; this is not a sauce you can keep warm or reheat. The amount of lemon juice is adjusted to taste or to complement different dishes. *Dolmades,* for example, need little lemon juice because of the astringency of the grape leaves, while a mellow-flavored chicken dish benefits from a larger amount.

Serves 4

3 large egg yolks
5–6 tablespoons strained freshly squeezed lemon juice, to taste
1 cup strained hot broth (from the dish to be sauced)

Whisk the yolks, using a hand whisk or electric mixer, for 2 minutes, or until pale and frothy. Slowly add the lemon juice and whisk 1 minute longer. Add one third of the broth in a thin steady stream, whisking steadily, then quickly whisk in the remainder. Transfer to a small heavy saucepan or the top of a double boiler set over very hot water. Gently heat, stirring constantly in a figure-8 motion, until just thick enough to lightly coat the back of a wooden spoon, about 4 minutes. Do not stop stirring the sauce or let it boil or it will curdle. When it is ready, immediately remove from the heat (and saucepan) and serve.

Whole Egg Avgolemono for Soups and Casseroles

Avgolemono made with both egg whites and yolks is a beautiful pale lemony color. However, egg whites cook faster than yolks so there is a risk of the sauce looking stringy. To avoid this Greek cooks whisk the egg whites until stiff before adding the yolks and lemon juice.

Serves 4 to 6

2 large eggs, separated
$1/2$ cup strained freshly squeezed lemon juice, or to taste
$1/2$ cup hot soup *or* broth (from dish to be sauced)

Whisk the egg whites with a hand whisk or electric beater until they hold stiff peaks. Add the yolks, whisk 1 minute longer, then add the lemon juice. Continue whisking until very pale and frothy. Pouring from a height of about 12 inches, slowly add the soup or broth to the egg and lemon juice mixture, whisking constantly. (By the time the liquid reaches the egg mixture it will no longer be hot enough to curdle the sauce.) Off the heat, add the *avgolemono* to the soup or casserole and stir or shake gently to blend the flavors. Set aside in a warm place for a few minutes; do not return to the heat. Serve immediately.

Garlic Almond Sauce
Skordalia

This thick and creamy blend of garlic, almonds, and olive oil has been a favorite since the days of the ancient Greeks. However, since almonds are now expensive, modern versions often substitute bread crumbs or potatoes for some or all of the ground almonds. For a truly excellent sauce use fresh sweet garlic and take a few minutes to blanch and grind fresh whole almonds. Serve *skordalia* with vegetable dishes such as fried zucchini and eggplants or baked beets or with grilled or baked fish or chicken.

Serves 6 to 8

1 cup ground almonds *or* ³/₄ cup ground almonds *and* ¹/₂ cup fresh bread crumbs (made from white *or* whole wheat bread, crusts removed)

4–6 large cloves garlic, crushed

Sea salt, to taste

¹/₂ teaspoon freshly ground white pepper, or to taste

4 tablespoons aged red wine vinegar *or* the juice of 1 large lemon

³/₄–1 cup extra virgin olive oil *or* ¹/₂ cup extra virgin olive oil *and* 5–8 tablespoons broth (from the dish to be sauced)

For serving

12 Elitses *or* Niçoise olives

Place the almonds (and bread crumbs), garlic, salt, and pepper in a food processor or blender container. With the machine running, slowly add half the vinegar and ³/₄ cup olive oil. Add some or all of the remaining vinegar and olive oil if necessary: The sauce should be creamy, with a slightly piquant flavor, and thick enough to hold its shape. Slightly more liquid is needed if you use bread crumbs. Serve immediately, or refrigerate for up to 24 hours in a tightly covered jar.

To make the traditional way Pound the almonds, garlic, salt, and pepper in a large wooden mortar until well mixed and fairly smooth. Add the bread crumbs, if using, and pound to mix. Gradually add the vinegar and olive oil, pounding constantly, until you have a thick sauce. It will not be as smooth as a food processor version but will have a superior flavor produced by the continual working together of the ingredients.

Note You can remove the powerful garlic aroma from a wooden bowl by wiping with lemon juice or baking soda.

Potato Skordalia
Skordalia me Patates

This sauce should be made only in a mortar or bowl, as food processors ruin the texture of cooked potatoes. Use firm good-quality boiling potatoes and, for a sauce with a glorious deep yellow color and rich flavor, add an egg yolk.

Serves 6 to 8

1 pound boiling potatoes *or* ¹/₂ pound boiling potatoes *and* 1 cup fresh bread crumbs (made from white bread, crusts removed)
4–6 large cloves fresh garlic, crushed
1 egg yolk, *optional*
Sea salt to taste
¹/₂ teaspoon freshly ground white pepper, or more to taste
4 tablespoons aged red wine vinegar, or more to taste
³/₄–1 cup extra virgin olive oil

Fill a large saucepan with slightly salted water and bring to a boil. Cut the potatoes into halves or quarters add to the boiling water, and cook 15 minutes, or until just tender. Drain, and peel when cool enough to handle. Push the potatoes through a potato ricer or food mill into a large mortar or bowl; add the bread crumbs, if using, the garlic, egg yolk, salt, and pepper. With a pestle or wooden spoon, pound until fairly smooth and well mixed. Gradually add the vinegar and then the olive oil, pounding constantly, until the sauce is thick. Add more vinegar, if liked. Serve immediately, or refrigerate in an airtight container for up to 3 hours.

Piquant Almond Sauce
Amigdalosaltsa Pikantiki

Fresh young almonds are a favorite *meze* wherever raki is enjoyed – as I discovered when I lived in a Cretan village house surrounded by magnificent almond trees. Sitting under their beautiful flowering branches in my first spring there I contemplated the lovely dishes I would make when the almonds were ready in the autumn – not realizing that my trees and their almonds were considered public property by the villagers! Along with everyone else I enjoyed "my" almonds in the village café where tables were piled high with them. The Greek love of almonds dates back to ancient times, as does this pungent sauce. Served with baked, poached, or steamed fish or chicken it elevates simply prepared food to the realms of elegance.

Serves 2 to 3

1/2 cup freshly ground almonds
2 tablespoons aged red wine vinegar, or more to taste
1 1/2 tablespoons dried *rigani* (see page 13)
2 tablespoons finely chopped flat leaf parsley
1/4 teaspoon powdered mustard
1 teaspoon aromatic honey, such as Hymettus
Sea salt *and* freshly ground black pepper, to taste
4 tablespoons extra virgin olive oil
1/4–1/2 cup Light Meat, Chicken *or* Fish Stock
   (pages 348, 343, and 345)

Place the almonds, vinegar, *rigani*, parsley, mustard, honey, and salt and pepper in a food processor or blender container. With the machine running, add the olive oil and then 4 tablespoons stock in a thin steady stream to make a thick sauce. For a thinner sauce, add up to 4 tablespoons additional stock. Add vinegar to taste, but its flavor should not be overpowering. Serve at room temperature or heat over low heat until warm.

Almond, Yogurt, and Coriander Sauce

Amigdalosaltsa me Yiaourti

This popular sauce, which can also be served as a *salata*, is delicious with grilled meats, *souvlakia*, eggplants, *pilafi*, fried fish, or vegetables.

Serves 3 to 4

1/2 cup freshly ground almonds
1/2 teaspoon ground coriander
1 clove garlic, finely chopped
1 teaspoon aromatic honey, such as Hymettus
Juice of 1 small lemon
Sea salt *and* freshly ground black pepper, to taste
1/2–1 cup Strained Yogurt (page 7)
4 tablespoons coarsely chopped flat-leaf parsley
4 tablespoons coarsely chopped cilantro

Place the almonds, ground coriander, garlic, honey, half the lemon juice, and salt and pepper in a food processor or blender container. With the machine running, add yogurt a tablespoon at a time until the sauce has the desired consistency. Add the parsley and cilantro and pulse or blend just to mix. Add salt, pepper, and/or lemon juice to taste and serve immediately.

Walnut Sauce
Karythosaltsa

Fresh walnuts are one of the incomparable delights of late summer and early autumn on the Greek islands and this is the sauce the islanders make with them. With its velvet texture and fine flavor it is the traditional accompaniment to fried mussels, grilled or fried fish, grilled or fried eggplants, and zucchini or chicken. New-crop walnuts with golden or pale brown inner skins are best for this sauce but if these are hard to find, use the freshest walnuts available. This sauce freezes exceptionally well – freeze it in small amounts and you'll have delicious instant sauce for a variety of grilled and fried dishes. It can also be used to thicken and enhance the pan juices of baked chicken or fish dishes.

Serves 6

2¼ cups walnut pieces

½ cup fresh bread crumbs (made from whole wheat bread, crusts removed), soaked for 5 minutes in 4 tablespoons broth (from the dish to be sauced) *or* milk (see Note)

2 tablespoons extra virgin olive oil (see Note)

1 large clove garlic, finely chopped

Sea salt *and* freshly ground white pepper, to taste

2–4 tablespoons freshly squeezed lemon juice *or* white wine vinegar, or to taste

Optional flavorings

½ teaspoon grated nutmeg *or* 1 teaspoon ground allspice (for chicken)

1 teaspoon finely grated horseradish *and* 1 small handful flat-leaf parsley, leaves coarsely chopped (for mussels, fish, or vegetables)

1 tablespoon finely chopped fresh thyme (for vegetables)

Walnuts with light-brown inner skins must be peeled: Blanch them in boiling water for 5 seconds and drain. Wrap in a clean dish towel, rub briskly to remove the skins, and set aside to dry.

Pulverize the walnuts and bread crumbs in a food processor container, then add the olive oil in a thin steady stream, processing until smooth. Add the garlic, salt, and pepper, half the lemon juice, and the chosen flavoring(s) and process until mixed. Add salt and pepper and/or the remaining lemon juice to taste. Add more broth if necessary to produce a thick but pouring sauce, or add more bread crumbs to thicken the sauce. Serve warm or cold.

To make the traditional way Pound the walnuts in a large wooden mortar with a pestle until the oil is released, 10–15 minutes. Add the bread crumbs and pound to mix. Slowly add the olive oil, pounding constantly. Add the garlic, salt, and pepper, lemon juice, and chosen flavoring and pound until creamy, fairly smooth, and of a pouring consistency (it will not be as smooth as a machine-made sauce).

Note The amount of oil in walnuts varies, so the texture of the sauce may be different each time you make it. Be prepared to add varying amounts of broth and/or olive oil.

Pine Nut Sauce
Koukounaria Saltsa

Along much of Greece's dramatic rocky coastline the magnificent umbrella-shaped Mediterranean pine dominates the landscape. Every three years the glossy brown cones mature and ripen, and inside each is the edible kernel known to us as the pine nut. This extended ripening period and the fact that these pine trees thrive only along coastlines mean that pine nuts have always been relatively scarce and, therefore, expensive. But the delicate creamy blend of nuts, lemon juice, olive oil, and fresh chives in this traditional sauce more than justifies the extravagance. Serve with grilled or baked chicken or fish.

Serves 4

1½ cups pine nuts
1 small clove garlic, finely chopped, *optional*
Sea salt, to taste
¼ teaspoon freshly ground white pepper, or to taste
2 tablespoons freshly squeezed lemon juice *or* 1 tablespoon aged red wine vinegar, or more to taste
3 tablespoons extra virgin olive oil, or more to taste
4–6 tablespoons broth (from the dish to be sauced) *or* additional extra virgin olive oil
4 tablespoons chopped fresh chives

Place the pine nuts, bread crumbs, if using, garlic, salt, and pepper in a food processor or blender container. With the machine running, gradually add the lemon juice, olive oil, and 4 tablespoons broth and process until the sauce resembles thick cream. Add broth or olive oil if a thinner consistency is desired, and add salt or a few drops of lemon juice to taste; take care not to overpower the delicate flavor of the pine nuts. Add the chives and pulse just to mix. Serve immediately.

To make the traditional way Place the pine nuts, garlic, salt, and pepper in a wooden mortar and pound with a pestle until smooth and well mixed, about 10 minutes. Add the bread crumbs, if using, and pound to mix. Gradually add the olive oil and broth, pounding constantly. The sauce will not be as smooth as a food processor version, but the flavor will be more distinctive. Stir in the chives just before serving.

Note Pine Nut Sauce can be refrigerated in an airtight container for up to 24 hours or frozen for up to 1 month, but do not add the chives until just before serving.

Mayonnaise
Mayonaiza

The flavor of mayonnaise is determined by the olive oil used. A light olive oil will produce the lightest mayonnaise, Kalamata or other extra virgin olive oils the fruity, traditional Greek version. Greek cooks sometimes add a few spoonfuls of yogurt to mayonnaise to lighten both color and flavor. Serve this mayonnaise with cold poached or baked fish, shellfish, chicken, and salads.

Serves 3 to 4

2 large egg yolks, at room temperature
Large pinch of powdered mustard
$^1/_2$ cup extra virgin olive oil
1–2 tablespoons freshly squeezed lemon juice, to taste
Sea salt *and* freshly ground white pepper, to taste
1–2 tablespoons Strained Yogurt (page 7), *optional*

Place the egg yolks and mustard in a large nonreactive bowl and whisk together 1 minute with a small whisk or 2 forks (held slightly apart, in the same hand). Add 4 tablespoons of the olive oil drop by drop, whisking constantly and pausing once or twice to add a few drops of lemon juice. Slowly add the remaining olive oil in a thin stream, whisking constantly. Add salt and pepper, whisk in the yogurt to taste, and serve.

Note To store, add 1 tablespoon boiling water to the finished mayonnaise. Cover tightly and refrigerate no longer than 4 hours.

To rescue curdled mayonnaise, place 1 room-temperature egg yolk in a clean bowl and slowly add the curdled mayonnaise, whisking constantly.

Garlic and Watercress Mayonnaise

Skortho ke Karthamon Mayonaiza

This piquant mayonnaise adds a delightful dash of the unexpected to *kephtedes* or everyday grilled chicken, and it can be quickly made in the food processor.

Serves 4

1 bunch fresh watercress, green leaves only
1 teaspoon finely grated fresh horseradish
Large pinch of powdered mustard
1 tablespoon capers, rinsed and patted dry
2–4 large cloves garlic, finely chopped, or to taste
Sea salt, to taste
2 egg yolks, at room temperature
$1/2$ cup extra virgin olive oil
Strained juice of $1/2$ lemon, or more to taste

Blanch the watercress in boiling water for 5 seconds, drain, spread between layers of paper towels, and blot dry.

Place the blanched watercress, horseradish, mustard, capers, garlic, salt, and egg yolks in a food processor or blender container and, with the machine running, add 4 tablespoons of the olive oil drop by drop. Gradually add the remaining olive oil and the lemon juice. Add more lemon juice and/or salt to taste and serve immediately.

To make the traditional way Boil 2 eggs for 4 minutes, peel, and remove the yolks with a small spoon. They should be soft but not runny. Chop together the blanched watercress, horseradish, mustard, and capers. Pound the garlic and a large pinch of salt to a puree in a large mortar or bowl. Add the egg yolks and watercress mixture and pound until well mixed. Add half the olive oil drop by drop, still pounding, then add the remaining olive oil and the lemon juice in a steady stream. The sauce should be thick and well mixed, but it will not be as smooth as a food processor version.

Green Grape Sauce

Agouritha

This unusual sauce is made from the juice of under-ripe grapes (known as verjuice). Made in traditional homes on Crete, it is used to flavor pork and game dishes and Stuffed Eggplants with Green Grape Sauce (page 84). The small hard pickling grapes are exactly right for this sauce, but they are very hard to find; if it proves impossible to procure suitable grapes, *agouritha* can also be made with gooseberries, rhubarb, crab apples, or lemons or limes (see below). With its clear sharp tang, this is a particularly effective flavoring for baked fish and chicken dishes and a perfect marinade for lamb. It can be frozen; since only a little sauce is required to flavor the dish, freeze it in an ice cube tray and store the cubes in a bag, ready to use.

Makes approximately 1 cup sauce

1 pound small hard white grapes (on the stem)

Blanch the grapes in boiling water for 5 seconds and remove with a slotted spoon. Drain between layers of paper towels and blot completely dry, then carefully separate the grapes from the stem.

Set a plastic sieve over a nonreactive bowl and push the grapes through with a wooden spoon. Don't be tempted to use a food processor because the metal blade reacts harshly with the sour juice, giving an unpleasant metallic flavor to the sauce. Even the plastic blade of a food processor will "overwork" the grape skins and spoil the delicate flavor. When you have extracted as much of the juice and pulp from the grapes as possible, rinse the sieve, line it with a layer of cheesecloth, and place over another clean nonreactive bowl. Press the puree through a second time; the result will be a lovely smooth sauce.

Refrigerate for up to 1 week in a covered jar or freeze for up to 2 months.

Substitutes
♦ Substitute ½ pound firm sour gooseberries for grapes; avoid large pink ones – they are usually sweet and watery. Snip off both ends with small scissors, and simmer 10 minutes in 4 tablespoons water. Large gooseberries may need a little longer to soften.
♦ Substitute ½ pound rhubarb, trimmed and the "strings" removed. Cut into ½-inch slices and simmer 10 minutes in 4 tablespoons water. Use pink rhubarb only when the green color of classic *agouritha* is not an integral part of the dish.
♦ Substitute 1 pound crab apples, peeled, cored, and cut into quarters. Simmer in a few tablespoons water until soft, about 30 minutes.
♦ If you can find neither under-ripe grapes nor a substitute, use the juice of 2 limes and 1 lemon (about ⅝ cup). However, this mixture does not have quite the same depth of flavor, nor does it have the property that turns the sauce slightly sweet when cooked, as do grapes, gooseberries, rhubarb, and crab apples, but it works well in such dishes as Stuffed Eggplants with Green Grape Sauce (page 84).

Tomato Sauce

Saltsa Domatas

The secret of the deliciously sweet tomato sauces of Greece is vine-ripened tomatoes (although when they are unavailable Greek cooks cheat a little by adding a spoonful of honey). You can vary this basic sauce depending on the herbs and spices used. Make large quantities whenever there is a good supply of high-quality tomatoes, and store for use later.

Makes approximately 1 quart sauce

4 tablespoons extra virgin olive oil
1 large onion, chopped
5 pounds ripe tomatoes, skinned and diced, juices reserved
4 tablespoons dry red wine *or* hot water
1 tablespoon tomato paste
1 tablespoon honey
Sea salt *and* freshly ground black pepper, to taste

Any one of the following groups of flavorings
1 teaspoon ground cinnamon *or* one 3-inch cinnamon stick *and* 4
  tablespoons chopped flat-leaf parsley *or* fresh mint *or* 2 tablespoons
  dried *rigani* (see page 13)
or
12 parsley sprigs *and* 4 bay leaves
or
4 tablespoons chopped fresh basil, parsley, *or* marjoram *and* 4 cloves *and* 1
large clove garlic, finely chopped
or
1 teaspoon ground cumin *and* 12 parsley sprigs

Warm the olive oil in a large nonreactive frying pan and sauté the onion over low heat until soft, about 10 minutes. Combine the red wine, tomato paste, and honey, and add to the frying pan. Stir in the tomatoes, salt and pepper, and the flavorings. Raise the heat and boil uncovered, stirring occasionally, 30–40 minutes, or until thick enough to stay separated for a few seconds when a wooden spoon is drawn across the bottom of the pan.

Set a strainer over a bowl. Remove the bay leaves or cinnamon stick, if using, and press the sauce through the sieve with the back of a wooden spoon. Add more salt and pepper to taste (if it is to be stored, season before using). Serve warm or cold.

Note To store, fill small sterilized jars with the sauce. Invert a metal spoon 1 inch above a jar and pour a thin stream of olive oil onto the spoon. It will reach the surface of the sauce at an angle, ensuring that it is not disturbed. Use only enough olive oil to make a thin layer for an airtight seal. Repeat with the remaining jars and cover tightly and refrigerate for up to 3 months. Use the sealing olive oil for cooking or stir into the sauce when serving.

Light Tomato Sauce
Saltsa Domatas Elafria

Make this elegant sauce when tomatoes are at their summer sweetest. Aromatized with cinnamon and pungent herbs it has a subtle fresh taste and a smooth thin consistency. It must be made as close as possible to serving time since the flavor begins to acidify in just a few hours.
This sauce is excellent with *macaronia* or *pilafi*, grilled fish or eggplants, and simple summer vegetable dishes.

Makes 1 to 1½ cups sauce

5 tablespoons extra virgin olive oil, or to taste
1 small onion, finely chopped
1 clove garlic, finely chopped, *optional*
4 large ripe tomatoes, skinned and diced
½ teaspoon honey
1 3-inch cinnamon stick, broken in half
Sea salt *and* freshly ground black pepper, to taste

Optional flavorings
2 tablespoons fresh mint, parsley, marjoram, basil, *or* oregano
or
1 tablespoon dried *rigani* (see page 13)
or
1 teaspoon dried thyme
or
1 tablespoon Mavrodaphne *or* Madeira wine, or to taste

Warm half the olive oil in a heavy frying pan and sauté the onion over low heat until barely soft, about 6 minutes. Chop the fresh herbs, if using, and add the garlic, tomatoes, honey, cinnamon stick, salt and pepper, and half the flavoring herb to the onions. Raise the heat and boil 3 minutes. Discard the cinnamon stick. Pour off any liquid in the pan and set aside.

Set a strainer, preferably plastic, over a bowl and press the sauce through with a wooden spoon. Stir in the wine, if using, and the remaining olive oil. The sauce should be the consistency of thin cream; if too thick, add some or all of the reserved cooking liquid. Season with salt and pepper and stir in the remaining flavoring herb. Serve warm or cold.

Roasted Tomato Sauce
Saltsa Domatas Kapsalismeni

When whole tomatoes are grilled until their skins blacken and blister, their flavor becomes wonderfully sweet and mellow – the perfect base for a full-flavored sauce. In tavernas, where the grill is in constant use, this sauce is made in vast quantities. It's simple to make and a wonderful complement to grilled or barbecued fish, chicken, or lamb, and vegetable *pilafi*.

Serves 3 to 4

4 large ripe tomatoes
1–2 teaspoons aromatic honey, such as Hymettus
1 large clove garlic, minced
1 tablespoon dried marjoram *or* 1½ tablespoons dried *rigani* (see page 13), crumbled
1 teaspoon ground paprika
Coarse-grain sea salt *and* cracked black pepper, to taste
1 small bunch flat-leaf parsley, leaves coarsely chopped
4 tablespoons extra virgin olive oil

Heat the broiler.

Set the tomatoes on a broiling pan close to the heat until blackened and blistered on top, about 5 minutes. Remove from the heat and, when cool enough to handle, skin, discard the seeds, and place the pulp in a sieve set over a bowl. Set aside to drain for a few minutes, and reserve the juice.

Transfer the pulp to a food processor or blender container and add the honey, garlic, marjoram, paprika, salt and pepper, and half the parsley. Pulse to mix, and add the olive oil in a thin steady stream, pulsing until well mixed and fairly smooth. Stir in the remaining parsley and enough of the reserved juice to make the desired consistency, and season to taste with salt and pepper. Serve at room temperature or heat gently to warm.

To make the traditional way Prepare the tomatoes as directed above.

Chop half the parsley, the garlic, the marjoram, paprika, and salt and pepper together to mix. Place in a large wooden mortar, pound 1 minute, then add the tomato pulp and honey and pound to blend. Continue pounding as you add olive oil. Stir in enough of the reserved juice to make the desired consistency, and stir in the remaining parsley. Season to taste.

Peloponnese Honey Sauce
Saltsa Peloponissou

This piquant sauce is perfect for grilled white-fleshed fish, especially bass or halibut, or for grilled pork, *souvlakia*, or sausages. It's simple to make but the flavors are complex and tantalizing. Make the sauce with a wooden mortar and pestle or in a ceramic or glass bowl using a wooden spoon – metal bowls or utensils will interact with the flavor of the egg yolk and subtly alter the taste of the finished sauce. Serve warm or cold.

Serves 3

2 soft-boiled eggs (boiled 4 minutes)
2 tablespoons aromatic honey, such as Hymettus
Sea salt, to taste
1 teaspoon cracked black pepper
4 tablespoons aged red wine vinegar *or* 2 tablespoons balsamic vinegar
    diluted with 2 tablespoons warm water
1 tablespoon small capers, rinsed
2 tablespoons finely chopped flat-leaf parsley

Slice the top third off each egg and spoon out the creamy yolk into a wooden mortar or nonreactive bowl. Add the honey, salt and pepper, and pound until smooth. Add the vinegar a few drops at a time, pounding constantly.

Transfer to a strainer, preferably plastic, set over a bowl and press the mixture through with the pounder. Stir in the capers and parsley and salt and pepper to taste. Serve immediately, or gently heat until warm. Do not let sauce become too hot or the egg yolks will curdle.

Anchovy Sauce
Saltsa Antsouyias

In a few Greek markets, such as Athinas in central Athens, it's still possible to buy whole anchovies preserved in brine, sometimes sold straight from the huge wooden barrels in which they were packed. Canned anchovies do not have the same special flavor but unless you can track down brine-preserved anchovies in a specialty shop or on-line, they are the kind to use for this creamy sauce. Make the sauce as close to serving time as possible. It's especially good with grilled tuna or swordfish.

Serves 3 to 4

1 large shallot, chopped *or* 2 scallions, white parts only, chopped
1 large clove garlic, cut into 2 or 3 pieces
6–8 salted anchovy fillets, rinsed, or to taste
Finely grated zest of 1/2 lemon
1 tablespoon capers, rinsed
Juice of 1 small lemon, or to taste
5 tablespoons extra virgin olive oil, or to taste
2 tablespoons finely chopped flat-leaf parsley
1/2 teaspoon cracked black pepper, or to taste

Place the shallot, garlic, anchovies, lemon zest, capers, and lemon juice in a food processor or blender container. With the machine running, add the olive oil in a thin steady stream. Add the parsley and pepper and pulse just to mix. The sauce will have the consistency of fairly thick cream. For a thinner sauce add more lemon juice, which will give a more piquant flavor, or olive oil, which will mellow the flavor. Serve at room temperature.

To make the traditional way Finely chop the shallot, garlic, anchovies, and capers together. Place in a wooden mortar and pound with the pestle until well mixed and fairly smooth, about 10 minutes. Slowly add the lemon juice and about 1/2 cup olive oil, pounding constantly, until thick. Stir in the parsley and pepper.

APPENDICES

Pickles
Toursia

Although *toursia* means "pickles," the term is generally now applied only to vegetables such as artichokes, cauliflower, cucumber, and peppers that have been traditionally prepared and flavored and stored in wine vinegar, sometimes spiced. Other vegetables and fruits of all kinds, are also pickled in great quantities: lemons are salted and stored in olive oil (see page 18), capers are packed in brine (see page 15), and tomatoes sun-dried and stored in olive oil. *Toursia* are served as *mezedakia* with ouzo (see page 341) or raki (see page 337), or with other *mezedes*, such as preserved meats, cheeses, radishes, wild artichokes, and young fava beans. They are rarely served with a main course.

Vegetables used for pickling must be fresh, unblemished, and very clean. Use an enameled, stainless steel, or other nonreactive saucepan and sterilized wide-necked jars with tight-fitting lids.

Spiced Pickled Peppers
Piperies Mikres Toursi

For pickling the Greeks use long, slender, waxy yellow or pale green peppers. They can be very mild, almost sweet, or quite tangy. If your peppers are tangy, omit the honey and cinnamon in the spiced vinegar, and add dried red chili peppers to the jar. These are delicious with tomato or beet salads, or with *feta* cheese.

Makes approximately 6¼ pints pickled peppers

36 slender peppers, 2–3 inches long, stems trimmed to ¼ inch
3 tablespoons coarse-grain sea salt
6 dried red chili peppers, *optional*
5 cups Spiced Vinegar (see page 328)
Olive oil, for sealing the jars

Place the peppers in a glass or ceramic bowl, sprinkle with the salt, and add water to barely cover. Cover and set aside for 6 hours, occasionally stirring the peppers.

Rinse the peppers and spread on paper towels to dry. Loosely pack into 1 quart-jars, add 1 or 2 red chili peppers to each jar, cover with the Spiced Vinegar, and seal with a thin layer of olive oil. Tightly cover and store at room temperature for at least 3 weeks, or up to 3 months, before using. Refrigerate after opening.

Pickled Tiny Stuffed Eggplants
Melitzanakia Yemista Toursi

For this pretty, delicate pickle choose slender baby eggplants about 2 inches long. To keep the filling in place, you use the stronger "strings" removed from the celery stalks (for Filling 1) or the parsley or wild celery stalks (for Filling 2). Store for up to 8 weeks at room temperature, and refrigerate and use within 1 week once the jar is opened.

Makes approximately 6¼ pints pickled eggplants

2 pounds small eggplants

Filling 1
2 large cloves garlic, finely chopped
2 large sticks of celery, tough strings removed and reserved, cut into 3-to-4-inch pieces
2 tablespoons finely chopped celery leaves (see wild celery, page 352)
1 red bell pepper, roasted, seeded, and skinned (see page 343), rinsed, and cut into thin strips
3 tablespoons finely chopped flat-leaf parsley
1 tablespoon olive oil

Filling 2
3 large cloves garlic, finely chopped
2 young carrots, peeled if desired, and grated
2 tablespoons finely chopped flat-leaf parsley
1 tablespoon finely chopped fresh mint
1 tablespoon olive oil
Pine nuts, small blanched almonds, *or* walnut pieces (1 for each eggplant)
Slender flat-leaf parsley *or* wild celery stalks (see page 352), each with a few leaves attached (1 stalk for each eggplant)
5 red chili peppers, *optional*
3 cups white wine vinegar *combined with* 2 cups water *and* 2 tablespoons coarse-grain sea salt *or* 5 cups Spiced Vinegar (see Note)
Olive oil, for sealing jars

Slice off the ends of the eggplants and carefully make a short lengthways incision in each eggplant. Blanch in boiling salted water for 2 minutes, remove with a slotted spoon, and dry between layers of paper towels.

Blanch the celery pieces for 5 minutes, remove with the slotted spoon, and drain on paper towels; finely chop. Blanch the celery strings or the parsley stalks for 6 seconds, and drain. Cut 6 of the pepper strips into ½-inch pieces and set aside; finely chop the rest.

Combine the garlic, celery, celery leaves, chopped bell pepper, parsley, and olive oil (for Filling 1), or combine the garlic, carrots, parsley, mint, and olive oil (for Filling 2). Loosely stuff the eggplants with the filling. Arrange the bell pepper strips along the eggplant incisions or place a pine nut in each eggplant. Firmly wrap a celery string around each eggplant (Filling 1) or wrap with a parsley stalk, starting with the leafy end over the filling but leaving the pine nut slightly exposed (Filling 2). Place the eggplants upright in pint jars, packing quite tightly. Push 1 red chili pepper down between the eggplants in each jar, cover with the vinegar, and seal with a thin layer of olive oil. Tightly cover the jars and set aside for 2 weeks before using.

Note To make Spiced Vinegar, combine 3 cups white wine vinegar, 2 cups water, 2 tablespoons coarse-grain sea salt, 12 allspice berries, 6 cloves, 1 teaspoon black peppercorns, 1 2-inch cinnamon stick, and 1 tablespoon honey in a large saucepan and bring to a boil. Simmer 5 minutes, strain, and let cool.

Pickled Cucumbers
Angourakia Toursi

Leave tiny (1–2 inch long) cucumbers whole, and cut larger ones lengthways into quarters or into thick slices. Store at room temperature for at least 2 weeks or up to 4 months before using, and refrigerate after opening. Use these as a garnish for Pork in Aspic (page 35) or Fried Cheese (page 38), or serve with other small appetizers.

Makes approximately 6½ pints pickled cucumbers

2 pounds pickling cucumbers, stems trimmed
2 large cloves garlic, cut into large slivers, *optional*
12 black peppercorns
6 sprigs fresh dill *or* 1 tablespoon dill seeds
12 small fresh grape leaves, tough stems trimmed, blanched in boiling water for 5 seconds, *optional*
2 cups white wine vinegar
3 tablespoons coarse-grain sea salt

½ teaspoon honey
Olive oil, for sealing the jars

Blanch the cucumbers in boiling water for 1 minute and dry between layers of paper towels. Fill three 1-quart jars with the cucumbers and divide the garlic, peppercorns, dill, and grape leaves between them. Combine the vinegar, salt, honey, and 1 cup water and pour over the cucumbers. Cover with a thin layer of olive oil and tightly cover the jars.

Jams and Preserves
Glyka

From the wide choice of fruits available to them, Greeks make a variety of delicious jams and preserves. Three of my particular favorites are those made from figs, quinces, and loquats. They are not difficult to make, calling for time, patience, and careful observation rather than professional skill, but the following tips may be helpful.

Jam sets thanks to the work of the enzyme pectin (present in large quantities in fruits such as apple and quince, in smaller amounts in other fruits – it's especially low in strawberries). But to work effectively pectin needs the help of both acid, in the fruit or in added lemon juice, and sugar, so it's important to judge the proportion of sugar to fruit carefully and to add the sugar at the right moment, usually when the fruit is already cooked or softened. At that point some of the fruit's own sugar will have started to work with the pectin. Once the sugar has been added, careful observation is crucial. If you do not boil the mixture sufficiently you will end up with a crystallized jam, while over-boiling will give you a runny syrup instead.

Another common problem is the formation of mold on top of the stored jam. To guard against this it's a good idea to add some form of alcohol to the jam mixture – whiskey, cognac, Armagnac, or, in true Greek fashion, raki, all serve the purpose. The same result is achieved by pouring melted wax over the surface of the jam, but the alcoholic option is easy and adds flavor as well.

Fresh Fig Jam
Sika Glyka

For this richly flavored jam you can use any variety of fig but the fruit must be ripe. If you have unsprayed figs the skin can be left on the fruit (almost all store-bought figs are sprayed) – they give the jam a beautiful deep color, especially if you use deep purple figs. Otherwise the figs must be peeled. The tart apples in this recipe serve a dual purpose: Rich in pectin, they help the jam to set, and they are also an economic way of increasing the amount of jam you can produce from a reasonable quantity of the more expensive figs.

Makes approximately 4 to 5 pints jam

2 pounds fresh ripe figs, rinsed or peeled, and stems trimmed
1 pound tart apples, such as Granny Smiths
1 teaspoon fennel seeds
Finely grated zest of 1 lemon
Strained juice of 3 large lemons
4½ cups sugar

Thoroughly wash and sterilize five 1-pint jam jars.

Cut each fig into 6 or 8 pieces. Peel, core, and thinly slice the apples. Place the fennel seeds on a small square of cheesecloth and tie up the edges to make a bag.

Place the figs, apples, bag of fennel seeds, lemon zest, and lemon juice, in a large heavy saucepan, cover, and bring slowly to a boil. Simmer 30 minutes or until the figs are tender, stirring occasionally to ensure that the fruit does not stick. Discard the bag of fennel seeds, add the sugar, stir well with a wooden spoon, and raise the heat. Boil 5 minutes, or until the setting point (220–222°F) is reached: To test, either use a candy thermometer or drop a small quantity of jam onto a chilled plate – if it appears to be covered by a light skin, it is ready. If not boil a few minutes longer and test once more; remove the saucepan from the heat each time you test and, to prevent the figs from burning, stir vigorously with a wooden spoon.

Pour into the jars and cover the surface of the jam with circles of waxed paper or with melted wax. Tightly cover the jars and store at room temperature.

Quince Jam
Glyka Kidoni

Throughout Greek myth and legend the quince is associated with love, marriage, and fertility, and it was actually a golden quince that Paris awarded to the goddess of love, Aphrodite, when he made the ill-fated judgement that sparked off the Trojan war. For Greeks the quince is still the love-fruit and its blossoms or fruit are an integral part of the Greek marriage ceremony.

In season Cretan markets display green-gold ripening quinces in abundance; in the U.S., they may be found in late autumn. If you spot quinces in your local shop, do not hesitate to buy them. They are versatile fruits to cook with: The ancient Greeks made them into a sweetmeat, but they can also be poached (see pages 288 to 289) or baked like apples and, when cooked, take on a beautiful deep red color. They are lovely baked with a little sweet white wine, sugar, and a few cloves or a vanilla bean (rinse and core the quinces, and bake in a low oven until tender). Half a quince, finely chopped, is also a wonderfully aromatic addition to apple and pear pies and tarts. Or use their delicately perfumed flavor in this delicious jam. Be sure to choose firm under-ripe quinces; ripe yellow ones are pulpy, and not suitable for jam.

Makes approximately 3 to 4 pints jam

2 pounds under-ripe quinces
2 small lemons
4½ cups sugar
2 teaspoons vanilla extract

Thoroughly wash and sterilize four 1-pint jam jars.

Fill a large bowl with ice water. Quarter 1 lemon, squeeze the juice into the bowl, and add the quarters. Squeeze the juice from the remaining lemon and set aside. Wipe the quinces to remove the fuzzy down on their skins. Peel, quarter, and core, and tie the peelings and cores up in a piece of cheesecloth to make a bag. Thinly slice or julienne the quinces, dropping them into the ice water. When all are prepared, drain the quinces, pat dry with paper towels, and place in a large heavy saucepan. Add the water and the cheesecloth bag. Slowly bring to a boil, and simmer 15 minutes. Remove the cheesecloth bag, squeeze it over the pan to extract as much juice as possible, and discard.

Add the sugar, reserved lemon juice, and the vanilla to the quinces and simmer until the sugar is dissolved. Raise the heat and rapidly boil until the setting point is reached (as directed on page 330).

Fill the jars, cover the surface of the jam with circles of waxed paper or with melted wax, and tightly cover the jars. Store at room temperature for up to 6 months.

Loquat Preserves
Glyka Mespilonta

The refreshing, delicately flavored loquat is native to China but throughout southern Greece and Crete loquat trees, laden with clusters of small orange-gold fruits, are a common sight. The loquat conveniently ripens in late spring, at the end of the orange season and before summer fruits appear in the markets. This lovely jam is absolutely delicious with cookies, pancakes, or almond cakes and it is especially good with Rich Cream (page 310).

Makes approximately 1 to 2 pints preserves

1½ pounds large unblemished loquats
Strained juice of 1 lemon
1 2–inch strip of lemon zest
1–1²/₃ sugar

Thoroughly wash and sterilize four ½–pint jam jars. Rinse the loquats and trim out their flower ends with a small paring knife. Cut into pieces and discard the pits. Work quickly – the fruit discolors easily.

Place the loquats in a heavy saucepan with the lemon juice, zest, and 4 tablespoons water, cover, and bring slowly to a boil. Reduce the heat and simmer 30–40 minutes, or until the loquats turn deep auburn. (This slow cooking is essential to release the loquats' sugar and to make well-flavored preserves.)

Fit a food-mill with the fine disc and set it over a nonreactive bowl. Discard the lemon zest and pass the loquats through the food mill. Measure the pulp, return it to the rinsed-out saucepan, and add exactly the same amount of sugar. Slowly bring to a boil and simmer for 5–20 minutes, or until the setting point (220–222°F) is reached (as directed on page 330).

Fill the jars, cover the surface of the jam with circles of waxed paper or with melted wax, and tightly cover the jars. Store at room temperature for up to 4 months.

Beverages
Pota

Greeks are connoisseurs of water and many will tell you without hesitation that cold water, pure and crystalline, is the only truly refreshing drink. As one English writer describes it, "The glass of water appears everywhere; it is an adjunct to every kind of sweetmeat and even to alcohol. It has a kind of biblical significance. When a Greek drinks water he *tastes* it and, pressing it against the palate, savours it." This fondness for water does not stop them, however, from delighting in a range of deliciously flavored non-alcoholic drinks. Some of the best are made with the syrup of spoon sweets or with the spoon sweet itself. Other popular traditional drinks are made with almonds, citrus fruits, and pomegranates.

Morello Cherry Syrup
Vissinatha

A popular and thirst-quenching drink is made from the syrup remaining from Morello Cherry Preserves (page 296). Fill a tall glass with ice, add syrup to taste, and fill with cold water.

The syrup of any spoon sweet can be used in the same way – lemon blossom syrup (see page 298) is especially good.

Submarines
Ypovrikhia

This is the colloquial name for a traditional way to serve preserves. A long-handled spoon is used to scoop up the sweet and then is immersed in a tall glass of ice-cold water. The fondant-like spoon sweet remains attached to the spoon, hence the drink's name. Favorite versions are those made from vanilla, Morello cherries (see page 296), or mastic (see page 13). Sipping *ypovrikhia* under a shady tree is an exceedingly pleasant way to while away the afternoon.

Almond Drink
Soumada

This refreshing drink, especially delicious on a hot summer's day, is the traditional beverage to serve at weddings. The classic way to make the syrup is to pound the almonds and sugar in a mortar, but a food processor will produce a similar flavor using far less time and energy. Process only a small quantity at a time or the almonds will not be properly pulverized. The syrup keeps indefinitely in airtight bottles.

Makes approximately 3³⁄₄ cups syrup

1 cup blanched almonds
3¹⁄₂ cups sugar
4¹⁄₃ cups water
Few drops almond extract, *optional*

With a nut grinder or a food processor, finely chop the almonds – but do not pulverize. Transfer 2 tablespoons of the chopped almonds to a mortar, or remove all but 2 tablespoons from the processor bowl and set aside. Add 1 tablespoon each of sugar and water to the smaller amount of almonds, and pulverize to a paste. Remove and set aside, and repeat with the remaining almonds, adding sugar and water to each 2 tablespoons of chopped almonds.

Combine the remaining sugar and water in a heavy saucepan, bring to a boil, and gently boil 10 minutes. Stir in the almond paste with a wooden spoon and boil 10 minutes longer, stirring frequently to prevent sticking; do not leave unattended – the syrup easily boils over. Set aside to cool. Strain into a bowl through 2 layers of cheesecloth, and squeeze the cheesecloth to extract all liquid. Add almond extract if desired – the almond flavor should be unmistakable, but not overpowering. Store at room temperature in airtight bottles.

To serve, pour syrup to taste over crushed ice in a tall glass and add cold water.

Lemonade
Lemonada

This is a simple and unusual way to make any citrus drink. The light syrup keeps in the refrigerator for up to 2 weeks.

Makes approximately 3 cups syrup

2⅞ cups sugar
3 cups water
Zest of 1 lemon
1 clove
1 2–inch cinnamon stick

For serving
Freshly squeezed lemon juice, to taste
Slices of lemon dipped in sugar

Combine the sugar, water, lemon zest, clove, and cinnamon stick in a heavy saucepan and bring to a boil. Gently boil 10 minutes and set aside to cool.

Strain into clean bottles or jars and refrigerate.

To serve, pour lemon juice and syrup to taste over ice in a tall glass, and add cold water. Balance a slice of lemon dipped in sugar on the rim of the glass.

Pomegranate Refresher
Granita

The flavor of this sweet and pretty drink is best when the pomegranates are juiced within an hour or two of serving.

Serves 4

4 large ripe pomegranates
Juice of ½ small lemon
5 tablespoons sugar, or to taste

For serving
Few drops orange-flower water *or* **rose water,** *optional*

Use a lemon squeezer or juice extractor, or a food processor fitted with the plastic blade, to juice the pomegranates (see page 291).

Strain the juice through 2 layers of cheesecloth into a nonreactive pitcher. Stir in the lemon juice and sugar with a wooden spoon and stir until the sugar has completely dissolved. Chill.

Serve over crushed ice, and sprinkle with orange-flower water or rose water if desired.

Coffee
Kafes

Old ways die hard in Greece and, although tradition is now changing slowly, the best coffee is still to be found in the *kafenion* (café) – until very recently, an exclusively male domain. Women generally drink coffee at home or in the *zacharoplasteion* (pastry shop). Coffee is rarely served in tavernas or traditional restaurants.

Greeks make coffee the way it is made throughout the Middle East – in a long-handled small brass pot (*briki*) with a broad lip, tapering toward the top. It is almost always served already sweetened, in tiny straight-sided cups. When you order your coffee you are asked how you would like it made, as sugar is added to the coffee grounds at the same time as the water. Some Greeks assert that there are at least 50 ways to make and flavor coffee but, in general, you are likely to be offered only *sketo* ("unsweetened"), *metrio* ("with some sugar"), and *glyko* ("sweet").

Greek coffee is made with thoroughly pulverized, well-roasted coffee beans. Brazilian is the coffee bean of choice although it is the length of time the beans are roasted that really defines Greek coffee's special character. Since the coffee grounds are poured into the cup it's essential that they are as fine as powder.

To make Greek Coffee at home you will need a *briki*. They are available in a range of sizes, from 1–cup to generous 8–cup versions. Both *brikia* and traditional cups can be bought from Greek and Middle Eastern shops; if you prefer to use larger espresso cups, increase the quantity of coffee and sugar by one half. Serve the coffee steaming hot.

Greek Coffee
Kafes

Greek coffee is always served with tall glasses of ice water.

Serves 4

---

4 coffee cups water
4 teaspoons finely ground coffee, or to taste
4 teaspoons sugar, or to taste

Bring the water to a boil in a 4– to 6–cup *briki*. Remove from the heat and sprinkle the coffee and sugar over the water. Bring to a boil again, and remove from the heat. Stir until the froth has disappeared, and return to a high heat. Remove from the heat, stir until the froth disappears, and bring to a boil one more time. (This process is necessary to infuse the coffee and make a thick froth; the alternative is a thin liquid.)

Divide the froth between the cups (it's said to bring good luck) and carefully pour in the coffee to the brim. The froth will rise to the surface. Serve at once.

Herbal Teas
Tsai Votana

In Greek villages tea means *faskomilo,* an infusion of the three-lobed sage (*salvia triloba*), a more aromatic member of the same botanical family as garden sage (*salvia officinalis*). Village folklore attributes great powers to sage tea, as a blood purifier or euphoric or to help relieve chest colds and upset stomachs. The sage is infused in boiling water for 3 to 5 minutes, according to taste, and the sweetener is honey.

Many other ancient herb teas are still enjoyed by Greeks today. Like sage tea these are not only refreshing and reviving drinks, but also have medicinal properties. Chamomile (*kamomili*) is the favorite, especially as a relaxing nighttime tea or to ease head colds. Mint (*thiosmos*) is taken for a fever, thyme (*thimari*) when bronchitis threatens, and Cretan dittany (*dictamos*) when health or spirits are low. Most of these teas can be bought in Greek grocery shops. Or, if you feel adventurous, take your symptoms to a herbalist in a Greek market, and try the recommended concoction!

Alcoholic Drinks
Pota Einopnevmatoða

In Greece grapes are used to make a variety of alcoholic drinks in addition to wine. Once the grapes have been harvested and pressed, their remnants are distilled to produce two distinctive popular and highly potent liquors.

Aniseed-flavored ouzo is the traditional accompaniment to *mezedes* throughout most of Greece. In the old-style cafés it is served straight, in a small glass, with a tall glass of cold water. Serving ouzo over ice is a modern innovation. The ouzo sold in Greece is usually much stronger than exported varieties.

Raki has a markedly different flavor, often somewhat similar to that of tequila. Only small quantities are bottled commercially but it is readily available in areas where it is produced (or in households with relatives in those areas). Until recently, it was made at home, or communally in the village, but today its manufacture requires a license. On the islands of Crete and Santorini and in other ancient wine-producing areas raki (known as *tsigouthia* or *tsipoura*) is the favorite liquor to drink with *mezedes*. Good raki is delicious; bad raki best avoided.

Other alcoholic drinks produced in Greece include brandy (frequently, slightly sweetened); *mastiha,* a mastic-flavored liquor; a refreshing lager-style beer; and a number of flavored liqueurs.

The Wines of Greece

Dionysus, the Greek god of wine, was the son of Zeus and the Theban princess Semele. The story runs that he passed on to the Greeks the secrets of wine making he had learned from the satyr Silenus. That much is myth: What is fact is that as their empire expanded the Greeks introduced both the grape and wine making to the rest of Western Europe.

Wine, along with bread and olives, has been part of Greek culture since the very earliest times and the poets of antiquity, Greek and Roman, praised the delights and variety of Greek wines. There is still an enormously rich variety of wines in Greece, and modern Greece has inherited grape varieties yielding wines that are often quite different in aroma and flavor from the well-known international varieties.

The Greek relationship with wine, as you might expect between old friends, is easy and natural. Greeks enjoy wine without fuss or unnecessary ceremony, without heated discussions of vintages or close scrutiny of labels. In general, Greek society still follows the precepts of the physician

Hippocrates, who advised that wine was beneficial if taken at the right time and in the right quantity.

For Greeks the right time to drink wine is with food, whether a full meal, *mezedes*, or a snack. Greek wine is the natural accompaniment to Greek food: A taverna meal and a glass of local wine, taken outside in the warm pine-scented air, perhaps with a view of the sea or the vine-covered hillsides, may not be the "hautest" of cuisines but it is a moment of inspired magic.

More importantly, the experience of Greek wine and food together brings us exciting new harmonies of flavor. Particularly stimulating to non-Greeks are the unexpected aromas of wines produced from grapes indigenous to Greece but unknown outside the country (see *Reading the Wine Label*, page 341).

The last 15 years have seen a tremendous renaissance in Greek wine making, with fresh, fruity wines now being made by all sections of the wine-producing industry – the major exporting giants such as Boutari, Kourtakis, and Tsantalis, the smaller boutique wineries, and some of the cooperative ventures. Exciting use is being made of a number of high-quality native Greek varieties as well as the noble ones of Cabernet Sauvignon, Chardonnay, and others. Stainless steel vats, temperature control, and new oak, allied to a better understanding of the grapes themselves on the part of an enthusiastic younger generation of winemakers, have resulted in many exciting wines, often offering a new flavor dimension, which are regularly winning prizes world wide. And it should not be forgotten that for many years Greece has been justly famous for great dessert wines such as Muscat of Samos, Lemnos, and Patras, and Mavrodaphne of Patras.

The wine most associated with Greece is, of course, retsina. The Greek taste for retsina dates back three thousand years; it is the pine-laced wine of the ancients. This very individual wine is not to everyone's taste but a chilled glass of retsina or *kokkineli* (the rosé version), with its surprising stringency, is just right with *mezedes*.

Retsina is not a true table wine but an aromatized wine. Its origins are very old and arise from the Greek habit of storing wine in airtight jars sealed with a mixture of clay and resin, the flavor of which seeped into the wine. Because of the exclusion of air, these wines kept far longer than was usual, but the ancients assumed that this was due to the resin instead, and began to add this to their wines.

In some quarters retsina is not taken very seriously, a pity since the finest retsina from Attica and Evia, made from the *savatiano* grape, has a delicate aroma and a distinctive, pleasant, and very refreshing flavor. In these areas, retsina is the true traditional accompaniment to the Easter feast of Paschal Lamb (page 141) and *kokoretsi* (page 143), and it marries well with dishes accompanied by a garlic sauce.

However, if you are entertaining friends at a Greek meal you may prefer a choice of wines. Since the annual wine production of many Greek vineyards is small, their wines are rarely exported and sampling them is a treat to be enjoyed during a visit to the country. Below you will find a consumer guide to some of the Greek wines that can occasionally be found here, and some helpful hints on reading a Greek wine label.

Once you start to sample Greek wines, you will begin to appreciate that they have a very special color, aroma, and flavor and that they enhance the dishes in this book as no other wines can.

Consumer's Guide to Greek Wines and Spirits

From a period of relative obscurity Greek wines are now appearing on the wine lists of the best Greek restaurants and on the shelves of some of our more intrepid vintners.

The Producers

The following list is alphabetical and by no means complete. It is based on producers whose wines are usually available on the export markets, rather than only in Greece, where many other fine wines can be found.

Antonopoulos:
Red and white wines, including Adoli Ghis, Mantinia, Cabernet Nea Dris and Chardonnay

Averoff:
Red Katogi

J. Boutari:
Large range of wines, including white Santorini, red Naoussa, and retsina

N. Cosmetatos:
White wines under the brand name of Gentilini

Emery:
Red, white, rosé, and sparkling wines

Gaia:
Red and white Notios, and white Thalassitis

Ktima Gerovassiliou:
Red and white wines

Ktima Hatzimichali:
Red and white wines, including ones from Chardonnay, Cabernet

Sauvignon, and Merlot grapes

Kourtakis S.A:
Wide range, including red and white Vins de Crete, Nemea and Patras, under the brand name of Kouros, retsina, and Mavrodaphne of Patras

Chateau Lazaridi:
Red, white, and rosé wines under the chateau name

Ktima Kosta Lazaridi:
Red, white, and rosé wines under the brand name of Amethystos and Chateau Julia

Markovitis:
Red Naoussa and Chateau Pegasos

Chateau Matsa:
White wines under chateau name and Laoutari

Ktima Mercouri:
Red wines under the ktima (domaine) name and white Foloe

Oenoforos:
White Asprolithi, rosé Esperitis, and red Cabernet

Ktima Papaioannou:
Red Nemea, white, and rosé wines

Parparoussis:
White wine and red Nemea

Samos Coop:
Every level of sweetness in muscat wines, notably the sweet Nectar

Semeli S.A:
White and rosé wines, and red Nemea and Chateau Semeli

Skouras Winery:
Cambello red, white, and rosé, a red Nemea, and red and white Megas Oenos

Ktima Spyropoulou:
White wines, including Mantinia

Strofilia:
White, rosé, and red wines under the Strofilia name

Tsantalis:
Wide range of red, white, and rosé wines, including red Nemea, Naoussa, and Rapsani. Also muscat wines and Mavrodaphne of Patras

Tselepos:
White Mantinia and red Ktima Tselepou

Spirits

Ouzo:
The traditional spirit flavored with aniseed. Producers include Tsantalis and Babatzim

Distillates:
Rarely available outside Greece at present. Producers include Averoff, Babatzim, Ktima Kosta Lazaridi, and Paparoussis.

Reading the Wine Label

Apart from the language itself, there are two possible areas of confusion for the Greek wine buyer – Greek Legislative Wine Categories and indigenous grape varieties.

Legislative Categories:
Appellation Greece follows EU viticultural policies. There are 27 appellations in Greece today. O.P.A.P. is equivalent to the French A.O.C., and O.P.E. is equivalent to V.D.Q.S. Many of the new top-quality wines do not qualify for O.P.A.P. or O.P.E. since they are made either outside a quality wine region or because different grape varieties than those permitted under quality wine legislation have been used. These wines are found labeled either as Vins de Pays or as Table Wine.

A few of the more common indigenous grape varieties:

White grapes:
Assyrtico Grown on Santorini and other Aegean islands; many styles of wine produced from bone-dry to sherry-like Visanto.
Lagorthi Once rare, this grape is making a comeback owing to its steely, lightly aromatic qualities.
Malagousia Rediscovered in the 1960s, this is now producing rich wines, and is increasingly used in high quality blends for its aromatic characteristics.
Moschofilero Produces some of the best Peloponnese white wines, with a delicate aromatic quality. At its best, very fine.
Muscat Grown on Samos and Cephalonia, and around Patras; yields wines from very dry to sweet, and sun-dried dessert wines.
Robola Popular on the Ionian islands; thought to have been introduced by the Venetians in the thirteenth century.
Roditis Grown extensively on the mainland; produces a wide spectrum of styles and quality.
Savatiano The predominant grape of Attica and Evia and the principal variety for retsina; also produces a range of branded table wines and vin de pays.

Vilana Unique to Crete; light, aromatic, and fresh when well-handled.

Red grapes:

Aghiorghitiko "St. George." One of the best red varietals, unique to Nemea, Peloponnese.

Liatiko A speciality of Crete and believed to be an ancient varietal; ripens very early and is often mixed with other grape varieties.

Limnio Originally from Lemnos but now grown in Khalkidiki and Drama, it is believed to be a very ancient varietal. It has a unique flavor, and marries well with oak.

Mandelaria An island grape, now grown mainly on the Cyclades, Rhodes, and Crete. It gives immense color to the wine.

Mavrodaphne Grows around Patras; the Greek name means "black laurel," and it makes a port-like dessert wine. It is increasingly used in blends.

Xynomavro The best red varietal of northern Greece; produces full-bodied wines such as Naoussa and Goumenissa. Quality can vary, vintages important.

GLOSSARY

Anchovies No Greek market would be complete without its large wooden barrels of anchovies, which owe their unique flavor to the traditional preservation methods used. The small whole anchovies (just the heads are removed) are immersed in a heavy brine, lightly dried in the sun until the brine crystallizes into salt, and then packed into barrels. A good anchovy packer uses the same brine several times and it's in this recycling that the secret of the Greek anchovies lies. Anchovies packed in reused brine have the strong traditional flavor familiar to the ancient Greeks, and these are the ones most sought after by today's connoisseurs. They can occasionally be found here; only the two fillets are used – lift each one from the backbone with the tip of a small knife. Imported canned or bottled anchovy fillets packed in olive oil are the best substitute.

Avgolemono Probably the best-known Greek flavor, this blend of lemon juice and eggs can become a delicious sauce for fish, chicken, or vegetables or a fine delicate soup based on a good Chicken Stock (see below).

Bell Peppers The distinctive flavor bell peppers impart to Greek dishes comes from a method of roasting (scorching) them over an open flame or hot embers. In Greece, large fleshy bell peppers are always stuffed; Greek cooks choose slender, mildly flavored varieties for roasting. These are difficult to find here but you can obtain a similar flavor by "scorching" bell peppers. Using tongs, hold the pepper over an open flame or hot embers (or use a grill), turning it until it is blistered and blackened on all sides. Cool in a paper bag or in a bowl covered with plastic wrap to make removing the skin easier. Remove the core and seeds and rub off the skin and any remaining seeds with your fingers. Do not rinse – water affects flavor and storage life. To store, cut roasted peppers into strips, place in sterile jars, cover with olive oil, and seal with a lid. Store for up to 2 months. Once the peppers are used, the storage oil can be used for flavorful grilling or cooking or on salads.

Cephalopods (squid, cuttlefish, and octopus) The name *cephalopod* derives from the Greek for "head and legs" – these sea creatures consist of just a head, tentacles, and a body bag or sac. Apart from the larger cuttlefish, which has a single bone in its sac, cephalopods have no bones. What they do have, however, is an ink sac that nature has provided for their protection. Under threat of attack from a predator the cephalopod squirts out ink and, under cover of the ensuing darkness, it slips away to safety. This ink not only protects the cephalopod but is useful to the cook too. It has a slightly salty flavor, lends a unique color and sheen to sauces, and acts as a thickener. Some fish purveyors will clean cephalopods for you (even tiny ones retain grains of sand in their body bags) but avoid ones that are already cleaned since these may not be fresh. See also Squid.

Chicken Stock Although Greek chickens are often scrawny, they are invariably free-range and have a superb flavor.

To make approximately 7½ cups of excellent stock: Cut up a chicken into 6 or 8 pieces, discard excess fat, trim the giblets, discarding the liver, and rinse the chicken and giblets. Place the chicken pieces and giblets in a large saucepan or stockpot along with 1 carrot (unpeeled), cut into large pieces; 1 stick of celery, cut into large pieces; 1 medium onion, peeled and quartered; 3 bay leaves; 3 sprigs parsley; 12 peppercorns; pinch of cayenne pepper; 2 cloves; ½ teaspoon saffron threads, gently heated in a small frying pan until fragrant; and 10 cups water (or enough to cover). Bring slowly to a boil, skim off any froth, cover, reduce the heat, and simmer 1¼ hours. Strain the stock and make fat-free (see Meat Stock) and, if desired, reduce for easier storage by rapid boiling.

To make Rich Chicken Stock: Boil the stock until reduced by one third. Use the chicken meat in pies, salads, or sandwiches.

See also Fish Stock, Lamb Stock, Meat Stock, and Vegetable Stock.

Croutons Crunchy, olive oil-rich crôutons give Greek soups and salads a very special character.

To make croutons: Remove the crusts from densely textured white or whole wheat bread, and cut the bread into ¼-inch cubes. Add a ⅛ inch–layer of extra virgin olive oil to a heavy frying pan and heat over moderate heat. Fry the bread cubes until golden brown on all sides. Drain on paper towels.

The secret of successful croutons is to use fruity olive oil and not to allow it to reach smoke point. In Greece it is common to see packages of croutons of very hard dark bread, made by the baker when he bakes Store Cupboard Bread (page 252).

Dolmas (Dolmades) These are small parcels of grape-leaf wrapped rice and herbs; sometimes meat and/or vegetables are added (see page 195 and page 197). Tiny *dolmades*, suitable for *meze,* are called *dolmadakia.* In winter *dolmades* are made with cabbage leaves (see page 90); in spring with squash blossoms (see page 198).

Farina (Semolina) Available in Greek shops and health food shops. Fine-ground *farina* has the texture of coarse flour and is used to make *macaronia* (see pages 236, 240, and 243). Medium- or coarse-grain *farina* is used in puddings (see page 304 and page 308) and coarse-grain *farina* is used in custards (pages 268, 272, 280, and 283).

Fava Bean This "Old World" bean is the one most frequently used in Greek cooking. Very young fava beans are shelled and eaten raw as *meze,* or cooked in the pod. Fresh favas are made into *salata* (see page 40), baked with lamb (see page 150) or chicken, eaten cold as a salad (page 53 and page 209), or warm as a vegetable dish (see page 194). They are dried for the winter and made into one of the most popular Greek *mezedes* (see page 52). *Fava* is also the name given to a *salata* made from fresh or dried fava beans (see page 41) or split peas.

Fish When buying fish your best guide is your nose – fresh fish smells good. It's also good to inspect the head – this is the first part of the fish to go bad. (In Greece all fish except anchovies and sardines are sold with their heads intact; headless fish are assumed to have been frozen). Check the eyes too – they should be dark, clear, and except for deep-water fish such as the grouper, protruding. Gills should be red and the flesh spring back when prodded. If you are in a any doubt, pick the fish up by its tail; if the body bends, do not buy it.

Cleaning and Scaling Fish Cleaning a fish means to gut it, leaving head and skin intact. To gut a fresh fish, which should be done as soon as possible, slit open the belly with a sharp knife and pull out everything in the cavity; run your finger and thumb along the inside of the fish to check. Trim the fins with scissors and pull out the gills; if necessary, loosen them with a small paring knife. With a scaling knife or the back of a table knife, remove the scales by scraping from the tail to the head, and thoroughly rinse the fish. If you plan to grill a large fish do not scale it – the scales will protect it from the fierce grilling heat; just gut and thoroughly rinse the fish.

Filleting Fish Agres of Rhodes, in the second century A.D., is said to have been the first person to think of filleting fish. Fish filleted just before cooking has the best flavor, so always fillet fish yourself. It is easy to remove fish fillets with a filleting knife, which has a long, thin, supple blade. First, to remove the skin, ease the point of the knife under the skin at the tail and firmly pull the skin toward the head. Then, run the point of the knife around the side of the fish and lift off the fillet.

Scoring Fish When grilling large fish you need to make sure they cook in the center but do not burn on the outside. To ensure that they cook through, make 2 or 3 deep parallel diagonal incisions on each side of the fish with a sharp knife.

Fish Stock Bony fish make the best-flavored stock, and including fish heads in the stock will produce a smooth velvety texture. In Greece, favorite fish to use as a base for stock are the John Dory (see page 346) and the scorpion fish (*scorpena*).

To make approximately 3³/₄ cups stock: Place 1¹/₂ pounds cleaned, gutted, and scaled fish (see above) or fish pieces in a large saucepan and add 1 sliced onion; 1 carrot (unpeeled), cut into large pieces; 2 bay leaves; 4 sprigs parsley or 4 tablespoons parsley stalks; 1 stalk celery, cut into large pieces, or a small handful wild celery leaves (see page 352); a large pinch of saffron threads, heated in a frying pan over low heat until fragrant, *optional*; 1 tablespoon olive oil; 6 peppercorns; and water to cover. Bring slowly to a boil, reduce the heat, and simmer 1 hour. Strain through a large sieve lined with 2 layers of cheesecloth, let cool, and refrigerate for up to 2 days.

Any flakes of fish can be seasoned and coated in a *rigani*/parsley-flavored *latholemono* sauce and served with olives and cheese, as a *meze*. Or lightly mix them with some mayonnaise (page 318) or add to *pilafi* (page 226).

Fournos The traditional clay oven that was once part of every Greek house (see page 23). Today when Greeks speak of the *fournos* they usually mean the local bakery. The baker will cook his customers' food in his oven once the day's bread is baked, saving time and money (the upkeep of a *fournos* is very expensive now). Casseroles, breads, pies, and vegetables baked in a *fournos* have a unique taste.

Game When dealing with game it is helpful to understand the principal of hanging, the process by which game is tenderized. Wild birds and animals, because of the action of internal bacteria, do not putrefy but rather dry after death. Domestic animals and birds, by contrast, are invaded by external bacteria that quickly cause decomposition, the effects of which are harmful to us. Therefore, it is essential that you know the origin of any bird or animal you wish to hang. Game that has been quickly and cleanly killed, that has only a few shot holes, can be hung; if the flesh is torn or the game has come into contact with our environment it should be prepared for the table right away. To hang game, choose a cool place inaccessible to flies (a cellar is ideal). The length of hanging time will depend on the weather, age of the game, and, above all, personal taste. The right moment is usually when a tail feather can be plucked. To enjoy game safely, avoid any you have not seen in its fur or feathers and cook only that which you have seen hung. For those who dislike the idea of dealing with hanging game, marinating is the answer. Game immersed in acids, such as wine or vinegar, undergo a process similar to hanging, and the meat is tenderized and flavor improved. See also Hare, Kid, Partridge, Pigeon/Squab.

Grape Leaves The grape leaves used to make *dolmades* (see page 344) must be tender enough to be edible, so they are picked from the top third of the vine and only a few are taken from each plant, in the spring and early summer. The leaves used to protect baked or grilled foods are discarded before the dish is served, so they are picked from any part of the vine, throughout summer. For a delicious country flavor, cover trays of stuffed vegetables or young fava beans in the pod with grape leaves before baking (see page 194) or wrap *kephtedes* (page 159)—made with rice instead of bread—in grape leaves and bake moistened with water, olive oil, and lemon juice. Both fresh leaves and those preserved in brine are used to make *dolmades;* only fresh leaves are used in grilled dishes.

Hare A hare is larger than a rabbit, usually weighing around 7–8 pounds (5 pounds after skinning). To cut a hare into serving pieces, cut off the front and back legs. Cut the body in half down the backbone. Cut each half into 4 or 5 pieces, similar in size to the legs. Hare meat can be tough, so it should be marinated for 1–2 days before cooking (see page 133).

John Dory (*Christopsaro*) John Dory, with its firm white flesh and sweetly delicious flavor, is popular for use in filleted fish dishes (see page 102). Since most of the fish is head and belly, it is the perfect choice for soups and dishes requiring a rich stock. Its Greek name, meaning, "Christ's fish," derives from the two black spots behind the enormous head, said by some Greek fishermen to be the fingerprints of St. Christopher, who plucked it from the water while he was carrying Christ on his back. As it is rarely exported to the United States, porgy (sea bream) makes a fine substitute.

Kephtedes Aromatic round, oblong, or square croquettes of meat, chicken, fish, or vegetables, unchanged in form and flavor since antiquity. *Kephtedes* vary in size from very small (*kephtedakia*), for a *meze,* to large enough for a main course. They can be grilled, fried, or poached and are served with a variety of sauces (see pages 31, 32, and 159).

Khorta Wild greens that grow in Greek meadows and on hillsides during the autumn, winter, and spring. These greens are rich in vitamins and minerals and have in common a slightly bitter flavor that makes them delicious with *latholemono* (see below) or *lathoxsithi* (an olive oil and vinegar sauce). Served cold, as a cooked greens salad, *khorta* becomes *khorta salatika* (page 222).

Kid In Greece, kid often replaces the Paschal Lamb (page 141) for the Easter Sunday feast. Spit-roasted kid makes an unusual centerpiece for an outdoor party. Whole kid can be bought during spring from speciality butchers or by mail order; leg of kid is often available until early summer. It can be prepared with the marinade on page 145. Usually older and larger than lamb when slaughtered, kid needs a longer roasting time, so the fire heat must be steadier and constant. Build the fires with coals spread out over a large area and leveled. When the fire is ready, arrange the spit about 60 cm/2 feet above the glowing coals but slightly to one side. Roast a 22–24–pound kid 3–3½ hours, slowly bringing the turning split closer to the embers, until the kid is only 5–6 inches away from the heat. Baste frequently, catching the juices in a pan. Near the end of the cooking time be especially careful that the less fleshy sections of meat do not burn – push most of the embers under the rump, leaving only a shallow layer under the shoulders and rib cage.

Klephtiko This term refers to dishes baked in paper, an ancient and practical cooking method (see page 155) that seals in all the delicious juices of the meat or fish. Modern cooks have discovered that vegetables taste delectable when cooked this way, too.

Lamb Stock Light and distinctively flavored lamb stock is a delicious ingredient of *souvlakia* (see page 351) and casseroles.

To make approximately 6¼ cups stock: Place 2 pounds cracked lamb bones and any scraps of lamb meat in a large heavy saucepan with 12 black peppercorns; 1 carrot (unpeeled), cut into large pieces; 1 sliced onion; 1 celery stalk, cut into large pieces; and water to cover. Bring to a boil, cover, reduce the heat, and simmer 3 hours. Strain and make fat-free (see **Meat Stock**). Use within 2 days or freeze.

Latholemono A light blend of fruity extra virgin olive oil and perfumed lemon juice, this is a fresh-tasting and traditional sauce for salads and sautéed or grilled meat and fish. Made with red wine vinegar instead of lemon juice *latholemono* becomes *lathoxsithi,* a sauce made in the kitchens of antiquity.

Lobster For home cooks, the easiest method of killing a live lobster is to plunge it head-first into a large pot of rapidly boiling water. Add 1 tablespoon salt and 4 tablespoons vinegar for each 5 cups of water. Once the water returns to the boil after the lobsters have been added, reduce the heat slightly and cook 6 (1–1½–pound lobsters) to 10 (larger ones) minutes longer. Drain, and blot dry with a cloth.

Macaronia Greek pasta; homemade pastas are also known as *zimarika* (literally, "dough"). A wide variety of *macaronia* is available here in Greek and Middle Eastern shops; one popular type of small pasta is called *kritharaki* (page 245).

Meat Stock Greeks have great faith in the sustaining powers of good meat stock; it is excellent on its own as a stock or as a basis for heartier soups, sauces, and casseroles. Most butchers will give you bones (veal bones produce a lovely gelatinous stock).

To make approximately 10 cups Light Meat Stock: Add 3 tablespoons olive oil to a heavy baking dish or roasting pan. Arrange 4 pounds beef, veal, or lamb bones (including shin, knuckle, and marrow bones, sawn through by the butcher and thoroughly rinsed) in a single layer, and add 1 large onion, sliced in half, cut sides down. Bake 1 hour at 375°F or until well browned. Transfer to a large stockpot or saucepan, add 10 cups water, bring to a boil, and remove any froth from the surface with a slotted spoon. Add 1 tablespoon black peppercorns; 2 bay leaves; 1 clove; 12 sprigs parsley; ½ teaspoon dried thyme; 2 large carrots (unpeeled), cut into large pieces; 1 small turnip, peeled and cut in half; and 2 diced tomatoes. Bring to a boil, reduce the heat, and simmer 3–4 hours. (Do not allow to boil).

Strain through a large sieve lined with 2 layers of cheesecloth and set aside to cool. Remove the fat from the surface of cooled stock with a spoon to produce almost fat-free stock. To make the stock completely fat-free, strain again through 2 layers of cheesecloth, or clarify as directed for Fat-Free Meat Stock (see below). Refrigerate for up to 2 days or freeze. Or reduce, if desired, to half the original volume by rapid boiling in an uncovered saucepan (to use in these recipes, use equal parts reduced stock and water) Cool before refrigerating or freezing.

To make approximately 7½ cups Meat Stock: Add 3 tablespoons olive oil to a heavy baking dish or roasting pan. Arrange a single layer of about 2 pounds beef shin bones (sawn through by the butcher and thoroughly rinsed) and bake 1 hour at 375F° or until well browned. Transfer to a large stockpot or saucepan, add 10 cups Light Meat Stock, and bring to a boil. Cover, reduce the heat, and simmer 4–5 hours. Strain through a large sieve lined with 2 layers of cheesecloth, let cool, and remove the fat from the surface of the stock to make it almost fat-free. Refrigerate for up to 2 days or freeze.

To make Fat-Free Meat Stock: Reduce the Meat Stock by rapid boiling to 5 cups, and let cool. Add 2 egg whites and bring slowly to a boil, stirring with a wooden spoon. Simmer uncovered, without stirring, for 15 minutes. Slowly strain the stock through a sieve lined with 2 layers of cheesecloth into a bowl, 1 ladleful at a time, disturbing the sediment on the bottom of the pot as little as possible. Remove any remaining fat by blotting the surface with paper towels.

See also **Chicken Stock, Fish Stock, Lamb Stock, Vegetable Stock.**

Meze (Mezedes) A small, usually savory, dish served with ouzo or raki (see page 337) or wine. Four to 25 *mezedes* are served at one time to compose a *meze* table. Small *mezedes,* such as olives, cucumber or tomato chunks, cheese, and almonds, are known as *mezedakia.* See Appetizers and First Courses, pages 26 to 380.

Onion Juice This is used in Greece as a marinade to tenderize and flavor fish and meat before grilling (see page 149). For the best flavor do not use metal utensils to prepare it.

To make onion juice: Chop 1 large onion, place it in a bowl, and stir in 4 tablespoons boiling water. Set aside to cool. Line a sieve with 2 layers of cheesecloth and set it over a bowl. Pour in the onion and any liquid, pull up the edges of the cheesecloth to make a bag, and squeeze as much juice as possible into the bowl. Use immediately.

Orange-Flower Water Used to flavor syrups for phyllo pastries (page 268) and cakes (see page 280). Available from Greek and Middle Eastern shops, and many supermarkets.

Orange or Lemon Zest When a recipe calls for just a delicate hint of citrus zest, remove the zest from the fruit with a stripper or zester and either blanch it or dry it. To blanch zest, drop it into boiling water for a minute, then drain, cool, and blot dry with paper towels before using. To dry zest, spread the strips of zest on a baking sheet and dry them for 30 minutes in a very low oven. Store dried zest for up to 3 months in an airtight container and use it in casseroles and pastries.

Partridge When choosing partridges, you need to know their age since this dictates the length of time you should cook them. (You can recognize an old partridge by the large knots on its lower legs, not present in young birds.) One large partridge will serve two people. They are delicious spit roasted; wrap first in grape leaves to flavor and protect from the fierce roasting heat. Always request the giblets from your supplier; they improve the flavor of the accompanying sauce.

Pastourmas Highly spiced and salted veal or pork. Thin slices of *pastourma* are served with pickles as a meze. *Pastourmas* also describes a type of flavor (see page 178).

Phyllo These very thin pastry sheets (the word means "leaves") are the basic ingredient for sublimely syrupy sweet pastries and aromatic savory pies. For information on making homemade phyllo pastry and on using homemade or commercial phyllo, see page 266 and specific recipes.

Pigeon/Squab Pigeons, or squab, are best braised, as in recipes such as Hunter's Pot (page 135); simply roasted, they tend to become dry. Always request the giblets from the supplier; they add to the flavor of the accompanying sauce.

Pilaf A savory rice dish flavored with herbs, to which can be added vegetables, fish or shellfish, chicken, or meat (see pages 225 to 235).

Pita Soft, flat bread, shaped into rounds or ovals (see page 253) that can be split through the center to make "pockets" to hold *souvlakia* and/or salads. Perfect with grilled meats or dishes served with a sauce, or with *mezedes,* especially *salates* (see below).

Pork Caul Fat This is the outer lining of a pig's stomach. In Greece it is sold in small blocks by street vendors as well as in butcher shops; here it is available from many butchers, in the same block form. Pork caul fat (*panes*) is stiff and easily torn; to separate the pieces, soak block in lightly vinegared warm water. Use to make sausages or parcels of ground or chopped meat for grilling, spit roasting, or baking. During cooking the fat melts away, leaving moist and tender aromatic meats.

Rose water A favorite flavoring for phyllo nut pastries (see page 266) and *kataifi* (Kataifi Custard Pie in Rose water Syrup, page 271).

Salata (Salates) Literally, this means "salad," but Greek salads do not always conform to our expectations of a salad. Many are purees (see Appetizers and First Courses, pages 38 to 46), others are composed vegetable salads. A green salad is called *salatika,* and one consisting of wild greens, *khorta salatika.*

Sardines in Olive Oil Greek sardines – lightly salted, immersed in fruity olive oil, and packed in barrels – have an unusual and appetizing flavor. Garnished with capers, cracked black pepper, and a little chopped mild onion they make a delicious *meze.* Greek shops occasionally stock barrels of sardines from Greece; other imported canned sardines packed in olive oil are the best substitute.

Sausage Casings To make a long sausage for smoking you need a long intestine – the ancient Greeks used pig's intestine but villagers today use a sheep's intestine. It is scrubbed inside and out with vinegar or wine, rinsed well, and then stuffed (pages 178 to 179). Speciality butchers occasionally stock cleaned and salted sheep's intestines; to prepare them, soak overnight and rinse thoroughly. Frozen sausage casings for 4– to 5–inch sausages are sold in most butcher shops – just rinse them before using.

Sea Urchins Only the roe (eggs) of sea urchins are eaten, and it is easiest to buy them ready to use. However, collecting sea urchins can be an enjoyable way to pass a few hours. You can find sea urchins in small clusters on rocks just below the water's surface (experienced divers will find a better harvest on rocks 12–15 feet below the surface). Look for female urchins, which are a deep reddish or chestnut brown. The greenish-black males can be left alone. The urchin's hard round shell is covered entirely in spikes except on the flattened underside where the mouth is. For instructions on how to prepare them see recipe, page 114 For the best harvest, gather sea urchins at the full moon. Greek sea urchins are usually quite small (1–3 inches across). Sea urchins must be very, very fresh so either collect them yourself or use a reputable supplier; they are usually inexpensive.

Skordalia The best version of this pungent, powerful garlic sauce is made with almonds (see page 313). Serve with Tiny Fried Fish (page 30), *khorta* (see page 222), or as a dip, with Pita Bread (page 253).

Snails Snails are very popular in Greece, especially on the islands, where they are made into *meze* (see page 37), *pilafi*, and a winter casserole. Gathered after a rain (the only time villagers consider them safe to eat), they are kept in large baskets containing bran, to dry the snails, and thyme, to sweeten their flavor. To deter the snails from escaping, salt is spread around the basket rim. The snails are left in a cool place for 3 or 4 days and thoroughly rinsed in lightly vinegared cold water before cooking.

When buying fresh snails make sure that the shell and the membrane covering the opening are both intact; at home discard any that break during preparation. Simmer snails 1 hour (or until cooked), adding a few tablespoons vinegar once the water boils (skim off the scum that forms on the surface). Remove membranes with a small paring knife, discard the tiny black "tail" of each snail – and they are then ready to use. Of course, although some flavor is lost it is much easier to buy canned snails – all you have to do is drain them.

Souvlaki (Souvlakia) Flavorful chunks of meat, fish, or vegetables are threaded on a skewer (*souvla*) and roasted over an open fire or grill. Lamb is the most popular meat but pork and chicken are also used and ground meat is wrapped in pork caul fat (see above) to make *sheftalia* (page 176). These are more familiar to many of us as *kebabs,* the Turkish name for the ancient cooking technique used. See also page 147.

Squid In Greece, succulently tender, flavorful squid (*calamaria*) is a favorite summer dish. Larger squid are stuffed, tiny ones (*calamarakia*) are fried whole. Fresh squid is firm and shiny with a lightly mottled, pink skin.

To prepare squid: Gently pull the head from the body or bag and cut off the two attached fins. Discard the contents of the bag (use your finger, or slit the bag from end to check) except for the elongated ink sac – set this aside in a small bowl. Cut off and discard the strip containing the eyes and press out the tough beak. Thoroughly rinse the squid, rubbing both tentacles and body bag with your fingers to remove any sand or purplish skin. Leave the body bags of small squid (and those to be stuffed) intact; cut others into 2.5 cm/1 inch strips for sautéing; leave in iced water until ready to use.

Taverna Despite its name, the Greek taverna is not primarily a drinking place but rather an eating place. Simpler, less expensive, and less pretentious than restaurants, many tavernas are located in spectacularly beautiful places – on terraced hillsides, in village squares, alongside beaches. Many (even in the heart of Athens) have vine-covered or shady courtyards or terraces and in most the owner stamps his personality on the décor in a very idiosyncratic way!

The way to find the most interesting food in a taverna is to follow the Greek example and take a look around at what's bubbling in the kitchen – written menus do not always alert the visitor to the day's speciality. Family-run tavernas usually have a welcoming casual atmosphere with the emphasis on relaxation – so don't expect a meal in a hurry. Tavernas often specialize – harborside establishments serve mostly fish, mountain tavernas mainly meat, while others make a speciality of a certain cooking method or type of dish.

Most tavernas serve local wine measured by the jug and perhaps a few bottles of national brands, too. You will not be offered fancy desserts – fresh fruit or perhaps yogurt and honey are traditional endings for a taverna meal – nor is coffee usually available. These will be found at the nearby pastry shop, or *zacharoplasteion*.

Toursi (Toursia) Vegetables pickled by a traditional method and with a distinctive flavor. See recipe, page 326.

Vegetable Stock This simple, fresh-tasting stock can be used as a substitute for meat or chicken stocks. Celery is the dominant flavor but add or substitute turnips, parsnips, or leeks if you prefer.

To make approximately 4 1/3 cups stock: Combine 3 stalks of celery, finely diced, 2 medium carrots, finely dined, 1 large onion, chopped; 2 bay leaves; 2 sprigs fresh dill (or fresh or dried thyme or marjoram); 2 sprigs parsley; pinch of salt; and 2 cups water in a heavy saucepan. Bring to a boil, cover, reduce the heat, and simmer 40 minutes. Discard the bay leaves and herb sprigs, transfer vegetables and cooking liquid to a blender or food processor, and puree until smooth. Or pass the vegetables through a food mill fitted with the fine disk into a bowl containing the cooking liquid. Set a fine-meshed sieve over a bowl and press the puree through with a wooden spoon. Discard any solids left in the sieve. Thin with water if desired, and season to taste with salt and pepper. Refrigerate for up to 2 days. See also Chicken Stock, Fish Stock, and Meat Stock.

Wild Celery A very popular flavoring in meat and fish casseroles, soups, and salads, and the most commonly available celery in Greece. Its natural habitat is marshland near the sea but in Greece it is semi-cultivated. The leaves, similar in appearance to flat-leaf parsley, are a beautiful shade of dark green; they have a mild, almost sweet, flavor, without any trace of the slightly bitter aftertaste of the pale leaves of large cultivated celery. During spring and summer Italian markets stock wild celery; if unavailable, use the darkest leaves of rib celery, but first blanch them briefly in boiling water.

MENUS FOR DIFFERENT OCCASIONS

Newcomers to Greek cooking may at first be unsure how to compose a balanced menu with dishes from various sections of this book. To help with this problem (although I am sure it will not remain a problem for long), I have suggested below a range of complete menus suitable for family meals, quick lunches or suppers, and for entertaining (both for small dinner parties and larger gatherings). Represented here are authentic, traditional dishes in which a variety of distinctively Greek flavors contrast and complement: Any of these menus will give you and your guests an ideal introduction to the enticing tastes and aromas of Greek food. The selection begins with menu suggestions for well-known Greek celebrations and the Lenten fast.

An Easter Feast
Mezedakia
Spit-Roasted Easter Sausages
Easter Bread
Paschal Lamb
Potatoes in a Clay Pot
Marinated Asparagus
Easter Green Salad with
Latholemono Sauce
Kos Lemon Pie

Drinks
White: Santorini Boutari
Reds: Semeli Nemea or Ktima
Mercouri

A Christmas Table
Mezedakia
Christmas Bread
Duckling Thessalía-Style
Turnips and Grapes in Aromatic
Sauce
Garlic Potatoes with Juniper Berries
Island Green Salad
Fruits in Sweet Wine and Honey
Honey Cakes

Drinks
Aperitif: Spyropoulous Mantinia
White: Strofilia Nafsika
Reds: Boutari Grand Reserve or
Chateau Semeli
Dessert: Muscat of Samos

New Year's Day
Mezedakia
Leeks the Classic Way
Saint Basil's Bread
Pheasant over a Fire *or*
Hunter's Pot
Potatoes in a Clay Pot
Purslane and Young Beets
Platter of Fresh Fruit
Manouri or myzithra cheese
with aromatic Greek honey
Honey Cakes

Drinks
Aperitif: Kouros white
White: Adoli Ghis (Anotonopoulos)
Reds: Gerovassiliou Red or Boutari
Goumenissa or Katogi Averoff
Dessert: Muscat of Limnos

The Lenten Fast

Salt-Dried Fish Roe Salata
Chickpea and Garlic Salata
Potato and Vegetable Kephtedakia
Marinated Olives
Peppered Dried Figs,
Pita Bread
Fava Beans and Sweet Carrot Pilaf
Wild Greens Salad
Almond Creams
Platter of Fresh Fruits

Drinks
A selection of waters

Easy Lunch

Macaronia with Chicken and Wild
Greens *or* Kritharaki with Brown
Butter and Cheese
Fragrant Eggplants with Olives
Sweet-Baked Figs *or*
Anoula's Dried Figs

Drinks
White: Gaia Notios
Dessert: Mavrodaphne of Patras

or

Peppery Grilled Liver
Rigani Cheese Bread *or* Olive Bread
Vanilla Rice Pudding

Drinks
White: Anotonopoulos Mantinia
Red: Tsantalis Rapsani

Family Dinner

Chicken Avgolemono Soup
Smyrna Sausages
Potatoes in a Clay Pot
Cucumber Salad with
Honey Vinegar Sauce
Honey Sesame Sweetmeats with
Vanilla Ice Cream

Drinks
White: Retsina
Red: Skouras Cambello
Dessert: Muscat

or

Potato Kephtedakia with Cheese
Pork Cutlets with Mustard Sauce
Pilaf with Green Lentils
Honey-Glazed Onions
Sticky Yogurt Cake

Drinks
White: Retsina
Red: Gerovassiliou
Dessert: Samos Nectar

Quick Supper for Friends

Black Olives and Lentil Salata
Pita Bread
Country Vegetable Omelet
Purslane Salad
Glazed Sweet Chestnuts

Drinks
White: Ktima Kosta Lazaridi
Dessert: Mavrodaphne of Patras

or (mostly made ahead)
Baked Cheese and Spinach Pies
Chicken in a Pot
Perfect Pilaf
Fruits in Sweet Wine and Honey

Drinks
Rosé: Ktima Kosta Lazaridi

A Casual Dinner Party

Sesame Spinach Pies
Bay-Scented Chicken with Figs
Tiny Cracked Potatoes
Kataifi Nut Rolls with
Caramel Syrup

Drinks
White: Gaia Thalassitis
Rosé: Semeli

or

Baked Eggplants to Make the Sultan
Swoon
Yogurt Lamb Souvlakia with
Saffron Rice
Purslane and Young Beets
Kataifi Custard Pie in
Rose Water Syrup

Drinks
Red: Ktima Papaioannou

Dinner Party
Mezedakia served with Drinks
Pork in Aspic
Marinated Olives
Purslane Salad
Cinnamon Lamb with Eggplants
Pilaf with Currants and Pine Nuts
Island Green Salad
Minoan Dates and Prunes

Drinks
White: Antonopoulos Chardonnay
Red: Skouras Megas Oenos
Dessert: Mavrodaphne of Patras

or

Mezedakia served with Drinks
Tiny Stuffed Vegetables
Cretan Chicken Pie
Green Salad with Feta Cheese
and Olives
Honey Ice Cream with
Fresh Fig Compote
Shortcakes

Drinks
White: Gerovassiliou
Reds: Gaia Notios or Ktima
Mercouri
Dessert: Samos Nectar

Vegetarian Dinner Party
Mushrooms à la Grecque
Spinach Bread *or* Fennel Bread
Baked Stuffed Eggplants, Tomatoes,
and Peppers
Purslane Salad *or*
Island Green Salad
Baked Figs
Hazelnut Cookies

Drinks
White: Oenoforos Asprolithi
Red: Boutari Naoussa

Meze Party
Most of the work for this menu can
be done 1 or 2 days in advance, and
some of the dishes can be frozen;
last-minute work is minimal.

Mezedakia, large selection
Grilled Eggplant Salata
Chickpea and Garlic Salata
Stuffed Grape Leaves with
Latholemono Sauce
Kephtedakia
Tiny Stuffed Vegetables
Honey-Glazed Onions
Purslane and Young Beets
Tiny Cracked Potatoes
Smoked Fish Salad
Small Pies
Souvlakia
Cheese Mint Bread
Olive Bread

Drinks
Whites: Semeli White or Boutari
Moschofilero
Red: Boutari Nemea

A Barbecue

**Some dishes baked and/or
prepared ahead**

Mezedakia
Black-Eyed Peas with Capers
Snails in Vinegar
Small Pies
The Villagers' Grilled Lamb *or*
Souvlaki Sausages

or
Mani Pork Souvlaki
Baked Summer Vegetables
Green Salad with
Feta Cheese and Olives
Shepherd's Bread
Country Bread
Phyllo Custard Pie

Drinks
Whites: Vin de Crete *or*
Boutari Kretikos
Red: Kourtaki Kouros

A Summer Buffet
Mezedakia
Green Lentil Salad
Traditional Tomato Salad
Fennel Bread, made with fresh fennel
and/or Pita Bread
Moussakas
Potatoes in a Clay Pot
Nut Pastries in
Fragrant Honey Syrup
A Platter of Fresh Fruits
Myzithra or manouri cheese
with aromatic Greek honey

Drinks
Whites: Strofilia or Cambello White
Rosés: Semeli or Tsantalis
Agoriotiko
Red: Strofilia

A Picnic
Marinated Olives
Peppered Dried Figs
Summer Bean Salad
Island Eggplants
Olive Bread *and/or* Pita Bread
Beets Island-Style
Cheese and Spinach Pie
Almond Cake in Honey Syrup
Platter of Fresh Fruits

Drinks
Whites: Retsina or Emery Villaré
Red: Vin de Crete

BIBLIOGRAPHY

While writing this book I consulted many written sources. Some were manuscripts and stored in archives, others were books long out of print and quite difficult to find. These are some of the more easily accessible works.

Brillat-Savarin, Jean Anthelme. *The Physiology of Taste*. Translated and annotated by M.F.K. Fisher. San Francisco: North Point Press, 1986.

Chatto, James and Martin, W.L. *A Kitchen in Corfu*. London: Weidenfeld and Nicholson, 1987.

Clusells, Sylvain. *Cooking on the Turning Spit and Grill*. London: Arthur Baker Ltd., 1961.

D'Andrea, Jeanne. *Ancient Herbs in the J. Paul Getty Museum Gardens*. Malibu, CA: J. Paul Getty Museum, 1982.

David, Elizabeth. *Mediterranean Food*. Revised ed. London: Penguin Books, 1955, and Elizabeth David Classics, Grub Street, 1999.

Davidson, Alan. *Mediterranean Seafood*. London: Penguin Books, 1972.

Durrell, Lawrence. *Prospero's Cell*. London: Faber & Faber, 1963.

Fermor, Patrick Leigh. *Roumeli*. London: John Murray, 1966, and Penguin Books, 1983.

Gissing, George. *By the Ionian Sea*. 1901. Reprint. London: Richards Press, 1956.

Graves, Robert. *Greek Myths*. 2 volumes. London: Penguin Books, 1956.

Gray, Patience. *Honey from a Weed*. London: Prospect Books, 1986.

Grigson, Jane. *Jane Grigson's Vegetable Book*. London: Michael Joseph, 1978.

Harrison, S. G.; Masefield, G.B.; and Wallis, Michael. *The Oxford Book of Food Plants*. Illustrations by B.E. Nicholson. London: Oxford University Press, 1969.

Homer. *The Iliad*.

Homer. *The Odyssey*.

Kochilas, Diane. *The Food and Wine of Greece*. New York: St. Martin's Press, 1990

Lambert-Gócs. *The Wines of Greece*. London: Faber & Faber, 1990

McConnell, Carol and Malcolm. *The Mediterranean Diet*. New York: W.W. Norton & Co., Inc., 1987.

Marks, Theonie. *Greek Islands Cooking*. Boston: Little Brown & Co., 1972.

Miller, Henry. *The Colossus of Maroussi*. 1941. Reprint. London: Penguin Books, 1963.

Niebuhr, Alta Dodds. *Herbs of Greece*. Sponsored by the New England Unit of the Herb Society of America, 1970.

Roden, Claudia. *A New Book of Middle Eastern Food*. London: Penguin Books, 1986

Salaman, Rena. *Greek Food*. London: Fontana Books, 1983.

Sculley, Victor. *The Earth, the Temple, and the Gods.* New Haven: Yale University Press, 1979.

Soyer, Alexis. *The Pantropheon.* New York: Paddington Press, 1977.

Stavroulakis, Nicholas. *Cookbook of the Jews of Greece.* New York: Cadmus Press, 1986.

Stobart, Tom. *Herbs, Spices, and Flavorings.* London: Grub Street, 1998.

Stubbs, Joyce M. *The Home Book of Greek Cookery.* London: Faber & Faber, 1963.

Tselementes, Nicholas. *Greek Cookery.* New York: D.C. Divry Inc., 1950.

Wolfert, Paula. *Mediterranean Cooking.* New York: Quadrangle/The New York Times Book Co., Inc., 1977.

INDEX